THE SELECTED POETRY OF
ROBINSON JEFFERS

The Selected
Poetry of
ROBINSON
JEFFERS

RANDOM HOUSE · NEW YORK

TO UNA JEFFERS

CONTENTS

CONTENTS

CONTENTS

ix

CONTENTS

FROM SOLSTICE

FROM SUCH COUNSELS YOU GAVE TO ME

CONTENTS

NEW POEMS AND FRAGMENTS

FOREWORD

THIS BOOK presents in one volume about half of my published work. In making the selection it was easy to eliminate the poems published in 1912 and 1916, which were only preparatory exercises, to say the best for them; and it was easy to omit a number of shorter poems from later volumes. After that the selection became more or less arbitrary. Several of the longer poems had to be omitted, for I have no desire to publish a "collected works" at this time, but there appears little reason to choose among them. *The Women at Point Sur* seems to me—in spite of grave faults—the most inclusive, and poetically the most intense, of any of my poems; it is omitted from this selection because it is the least understood and least liked, and because it is the longest. *Dear Judas* also was not liked and is therefore omitted, though I think it has value, if any of these poems has. *Such Counsels You Gave to Me* is omitted in order to make room for a number of shorter pieces from the same volume. The omission of *Cawdor* is purely arbitrary and accidental; I had finally to choose between this and *Thurso's Landing*; and there was no ground for choice; I simply drew lots in my mind.

The arrangement of the book is merely chronological; the long poems are presented in the order of their writing, the short ones in groups as they were first published. The earliest of the long poems was written, I think, in 1921 and 1922; the earliest of the short ones in 1917. This is *The Songs of the Dead Men to the Three Dancers*—choruses from a wartime play—reprinted here only as a sample of the metrical experiments that occupied my mind for awhile.

A good friend of mine, who is also my publisher, wants me

to turn this foreword to some account; he says that a number of people have written pro and con about my verses, and it is high time for the author himself to say something. Very likely. But I do not wish to commend or defend them, though sufficiently attacked; and it seems to me that their meaning is not obscure. Perhaps a few notes about their origins may be of interest to anyone who is interested in the verses themselves.

Long ago, before anything included here was written, it became evident to me that poetry—if it was to survive at all—must reclaim some of the power and reality that it was so hastily surrendering to prose. The modern French poetry of that time, and the most "modern" of the English poetry, seemed to me thoroughly defeatist, as if poetry were in terror of prose, and desperately trying to save its soul from the victor by giving up its body. It was becoming slight and fantastic, abstract, unreal, eccentric; and was not even saving its soul, for these are generally anti-poetic qualities. It must reclaim substance and sense, and physical and psychological reality. This feeling has been basic in my mind since then. It led me to write narrative poetry, and to draw subjects from contemporary life; to present aspects of life that modern poetry had generally avoided; and to attempt the expression of philosophic and scientific ideas in verse. It was not in my mind to open new fields for poetry, but only to reclaim old freedom.

Still it was obvious that poetry and prose are different things; their provinces overlap, but must not be confused. Prose, of course, is free of all fields; it seemed to me, reading poetry and trying to write it, that poetry is bound to concern itself chiefly with permanent things and the permanent aspects of life. That was perhaps the great distinction between them, as regards subject and material. Prose can discuss matters of the moment; poetry must deal with things that a reader two thousand years away could understand and be moved by. This excludes much of the circumstance of modern life, especially in the cities. Fashions, forms of machinery, the more complex social, financial, political adjustments, and so forth, are all ephemeral, exceptional; they exist but will never exist again. Poetry must concern itself with (relatively) permanent things. These have poetic value; the ephemeral has only news value.

Another formative principle came to me from a phrase of Nietzsche's: "The poets? The poets lie too much." I was nineteen when the phrase stuck in my mind; a dozen years passed before it worked effectively, and I decided not to tell lies in verse. Not to feign any emotion that I did not feel; not to pretend to believe in optimism or pessimism, or unreversible progress; not to say anything because it was popular, or generally accepted, or fashionable in intellectual circles, unless I myself believed it; and not to believe easily. These negatives limit the field; I am not recommending them but for my own occasions.

Here are the principles that conditioned the verse in this book before it was written; but it would not have been written at all except for certain accidents that changed and directed my life. (Some kind of verse I should have written, of course, but not this kind.) The first of these accidents was my meeting with the woman to whom this book is dedicated, and her influence, constant since that time. My nature is cold and undiscriminating; she excited and focused it, gave it eyes and nerves and sympathies. She never saw any of my poems until they were finished and typed, yet by her presence and conversation she has co-authored every one of them. Sometimes I think there must be some value in them, if only for that reason. She is more like a woman in a Scotch ballad, passionate, untamed and rather heroic—or like a falcon—than like any ordinary person.

A second piece of pure accident brought us to the Monterey coast mountains, where for the first time in my life I could see people living—amid magnificent unspoiled scenery—essentially as they did in the Idyls or the Sagas, or in Homer's Ithaca. Here was life purged of its ephemeral accretions. Men were riding after cattle, or plowing the headland, hovered by white sea-gulls, as they have done for thousands of years, and will for thousands of years to come. Here was contemporary life that was also permanent life; and not shut from the modern world but conscious of it and related to it; capable of expressing its spirit, but unencumbered by the mass of poetically irrelevant details and complexities that make a civilization.

By this time I was nearing thirty, and still a whole series of accidents was required to stir my lazy energies to the point of writing verse that seemed to be—whether good or bad—at least my own voice.

So much for the book as a whole: a few notes may be added as to the origins of particular poems.

Tamar grew up from the biblical story, mixed with a reminiscence of Shelley's *Cenci*, and from the strange, introverted and storm-twisted beauty of Point Lobos. *Roan Stallion* originated from an abandoned cabin that we discovered in a roadless hollow of the hills. When later we asked about its history no one was able to tell us anything except that the place had been abandoned ever since its owner was killed by a stallion.

This is the only one of my poems of which I can remember clearly the moment of conception. I had just finished *The Tower Beyond Tragedy* and was looking about for another subject—which was to be contemporary, because I repented of using a Greek story when there were so many new ones at hand. I was quarrying granite under the sea-cliff to build our house with, and slacking on the job sat down on a wet rock to look at the sunset and think about my next poem. The stallion and the desolate cabin came to mind; then immediately, for persons of the drama, came the Indian woman and her white husband, real persons whom I had often seen driving through our village in a ramshackle buggy. The episode of the woman swimming her horse through a storm-swollen ford at night came also; it was part of her actual history. . . . So that when I stood up and began to handle stones again, the poem had already made itself in my mind.

The Tower Beyond Tragedy was suggested to me by the imposing personality of a Jewish actress who was our guest for a day or two. She was less than successful on the stage, being too tall, and tragic in the old-fashioned manner; but when she stood up in our little room under the low ceiling and recited a tragic ballad—"Edward, Edward"—for a few people gathered there, the experience made me want to build a heroic poem to match her formidable voice and rather colossal beauty. I thought these would be absurdly out of place in any contemporary story, so I looked back toward the feet of Aeschylus, and cast this woman for the part of Cassandra in my poem.

Apology for Bad Dreams originated from the episode of the woman and her sons torturing a horse, a thing which happened on our coast. Cruelty is a part of nature, at least of human nature, but it is the one thing that seems unnatural to us; the tension of the mind trying to recognize cruelty and evil as part of the sum of things is what made the poem. (This woman a few years later was killed by another horse: an unusual piece of justice.)

The story of *The Loving Shepherdess* was suggested by a footnote in one of the novels of Walter Scott, which I was reading aloud to our sons. I cannot remember which novel it was. The note tells about a half-insane girl who wandered up and down Scotland with a dwindling flock of sheep, that perished one by one.

The story of *Thurso's Landing* was suggested entirely, I think, by the savage beauty of the canyon and sea-cliff that are its scene, and by the long-abandoned lime-works there.

I cannot remember planning the story at all. When we first saw this place, in 1914, the heavy steel cable was hanging across the sky of the canyon, still supporting a rusted skip. During the war it was taken down for scrap-iron.

The phrase "Give your heart to the hawks" swam about in my mind for several years as a good title for a poem; then one day I noticed the scene and farmhouse that seemed to fit the title, in Sycamore Canyon, just south of Big Sur; and between the title and the scene the poem unrolled itself.

At the Birth of an Age had a more calculated origin. I was considering the main sources of our civilization, and listed them roughly as Hebrew-Christian, Roman, Greek, Teutonic. Then it occurred to me that I had written something about the Hebrew-Christian source in *Dear Judas*, and that *The Tower Beyond Tragedy* might pass for a recognition of the Greek source. About the Roman source I should probably never write anything, for it is less sympathetic to me. Recognition of the Teutonic source might be an interesting theme for a new poem, I thought . . . and the Volsung Saga might serve for fable. Only as the poem progressed did the Teutonic element begin to warp and groan under the tension of Christian influence. The symbol of the self-tortured God, that closes the poem, had appeared to me long before in *Apology for Bad Dreams* and in *The Women at Point Sur*—Heautontimoroumenos, the self-tormentor—but it stands most clearly in the self-hanged Odin of Norse mythology.

ROBINSON JEFFERS

THE SELECTED POETRY OF
ROBINSON JEFFERS

TAMAR

A night the half-moon was like a dancing-girl,
No, like a drunkard's last half-dollar
Shoved on the polished bar of the eastern hill-range,
Young Cauldwell rode his pony along the sea-cliff;
When she stopped, spurred; when she trembled, drove
The teeth of the little jagged wheels so deep
They tasted blood; the mare with four slim hooves
On a foot of ground pivoted like a top,
Jumped from the crumble of sod, went down, caught, slipped;
Then, the quick frenzy finished, stiffening herself
Slid with her drunken rider down the ledges,
Shot from sheer rock and broke
Her life out on the rounded tidal boulders.

The night you know accepted with no show of emotion the little
    accident; grave Orion
Moved northwest from the naked shore, the moon moved to
    meridian, the slow pulse of the ocean
Beat, the slow tide came in across the slippery stones; it drowned
    the dead mare's muzzle and sluggishly
Felt for the rider; Cauldwell's sleepy soul came back from the
    blind course curious to know
What sea-cold fingers tapped the walls of its deserted ruin.
    Pain, pain and faintness, crushing
Weights, and a vain desire to vomit, and soon again
The icy fingers, they had crept over the loose hand and lay in the
    hair now. He rolled sidewise
Against mountains of weight and for another half-hour lay still.
    With a gush of liquid noises
The wave covered him head and all, his body
Crawled without consciousness and like a creature with no bones,
    a seaworm, lifted its face

3

Above the sea-wrack of a stone; then a white twilight grew about
    the moon, and above
The ancient water, the everlasting repetition of the dawn. You
    shipwrecked horseman
So many and still so many and now for you the last. But when it
    grew daylight
He grew quite conscious; broken ends of bone ground on each
    other among the working fibers
While by half-inches he was drawing himself out of the sea-
    wrack up to sandy granite,
Out of the tide's path. Where the thin ledge tailed into flat cliff
    he fell asleep. . . .
                Far seaward
The daylight moon hung like a slip of cloud against the horizon.
    The tide was ebbing
From the dead horse and the black belt of sea-growth. Cauldwell
    seemed to have felt her crying beside him,
His mother, who was dead. He thought "If I had a month or two
    of life yet
I would remember to be decent, only it's now too late, I'm fin-
    ished, mother, mother,
I'm sorry." After that he thought only of pain and raging thirst
    until the sundown
Reddened the sea, and hands were reaching for him and drawing
    him up the cliff.

            His sister Tamar
Nursed him in the big westward bedroom
Of the old house on Point Lobos. After fever
A wonderful day of peace and pleasant weakness
Brought home to his heart the beauty of things. "O Tamar
I've thrown away years like rubbish. Listen, Tamar,
It would be better for me to be a cripple,
Sit on the steps and watch the forest grow up the hill
Or a new speck of moss on some old rock
That takes ten years agrowing, than waste
Shame and my spirit on Monterey rye whiskey,
And worse, and worse. I shan't be a cripple, Tamar.

We'll walk along the blessed old gray sea,
And up in the hills and watch the spring come home."

Youth is a troublesome but a magical thing,
There is little more to say for it when you've said
Young bones knit easily; he that fell in December
Walked in the February fields. His sister Tamar
Was with him, and his mind ran on her name,
But she was saying, "We laugh at poor Aunt Stella
With her spirit visitors: Lee, something told her truth.
Last August, you were hunting deer, you had been gone
Ten days or twelve, we heard her scream at night,
I went to the room, she told me
She'd seen you lying all bloody on the sea-beach
By a dead deer, its blood dabbling the black weeds of the ebb."
"I was up Tassajara way," he answered,
"Far from the sea." "We were glad when you rode home
Safe, with the two bucks on the packhorse. But listen,
She said she watched the stars flying over you
In her vision, Orion she said, and made me look
Out of her window southward, where I saw
The stars they call the Scorpion, the red bead
With the curling tail. 'Then it will be in winter,'
She whispered to me, 'Orion is winter.' " "Tamar, Tamar,
Winter is over, visions are over and vanished,
The fields are winking full of poppies,
In a week or two I'll fill your arms with shining irises."

The winter sun went under and all that night there came a roaring
     from the south; Lee Cauldwell
Lay awake and heard the tough old house creak all her timbers;
     he was miserably lonely and vacant,
He'd put away the boyish jets of wickedness, loves with dark
     eyes in Monterey back-streets, liquor
And all its fellowship, what was left to live for but the farm-
     work, rain would come and hinder?
He heard the cypress trees that seemed to scream in the wind,
     and felt the ocean pounding granite.

His father and Tamar's, the old man David Cauldwell, lay in the
    eastern chamber; when the storm
Wakened him from the heartless fugitive slumber of age he rose
    and made a light, and lighted
The lamp not cold yet; night and day were nearly equal to him,
    he had seen too many; he dressed
Slowly and opened his Bible. In the neighboring rooms he heard
    on one side Stella Moreland,
His dead wife's sister, quieting his own sister, the idiot Jinny
    Cauldwell, who laughed and chuckled
Often for half the night long, an old woman with a child's mind
    and mostly sleepless; in the other
Chamber Tamar was moaning, for it seemed that nightmare
Within the house answered to storm without.
To Tamar it seemed that she was walking by the seaside
With her dear brother, who said "Here's where I fell,
A bad girl that I knew in Monterey pushed me over the cliff,
You can see blood still on the boulders." Where he vanished to
She could not tell, nor why she was crying "Lee. No.
No dearest brother, dearest brother no." But she cried vainly,
Lee was not there to help her, a wild white horse
Came out of the wave and trampled her with his hooves,
The horror that she had dreaded through her dreaming
With mystical foreknowledge. When it wakened her,
She like her father heard old Jinny chuckling
And Stella sighing and soothing her, and the southwind
Raging around the gables of the house and through the forest of
    the cypresses.
"When it rains it will be quieter," Tamar thought. She slept
    again, all night not a drop fell.
Old Cauldwell from his window saw the cloudy light seep up
    the sky from the overhanging
Hilltops, the dawn was dammed behind the hills but overflowed
    at last and ran down on the sea.

II

Lee Cauldwell rode across the roaring southwind to the winter
    pasture up in the hills.

A hundred times he wanted Tamar, to show her some new beauty
    of canyon wildflowers, water
Dashing its ferns, or oaktrees thrusting elbows at the wind, black-
    oaks smoldering with foliage
And the streaked beauty of white-oak trunks, and redwood
    glens; he rode up higher across the rainwind
And found his father's cattle in a quiet hollow among the hills,
    their horns to the wind,
Quietly grazing. He returned another way, from the headland
    over Wildcat Canyon,
Saw the immense water possessing all the west and saw Point
    Lobos
Gemmed in it, and the barn-roofs and the house-roof
Like ships' keels in the cypress tops, and thought of Tamar.
Toward sundown he approached the house; Will Andrews
Was leaving it and young Cauldwell said, "Listen, Bill Andrews,
We've had gay times together and ridden at night.
I've quit it, I don't want my old friends to visit my sister.
Better keep off the place." "I will," said the other,
"When Tamar tells me to." "You think my bones
Aren't mended yet, better keep off." Lee Cauldwell
Rode by to the stable wondering why his lips
Twitched with such bitter anger; Tamar wondered
Why he went upstairs without a word or smile
Of pleasure in her. The old man David Cauldwell,
When Lee had told him news of the herd and that Ramon
Seemed faithful, and the calves flourished, the old man answered:
"I hear that there's a dance at Notley's Landing Saturday. You'll
    be riding
Down the coast, Lee. Don't kill the horse, have a good time."
    "No, I've had all I want, I'm staying
At home now, evenings." "Don't do it; better dance your pony
    down the cliffs again than close
Young life into a little box; you've been too wild; now I'm worn
    out, but I remember
Hell's in the box." Lee answered nothing, his father's lamp of
    thought was hidden awhile in words,

7

An old man's words, like the dry evening moths that choke a
  candle. A space, and he was saying,
"Come summer we'll be mixed into the bloody squabble out there,
  and you'll be going headforemost
Unless you make your life so pleasant you'd rather live it. I
  mayn't be living
To see you home or hear you're killed." Lee, smiling at him,
"A soldier's what I won't be, father." That night
He dreamed himself a soldier, an aviator
Duelling with a German above a battle
That looked like waves, he fired his gun and mounted
In steady rhythm; he must have been winged, he suddenly
Plunged and went through the soft and deadly surface
Of the deep sea, wakening in terror.
He heard his old Aunt Jinny chuckling,
Aunt Stella sighing and soothing her, and the southwind
Raging around the gables of the house and through the forest of
  the cypresses.

III

They two had unbridled the horses
And tied them with long halters near the thicket
Under Mal Paso bridge and wandered east
Into the narrow cleft, they had climbed the summit
On the right and looked across the sea.
The steep path down, "What are we for?" said Tamar wearily,
  "to want and want and not dare know it."
"Because I dropped the faded irises," Lee answered, "you're un-
  happy. They were all withered, Tamar.
We have grown up in the same house." "The withered house
Of an old man and a withered woman and an idiot woman. No
  wonder if we go mad, no wonder."
They came to the hid stream and Tamar said, "Sweet, green and
  cool,
After the mad white April sun: you wouldn't mind, Lee?
Here where it makes a pool: you mustn't look; but you're my
  brother. And then

8

I will stand guard for you." The murmur and splash of water
    made his fever fierier; something
Unfelt before kept his eyes seaward: why should he dread to see
    the round arm and clear throat
Flash from the hollow stream? He trembled, thinking "O we are
    beasts, a beast, what am I for?
Was the old man right, I must be drunk and a dancer and feed on
    the cheap pleasures, or it's dangerous?
Lovely and thoughtless, if she knew me how she'd loathe and
    avoid me. Her brother, brother. My sister.
Better the life with the bones, and all at once have broken."
    Meanwhile Tamar
Uneasily dipped her wrists, and crouching in the leaf-grown bank
Saw her breasts in the dark mirror, she trembled backward
From a long ripple and timidly wading entered
The quiet translucence to the thighs. White-shining
Slender and virgin pillar, desire in water
Unhidden and half reflected among the interbranching ripples,
Arched with alder, over-woven with willow.
Ah Tamar, stricken with strange fever and feeling
Her own desirableness, half-innocent Tamar
Thought, "If I saw a snake in the water he would come now
And kill the snake, he is keen and fearless but he fears
Me I believe." Was it the wild rock coast
Of her breeding, and the reckless wind
In the beaten trees and the gaunt booming crashes
Of breakers under the rocks, or rather the amplitude
And wing-subduing immense earth-ending water
That moves all the west taught her this freedom? Ah Tamar,
It was not good, not wise, not safe, not provident,
Not even, for custom creates nature, natural,
Though all other license were; and surely her face
Grew lean and whitened like a mask, the lips
Thinned their rose to a split thread, the little breasts
Erected sharp bright buds but the white belly
Shuddered, sucked in. The lips writhed and no voice
Formed, and again, and a faint cry. "Tamar?"
He answered, and she answered, "Nothing. A snake in the water

9

Frightened me." And again she called his name.
"What is it, Tamar?" "Nothing. It is cold in the water.
Come, Lee, I have hidden myself all but the head.
Bathe, if you mean to bathe, and keep me company.
I won't look till you're in." He came, trembling.
He unclothed himself in a green depth and dared not
Enter the pool, but stared at the drawn scars
Of the old wound on his leg. "Come, Lee, I'm freezing.
Come, I won't look." He saw the clear-skinned shoulders
And the hollow of her back, he drowned his body
In the watery floor under the cave of foliage,
And heard her sobbing. When she turned, the great blue eyes
Under the auburn hair, streamed. "Lee.
We have stopped being children; I would have drowned myself;
If you hadn't taught me swimming—long ago—long ago, Lee—
When we were children." "Tamar, what is it, what is it?"
"Only that I want . . . death. You lie if you think
Another thing." She slipped face down and lay
In the harmless water, the auburn hair trailed forward
Darkened like weeds, the double arc of the shoulders
Floated, and when he had dragged her to the bank both arms
Clung to him, the white body in a sobbing spasm
Clutched him, he could not disentangle the white desire,
So they were joined (like drowning folk brought back
By force to bitter life) painfully, without joy.
The spasm fulfilled, poor Tamar, like one drowned indeed, lay
     pale and quiet
And careless of her nakedness. He, gulfs opening
Between the shapes of his thought, desired to rise and leave her
     and was ashamed to.
He lay by her side, the cheek he kissed was cold like a smooth
     stone, the blue eyes were half open,
The bright smooth body seemed to have suffered pain, not love.
     One of her arms crushed both her breasts,
The other lay in the grass, the fingers clutching toward the
     roots of the soft grass. "Tamar,"
He whispered, then she breathed shudderingly and answered,
     "We have it, we have it. Now I know.

It was my fault. I never shall be ashamed again." He said, "What
 shall I do? Go away?
Kill myself, Tamar?" She contracted all her body and crouched
 in the long grass, shivering.
"It hurts, there is blood here, I am too cold to bathe myself
 again. O brother, brother,
Mine and twice mine. You knew already, a girl has got to learn.
 I love you, I chose my teacher.
Mine, it was my doing." She flung herself upon him, cold white
 and smooth, with sobbing kisses.
"I am so cold, dearest, dearest." The horses at the canyon mouth
 tugged at their halters,
Dug pits under the restless forehooves, shivered in the hill-wind
At sundown, were not ridden till dark, it was near midnight
They came to the old house.

IV

When Jinny Cauldwell slept, the old woman with a child's mind,
 then Stella Moreland
Invoked her childish-minded dead, or lying blank-eyed in the
 dark egged on her dreams to vision,
Suffering for lack of audience, tasting the ecstasy of vision. This
 was the vaporous portion
She endured her life in the strength of, in the sea-shaken lone-
 liness, little loved, nursing an idiot,
Growing bitterly old among the wind-torn Lobos cypress trunks.
 (O torture of needled branches
Doubled and gnarled, never a moment of quiet, the northwind
 or the southwind or the northwest.
For up and down the coast they are tall and terrible horsemen on
 patrol, alternate giants
Guarding the granite and sand frontiers of the last ocean; but
 here at Lobos the winds are torturers,
The old trees endure them. They blew always thwart the old
 woman's dreams and sometimes by her bedside
Stood, the south in russety black, the north in white, but the
 northwest wave-green, sea-brilliant,

Scaled like a fish. She had also the sun and moon and mightier
  presences in her visions.) Tamar
Entered the room toward morning and stood ghost-like among
  the old woman's ghosts. The rolled-up eyes,
Dull white, with little spindles of iris touching the upper lids,
  played back the girl's blown candle
Sightlessly, but the spirit of sight that the eyes are tools of and
  it made them, saw her. "Ah, Helen,"
Cried out the entranced lips, "We thought you were tired of the
  wind, we thought you never came now.
My sister's husband lies in the next room, go waken him, show
  him your beauty, call him with kisses.
He is old and the spittle when he dreams runs into his beard, but
  he is your lover and your brother."
"I am not Helen," she said, "what Helen, what Helen?" "Who
  was not the wife but the sister of her man,
Mine was his wife." "My mother?" "And now he is an old hulk
  battered ashore. Show him your beauty,
Strip for him, Helen, as when he made you a seaweed bed in the
  cave. What if the beard is slimy
And the eyes run, men are not always young and fresh like you
  dead women." But Tamar clutching
The plump hand on the coverlet scratched it with her nails, the
  old woman groaned but would not waken,
And Tamar held the candle flame against the hand, the soot
  striped it, then with a scream
The old woman awoke, sat up, and fell back rigid on the bed.
  Tamar found place for the candle
On a little table at the bedside, her freed hands could not awaken
  a second answer
In the flesh that now for all its fatness felt like a warmed stone.
  But the idiot waked and chuckled,
Waved both hands at the candle saying, "My little star, my little
  star, come little star."
And to these three old Cauldwell sighing with sleeplessness
Entered, not noticed, and he stood in the open door. Tamar was
  bending
Over the bed, loose hair like burnished metal

12

Concealed her face and sharply cut across one rounded shoulder
The thin night-dress had slipped from. The old man her father
Feared, for a ghost of law-contemptuous youth
Slid through the chilly vaults of the stiff arteries,
And he said, "What is it, Tamar?" "She was screaming in a
     dream,
I came to quiet her, now she has gone stiff like iron.
Who is this woman Helen she was dreaming about?"
"Helen? Helen?" he answered slowly and Tamar
Believed she saw the beard and the hands tremble.
"It's too cold for you, Tamar, go back to bed
And I'll take care of her. A common name for women."
Old Jinny clapped her hands, "Little star, little star,
Twinkle all night!" and the stiff form on the bed began to speak,
In a changed voice and from another mode of being
And spirit of thought: "I cannot think that you have forgotten.
I was walking on the far side of the moon,
Whence everything is seen but the earth, and never forgot.
This girl's desire drew me home, we also had wanted
Too near our blood,
And to tangle the interbranching net of generations
With a knot sideways. Desire's the arrow-sprayer
And shoots into the stars. Poor little Tamar
He gave you a luckless name in memory of me
And now he is old forgets mine." "You are that Helen,"
Said Tamar leaning over the fat shape
The quiet and fleshless voice seemed issuing from,
A sound of youth from the old puffed lips, "What Helen? This
     man's . . .
Sister, this body was saying?" "By as much more
As you are of your brother." "Why," laughed Tamar trembling,
"Hundreds of nasty children do it, and we
Nothing but children." Then the old man: "Lies, lies, lies.
No ghost, a lying old woman. Your Aunt Helen
Died white as snow. She died before your mother died.
Your mother and this old woman always hated her,
This liar, as they hated me. I was too hard a nature
To die of it. Lily and Stella." "It makes me nothing,

My darling sin a shadow and me a doll on wires,"
Thought Tamar with one half her spirit; and the other half said,
"Poor lies, words without meaning. Poor Aunt Stella,
The voices in her have no minds." "Poor little Tamar,"
Murmured the young voice from the swollen cavern,
"Though you are that woman's daughter, if we dead
Could be sorrowful for anyone but ourselves
I would be sorrowful for you, a trap so baited
Was laid to catch you when the world began,
Before the granite foundation. I too have tasted the sweet bait.
But you are the luckier, no one came home to me
To say there are no whips beyond death—but only memory,
And that can be endured." The room was quiet a moment,
And Tamar heard the wind moving outdoors. Then the idiot
     Jinny Cauldwell
Whose mind had been from birth a crippled bird but when she
     was twelve years old her mind's cage
Was covered utterly, like a bird-cage covered with its evening
     cloth when lamps are lighted,
And her memory skipped the more than forty years between but
     caught stray gleams of the sun of childhood,
She in her crumpled voice: "I'd rather play with Helen, go away
     Stella. Stella pinches me,
Lily laughs at me, Lily and Stella are not my sisters." "Jinny,
     Jinny,"
Said the old man shaking like a thin brick house-wall in an earth-
     quake, "do you remember, Jinny?"
"Jinny don't like the old man," she answered, "give me the star,
     give me my star,"
She whined, stretching from bed to reach the candle, "why have
     they taken my little star?
Helen would give it to Jinny." Then Stella waking from the
     trance sighed and arose to quiet her
According to her night's habit. Tamar said, "You were screaming
     in your sleep." "I had great visions.
And I have forgotten them. There Jinny, there, there. It'll have
     the candle, will it? Pretty Jinny.

Will have candle to-morrow. Little Jinny let Aunt Stella sleep
   now." Old Cauldwell tottering
Went to his room; then Tamar said, "You were talking about
   his sister Helen, my aunt Helen,
You never told me about her." "She has been dead for forty
   years, what should we tell you about her?
Now little Jinny, pretty sister." And laying her hands upon the
   mattress of the bed
The old woman cradled it up and down, humming a weary song.
   Tamar stood vainly waiting
The sleep of the monstrous babe; at length because it would not
   sleep went to her room and heard it
Gurgle and whimper an hour; and the tired litanies of the lulla-
   bies; not quiet till daylight.

v

O swiftness of the swallow and strength
Of the stone shore, brave beauty of falcons,
Beauty of the blue heron that flies
Opposite the color of evening
From the Carmel River's reed-grown mouth
To her nest in the deep wood of the deer
Cliffs of peninsular granite engirdle,
O beauty of the fountains of the sun
I pray you enter a little chamber,
I have given you bodies, I have made you puppets,
I have made idols for God to enter
And tiny cells to hold your honey.
I have given you a dotard and an idiot,
An old woman puffed with vanity, youth but botched with
   incest,
O blower of music through the crooked bugles,
You that make signs of sins and choose the lame for angels,
Enter and possess. Being light you have chosen the dark lamps,
A hawk the sluggish bodies: therefore God you chose
Me; and therefore I have made you idols like these idols
To enter and possess.
Tamar, finding no hope,

15

Slid back on passion, she had sought counsel of the dead
And found half-scornful pity and found her sin
Fore-dated; there was honey at least in shame
And secrecy in silence, and her lover
Could meet her afield or slip to her room at night
In serviceable safety. They learned, these two,
Not to look back nor forward; and but for the hint
Of vague and possible wreck every transgression
Paints on the storm-edge of the sky, their blue
Though it dulled a shade with custom shone serene
To the fifth moon, when the moon's mark on women
Died out of Tamar. She kept secret the warning,
How could she color such love with perplexed fear?
Her soul walked back and forth like a new prisoner
Feeling the plant of unescapable fate
Root in her body. There was death; who had entered water
To compass love might enter again to escape
Love's fruit; "But O, but O," she thought, "not to die now.
It is less than half a year
Since life turned sweet. If I knew one of the girls
My lover has known
She'd tell me what to do, how to be fruitless,
How to be . . . happy? They do it, they do it, all sin
Grew nothing to us that day in Mal Paso water.
A love sterile and sacred as the stars.
I will tell my lover, he will make me safe,
He will find means . . .
Sterile and sacred, and more than any woman
. . . Unhappy. Miserable," she sobbed, "miserable,
The rough and bitter water about the cliff's foot
Better to breathe."
              When Lee was not by her side
She walked the cliffs to tempt them. The calm and large
Pacific surge heavy with summer rolling southeast from a far
    origin
Battered to foam among the stumps of granite below.
Tamar watched it swing up the little fjords and fountain
Not angrily in the blowholes; a gray vapor

TAMAR

Breathed up among the buttressed writhings of the cypress trunks
And branches swollen with blood-red lichen. She went home
And her night was full of foolish dreams, two layers of dream,
  unrelative in emotion
Or substance to the pain of her thoughts. One, the undercurrent
  layer that seemed all night continuous,
Concerned the dead (and rather a vision than a dream, for visions
  gathered on that house
Like corposant fire on the hoar mastheads of a ship wandering
  strange waters), brown-skinned families
Came down the river and straggled through the wood to the sea,
  they kindled fires by knobs of granite
And ate the sea-food that the plow still turns up rotting shells of,
  not only around Point Lobos
But north and south wherever the earth breaks off to sea-rock;
  Tamar saw the huddled bodies
Squat by the fires and sleep; but when the dawn came there was
  throbbing music meant for daylight
And that weak people went where it led them and were nothing;
  then Spaniards, priests and horseback soldiers,
Came down the river and wandered through the wood to the sea,
  and hearing the universal music
Went where it led them and were nothing; and the English-
  speakers
Came down the river and wandered through the wood to the sea,
  among them Tamar saw her mother
Walking beside a nameless woman with no face nor breasts; and
  the universal music
Led them away and they were nothing; but Tamar led her father
  from that flood and saved him,
For someone named a church built on a rock, it was beautiful
  and white, not fallen to ruin
Like the ruin by Carmel River; she led him to it and made him
  enter the door, when he had entered
A new race came from the door and wandered down the river
  to the sea and to Point Lobos.
This was the undertow of the dream, obscured by a brighter
  surface layer but seeming senseless.

17

The tides of the sea were quiet and someone said "because the
    moon is lost." Tamar looked up
And the moon dwindled, rocketing off through lonely space, and
    the people in the moon would perish
Of cold or of a star's fire: then Will Andrews curiously wounded
    in the face came saying
"Tamar, don't cry. What do you care? I will take care of you."
    Wakening, Tamar thought about him
And how he had stopped coming to see her. Perhaps it was
    another man came through her dream,
The wound in the face disguised him, but that morning Lee
    having ridden to Mill Creek
To bargain about some fields of winter pasture
Now that the advancing year withered the hill-grass,
Tamar went down and saddled her own pony,
A four-year-old, as white as foam, and cantered
Past San Jose creek-mouth and the Carrows' farm
(Where David Carrow and his fanatical blue eyes,
That afterward saw Christ on the hill, smiled at her passing)
And three miles up the Carmel Valley came
To the Andrews place where the orchards ran to the river
And all the air was rich with ripening apples.
She would not go to the house; she did not find
Whom she was seeking; at length sadly she turned
Homeward, for Lee might be home within two hours,
And on the Carmel bridge above the water
(Shrunken with summer and shot with water lichen,
The surface scaled with minute scarlet leaves,
The borders green with slimy threads) met whom she sought.
"Tamar," he said, "I've been to see you." "You hadn't
For a long time." "I had some trouble with Lee,
I thought you didn't want me." While they talked
Her eyes tasted his face: was it endurable?
Though it lacked the curious gash her dream had given him. . . .
"I didn't want you, you thought?" "Lee said so." "You might
    have waited
Till Tamar said so." "Well," he answered, "I've been,
And neither of you was home but now I've met you."

—Well-looking enough; freckles, light hair, light eyes;
Not tall, but with a chest and hard wide shoulders,
And sitting the horse well—"O I can do it, I can do it,
Help me, God," murmured Tamar in her mind,
"How else—what else can I do?" and said, "Luck, isn't it?
What did you want to see me about?" "I wanted . . .
Because I . . . like you, Tamar."—"Why should I be careful,"
She thought, "if I frighten him off what does it matter,
I have got a little beyond caring." "Let's go down
Into the willow," she said, "we needn't be seen
Talking and someone tell him and make trouble
Here on the bridge." They went to the hidden bank
Under the deep green willows, colored water
Stagnated on its moss up to the stems,
Coarse herbage hid the stirrups, Tamar slid from the saddle
As quietly as the long unwhitening wave
Moulds a sunk rock, and while he tethered the horses,
"I have been lonely," she said. "Not for me, Tamar."
"You think not? Will, now that all's over
And likely we'll not see each other again
Often, nor by ourselves, why shouldn't I tell you . . ."
"What, Tamar?" "There've been moments . . . hours then . . .
When anything you might have asked me for
Would have been given, I'd have done anything
You asked me to, you never asked anything, Will.
I'm telling you this so that you may remember me
As one who had courage to speak truth, you'll meet
So many others." "But now"—he meant to ask,
"Now it's too late, Tamar?" and hadn't courage,
And Tamar thought "Must I go farther and say more?
Let him despise me as I despise myself.
I have got a little beyond caring." "Now?" she said.
"Do you think I am changed? You have changed, Will, you
     have grown
Older, and stronger I think, your face is firmer;
And carefuller: I have not changed, I am still reckless
To my own injury, and as trustful as a child.

Would I be with you here in the green thicket
If I weren't trustful? If you should harm me, Will,
I'd think it was no harm." She had laid her hand
On the round sunburnt throat and felt it throbbing,
And while she spoke the thought ran through her mind,
"He is only a little boy but if he turns pale
I have won perhaps, for white's the wanting color.
If he reddens I've lost and it's no matter." He did not move
And seemed not to change color and Tamar said,
"Now I must go. Lee will be home soon.
How soft the ground is in the willow shadow.
I have ended with you honestly, Will; remember me
Not afraid to speak truth and not ashamed
To have stripped my soul naked. You have seen all of me.
Good-bye." But when she turned he caught her by the arm,
She sickened inward, thinking, "Now it has come.
I have called and called it and I can't endure it.
Ah. A dumb beast." But he had found words now and said,
"How would you feel, Tamar, if all of a sudden
The bird or star you'd broken your heart to have
Flew into your hands, then flew away. O Tamar, Tamar,
You can't go now, you can't." She unresisting
Took the hot kisses on her neck and hair
And hung loose in his arms the while he carried her
To a clean bank of grass in the deep shadow.
He laid her there and kneeling by her: "You said you trusted
    me.
You are wise, Tamar; I love you so much too well
I would cut my hands off not to harm you." But she,
Driven by the inward spark of life and dreading
Its premature maturity, could not rest
On harmless love, there were no hands to help
In the innocence of love, and like a vision
Came to her the memory of that other lover
And how he had fallen a farther depth
From firmer innocence at Mal Paso, but the stagnant
Autumn water of Carmel stood too far

From the April freshet in the hills. Tamar pushed off
His kisses and stood up weeping and cried
"It's no use, why will you love me till I cry?
Lee hates you and my father is old and old, we can't
Sour the three years he has before he dies."
"I'll wait for you," said the boy, "wait years, Tamar." Then
    Tamar
Hiding her face against his throat
So that he felt the tears whispered, "But I . . ."
She sobbed, "Have no patience . . . I can't wait. Will . . .
When I made my soul naked for you
There was one spot . . . a fault . . . a shame
I was ashamed to uncover." She pressed her mouth
Between the muscles of his breast: "I want you and want you.
You didn't know that a clean girl could want a man.
Now you will take me and use me and throw me away
And I've . . . earned it." "Tamar, I swear by God
Never to let you be sorry, but protect you
With all my life." "This is our marriage," Tamar answered.
"But God would have been good to me to have killed me
Before I told you." The boy feeling her body
Vibrant and soft and sweet in its weeping surrender
Went blind and could not feel how she hated him
That moment; when he awakened she was lying
With the auburn hair muddied and the white face
Turned up to the willow leaves, her teeth were bared
And sunk in the under lip, a smear of blood
Reddening the corner of the lips. One of her arms
Crushed both her breasts, the other lay in the grass,
The fingers clutching toward the roots of the soft grass. "O
    Tamar,"
Murmured the boy, "I love you, I love you. What shall I do?
    Go away?
Kill myself, Tamar?" She contracted all her body and crouched
    in the long grass, thinking
"That Helen of my old father's never fooled him at least," and
    said, "There is nothing to do, nothing.

It is horribly finished. Keep it secret, keep it secret, Will. I too
   was to blame a little.
But I didn't mean . . . this." "I know," he said, "it was my
   fault, I would kill myself, Tamar,
To undo it but I loved you so, Tamar." "Loved? You have hurt
   me and broken me, the house is broken
And any thief can enter it." "O Tamar!" "You have broken
   our crystal innocence, we can never
Look at each other freely again." "What can I do, Tamar?"
   "Nothing. I don't know. Nothing.
Never come to the farm to see me." "Where can I see you,
   Tamar?" "Lee is always watching me,
And I believe he'd kill us. Listen, Will. To-morrow night I'll
   put a lamp in my window,
When all the house is quiet, and if you see it you can climb up
   by the cypress. I must go home,
Lee will be home. Will, though you've done to me worse than
   I ever dreamed, I love you, you have my soul,
I am your tame bird now."

VI

This was the high plateau of summer and August waning; white
   vapors
Breathed up no more from the brown fields nor hung in the hills;
   daily the insufferable sun
Rose, naked light, and flaming naked through the pale transpar-
   ent ways of the air drained gray
The strengths of nature; all night the eastwind streamed out of
   the valley seaward, and the stars blazed.
The year went up to its annual mountain of death, gilded with
   hateful sunlight, waiting rain.
Stagnant waters decayed, the trickling springs that all the misty-
   hooded summer had fed
Pendulous green under the granite ocean-cliffs dried and turned
   foul, the rock-flowers faded,
And Tamar felt in her blood the filth and fever of the season.
   Walking beside the house-wall

Under her window, she resented sickeningly the wounds in the
    cypress bark, where Andrews
Climbed to his tryst, disgust at herself choked her, and as a fire
    by water
Under the fog-bank of the night lines all the sea and sky with
    fire, so her self-hatred
Reflecting itself abroad burned back against her, all the world
    growing hateful, both her lovers
Hateful, but the intolerably masculine sun hatefullest of all.
    The heat of the season
Multiplied centipedes, the black worms that breed under loose
    rock, they call them thousand-leggers,
They invaded the house, their phalloid bodies cracking under-
    foot with a bad odor, and dropped
Ceiling to pillow at night, a vile plague though not poisonous.
    Also the sweet and female sea
Was weak with calm, one heard too clearly a mounting cormo-
    rant's wing-claps half a mile off shore;
The hard and dry and masculine tyrannized for a season. Rain
    in October or November
Yearly avenges the balance; Tamar's spirit rebelled too soon, the
    female fury abiding
In so beautiful a house of flesh. She came to her aunt the ghost-
    seer. "Listen to me, Aunt Stella.
I think I am going mad, I must talk to the dead; Aunt Stella,
    will you help me?" That old woman
Was happy and proud, no one for years had sought her for
    her talent. "Dear Tamar, I will help you.
We must go down into the darkness, Tamar, it is hard and pain-
    ful for me." "I am in the darkness
Already, a fiery darkness." "The good spirits will guide you,
    it is easy for you; for me, death.
Death, Tamar, I have to die to reach them." "Death's no bad
    thing," she answered, "each hour of the day
Has more teeth." "Are you so unhappy, Tamar, the good spirits
    will help you and teach you." "Aunt Stella,
To-night, to-night?" "I groan when I go down to death, your
    father and brother will come and spoil it."

"In the evening we will go under the rocks by the sea." "Well,
   in the evening." "If they talk to us
I'll buy you black silk and white lace."

                  In and out of the little fjord swam the weak waves
Moving their foam in the twilight. Tamar at one flank, old
   Stella at the other, upheld poor Jinny
Among the jags of shattered granite, so they came to the shingle.
   Rich, damp and dark the sea's breath
Folding them made amend for days of sun-sickness, but Jinny
   among the rubble granite
(They had no choice but take her along with them, who else
   would care for the idiot?) slipped, and falling
Gashed knees and forehead, and she whimpered quietly in the
   darkness. "Here," said Tamar, "I made you
A bed of seaweed under the nose of this old rock, let Jinny lie
   beside you, Aunt Stella,
I'll lay the rug over you both." They lay on the odorous kelp,
   Tamar squatted beside them,
The weak sea wavered in her rocks and Venus hung over the
   west between the cliff-butts
Like the last angel of the world, the crystal night deepening.
   The sea and the three women
Kept silence, only Tamar moved herself continually on the fret
   of her taut nerves,
And the sea moved, on the obscure bed of her eternity, but
   both were voiceless. Tamar
Felt her pulse bolt like a scared horse and stumble and stop,
   for it seemed to her a wandering power
Essayed her body, something hard and rounded and invisible
   pressed itself for entrance
Between the breasts, over the diaphragm. When she was forced
   backward and lay panting, the assault
Failed, the presence withdrew, and in that clearance she heard
   her old Aunt Stella monotonously muttering
Words with no meaning in them; but the tidal night under
   the cliff seemed full of persons

With eyes, although there was no light but the evening planet's
  and her trail in the long water.
Then came a man's voice from the woman, saying, "Que quieres
  pobrecita?" and Tamar, "Morir,"
Trembling, and marveling that she lied for no reason, and said,
  "Es porque no entiendo,
Anything but ingles." To which he answered, "Ah pobrecita,"
  and was silent. And Tamar
Cried, "I will talk to that Helen." But instead another male throat
  spoke out of the woman's
Unintelligible gutturals, and it ceased, and the woman changing
  voice, yet not to her own:
"An Indian. He says his people feasted here and sang to their
  Gods and the tall Gods came walking
Between the tide-marks on the rocks; he says to strip and dance
  and he will sing, and his Gods
Come walking." Tamar answered, crying, "I will not, I will
  not, tell him to go away and let me
Talk to that Helen." But old Stella after a silence: "He says No,
  no, the pregnant women
Would always dance here and the shore belongs to his people's
  ghosts nor will they endure another
Unless they are pleased." And Tamar said, "I cannot dance,
  drive him away," but while she said it
Her hands accepting alien life and a strange will undid the
  fastenings of her garments.
She panted to control them, tears ran down her cheeks, the
  male voice chanted
Hoarse discords from the old woman's body, Tamar drew her
  beauty
Out of its husks; dwellers on eastern shores
Watch moonrises as white as hers
When the half-moon about midnight
Steps out of her husk of water to dance in heaven:
So Tamar weeping
Slipped every sheath down to her feet, the spirit of the place
Ruling her, she and the evening star sharing the darkness,
And danced on the naked shore

Where a pale couch of sand covered the rocks,
Danced with slow steps and streaming hair,
Dark and slender
Against the pallid sea-gleam, slender and maidenly
Dancing and weeping . . .
It seemed to her that all her body
Was touched and troubled with polluting presences
Invisible, and whatever had happened to her from her two lovers
She had been until that hour inviolately a virgin,
Whom now the desires of dead men and dead Gods and a dead
    tribe
Used for their common prey . . . dancing and weeping,
Slender and maidenly . . . The chant was changed,
And Tamar's body responded to the change, her spirit
Wailing within her. She heard the brutal voice
And hated it, she heard old Jinny mimic it
In the cracked childish quaver, but all her body
Obeyed it, wakening into wantonness,
Kindling with lust and wilder
Coarseness of insolent gestures,
The senses cold and averse, but the frantic too-governable flesh
Inviting the assaults of whatever desired it, of dead men
Or Gods walking the tide-marks,
The beautiful girlish body as gracile as a maiden's
Gone beastlike, crouching and widening,
Agape to be entered, as the earth
Gapes with harsh heat-cracks, the inland adobe of sun-worn
    valleys
At the end of summer
Opening sick mouths for its hope of the rain,
So her body gone mad
Invited the spirits of the night, her belly and her breasts
Twisting, her feet dashed with blood where the granite had
    bruised them,
And she fell, and lay gasping on the sand, on the tide-line.
                                                    Darkness
Possessed the shore when the evening star was down; old Stella

Was quiet in her trance; old Jinny the idiot clucked and par-
roted to herself, there was none but the idiot

Saw whether a God or a troop of Gods came swaggering along
the tide-marks unto Tamar, to use her

Shamefully and return from her, gross and replete shadows,
swaggering along the tide-marks

Against the sea-gleam. After a little the life came back to that
fallen flower; for fear or feebleness

She crept on hands and knees, returning so to the old medium
of this infamy. Only

The new tide moved in the night now; Tamar with her back
bent like a bow and the hair fallen forward

Crouched naked at old Stella's feet, and shortly heard the voice
she had cried for. "I am your Helen.

I would have wished you choose another place to meet me and
milder ceremonies to summon me.

We dead have traded power for wisdom, yet it is hard for us
to wait on the maniac living

Patiently, the desires of you wild beasts. You have the power."
And Tamar murmured, "I had nothing,

Desire nor power." And Helen, "Humbler than you were. She
has been humbled, my little Tamar.

And not so clean as the first lover left you, Tamar. Another and
half a dozen savages,

Dead, and dressed up for Gods." "I have endured it," she an-
swered. Then the sweet disdainful voice

In the throat of the old woman: "As for me, I chose rather to
die." "How can I kill

A dead woman," said Tamar in her heart, not moving the lips,
but the other listened to thought

And answered, "O, we are safe, we shan't fear murder. But,
Tamar, the child will die, and all for nothing

You were submissive by the river, and lived, and endured fouling.
I have heard the wiser flights

Of better spirits, that beat up to the breasts and shoulders of our
Father above the star-fire,

Say, 'Sin never buys anything.'" Tamar, kneeling, drew the
thickness of her draggled hair

Over her face and wept till it seemed heavy with blood; and
    like a snake lifting its head
Out of a fire, she lifted up her face after a little and said, "It
    will live, and my father's
Bitch be proved a liar." And the voice answered, and the tone
    of the voice smiled, "Her words
Rhyme with her dancing. Tamar, did you know there were
    many of us to watch the dance you danced there,
And the end of the dance? We on the cliff; your mother, who
    used to hate me, was among us, Tamar.
But she and I loved each only one man, though it were the
    same. We two shared one? You, Tamar,
Are shared by many." And Tamar: "This is your help, I dug
    down to you secret dead people
To help me and so I am helped now. What shall I ask more?
    How it feels when the last liquid morsel
Slides from the bone? Or whether you see the worm that bur-
    rows up through the eye-socket, or thrill
To the maggot's music in the tube of a dead ear? You stinking
    dead. That you have no shame
Is nothing: I have no shame: see I am naked, and if my thighs
    were wet with dead beasts' drippings
I have suffered no pollution like the worms in yours; and if I
    cannot touch you I tell you
There are those I can touch. I have smelled fire and tasted fire,
And all these days of horrible sunlight, fire
Hummed in my ears, I have worn fire about me like a cloak and
    burning for clothing. It is God
Who is tired of the house that thousand-leggers crawl about in,
    where an idiot sleeps beside a ghost-seer,
A doting old man sleeps with dead women and does not know it,
And pointed bones are at the doors
Or climb up trees to the window. I say He has gathered
Fire all about the walls and no one sees it
But I, the old roof is ripe and the rafters
Rotten for burning, and all the woods are nests of horrible things,
    nothing would ever clean them

But fire, but I will go to a clean home by the good river." "You
    danced, Tamar," replied
The sweet disdainful voice in the mouth of the old woman, "and
    now your song is like your dance,
Modest and sweet. Only you have not said it was you,
Before you came down by the sea to dance,
That lit a candle in your closet and laid
Paper at the foot of the candle. We were watching.
And now the wick is nearly down to the heap,
It's God will have fired the house? But Tamar,
It will not burn. You will have fired it, your brother
Will quench it, I think that God would hardly touch
Anything in that house." "If you know everything,"
Cried Tamar, "tell me where to go.
Now life won't do me and death is shut against me
Because I hate you. O believe me I hate you dead people
More than you dead hate me. Listen to me, Helen.
There is no voice as horrible to me as yours,
And the breasts the worms have worked in. A vicious berry
Grown up out of the graveyard for my poison.
But there is no one in the world as lonely as I,
Betrayed by life and death." Like rain breaking a storm
Sobs broke her voice. Holding by a jag of the cliff
She drew herself full height. God who makes beauty
Disdains no creature, nor despised that wounded
Tired and betrayed body. She in the starlight
And little noises of the rising tide
Naked and not ashamed bore a third part
With the ocean and keen stars in the consistence
And dignity of the world. She was white stone,
Passion and despair and grief had stripped away
Whatever is rounded and approachable
In the body of woman, hers looked hard, long lines
Narrowing down from the shoulder-bones, no appeal,
A weapon and no sheath, fire without fuel,
Saying, "Have you anything more inside you
Old fat and sleepy sepulcher, any more voices?
You can do better than my father's by-play

And the dirty tricks of savages, decenter people
Have died surely. I have so passed nature
That God himself, who's dead or all these devils
Would never have broken hell, might speak out of you
Last season thunder and not scare me." Old Stella
Groaned but not spoke, old Jinny lying beside her
Wakened at the word thunder and suddenly chuckling
Began to mimic a storm, "whoo-whoo" for wind
And "boom-boom-boom" for thunder. Other voices
Wakened far off above the cliff, and suddenly
The farm-bell ringing fire; and on the rock-islets
Sleepy cormorants cried at it. "Why, now He speaks
Another way than out of the fat throat,"
Cried Tamar, and prayed, "O strong and clean and terrible
Spirit and not father punish the hateful house.
Fire eat the walls and roofs, drive the red beast
Through every wormhole of the rotting timbers
And into the woods and into the stable, show them,
These liars, that you are alive." Across her voice
The bell sounded and old Jinny mimicking it,
And shouts above the cliff. "Look, Jinny, look,"
Cried Tamar, "the sky'll be red soon, come and we'll dress
And watch the bonfire." Yet she glanced no thought
At her own mermaid nakedness but gathering
The long black serpents of beached seaweed wove
Wreaths for old Jinny and crowned and wound her. Meanwhile
The bell ceased ringing and Stella ceased her moan,
And in the sudden quietness, "Tamar," she said
In the known voice of Helen so many years
Dead, "though you hate me utterly, Tamar, I
Have nothing to give back, I was quite emptied
Of hate and love and the other fires of the flesh
Before your mother gave the clay to my lover
To mould you a vessel to hold them." Tamar, winding
Her mindless puppet in the sea-slough mesh
Said over her shoulder, hardly turning, "Why then
Do you trouble whom you don't hate?" "Because we hunger
And hunger for life," she answered. "Did I come uncalled?

You called me, you have more hot and blind, wild-blooded
And passionate life than any other creature.
How could I ever leave you while the life lasts?
God pity us both, a cataract life
Dashing itself to pieces in an instant.
You are my happiness, you are my happiness and death eats you.
I'll leave you when you are empty and cold and join us.
Then pity me, then Tamar, me flitting
The chilly and brittle pumice-tips of the moon,
While the second death
Corrodes this shell of me, till it makes my end."
But Tamar would not listen to her, too busily
Decking old Jinny for the festival fire,
And sighing that thin and envious ghost forsook
Her instrument, and about that time harsh pain
Wrung Tamar's loins and belly, and pain and terror
Expelled her passionate fancies, she cried anxiously,
"Stella, Aunt Stella, help me, will you?" and thinking,
"She hears when Jinny whimpers," twistingly pinched
Her puppet's arm until it screamed. Old Stella
Sat up on the seaweed bed and turned white eyes
No pupils broke the diffused star-gleam in
Upon her sixty-year-old babe, that now
Crouched whimpering, huddled under the slippery leaves
And black whips of the beach; and by it stood gleaming
Tamar, anguished, all white as the blank balls
That swept her with no sight but vision: old Stella
Did not awake yet but a voice blew through her,
Not personal like the other, and shook her body
And shook her hands: "It was no good to do too soon, your
    fire's out, you'd been patient for me
It might have saved two fires." But Tamar: "Stella.
I'm dying: or it is dying: wake up Aunt Stella.
O pain, pain, help me." And the voice: "She is mine while I
    use her. Scream, no one will hear but this one
Who has no mind, who has not more help than July rain." And
    Tamar, "What are you, what are you, mocking me?

More dirt and another dead man? O," she moaned, pressing her
  flanks with both her hands, and bending
So that her hair across her knees lay on the rock. It answered,
  "Not a voice from carrion.
Breaker of trees and father of grass, shepherd of clouds and
  waters, if you had waited for me
You'd be the luckier." "What shall I give you?" Tamar cried,
  "I have given away——" Pain stopped her, and then
Blood ran, and she fell down on the round stones, and felt nor
  saw nothing. A little later
Old Stella Moreland woke out of her vision, sick and shaking.

                               Tamar's mind and suffering
Returned to her neither on the sea-rocks of the midnight nor
  in her own room; but she was lying
Where Lee her brother had lain, nine months before, after his
  fall, in the big westward bedroom.
She lay on the bed, and in one corner was a cot for Stella who
  nursed her, and in the other
A cot for the idiot, whom none else would care for but old
  Stella. After the ache of awakening
And blank dismay of the spirit come home to a spoiled house,
  she lay thinking with vacant wonder
That life is always an old story, repeating itself always like the
  leaves of a tree
Or the lips of an idiot; that herself like Lee her brother
Was picked up bleeding from the sea-boulders under the sea-
  cliff and carried up to be laid
In the big westward bedroom . . . was he also fouled with
  ghosts before they found him, a gang
Of dead men beating him with rotten bones, mouthing his body,
  piercing him? "Stella," she whispered,
"Have I been sick long?" "There, sweetheart, lie still; three or
  four days." "Has Lee been in to see me?"
"Indeed he has, hours every day." "He'll come, then," and she
  closed her eyes and seemed to sleep.
Someone tapped at the door after an hour and Tamar said,
  "Come, Lee." But her old father

Came in, and he said nothing, but sat down by the bed; Tamar
    had closed her eyes. In a little

Lee entered, and he brought a chair across the room and sat by
    the bed. "Why don't you speak,

Lee?" And he said, "What can I say except I love you, sister?"
    "Why do you call me sister,

Not Tamar?" And he answered, "I love you, Tamar." Then old
    Aunt Stella said, "See, she's much better.

But you must let her rest. She'll be well in a few days; now kiss
    her, Lee, and let her rest."

Lee bent above the white pure cameo-face on the white pillow,
    meaning to kiss the forehead.

But Tamar's hands caught him, her lips reached up for his: while
    Jinny the idiot clapped and chuckled

And made a clucking noise of kisses; then, while Lee sought to
    untwine the arms that yoked his neck,

The old man, rising: "I opened the Book last night thinking
    about the sorrows of this house,

And it said, 'If a man find her in the field and force her and lie
    with her, nevertheless the damsel

Has not earned death, for she cried out and there was none to
    save her.' Be glad, Tamar, my sins

Are only visited on my son, for you there is mercy." "David,
    David,

Will you be gone and let her rest now," cried old Stella, "do
    you mean to kill her with a bible?"

"Woman," he answered, "has God anything to do with you?
    She will not die, the Book

Opened and said it." Tamar, panting, leaned against the pillow
    and said, "Go, go. To-morrow

Say all you please; what does it matter?" And the old man said,
    "Come, Lee, in the morning she will hear us."

Tamar stretched out her trembling hand, Lee did not touch it,
    but went out ahead of his father.

So they were heard in the hall, and then their footsteps on the
    stair. Tamar lay quiet and rigid,

With open eyes and tightening fists, with anger like a coiled steel
    spring in her throat but weakness

And pain for the lead weights. After an hour she said, "What
    does he mean to do? Go away?
Kill himself, Stella?" Stella answered, "Nothing, nothing, they
    talk, it's to keep David quiet.
Your father is off his head a little, you know. Now rest you,
    little Tamar, smile and be sleepy,
Scold them to-morrow." "Shut the sun out of my eyes then,"
    Tamar said, but the idiot Jinny
Made such a moaning when the windows were all curtained they
    needed to let in one beam
For dust to dance in; then the idiot and the sick girl slept. About
    the hour of sundown
Tamar was dreaming trivially—an axman chopping down a tree
    and field-mice scampering
Out of the roots—when suddenly like a shift of wind the dream
Changed and grew awful, she watched dark horsemen coming
    out of the south, squadrons of hurrying horsemen
Between the hills and the dark sea, helmeted like the soldiers of
    the war in France,
Carrying torches. When they passed Mal Paso Creek the columns
Veered, one of the riders said, "Here it began," but another
    answered, "No. Before the granite
Was bedded to build the world on." So they formed and gal-
    loped north again, hurrying squadrons,
And Tamar thought, "When they come to the Carmel River
    then it will happen. They have passed Mal Paso."

                             Meanwhile—
Who has ever guessed to what odd ports, what sea buoying the
    keels, a passion blows its bulkless
Navies of vision? High up in the hills
Ramon Ramirez, who was herdsman of the Cauldwell herds,
    stood in his cabin doorway
Rolling a cigarette a half-hour after sundown, and he felt puffs
    from the south
Come down the slope of stunted redwoods, so he thought the
    year was turning at last, and shortly

There would come showers; he walked therefore a hundred
  yards to westward, where a point of the hill
Stood over Wildcat Canyon and the sea was visible; he saw
  Point Lobos gemmed in the darkening
Pale yellow sea; and on the point the barn-roofs and the house-
  roof breaking up through the blackness
Of twilight cypress tops, and over the sea a cloud forming. The
  evening darkened. Southwestward
A half-mile loop of the coast-road could be seen, this side Mal
  Paso. Suddenly a nebular company
Of lights rounded the hill, Ramirez thought the headlights of
  a car sweeping the road,
But in a moment saw that it was horsemen, each carrying a light,
  hurrying northward,
Moving in squads he judged of twenty or twenty-five, he counted
  twelve or thirteen companies
When the brush broke behind him and a horseman rode the
  headlong ridge like level ground,
Helmeted, carrying a torch. Followed a squad of twelve, hel-
  meted, cantering the headlong ridge
Like level ground. He thought in the nervous innocence of the
  early war, they must be Germans.

Tamar awoke out of her dream and heard old Jinny saying,
  "Dear sister Helen, kiss me
As you kiss David. I was watching under a rock, he took your
  clothes off and you kissed him
So hard and hard, I love you too, Helen; you hardly ever kiss
  me." Tamar lay rigid,
Breathless to listen to her; it was well known in the house that
  under the shell of imbecility
Speech and a spirit, however subdued, existed still; there were
  waking flashes, and more often
She talked in sleep and proved her dreams were made out of
  clear memories, childhood sights and girlhood
Fancies, before the shadow had fallen; so Tamar craving food
  for passion listened to her,

And heard: "Why are you cross, Helen? I won't peek if you'd
    rather I didn't. Darling Helen,
I love him, too; I'd let him play with me the way he does with
    you if he wanted to.
And Lily and Stella hate me as much as they hate you." All
    she said after was so mumbled
That Tamar could not hear it, could only hear the mumble, and
    old Aunt Stella's nasal sleep
And the sea murmuring. When the mumbled voice was quiet it
    seemed to Tamar
A strange thing was preparing, an inward pressure
Grew in her throat and seemed to swell her arms and hands
And join itself with a fluid power
Streaming from somewhere in the room—from Jinny?
From Stella?—and in a moment the heavy chair
That Lee had sat in, tipped up, rose from the floor,
And floated to the place he had brought it from
Five hours ago. The power was then relaxed,
And Tamar could breathe and speak. She awaked old Stella
And trembling told her what she had seen; who laughed
And answered vaguely so that Tamar wondered
Whether she was still asleep, and let her burrow
In her bed again and sleep. Later that night
Tamar too slept, but shudderingly, in snatches,
For fear of dreaming. A night like years. In the gray of morning
A horse screamed from the stableyard and Tamar
Heard the thud of hooves lashing out and timbers
Splintering, and two or three horses broken loose
Galloped about the grounds of the house. She heard men calling,
And downstairs Lee in a loud angry tone
Saying "Someone's pitched the saw-buck and the woodpile
Into the horse-corral." Then Tamar thought
"The same power moved his chair in the room, my hatred, my
    hatred,
Disturbing the house because I failed to burn it.
I must be quiet and quiet and quiet and keep
The serving spirits of my hid hatred quiet
Until my time serves too. Helen you shadow

Were never served so handily." Stella had awakened,
And Tamar asking for a drink of water
She waddled to fetch it and met Lee at the door.
"O Lee," she said, "that noise—what ever has happened?"
He: "I don't know. Some fool has pitched the whole woodpile
Into the horse-corral. Is Tamar awake?
I want to see Tamar." He entered the room
As Stella left it. Old withered Aunt Jinny
Sat up in her bed saying "David, David," but Lee
Kneeling at Tamar's bedside, "O Tamar, Tamar.
The old man's outdoors tottering after the horses
So I can see you a minute. O why, why, why,
Didn't you tell me Tamar? I'd have taken you up
In my arms and carried you to the end of the world."
"How it's turned sour," she thought, "I'd have been glad of this
Yesterday," and she clinched her finger-nails
Into her palms under the bed-covers,
Saying, "Tell you—what? What have they told you," she asked
With a white sidelong smile, "people are always lying?"
"Tamar, that you—that we . . . O I've lived hell
Four or five days now." "You look well enough,"
She answered, "put yours by mine," laying her white, lean,
And somewhat twitching hand on the counterpane,
"Mine used to manage a bridle as well as yours
And now look at them. I don't suppose you want me
Now, but it doesn't matter. You used to come to my bed
With something else than pity, convenient, wasn't it?
Not having to ride to Monterey?" He answered frowning,
"However much you hurt me I am very glad too
That all the joys and memories of a love
As great and as forbidden as ours are nothing to you
Or worse than nothing, because I have to go away,
Two days from now, and stay till the war's over
And you are married and father is dead. I've promised him
Never to see him again, never to see his face.
He didn't ask it because he thinks his Book
Told him I'm to be killed. That's foolishness,
But makes your peace with him and thank God for that.

37

What his Book told him." "So here's the secret
I wasn't strong enough yesterday to hear.
I thought maybe you meant to kill yourself."
"Thanks, Tamar. The old man thinks I don't need to." "O,
You beast," she said, "you runaway dog.
I wish you joy of your dirty Frenchwomen
You want instead of me. Take it, take it.
Old people in their dotage gabble the truth,
You won't live long." "What can I say, Tamar?
I'm sorry, I'm sorry, I'm sorry." "But go away,"
She said, "and if you'll come again to-night
Maybe I'll tell you mine, my secret."

        That morning
Ramon Ramirez who watched the Cauldwell cattle
Up in the hills kept thinking of his vision
Of helmets carrying torches; he looked for tracks
On the ridge where he had seen the riders cantering,
And not a bush was broken, not a hoof-mark
Scarred the sear grass. At noon he thought he'd ride
To Vogel's place taking his lunch in the saddle
And tell someone about it. At the gap in the hill
Where storm-killed redwoods line both sides he met
Johnny Cabrera with a flaming bundle
Of dead twigs and dry grass tied with brown cord.
He smelled the smoke and saw the flame sag over
On a little wind from the east, and said in Spanish
"Eh Johnny, are you out of matches?" who answered flashing
His white teeth in a smile, "I'm carrying fire to Lobos
If God is willing," and walked swinging ahead,
Singing to himself the fool south-border couplet
"No tengo tabaco, no tengo papel,
No tengo dinero, God damn it to hell,"
And Ramon called "Hey Johnny," but he would not stop
Nor answer, and thinking life goes wild at times
Ramon came to the hill-slope under Vogel's
And smelled new smoke and saw the clouds go up
And this same Johnny with two other men
Firing the brush to make spring pasture. Ramon

Felt the scalp tighten on his temples and thought best
Not to speak word of either one of his visions,
Though he talked with the men, they told him Tamar Cauldwell
Was sick, and Lee had enlisted.

                The afternoon
Was feverish for so temperate a sea-coast
And terribly full of light, the sea like a hard mirror
Reverberated the straight and shining serpents
That fell from heaven and Tamar dreamed in a doze
She was hung naked by that tight cloth bandage
Half-way between sea and sky, beaten on by both,
Burning with light; wakening she found she had tumbled
The bed-clothes to the floor and torn her nightgown
To rags, and was alone in the room, and blinded
By the great glare of sun in the western windows.
She rose and shut the curtains though they had told her
She mustn't get out of bed, and finding herself
Able to walk she stood by the little window
That looked southeast from the south bay of the room
And saw the smoke of burning brushwood slopes
Tower up out of the hills in the windless weather
Like an enormous pinetree, "Everybody
But me has luck with fire," she thought to herself,
"But I can walk now," and returned to bed
And drew the sheets over her flanks, but leaving
The breasts and the shoulders bare. In half an hour
Stella and old Jinny came into the room
With the old man David Cauldwell. Stella hastily
Drew up the sheet to Tamar's throat but Tamar
Saying, "You left the curtains open and the sun
Has nearly killed me," doubled it down again,
And David Cauldwell, trembling: "Will you attempt
Age and the very grave, uncovering your body
To move the old bones that seventy years have broken
And dance your bosoms at me through a mist of death?
Though I know that you and your brother have utterly despised
The bonds of blood, and daughter and father are no closer
    bound,

And though this house spits out all goodness, I am old, I am old,
 I am old,
What do you want of me?" He stood tottering and wept,
Covering his eyes and beard with shaken old hands,
And Tamar, having not moved, "Nothing," she said,
"Nothing, old man. I have swum too deep into the mud
For this to sicken me; and as you say, there are neither
Brother nor sister, daughter nor father, nor any love
This side the doorways of the damnable house.
But I have a wildbeast of a secret hidden
Under the uncovered breast will eat us all up
Before Lee goes." "It is a lie, it is a lie, it is all a lie.
Stella you must go out, go out of the room Stella,
Not to hear the sick and horrible imaginations
A sick girl makes for herself. Go Stella." "Indeed I won't,
David." "You—you—it is still my house." "To let you kill her
 with bad words
All out of the bible—indeed I won't." "Go, Stella," said Tamar,
"Let me talk to this old man, and see who has suffered
When you come back. I am out of pity, and you and Jinny
Will be less scorched on the other side of the door." After a
 third refusal
The old woman went, leading her charge, and Tamar: "You
 thought it was your house? It is me they obey.
It is mine, I shall destroy it. Poor old man I have earned
 authority." "You have gone mad," he answered.
And she: "I'll show you our trouble, you sinned, your old book
 calls it, and repented: that was foolish.
I was unluckier, I had no chance to repent, so I learned some-
 thing, we must keep sin pure
Or it will poison us, the grain of goodness in a sin is poison.
 Old man, you have no conception
Of the freedom of purity. Lock the door, old man, I am telling
 you a secret." But he trembling,
"O God thou hast judged her guiltless, the Book of thy word
 spake it, thou hast the life of the young man
My son . . ." and Tamar said, "Tell God we have revoked
 relationship in the house, he is not

Your son nor you my father." "Dear God, blot out her words,
    she has gone mad. Tamar, I will lock it,
Lest anyone should come and hear you, and I will wrestle for
    you with God, I will not go out
Until you are His." He went and turned the key and Tamar
    said, "I told you I have authority.
You obey me like the others, we pure have power. Perhaps
    there are other ways, but I was plunged
In the dirt of the world to win it, and, O father, so I will call
    you this last time, dear father
You cannot think what freedom and what pleasure live in having
    abjured laws, in having
Annulled hope, I am now at peace." "There is no peace, there
    is none, there is none, there is no peace
But His," he stammered, "but God's." "Not in my arms, old
    man, on these two little pillows? Your son
Found it there, and another, and dead men have defiled me.
    You that are half dead and half living,
Look, poor old man. That Helen of yours, when you were
    young, where was her body more desirable,
Or was she lovinger than I? You know it is forty years ago
    that we revoked
Relationships in the house." "He never forgives, He never for-
    gives, evil punishes evil
With the horrible mockery of an echo." "Is the echo louder
    than the voice, I have surpassed her,
Yours was the echo, time stands still old man, you'll learn when
    you have lived at the muddy root
Under the rock of things; all times are now, to-day plays on
    last year and the inch of our future
Made the first morning of the world. You named me for the
    monument in a desolate graveyard,
Fool, and I say you were deceived, it was out of me that fire lit
    you and your Helen, your body
Joined with your sister's
Only because I was to be named Tamar and to love my brother
    and my father.

I am the fountain." But he, shuddering, moaned, "You have gone
    mad, you have gone mad, Tamar,"
And twisted his old hands muttering, "I fear hell. O Tamar, the
    nights I have spent in agony,
Ages of pain, when the eastwind ran like glass under the peeping
    stars or the southwest wind
Plowed in the blackness of the tree. You—a little thing has
    driven you mad, a moment of suffering,
But I for more than forty years have lain under the mountains
    and looked down into hell."
"One word," she said, "that was not written in the book of my
    fears. I did indeed fear pain
Before peace found me, or death, never that dream. Old man,
    to be afraid is the only hell
And dead people are quit of it, I have talked with the dead."
    "Have you—with her?" "Your pitiful Helen?
She is always all about me; if you lay in my arms old man you
    would be with her. Look at me,
Have you forgotten—your Helen?" He in torture
Groaned like a beast, but when he approached the bed she
    laughed, "Not here, behind you." And he blindly
Clutching at her, she left the coverlet in his hands and slipping
    free at the other side
Saw in a mirror on the wall her own bright throat and shoulder
    and just beyond them the haggard
Open-mouthed mask, the irreverend beard and blind red eyes.
    She caught the mirror from its fastening
And held it to him, reverse. "Here is her picture, Helen's pic-
    ture, look at her, why is she always
Crying and crying?" When he turned the frame and looked,
    then Tamar: "See that is her lover's.
The hairy and horrible lips to kiss her, the drizzling eyes to eat
    her beauty, happiest of women
If only he were faithful; he is too young and wild and lovely,
    and the lusts of his youth
Lead him to paw strange beds." The old man turned the glass
    and gazed at the blank side, and turned it

Again face toward him, he seemed drinking all the vision in it,
and Tamar: "Helen, Helen,

I know you are here present; was I humbled in the night lately
and you exulted?

See here your lover. I think my mother will not envy you now,
your lover, Helen, your lover,

The mouth to kiss you, the hands to fondle secret places." Then
the old man sobbing, "It is not easy

To be old, mocked, and a fool." And Tamar, "What, not yet,
you have not gone mad yet? Look, old fellow.

These rags drop off, the bandages hid something but I'm done
with them. See . . . I am the fire

Burning the house." "What do you want, what do you want?"
he said, and stumbled toward her, weeping.

"Only to strangle a ghost and to destroy the house. Spit on the
memory of that Helen

You might have anything of me." And he groaning, "When I
was young

I thought it was my fault, I am old and know it was hers, night
after night, night after night

I have lain in the dark, Tamar, and cursed her." "And now?"
"I hate her, Tamar." "O," said Tamar gently,

"It is enough, she has heard you. Now unlock the door, old
father, and go, and go." "Your promise,

Tamar, the promise, Tamar." "Why I might do it, I have no
feeling of revolt against it.

Though you have forgotten that fear of hell why should I let
you

Be mocked by God?" And he, the stumpage of his teeth knock-
ing together, "You think, you think

I'll go to the stables and a rope from a rafter

Finish it for you?" "Dear, I am still sick," she answered, "you
don't want to kill me? A man

Can wait three days: men have lived years and years on the
mere hope."

     Meanwhile the two old women

Sat in their room, old Stella sat at the window looking south
into the cypress boughs, and Jinny

On her bed's edge, rocking her little withered body backward
and forward, and said vacantly,
"Helen, what do you do the times you lock the door to be
alone, and Lily and Stella
Wonder where David's ridden to?" After a while she said again,
"Do tell me, sister Helen,
What you are doing the times you lock the door to be alone,
and Lily and Stella wonder
Where David's ridden to?" And a third time she repeated,
"Darling sister Helen, tell me
What you are doing the times you lock the door to be alone,
and Lily and Stella wonder
Where David's riding?" Stella seemed to awake, catching at
breath, and not in her own voice,
"What does she mean," she said, "my picture, picture? O! the
mirror—I read in a book Jinny.
A story about lovers; I never had a lover, I read about them;—
I won't look, though.
With all that blind abundance, so much of life and blood, that
sweet and warming blaze of passion,
She has also a monkey in her mind." "Tell me the story about
the picture." "Ugh, if she plans
To humble herself utterly . . . You may peek, Jinny,
Try if you can, shut both eyes, draw them back into your fore-
head, and look, look, look
Over the eyebrows, no, like this, higher up, up where the hair
grows, now peek Jinny. Can't you
See through the walls? You can. Look, look, Jinny. As if they'd
cut a window. I used to tell you
That God could see into caves: you are like God now: peek,
Jinny." "I can see something.
It's in the stable, David's come from Monterey, he's hanging
the saddle on a peg there . . ."
"Jinny, I shall be angry. That's not David,
It's Lee, don't look into the stable, look into the bedroom, you
know, Jinny, the bedroom,
Where we left Tamar on the bed." "O that's too near, it hurts
me, it hurts my head, don't scold me, Helen.

How can I see if I'm crying? I see now clearly."
"What do you see?" "I see through walls, O, I'm like God,
    Helen. I see the wood and plaster
And see right through them." "What? What are they doing?"
    "How can you be there and here, too, Helen?"
"It's Tamar, what is she doing?" "I know it's you Helen, be-
    cause you have no hair
Under the arms, I see the blue veins under the arms." "Well, if
    it's me, what is she doing?
Is she on the bed? What is she saying?" "She is on fire Helen,
    she has white fire all around you
Instead of clothes, and that is why you are laughing with so
    pale a face." "Does she let him do
Whatever he wants to, Jinny?" "He says that he hates . . .
    somebody . . . and then you laughed for he had a rope
Around his throat a moment, the beard stuck out over it." "O
    Jinny it wasn't I that laughed
It was that Tamar, Tamar, Tamar, she has bought him for
    nothing. She and her mother both to have him,
The old hollow fool." "What do they want him for, Helen?"
    "To plug a chink, to plug a chink, Jinny,
In the horrible vanity of women. Lee's come home, now I
    could punish her, she's past hurting,
Are they huddled together Jinny? What, not yet, not yet?"
    "You asked for the key but when he held it
You ran away from him." "What do I want, what do I want,
    it is frightful to be dead, what do I . . .
Without power, and no body or face. To kill her, kill her?
There's no hell and curse God for it . . ."

                                        Lee Cauldwell childishly
Loved hearing the spurs jingle, and because he felt
"After to-morrow I shan't wear them again,
Nor straddle a pony for many a weary month and year,
Maybe forever," he left them at his heels
When he drew off the chaps and hung the saddle
On the oak peg in the stable-wall. He entered the house
Slowly, he had taken five drinks in Monterey

45

And saw his tragedy of love, sin, and war
At the disinterested romantic angle
Misted with not unpleasing melancholy,
Over with, new adventure ahead, a perilous cruise
On the other ocean, and great play of guns
On the other shore . . . at the turn of the stair he heard
Hands hammering a locked door, and a voice unknown to him
Crying, "Tamar, I loved you for your flame of passion
And hated you for its deeds, all that we dead
Can love or hate with: and now will you crust flame
With filth, submit? Submit? Tamar,
The defilement of the tideline dead was nothing
To this defilement." Then Lee jingling his spurs,
Jumped four steps to the landing, "Who is there? You,
Aunt Stella?" Old gray Aunt Jinny like a little child
Moaning drew back from him, and the mouth of Stella:
"A man that's ready to cross land and water
To set the world in order can't be expected
To leave his house in order." And Lee, "Listen, Aunt Stella,
Who are you playing, I mean what voice out of the world of
    the dead
Is speaking from you?" She answered, "Nothing. I was some-
    thing
Forty years back but now I'm only the bloodhound
To bay at the smell of what they're doing in there."
"Who? Tamar? Blood?" "Too close in blood, I am the blood-
    stain
On the doorsill of a crime, she does her business
Under her own roof mostly." "Tamar, Tamar,"
Lee called, shaking the door. She from within
Answered "I am here, Lee. Have you said good-by
To Nita and Conchita in Monterey
And your fat Fanny? But who is the woman at the door
Making the noise?" He said, "Open the door;
Open the door, Tamar." And she, "I opened it for you,
You are going to France to knock at other doors.
I opened it for you and others." "What others?" "Ask her,"
Said the young fierce voice from old Aunt Stella's lips,

"What other now?" "She is alone there," he answered,
"A devil is in you. Tamar," he said, "tell her
You are alone." "No, Lee, I am asking in earnest,
Who is the woman making the noise out there?
Someone you've brought from Monterey? Tell her to go:
Father is here." "Why have you locked it, why have you
    locked it?"
He felt the door-knob turning in his hand
And the key shook the lock; Tamar stood in the doorway
Wrapped in a loose blue robe that the auburn hair
Burned on, and beyond her the old man knelt by the bed,
His face in the lean twisted hands. "He was praying for me,"
Tamar said quietly. "You are leaving to-morrow,
He has only one child." Then the old man lifting a face
From which the flesh seemed to have fallen, and the eyes
Dropped and been lost: "What will you do to him, Tamar?
Tamar, have mercy.
He was my son, years back." She answered, "I am glad
That you know who has power in the house"; and he
Hid the disfigured face, between his wrists
The beard kept moving, they thought him praying to God.
And Tamar said, "It is coming to the end of the bad story,
That needn't have been bad only we fools
Botch everything, but a dead fool's the worst,
This old man's sister who rackets at the doors
And drove me mad, although she is nothing but a voice,
Dead, shelled, and the shell rotted, but she had to meddle
In the decencies of life here. Lee, if you truly
Lust for the taste of a French woman I'll let you go
For fear you die unsatisfied and plague
Somebody's children with a ghost's hungers
Forty years after death. Do I care, do I care?
You shan't go, Lee. I told the old man I have a secret
That will eat us all up . . . and then, dead woman,
What will you have to feed on? You spirits flicker out
Too speedily, forty years is a long life for a ghost
And you will only famish a little longer
To whom I'd wish eternity." "O Tamar, Tamar,"

It answered out of Stella's mouth, "has the uttermost
Not taught you anything yet, not even that extinction
Is the only terror?" "You lie too much," she answered,
"You'll enter it soon and not feel any stitch
Of fear afterwards. Listen, Lee, your arms
Were not the first man's to encircle me, and that spilled life
Losing which let me free to laugh at God,
I think you had no share in." He trembled, and said
"O Tamar has your sickness and my crime
Cut you so deep? A lunatic in a dream
Dreams nearer things than this." "I'd never have told you,"
She answered, "if his vicious anger—after I'd balanced
Between you a long time and then chose you—
Hadn't followed his love's old night-way to my window
And kindled fire in the room when I was gone,
The spite-fire that might easily have eaten up
And horribly, our helpless father, or this innocent
Jinny . . ." "He did it, he did it, forgive me, Tamar.
I thought that you gone mad . . . Tamar, I know
That you believe what you are saying but I
Do not believe you. There was no one." "The signal
Was a lamp in the window, perhaps some night
He'd come still if you'd set a lamp into my window.
And when he climbed out of the cypress tree
Then you would know him." "I would mark him to know.
But it's not true." "Since I don't sleep there now
You might try for the moth; if he doesn't come
I'll tell you his name to-morrow." Then the old man jerking
Like dry bones wired pulled himself half erect
With clutching at the bed-clothes: "Have mercy, Tamar.
Lee, there's a trick in it, she is a burning fire,
She is packed with death. I have learned her, I have learned her,
    I have learned her,
Too cruel to measure strychnine, too cunning-cruel
To snap a gun, aiming ourselves against us."
Lee answered, "There is almost nothing here to understand.
If we all did wrong why have we all gone mad
But me, I haven't a touch of it. Listen, dead woman,

Do you feel any light here?" "Fire—as much light
As a bird needs," the voice from the old woman
Answered, "I am the gull on the butt of the mast
Watching the ship founder, I'll fly away home
When you go down, or a swallow above a chimney
Watching the brick and mortar fly in the earthquake."
"I'll just go look at the young cypress bark
Under her window," he said, "it might have taken
The bite of a thief's hobnails." When he was gone
And jingling down the stair, then Tamar: "Poor people,
Why do you cry out so? I have three witnesses,
The old man that died to-day, and a dead woman
Forty years dead, and an idiot, and only one of you
Decently quiet. There is the great and quiet water
Reaching to Asia, and in an hour or so
The still stars will show over it but I am quieter
Inside than even the ocean or the stars.
Though I have to kindle paper flares of passion
Sometimes, to fool you with. But I was thinking
Last night, that people all over the world
Are doing much worse and suffering much more than we
This wartime, and the stars don't wink, and the ocean
Storms perhaps less than usual." Then the dead woman,
"Wild life, she has touched the ice-core of things and learned
Something, that frost burns worse than fire." "O, it's not true,"
She answered, "frost is kind; why, almost nothing
You say is true. Helen, do you remember at all
The beauty and strangeness of this place? Old cypresses
The sailor wind works into deep-sea knots
A thousand years; age-reddened granite
That was the world's cradle and crumbles apieces
Now that we're all grown up, breaks out at the roots;
And underneath it the old gray-granite strength
Is neither glad nor sorry to take the seas
Of all the storms forever and stand as firmly
As when the red hawk wings of the first dawn
Streamed up the sky over it: there is one more beautiful thing,
Water that owns the north and west and south

And is all colors and never is all quiet,
And the fogs are its breath and float along the branches of
    the cypresses.
And I forgot the coals of ruby lichen
That glow in the fog on the old twigs. To live here
Seventy-five years or eighty, and have children,
And watch these things fill up their eyes, would not
Be a bad life . . . I'd rather be what I am,
Feeling this peace and joy, the fire's joy's burning,
And I have my peace." Then the old man in the dull
And heartless voice answered, "The strangest thing
Is that He never speaks: we know we are damned, why should
    He speak? The book
Is written already. Cauldwell, Cauldwell, Cauldwell, Cauldwell.
Eternal death, eternal wrath, eternal torture, eternity, eternity,
    eternity . . .
That's after the judgment." "You needn't have any fear, old
    father,
Of anything to happen after to-morrow," Tamar answered, "we
    have turned every page
But the last page, and now our paper's so worn out and tissuey
    I can read it already
Right through the leaf, print backwards."

                                    It was twilight in the
    room, the shiny side of the wheel
Dipping toward Asia; and the year dipping toward winter en-
    crimsoned the grave spokes of sundown;
And jingling in the door Lee Cauldwell with the day's-death
    flush upon his face: "Father:
There are marks on the cypress: a hell of a way to send your
    soldier off: I want to talk to her
Alone. You and the women——" he flung his hand out, meaning
    "go." The old man without speaking
Moved to the door, propping his weakness on a chair and on
    the door-frame, and Lee entering
Passed him and the two women followed him—three, if Stella
    were one—but when they had passed the doorway

Old Cauldwell turned, and tottering in it: "Death is the horror,"
  he said, "nothing else lasts, pain passes,
Death's the only trap. I am much too wise to swing myself in
  the stable on a rope from a rafter. Helen, Helen,
You know about death." "It is cold," she answered from the
  hallway; "unspeakably hopeless . . ." "You curse of talkers,
Go," he said, and he shut the door against them and said, "Slut,
  how many, how many?" She, laughing,
"I knew you would be sweet to me: I am still sick: did you find
  marks in the bark? I am still sick, Lee;
You don't intend killing me?" "Flogging, whipping, whipping,
  is there anything male about here
You haven't used yet? Agh you mouth, you open mouth. But
  I won't touch you." "Let me say something,"
She answered, standing dark against the west in the window, the
  death of the winter rose of evening
Behind her little high-poised head, and threading the brown
  twilight of the room with the silver
Exultance of her voice, "My brother can you feel how happy
  I am but how far off too?
If I have done wrong it has turned good to me, I could almost
  be sorry that I have to die now
Out of such freedom; if I were standing back of the evening
  crimson on a mountain in Asia
All the fool shames you can whip up into a filth of words would
  not be farther off me,
Nor any fear of anything, if I stood in the evening star and saw
  this dusty dime's worth
A dot of light, dropped up the star-gleam. Poor brother, poor
  brother, you played the fool too
But not enough, it is not enough to taste delight and passion and
  disgust and loathing
And agony, you have to be wide alive, 'an open mouth' you
  said, all the while, to reach this heaven
You'll never grow up to. Though it's possible if I'd let you
  go asoldiering, there on the dunghills
Of death and fire . . . ah, you'd taste nothing even there but
  the officers' orders, beef and brandy,

And the tired bodies of a few black-eyed French dance-girls:
    it is better for you
To be lost here than there." "You are up in the evening star,"
    he said, "you can't feel this," flat-handed
Striking her cheek, "you are up on a mountain in Asia, who
    made you believe that you could keep me
Or let me go? I am going to-morrow, to-night I set the house
    in order." "There is nothing now
You can be sorry for," she answered, "not even this, it is out
    of the count, the cup ran over
Yesterday." He turned and left the room, the foolish tune of
    the spurs tinkled
Hallway and stair. Tamar, handling the fiery spot upon her
    cheek smiled in the darkness,
Feeling so sure of the end. "Night after night he has ridden to
    the granite at the rivermouth
And missed my light, to-night he will see it, the Lobos star he
    called it, and look and look to be sure
It is not a ship's light nor a star's, there in the south, then he
    will come, and my three lovers
Under one roof."

VII

Lee Cauldwell felt his way in the dark among the cypress trees,
    and turning
At the stable-door saw the evening star, he felt for the lantern
Hung on the bent nail to the right of the door,
Lighted it, and in the sweet hay-dusty darkness
Found the black quirt that hung beside the saddle
And seemed a living snake in the hand, then he opened
A locker full of hunter's gear and tumbled
Leather and iron to the floor for an old sheath-knife
Under all the rest; he took the knife and whip
And Tamar in the dark of the westward bedroom heard him
Tinkle on the stair and jingle in the hall, slow steps
Moving to hers, the room that had been her room
Before this illness; she felt him as if she had been there
Lighting her lamp and setting it on the sill,

Then felt him look about the little room and feel it
Breathing and warm with her once habitancy
And the hours of hers and his there, and soften almost
To childish tears at trifles on the wall;
And then he would look at the bed and stiffen
In a brittle rage, feel with thrust under-lip
Virtuous, an outcrop of morality in him
To grow ridiculous and wish to be cruel,
And so return to her. Hastily, without light,
She redded up some of the room's untidiness,
Thrust into the stove the folds of bandage-cloth,
Straightened the bed a little, and laying aside
The loose blue robe lay down in the bed to await him,
Who, throwing open the door, "Tamar: I've got no right
To put my hands into your life, I see
That each of us lives only a little while
And must do what he can with it: so, I'm going
To-night; I'd nearly worked myself to the act
Of some new foolishness: are you there, Tamar?
The lamp?" He struck a match and saw her eyes
Shine on him from the pillow and when the lamp
Was lighted he began again: "It's all such foolishness.
Well, you and I are done. I set your lamp for a signal on the
    sill,
I'll take it away or help you to that room,
Whichever you like. That'll be my last hand in the game.
It won't take me ten minutes to pack and go, my plan's
Not to risk losing temper and have half-decent
Thoughts of you while I'm gone, and you of me, Tamar."
She lay too quietly and the shining eyes
Seemed not to hide amusement, he waited for her
To acknowledge not in direct words perhaps
His generosity, but she silent, "Well, shall I leave the lamp?"
He said, not all so kindly, and Tamar, "I've no one else
If you are going. But if you'd stay I wouldn't
Touch you again, ever. Agh, you can't wait
To get to France to crawl into strange beds,
But Monterey to-night. You—what a beast.

TAMAR

You like them dirty." He said, "You're a fool, Tamar.
Well, so I'll leave the lamp. Good-by, Tamar."
"You said you'd help me down the hall." "Yes, even that.
What must I do, carry you?" "Is the bed together?
See whether there are sheets and covers on it."
He went, and returned icy-pale. "It hasn't been changed
Since I smelled fire and ran into the room
Six or eight days ago. The cupboard door-frame
Is all charcoal. By God, Tamar,
If I believed he'd done it—who is he, Andrews?—
You and your lies have made a horror in the house.
What, shall I go, shall I go?" "Me? who made *me*
Believe that I could keep you or let you go.
Didn't you say?" "You still believe it," he answered,
Doubling his fists to hold in anger, the passionate need
Of striking her like a torrent in his throat,
"Believe it, fool." "Poor brother. You will never see France.
Never wear uniform nor learn how to fasten
A bayonet to a gun-barrel." "Come. Stop talking.
Get up, come to your room." "Carry me," she answered.
"Though I am not really much too tired to walk.
You used to like me." "Well, to get done and be gone,"
He said, bending above her, she enlaced his neck
Softly and strongly and raised her knees to let
His arms slip under them, he like a man stung by a serpent
Felt weakness and then rage, panted to lift her
And staggered in the doorway and in the dark hallway
Grew dizzy, and difficultly went on and groaning
Dropped her on the bed in her own room, she did not move
To cover herself, then he drawing his palm
Across his forehead found it streaming wet
And said, "You whore, you whore, you whore. Well, you shall
    have it,
You've earned it," and he twisted himself to the little table
And took the whip, the oiled black supple quirt,
Loaded at the handle, that seemed a living snake in the hand,
And felt the exasperate force of his whole baffled
And blindfold life flow sideways into the shoulder

54

Swinging it, and half repenting while it dropped
Sickened to see the beautiful bare white
Blemishless body writhe under it before it fell,
The loins pressed into the bed, the breast and head
Twisting erect, and at the noise of the stroke
He made a hoarse cry in his throat but she
Took it silently, and lay still afterward,
Her head so stricken backward that the neck
Seemed strained to breaking, the coppery pad of her hair
Crushed on the shoulder-blades, while that red snake-trail
Swelled visibly from the waist and flank down the left thigh.
"O God, God, God," he groaned; and she, her whole body
Twitching on the white bed whispered between her teeth
"It was in the bargain," and from her bitten lip
A trickle of blood ran down to the pillow.

                                      That one light in the room,
The lamp on the sill, did not turn redder for blood nor with the
    whipstripe
But shone serene and innocent up the northward night, writing
    a long pale-golden track
In the river's arm of sea, and beyond the river's mouth where
    the old lion's teeth of blunted granite
Crop out of the headland young Will Andrews kissed it with
    his eyes, rode south and crossed the river's
Late-summer sand-lock. Figures of fire moved in the hills on
    the left, the pasture-fires and brush-fires
Men kindle before rain, on a southerly wind the smell of the
    smoke reached him, the sea on his right
Breathed; when he skirted the darkness of the gum-tree grove
    at San Jose creek-mouth he remembered
Verdugo killed there; Sylvia Vierra and her man had lived in
    the little white-washed farm-hut
Under the surf-reverberant blue-gums, two years ago they had
    had much wine in the house, their friend
Verdugo came avisiting, he being drunk on the raw plenty of
    wine they thought abused

Nine-year-old Mary, Sylvia's daughter, they struck him from
    behind and when he was down unmanned him
With the kitchen knife, then plotted drunkenly—for he seemed
    to be dead—where to dispose the body.
That evening Tamar Cauldwell riding her white pony along
    the coast-road saw a great bonfire
Periling the gum-tree grove, and riding under the smoke met evil
    odors, turning in there
Saw by the firelight a man's feet hang out of the fire; then Tamar
    never having suffered
Fear in her life, knocked at the hut's door and unanswered en-
    tered, and found the Vierras asleep
Steaming away their wine, but little Mary weeping. She had
    taken the child and ridden homeward.
Young Andrews thinking of that idyll of the country gulped at
    the smoke from the hills and tethered
His horse in the hiding of a clump of pines, and climbed the
    line-fence.
           Turning a cypress thicket
He saw a figure sway in the starlight, and stood still, breathless.
    A woman: Tamar? Not Tamar:
No one he knew: it faced the east gables of the house and seemed
    twisting its hands and suddenly
Flung up both arms to its face and passed out of the patch of
    starlight. The boy, troubled and cautious,
Turned the other way and circling to the south face of the
    house peered from behind the buttressed
Base of a seventy-year-old trunk that yellow light on the other
    side clothed, and he saw
A lamp on the table and three people sitting by it; the old man,
    stiff-jointed as a corpse,
Grotesquely erect, and old Aunt Stella her lips continually in
    motion, and old Jinny
Cross-legg'd having drawn up her ankles into her chair, nodding
    asleep. At length Aunt Stella
Ceased talking, none of the three stirred. Young Andrews backed
    into the wood and warily finishing

His circuit stood in the darkness under Tamar's window. The
strong young tree to help him to it
Still wore on its boughs her lamplight, then he climbed and set
his hands on the sill, his feet on the ledge
Under it, and Tamar came to the window and took up the lamp
to let him enter. Her face
White in the yellow lamp's glow, with sharp shadows under the
eyes and a high look of joy
He had never seen there frightened him, and she said, "I have
been sick, you know." "I heard," he answered,
"O Tamar, I have been lonely. We must let them know, we
can't go on, my place is with you
When you most need me." "We will tell them to-night," she
said, and kissed his mouth and called, "Lee, Lee,
Come. He has come." "What? Now," he said. "I have told Lee.
I was sick, he was sorry for me, he is going
To camp to-morrow, he wants to see you and say good-by."
Lee entered while she spoke and quietly
Held out his hand and Andrews took it. "Talk to each other,"
Tamar said, "I am very tired
And must lie down." Lee muttered "She's been awfully sick, it
scared us, you were lucky, Bill Andrews,
Not to be here." "I didn't think so," he answered, "what was it,
Lee?" "Well, it's all over," Lee said,
Shifting his feet, "I'm off to-morrow. I'm glad we're friends to
say good-by. Be good to her, won't you."
And the other, "O God knows I will. All I can do. But of course
. . . Lee . . . if they need me
She knows I won't beg off because I'm . . . married . . .
maybe I'll see you over there." "O," said Tamar
Laughing, "you too?" and she sat up on the bed saying, "Lee:
go and call father if he's able.
We ought to tell him, he ought to meet my—husband." "I'll see
if he can," Lee answered, "he was unwell
To-day, and if he's in bed . . ." He left the room, then Tamar:
"Look. Bring the lamp. What Lee did to me."
She opened the blue robe and bared her flank and thigh showing
the long whip-mark. "I have a story.

You must see this to believe it." He turned giddy, the sweet
slenderness
Dazzling him, and the lamp shook in his hand, for the sharp spasm
of physical pain one feels
At sight of a wound shot up his entrails. That long welt of red on
the tender flesh, the blood-flecks
And tortured broken little channels of blood crossing it. "Tamar,
Tamar!" "Put down the lamp,
And when they come I'll tell you the story." "What shall I do?"
"Why, nothing, nothing. Poor boy," she said,
Pityingly, "I think you are too glad of your life to have come
Into this house, you are not hard enough, you are like my mother,
only stone or fire
Should marry into this house." Then he bewildered looking at
the blackened door-frame, "Why, yes,"
Laughed Tamar, "it is here, it has been here, the bridegroom's
here already. O Will I have suffered . . .
Things I daren't tell." "What do you mean, Tamar?" "Nothing,
I mustn't tell you, you are too high-tempered,
You would do something. Dear, there are things so wicked that
nothing you can do can make them better,
So horrible now they are done that even to touch or try to mend
or punish them is only to widen
Horror: like poking at a corpse in a pool. And father's old and
helpless." "Your father, Tamar?"
"And not to blame. I think he hardly even knew what Lee—"
"Lee?" "This much I'll tell you,
You have to know it . . . our love, your love and mine, had . . .
fruit, would have been fruitful, we were going to have
A child, and I was happy and frightened, and it is dead. O God,
O God, O God, I wish
I too had been born too soon and died with the eyes unopened,
not a cry, darkness, darkness,
And to be hidden away. They did it to me; with other abuse,
worse violence." Meanwhile Lee Cauldwell
Finding his father with the two old women in the room down-
stairs, "Father," he said,

"Tamar was asking for you . . ." and Helen's voice through old
 Aunt Stella answered, "She has enough,
Tell her she has enough." "Aunt Stella," he said, "how long will
 you keep it up? Our trouble's clearing,
Let your ghosts be." "She has you and the other," she answered,
 "let me have this one. Are we buzzards to quarrel
Over you dead, we ghosts?" Then Lee turning his shoulder at her,
 "You must come up, father.
Do you remember the Andrews place that's up the valley? Young
 Andrews is upstairs with Tamar,
He wants to marry her. You know I have to go away to-morrow,
 remember? and I'll go happier
To leave her . . . taken care of. So you'll see him, father?"
 "Who is it?" asked the old man. "The bridegroom,"
Said Helen's voice, "a bridegroom for your Tamar, and the priest
 will be fire and blood the witness,
And they will live together in a house where the mice are moles."
 "Why do you plague me," he answered
Plaintively, and Lee: "Come, father," and he lifting his face,
 "I have prayed to the hills to come and cover me,
We are on the drop-off cliff of the world and dare not meet Him,
 I with two days to live, even I
Shall watch the ocean boiling and the sea curl up like paper in a
 fire and the dry bed
Crack to the bottom: I have good news for her, I will see her."
 "And I to tell her she may take
Two but not three," said Helen. "Stay here, stay here, be quiet,"
 Lee answered angrily, "can I take up
The whole menagerie, raving?" He turned in the door and heard
 his father move behind him and said,
"If you come up, be quiet," and at the door upstairs, "Father is
 tired and sick, he'll only
Speak to you, Andrews, and must go to bed; he's worried about
 my going away to-morrow.
This is Bill Andrews, father." And Tamar coming to the door,
 "Let him come in, it's dark here,
No, bring him in. Father come in. What, shall the men that made
 your war suck up their millions,

Not I my three?" Then Andrews: "If Tamar is well enough to
  go to-night I will take her to-night.
You will be well when you are out of this house." "You hate it
  still," said Tamar. "He hates the house,"
She said to Lee, leading his eyes with the significance in hers to
  the blackened door-frame,
"Well, I will go with you to-morrow." And Lee, "Listen, Will
  Andrews, I heard from somebody
You know who set the fire here." "No, not that," he answered,
  "but I know other worse things
That have been done here." "Fire, fire," moaned the old man,
  "the fire of the Lord coming in judgment. Tamar,
It is well with us, be happy, He won't torture the wicked, He will
  rub them out and suddenly
With instant fire. We shall be nothing." "Come, Tamar," An-
  drews cried, "to-night. I daren't leave you."
"For fear I ask her," said Lee. "You did it, then. You set the fire."
  "No, that's too idiot
A lie to answer," he said, "what do I know about your fires?
  I know something
Worse than arson. And saw the horrible new scar of a whip
Not to be paid—this way!" He felt the jerk of his arm striking
And his fist hitting the sharp edge of the jawbone, but yet
When Lee staggered and closed in with a groan,
Clutching him, fumbling for his throat, Will thought "What
  a fool
To make a nasty show of us before Tamar
And the others, why does he want to fight?" and indignantly
Pushed him off and struck twice, both fists, Lee dropped
And scrambled on hands and knees by the little table.
Then the old man cried, "We shall be nothing, nothing.
O but that's frightful."
And Will turning to Tamar saw such hatred
Wrinkle her face he felt a horrible surge
Of nausea in him, then with bare teeth she smiled at him
And he believed the hate was for her brother
And said, "Ah Tamar, come." Meanwhile the Helen
That spoke out of the lungs and ran in the nerves

Of old Aunt Stella caught the old man David Cauldwell
By the loose flapping sleeve and the lean arm,
Saying in a clotted amorous voice, "Come, David,
My brother, my lover, O honey come, she has no eyes for you,
She feasts on young men. But you to me, to me,
Are as beautiful as when we dared
Desperate pleasure, naked, ages ago,
In the room and by the sea." "Father," said Tamar,
"It is only an hour to the end, whom do you want
To-night? Stay here by me." "I was hunting for something," said Lee Cauldwell,
"Here it is, here it is," and had the sheath-knife bared
And struck up from the floor, rising, the blade
Ripped cloth and skin along his enemy's belly
And the leather belt catching it deflected the point
Into the bowels, Andrews coughed and fell backward
And Lee falling across him stabbed at his throat
But struck too high and opened the right cheek,
The knife scraping on bone and teeth, then Tamar
In a sea-gull voice, "I dreamed it in his face,
I dreamed a T cut in his face——" "You and your dreams
Have done for us," Lee groaned answer. "Akh, all blood, blood.
What did you say to make him hit me?"

                        Though it is not thought
That the dead intervene between the minds
And deeds of the living, that they are witnesses,
If anything of their spirits with any memory
Survive and not in prison, would seem as likely
As that an exile should look longingly home:
And the mist-face of that mother at the window
Wavering was but a witness, could but watch,
Neither prevent nor cause: no doubt there are many
Such watchers in the world: the same whom Andrews,
Stepping like a thief among the cypress clumps an hour before
Saw twist her hands and suddenly fling up both vaporous arms
    and sway out of the starlight,
She now was watching at the downstairs window

Old Jinny alone in the room, and saw, as the dead see, the thoughts
More clearly than the cloth and skin; the child mind
In that old flesh gathered home on itself
In coils, laboring to warm a memory,
And worked on by an effluence, petulantly pushing away
The easier memories of its open time
Forty years back, power flowing from someone in that house
Belting it in, pressing it to its labor,
Making it shape in itself the memory of to-day's
Vision, the watcher saw it, how could she know it
Or know from whence? a girl naked, no, wrapped in fire,
Filmed in white sheets of fire. "Why, I'm like God,"
Old Jinny had said, "I see through walls," a girl
Naked though clothed in fire, and under the arms
Naked, no hair,—"Ah to be like her, to be like her, probably
Cloth, hair, burned off"; displaying herself before a wild old man
Who appeared part of the joy: "Ah, to be like her,
Fire is so sweet, they never let me play with it,
No one loves Jinny, wouldn't fire be a father
And hold her in his arms? Fire is so sweet,"
She hovered the hot lamp, "sweet fire, sweet light,"
She held a rag of paper above it, "O dear, dear fire,
Come and kiss Jinny, no one's looking,
Jinny's alone. Dear star, dear light, O lovely fire
Won't you come out, why is it turning black,
Ah come, Ah come, hug Jinny." The hungry beautiful bird
Hopped from its bird-cage to her. "I've got my star
Ah love, Ah love, and here's more paper
And a little of Jinny's dress, love, lovely light,
Jinny so loves you, Jinny's baby, Jinny's baby,
O," she screamed, "Oo, Oo, Oo," and ran to the window, folded
In a terrible wreath, and at her side the curtains
Danced into flame, and over her head; the gasp
That followed on a cry drew down a sword
Of flame to her lungs, pain ceased, and thinking "Father"
She dropped herself into the arms of the fire,
Huddling under the sill, and her spirit unprisoned

Filled all the room and felt a nuptial joy
In mixing with the bright and eager flame.
While from that blackened morsel on the floor
Fire spread to the wall and gnawed it through, and the window-
glass
Crackling and tinkling a rush of south wind fed
The eagerness in the house. They heard upstairs
That brutal arch of crying, the quick crescendo,
The long drop and the following moan, Will Andrews
Struggled to rise and like a gopher-snake that a child
Has mashed the head of with a stone, he waggled
The blood-clot of his head over the floor
Gulping "You devils, you devils." Lee would have run down
But Tamar clung to him, the old man on his knees
Muttered to God, and old Aunt Stella
In no voice but her own screamed, screamed. Then fire
Was heard roaring, the door leaked threads of smoke,
Lee caught up Tamar in his arms and turned
To the window, the cypress-ladder, but his first step,
Blind, with the burden in his arms, the smoke in his eyes,
Trampled his murdered man on the floor who turning
Caught the other ankle and Lee went down and Tamar
So lovingly wound him that he could not rise
Till the house was full of its bright death; then Tamar:
"I will not let you take me. Go if you want."
He answered, "You devil, shall I go?" "You wouldn't stay!
Think of your black-eyed French girls." "We are on the edge
of it," he answered,
"Tamar, be decent for a minute." "I have my three lovers
Here in one room, none of them will go out,
How can I help being happy? This old man
Has prayed the end of the world onto us all,
And which of you leaves me?" Then the old man: "O what
mountain,
What mountain, what mountain?" And Lee, "Father. The
window
We'll follow you." But he kneeling would not rise,
While the house moved and the floor sagged to the south

And old Aunt Stella through the opening door
Ran into the red and black, and did not scream
Any more; then Tamar, "Did you think you would go
Laughing through France?" And the old man, "Fierce, fierce
    light,
Have pity, Christ have pity, Christ have pity, Christ have pity,
Christ have pity,
Christ have pity . . ."
And Tamar with her back to the window embraced
Her brother, who struggled toward it, but the floor
Turned like a wheel.

                Grass grows where the flame flowered;
A hollowed lawn strewn with a few black stones
And the brick of broken chimneys; all about there
The old trees, some of them scarred with fire, endure the sea
    wind.

DIVINELY SUPERFLUOUS BEAUTY

The storm-dances of gulls, the barking game of seals,
Over and under the ocean . . .
Divinely superfluous beauty
Rules the games, presides over destinies, makes trees grow
And hills tower, waves fall.
The incredible beauty of joy
Stars with fire the joining of lips, O let our loves too
Be joined, there is not a maiden
Burns and thirsts for love
More than my blood for you, by the shore of seals while the
    wings
Weave like a web in the air
Divinely superfluous beauty.

THE MAID'S THOUGHT

Why listen, even the water is sobbing for something.
The west wind is dead, the waves
Forget to hate the cliff, in the upland canyons
Whole hillsides burst aglow
With golden broom. Dear how it rained last month,
And every pool was rimmed
With sulphury pollen dust of the wakening pines.
Now tall and slender suddenly
The stalks of purple iris blaze by the brooks,
The penciled ones on the hill;
This deerweed shivers with gold, the white globe-tulips
Blow out their silky bubbles,
But in the next glen bronze-bells nod, the does
Scalded by some hot longing
Can hardly set their pointed hoofs to expect
Love but they crush a flower;
Shells pair on the rock, birds mate, the moths fly double.
O it is time for us now
Mouth kindling mouth to entangle our maiden bodies
To make that burning flower.

THE SONGS OF THE DEAD MEN TO
THE THREE DANCERS

I · TO DESIRE

(Here a dancer enters and dances.)

Who is she that is fragrant and desirable,
Clothed but enough to wake wantonness,
And proud of her polished lithe body and her narrowing of
    kohl-darkened eyelids with arrows between them?
Ah, ah, ah! Goddess of the world,
Young serpent in the veins of the rock,
In the mountain of jewels a young serpent, in the veins of a
    man a sweet viper all emerald: ah Goddess
Are we proof to the hilt, are you pleased with us
When the splendor of your undulant insolence
Pricks the dark entrails of death, his foregathered grow hot for
    you, the skeleton stands up to be amorous?
Ah, ah, ah! Goddess of the flesh
Will you think it a gift lacking grace
That the gates of the grave have been battered before you, the
    iron doors to us dead in the deepest abysm?
For who has gone down to the dead or has touched them?
Did Jesus of Nazareth when he lay in deep hell
For three days and since lived as they say and has failed us?
No man nor no woman has gone down to us dead
Living until now, but the proof is here now, ah beautiful torture
    us again and again.
We are fleshless, we tremble to your flesh,
Dear Goddess to taste of the dew
On your arms when you dance or to lip at the glitter of your
    burnished thighs or the breast of your barrenness.
In the book of your triumphs with no term
Inscribe a more wonderful deed,
That you quickened the dead, that you lifted the flesh of the
    fleshless, ah Goddess, ah! dancing, us dead men.

(The dancer goes out.)

SONGS OF THE DEAD MEN

II · TO DEATH

(A second dancer enters and dances.)

Was it lovely to lie among violets ablossom in the valleys of
    love on the breast of the south?
It was lovely but lovelier now
To behold the calm head of the dancer we dreaded, his curls are
    as tendrils of the vineyard, O Death
Sweet and more sweet is your dancing.
Like the swoon of fulfilment of love in some lonelier vale among
    flowers is the languor that flushes us,
O why did we fear him, for Death
Is a beautiful youth and his eyes are sleepy, the lids droop heavily
    with wine when he wakens,
And his breast is more smooth than a dove's.
Fair Garda, gay water with olives engarlanded, lake of blue
    laughter in a bay of the Alps
It is better for our spirits to be here
In the desolate hollows of darkness beholding the beauty of our
    dancer than at rest on your hills
Of anemones and jonquils immingled.
And gay from the glacier womb, boy-throated for gladness to
    shout where the snow-crags throng
Ran foaming the rivulet Rhone,
When the mountains were sprung for his passage, the ridges of
    granite were splintered; and lovely the lake was
Under the vineyards of Vaud,
And at evening empurpling the peaks of the Chablais were
    painted on the sleep and deep shadow of its waters
When the sundown was flame on la Dole.
But the best of the course is the last broad slumber, O river of
    France to forget and go down
Slow-gliding and sultrily stagnant
Past Arles to the Gulf of the Lion and that azure and beautiful
    grave in the waves of the south
That are warmest and best . . . and an end . . .

(The dancer has gone out.)

III · TO VICTORY

(A third dancer enters and dances.)

Use us again, you in the world only of goddesses worshipful
    now or adored,
Helmeted victory!
How did we bow, even in dream, visions betraying us, unto some
    other and base
Power when your splendor there
Struck on the gates? Use us again, awfully beautiful. Blood will
    reblossom from death
Burning to minister
All its revived fire at your feet, only to merit an eye-glance, or
    flash of your hand's
Gauntleted majesty.
Pounding of guns clear you a path, trample the ports of decision
    and triumph on the slain.
Men when they fall in it
Gayly they die, scattering for flowers rosy and white at your
    feet the red blood and pale brains
Carpeting battlefields.
Towering in steel, terribly armed, which of the daughters of
    heaven is so hotly desired?
None has embraced you yet,
All of us burn, beautifully mad, frantic with lust of your beauty
    and with thirst of your mouth's
Terrible maidenhood;
Holy and white, under the steel, hide the sweet limbs of our
    longing desire in a deep
Sacred virginity.
Emperors and lords gave her in vain cities of gold and whole
    nations of blood, for she took
Gifts, but rejected them.
Neither a king's bribe nor a bold armorer's hammer prevails to
    unrivet the steel
Belt of her maidenhood,

Yet shall our prayer surely be heard. Goddess of glory revoke our
    exemption of death,
Twice let us die for you.
Use us again, though but an hour: surely the prayer is as humble
    as the gift would be great,
Helmeted Victory.

(The dancer goes out.)

TO HIS FATHER

Christ was your lord and captain all your life,
He fails the world but you he did not fail,
He led you through all forms of grief and strife
Intact, a man full-armed, he let prevail
Nor outward malice nor the worse-fanged snake
That coils in one's own brain against your calm,
That great rich jewel well guarded for his sake
With coronal age and death like quieting balm.
I Father having followed other guides
And oftener to my hurt no leader at all,
Through years nailed up like dripping panther hides
For trophies on a savage temple wall
Hardly anticipate that reverend stage
Of life, the snow-wreathed honor of extreme age.

THE TRUCE AND THE PEACE

(NOVEMBER, 1918)

I

Peace now for every fury has had her day,
Their natural make is moribund, they cease,
They carry the inward seeds of quick decay,
Build breakwaters for storm but build on peace.
The mountains' peace answers the peace of the stars,
Our petulances are cracked against their term.
God built our peace and plastered it with wars,
Those frescoes fade, flake off, peace remains firm.
In the beginning before light began
We lay or fluttered blind in burdened wombs,
And like that first so is the last of man,
When under death for husband the amorous tombs
Are covered and conceived; nine months go by
No midwife called, nine years no baby's cry.

II

Peace now, though purgatory fires were hot
They always had a heart something like ice
That coldly peered and wondered, suffering not
Nor pleased in any park, nor paradise
Of slightly swelling breasts and beautiful arms
And throat engorged with very carnal blood.
It coldly peered and wondered, "Strong God your charms
Are glorious, I remember solitude.
Before youth towered we knew a time of truth
To have eyes was nearly rapture." Peace now, for war
Will find the cave that childhood found and youth.
Ten million lives are stolen and not one star
Dulled; wars die out, life will die out, death cease,
Beauty lives always and the beauty of peace.

III

Peace to the world in time or in a year,
In the inner world I have touched the instant peace.
Man's soul's a flawless crystal coldly clear,
A cold white mansion that he yields in lease
To tenant dreams and tyrants from the brain
And riotous burnings of the lovelier flesh.
We pour strange wines and purples all in vain.
The crystal remains pure, the mansion fresh.
All the Asian bacchanals and those from Thrace
Lived there and left no wine-mark on the walls.
What were they doing in that more sacred place
All the Asian and the Thracian bacchanals?
Peace to the world to-morrow or in a year,
Peace in that mansion white, that crystal clear.

IV

Peace now poor earth. They fought for freedom's sake,
She was starving in a corner while they fought.
They knew not whom they stabbed by Onega Lake,
Whom lashed from Archangel, whom loved, whom sought.
How can she die, she is the blood unborn,
The energy in earth's arteries beating red,
The world will flame with her in some great morn,
The whole great world flame with her, and we be dead.
Here in the west it grows by dim degrees,
In the east flashed and will flame terror and light.
Peace now poor earth, peace to that holier peace
Deep in the soul held secret from all sight.
That crystal, the pure home, the holier peace,
Fires flaw not, scars the cruelest cannot crease.

V

South of the Big Sur River up the hill
Three graves are marked thick weeds and grasses heap,
Under the forest there I have stood still

73

Hours, thinking it the sweetest place to sleep . . .
Strewing all-sufficient death with compliments
Sincere and unrequired, coveting peace . . .
Boards at the head not stones, the text's rude paints
Mossed, rain-rubbed . . . wasting hours of scanty lease
To admire their peace made perfect. From that height
But for the trees the whole valley might be seen,
But for the heavy dirt, the eye-pits no light
Enters, the heavy dirt, the grass growing green
Over the dirt, the molelike secretness,
The immense withdrawal, the dirt, the quiet, the peace.

VI

Women cried that morning, bells rocked with mirth,
We all were glad a long while afterward,
But still in dreary places of the earth
A hundred hardly fed shall labor hard
To clothe one belly and stuff it with soft meat,
Blood paid for peace but still those poor shall buy it,
This sweat of slaves is no good wine but yet
Sometimes it climbs to the brain. Be happy and quiet,
Be happy and live, be quiet or God might wake.
He sleeps in the mountain that is heart of man's heart,
He also in promontory fists, and make
Of stubborn-muscled limbs, he will not start
For a little thing . . . his great hands grope, unclose,
Feel out for the main pillars . . . pull down the house . . .

VII

After all, after all we endured, who has grown wise?
We take our mortal momentary hour
With too much gesture, the derisive skies
Twinkle against our wrongs, our rights, our power.
Look up the night, starlight's a steadying draught
For nerves at angry tension. They have all meant well,
Our enemies and the knaves at whom we've laughed,
The liars, the clowns in office, the kings in hell,

They have all meant well in the main . . . some of them tried
The mountain road of tolerance . . . They have made war,
Conspired, oppressed, robbed, murdered, lied and lied,
Meant well, played the loud fool . . . and star by star
Winter Orion pursues the Pleiades
In pale and huge parade, silence and peace.

VIII

That ice within the soul, the admonisher
Of madness when we're wildest, the unwinking eye
That measures all things with indifferent stare,
Choosing far stars to check near objects by,
That quiet lake inside and underneath,
Strong, undisturbed by any angel of strife,
Being so tranquil seems the presence of death,
Being so central seems the essence of life.
Is it perhaps that death and life make truce
In neutral zone while their old feud beyond
Fires the towered cities? Surely for a strange use
He sphered that eye of flawless diamond.
It does not serve him but with line and rod
Measures him, how indeed should God serve God?

IX

It does not worship him, it will not serve.
And death and life within that Eye combine,
Within that only untorturable nerve
Of those that make a man, within that shrine
Which there is nothing ever can profane,
Where life and death are sister and brother and lovers,
The golden voice of Christ were heard in vain,
The holy spirit of God visibly hovers.
Small-breasted girls, lithe women heavy-haired,
Loves that once grew into our nerves and veins,
Yours Freedom was desire that deeper dared
To the citadel where mastery remains,
Yours to the spirit . . . discount the penny that is
Ungivable, this Eye, this God, this Peace.

X

All in a simple innocence I strove
To give myself away to any power,
Wasting on women's bodies wealth of love,
Worshipping every sunrise mountain tower;
Some failure mocked me still denying perfection,
Parts of me might be spended not the whole,
I sought of wine surrender and self-correction,
I failed, I could not give away my soul.
Again seeking to give myself I sought
Outward in vain through all things, out through God,
And tried all heights, all gulfs, all dreams, all thought.
I found this wisdom on the wonderful road,
The essential. Me cannot be given away,
The single Eye, God cased in blood-shot clay.

XI

Peace to the world in time or in a year,
But always all our lives this peace was ours.
Peace is not hard to have, it lies more near
Than breathing to the breast. When brigand powers
Of anger or pain or the sick dream of sin
Break our soul's house outside the ruins we weep.
We look through the breached wall, why there within
All the red while our peace was lying asleep.
Smiling in dreams while the broad knives drank blood,
The robbers triumphed, the roof burned overhead,
The eternal living and untroubled God
Lying asleep upon a lily bed.
Men screamed, the bugles screamed, walls broke in the air,
We never knew till then that He was there.

NATURAL MUSIC

The old voice of the ocean, the bird-chatter of little rivers,
(Winter has given them gold for silver
To stain their water and bladed green for brown to line their
   banks)
From different throats intone one language.
So I believe if we were strong enough to listen without
Divisions of desire and terror
To the storm of the sick nations, the rage of the hunger-smitten
   cities,
Those voices also would be found
Clean as a child's; or like some girl's breathing who dances alone
By the ocean-shore, dreaming of lovers.

POINT JOE

Point Joe has teeth and has torn ships; it has fierce and solitary
    beauty;
Walk there all day you shall see nothing that will not make part
    of a poem.

I saw the spars and planks of shipwreck on the rocks, and beyond
    the desolate
Sea-meadows rose the warped wind-bitten van of the pines, a
    fog-bank vaulted

Forest and all, the flat sea-meadows at that time of year were
    plated
Golden with the low flower called footsteps of the spring, mil-
    lions of flowerets,

Whose light suffused upward into the fog flooded its vault, we
    wandered
Through a weird country where the light beat up from earth-
    ward, and was golden.

One other moved there, an old Chinaman gathering seaweed
    from the sea-rocks,
He brought it in his basket and spread it flat to dry on the edge of
    the meadow.

Permanent things are what is needful in a poem, things tem-
    porally
Of great dimension, things continually renewed or always
    present.

Grass that is made each year equals the mountains in her past
    and future;
Fashionable and momentary things we need not see nor speak of.

POINT JOE

Man gleaning food between the solemn presences of land and
    ocean,
On shores where better men have shipwrecked, under fog and
    among flowers,

Equals the mountains in his past and future; that glow from the
    earth was only
A trick of nature's, one must forgive nature a thousand graceful
    subtleties.

THE CYCLE

The clapping blackness of the wings of pointed cormorants,
the great indolent planes
Of autumn pelicans nine or a dozen strung shorelong,
But chiefly the gulls, the cloud-caligraphers of windy spirals
before a storm,
Cruise north and south over the sea-rocks and over
That bluish enormous opal; very lately these alone, these and the
clouds
And westering lights of heaven, crossed it; but then
A hull with standing canvas crept about Point Lobos . . . now
all day long the steamers
Smudge the opal's rim; often a seaplane troubles
The sea-wind with its throbbing heart. These will increase, the
others diminish; and later
These will diminish; our Pacific has pastured
The Mediterranean torch and passed it west across the fountains
of the morning;
And the following desolation that feeds on Crete
Feed here; the clapping blackness of the wings of pointed cor-
morants, the great sails
Of autumn pelicans, the gray sea-going gulls,
Alone will streak the enormous opal, the earth have peace like the
broad water, our blood's
Unrest have doubled to Asia and be peopling
Europe again, or dropping colonies at the morning star: what
moody traveler
Wanders back here, watches the sea-fowl circle
The old sea-granite and cemented granite with one regard, and
greets my ghost,
One temper with the granite, bulking about here?

SALMON-FISHING

The days shorten, the south blows wide for showers now,
The south wind shouts to the rivers,
The rivers open their mouths and the salt salmon
Race up into the freshet.
In Christmas month against the smoulder and menace
Of a long angry sundown,
Red ash of the dark solstice, you see the anglers,
Pitiful, cruel, primeval,
Like the priests of the people that built Stonehenge,
Dark silent forms, performing
Remote solemnities in the red shallows
Of the river's mouth at the year's turn,
Drawing landward their live bullion, the bloody mouths
And scales full of the sunset
Twitch on the rocks, no more to wander at will
The wild Pacific pasture nor wanton and spawning
Race up into fresh water.

TO THE HOUSE

I am heaping the bones of the old mother
To build us a hold against the host of the air;
Granite the blood-heat of her youth
Held molten in hot darkness against the heart
Hardened to temper under the feet
Of the ocean cavalry that are maned with snow
And march from the remotest west.
This is the primitive rock, here in the wet
Quarry under the shadow of waves
Whose hollows mouthed the dawn; little house each stone
Baptized from that abysmal font
The sea and the secret earth gave bonds to affirm you.

TO THE ROCK THAT WILL BE A CORNERSTONE OF THE HOUSE

Old garden of grayish and ochre lichen,
How long a time since the brown people who have vanished from
    here
Built fires beside you and nestled by you
Out of the ranging sea-wind? A hundred years, two hundred,
You have been dissevered from humanity
And only known the stubble squirrels and the headland rabbits,
Or the long-fetlocked plowhorses
Breaking the hilltop in December, sea-gulls following,
Screaming in the black furrow; no one
Touched you with love, the gray hawk and the red hawk touched
    you
Where now my hand lies. So I have brought you
Wine and white milk and honey for the hundred years of famine
And the hundred cold ages of sea-wind.

I did not dream the taste of wine could bind with granite,
Nor honey and milk please you; but sweetly
They mingle down the storm-worn cracks among the mosses,
Interpenetrating the silent
Wing-prints of ancient weathers long at peace, and the older
Scars of primal fire, and the stone
Endurance that is waiting millions of years to carry
A corner of the house, this also destined.
Lend me the stone strength of the past and I will lend you
The wings of the future, for I have them.
How dear you will be to me when I too grow old, old comrade.

TO THE STONE-CUTTERS

Stone-cutters fighting time with marble, you foredefeated
Challengers of oblivion
Eat cynical earnings, knowing rock splits, records fall down,
The square-limbed Roman letters
Scale in the thaws, wear in the rain. The poet as well
Builds his monument mockingly;
For man will be blotted out, the blithe earth die, the brave sun
Die blind and blacken to the heart:
Yet stones have stood for a thousand years, and pained thoughts
found
The honey of peace in old poems.

SUICIDE'S STONE

Peace is the heir of dead desire,
Whether abundance killed the cormorant
In a happy hour, or sleep or death
Drowned him deep in dreamy waters,
Peace is the ashes of that fire,
The heir of that king, the inn of that journey.

This last and best and goal: we dead
Hold it so tight you are envious of us
And fear under sunk lids contempt.
Death-day greetings are the sweetest.
Let trumpets roar when a man dies
And rockets fly up, he has found his fortune.

Yet hungering long and pitiably
That way, you shall not reach a finger
To pluck it unripe and before dark
Creep to cover: life broke ten whipstocks
Over my back, broke faith, stole hope,
Before I denounced the covenant of courage.

WISE MEN IN THEIR BAD HOURS

Wise men in their bad hours have envied
The little people making merry like grasshoppers
In spots of sunlight, hardly thinking
Backward but never forward, and if they somehow
Take hold upon the future they do it
Half asleep, with the tools of generation
Foolishly reduplicating
Folly in thirty-year periods; they eat and laugh too,
Groan against labors, wars and partings,
Dance, talk, dress and undress; wise men have pretended
The summer insects enviable;
One must indulge the wise in moments of mockery.
Strength and desire possess the future,
The breed of the grasshopper shrills, "What does the future
Matter, we shall be dead?" Ah, grasshoppers,
Death's a fierce meadowlark: but to die having made
Something more equal to the centuries
Than muscle and bone, is mostly to shed weakness.
The mountains are dead stone, the people
Admire or hate their stature, their insolent quietness,
The mountains are not softened nor troubled
And a few dead men's thoughts have the same temper.

CONTINENT'S END

At the equinox when the earth was veiled in a late rain, wreathed
    with wet poppies, waiting spring,
The ocean swelled for a far storm and beat its boundary, the
    ground-swell shook the beds of granite.

I gazing at the boundaries of granite and spray, the established
    sea-marks, felt behind me
Mountain and plain, the immense breadth of the continent, before
    me the mass and doubled stretch of water.

I said: You yoke the Aleutian seal-rocks with the lava and coral
    sowings that flower the south,
Over your flood the life that sought the sunrise faces ours that has
    followed the evening star.

The long migrations meet across you and it is nothing to you, you
    have forgotten us, mother.
You were much younger when we crawled out of the womb and
    lay in the sun's eye on the tideline.

It was long and long ago; we have grown proud since then and
    you have grown bitter; life retains
Your mobile soft unquiet strength; and envies hardness, the
    insolent quietness of stone.

The tides are in our veins, we still mirror the stars, life is your
    child, but there is in me
Older and harder than life and more impartial, the eye that
    watched before there was an ocean.

That watched you fill your beds out of the condensation of thin
    vapor and watched you change them,
That saw you soft and violent wear your boundaries down, eat
    rock, shift places with the continents.

Mother, though my song's measure is like your surf-beat's ancient
rhythm I never learned it of you.

Before there was any water there were tides of fire, both our
tones flow from the older fountain.

THE TOWER BEYOND TRAGEDY

You'd never have thought the Queen was Helen's sister—Troy's
burning-flower from Sparta, the beautiful sea-flower
Cut in clear stone, crowned with the fragrant golden mane, she
the ageless, the uncontaminable—
This Clytemnestra was her sister, low-statured, fierce-lipped, not
dark nor blonde, greenish-gray-eyed,
Sinewed with strength, you saw, under the purple folds of the
queen-cloak, but craftier than queenly,
Standing between the gilded wooden porch-pillars, great steps of
stone above the steep street,
Awaiting the King.
                    Most of his men were quartered on the town;
he, clanking bronze, with fifty
And certain captives, came to the stair. The Queen's men were
a hundred in the street and a hundred
Lining the ramp, eighty on the great flags of the porch; she
raising her white arms the spear-butts
Thundered on the stone, and the shields clashed; eight shining
clarions
Let fly from the wide window over the entrance the wildbirds of
their metal throats, air-cleaving
Over the King come home. He raised his thick burnt-colored
beard and smiled; then Clytemnestra,
Gathering the robe, setting the golden-sandaled feet carefully,
stone by stone, descended
One half the stair. But one of the captives marred the comeliness
of that embrace with a cry
Gull-shrill, blade-sharp, cutting between the purple cloak and
the bronze plates, then Clytemnestra:
Who was it? The King answered: A piece of our goods out of
the snatch of Asia, a daughter of the king,
So treat her kindly and she may come into her wits again. Eh,
you keep state here my queen.

You've not been the poorer for me.—In heart, in the widowed
  chamber, dear, she pale replied, though the slaves
Toiled, the spearmen were faithful. What's her name, the slave-
  girl's?

AGAMEMNON Come up the stair. They tell me my kinsman's
Lodged himself on you.

CLYTEMNESTRA Your cousin Ægisthus? He was out of refuge,
  flits between here and Tiryns.

Dear: the girl's name?

AGAMEMNON Cassandra. We've a hundred or so other
  captives; besides two hundred
Rotted in the hulls,—they tell odd stories about you and your
  guest: eh? no matter:—the ships
Ooze pitch and the August road smokes dirt, I smell like an
  old shepherd's goatskin, you'll have bath-water?

CLYTEMNESTRA
They're making it hot. Come, my lord. My hands will pour it.
                              (*They enter the palace.*)

CASSANDRA
In the holy city,
In Troy, when the stone was standing walls and the ash
Was painted and carved wood and pictured curtains,
And those lived that are dead, they had caged a den
Of wolves out of the mountain, and I a maiden
Was led to see them: it stank and snarled,
The smell was the smell here, the eyes were the eyes
Of steep Mycenæ: O God guardian of wanderers
Let me die easily.
So cried Cassandra the daughter of King Priam, treading the steps
  of the palace at Mycenæ.
Swaying like a drunken woman, drunk with the rolling of the
  ship, and with tears, and with prophecy.
The stair may yet be seen, among the old stones that are Mycenæ;
  tall dark Cassandra, the prophetess,
The beautiful girl with whom a God bargained for love, high-
  nurtured, captive, shamefully stained
With the ship's filth and the sea's, rolled her dark head upon her
  shoulders like a drunken woman

And trod the great stones of the stair. The captives, she among
    them, were ranked into a file
On the flagged porch, between the parapet and the spearmen.
    The people below shouted for the King,
King Agamemnon, returned conqueror, after the ten years of
    battle and death in Asia.
Then cried Cassandra:
Good spearmen you did not kill my father, not you
Violated my mother with the piercing
That makes no life in the womb, not you defiled
My tall blond brothers with the masculine lust
That strikes its loved one standing,
And leaves him what no man again nor a girl
Ever will gaze upon with the eyes of desire:
Therefore you'll tell me
Whether it's an old custom in the Greek country
The cow goring the bull, break the inner door back
And see in what red water how cloaked your King
Bathes, and my brothers are avenged a little.
One said: Captive be quiet. And she: What have I to be quiet for,
    you will not believe me.
Such wings my heart spreads when the red runs out of any
    Greek, I must let the bird fly. O soldiers
He that mishandled me dies! The first, one of your two brute
    Ajaxes, that threw me backward
On the temple flagstones, a hard bride-bed, I enduring him
    heard the roofs of my city breaking,
The roar of flames and spearmen: what came to Ajax? Out of a
    cloud the loud-winged falcon lightning
Came on him shipwrecked, clapped its wings about him, clung
    to him, the violent flesh burned and the bones
Broke from each other in that passion; and now this one, returned
    safe, the Queen is his lightning.
While she yet spoke a slave with haggard eyes darted from the
    door; there were hushed cries and motions
In the inner dark of the great hall. Then the Queen Clytem-
    nestra issued, smiling. She drew

Her cloak up, for the brooch on the left shoulder was broken; the
    fillet of her hair had come unbound;
Yet now she was queenly at length; and standing at the stair-
    head spoke: Men of Mycenæ, I have made
Sacrifice for the joy this day has brought to us, the King come
    home, the enemy fallen, fallen,
In the ashes of Asia. I have made sacrifice. I made the prayer
    with my own lips, and struck the bullock
With my own hand. The people murmured together, She's not
    a priestess, the Queen is not a priestess,
What has she done there, what wild sayings
Make wing in the Queen's throat?
CLYTEMNESTRA   I have something to tell you.
    Too much joy is a message-bearer of misery.
A little is good; but come too much and it devours us. Therefore
    we give of a great harvest
Sheaves to the smiling Gods; and therefore out of a full cup we
    pour the quarter. No man
Dare take all that God sends him, whom God favors, or de-
    struction
Rides into the house in the last basket. I have been twelve years
    your shepherdess, I the Queen have ruled you
And I am accountable for you.
CASSANDRA
Why should a man kill his own mother?
The cub of the lion being grown
Will fight with the lion, but neither lion nor wolf
Nor the unclean jackal
Bares tooth against the womb that he dropped out of:
Yet I have seen—
CLYTEMNESTRA
Strike that captive woman with your hand, spearman; and then
    if the spirit
Of the she-wolf in her will not quiet, with the butt of the spear.
CASSANDRA   —the blade in the child's hand
Enter the breast that the child sucked—that woman's—
The left breast that the robe has dropped from, for the brooch is
    broken,

That very hillock of whiteness, and she crying, she kneeling—
(*The spearman who is nearest* CASSANDRA *covers her mouth with his hand.*)

CLYTEMNESTRA

My sister's beauty entered Troy with too much gladness. They
forgot to make sacrifice.

Therefore destruction entered; therefore the daughters of Troy
cry out in strange dispersals, and this one

Grief has turned mad. I will not have that horror march under
the Lion-gate of Mycenæ

That split the citadel of Priam. Therefore I say I have made
sacrifice; I have subtracted

A fraction from immoderate joy. For consider, my people,

How unaccountably God has favored the city and brought home
the army. King Agamemnon,

My dear, my husband, my lord and yours,

Is yet not such a man as the Gods love; but insolent, fierce, over-
bearing, whose folly

Brought many times many great evils

On all the heads and fighting hopes of the Greek force. Why,
even before the fleet made sail,

While yet it gathered on Bœotian Aulis, this man offended. He
slew one of the deer

Of the sacred herd of Artemis, out of pure impudence, hunter's
pride that froths in a young boy

Laying nock to string of his first bow: this man, grown, a grave
king, leader of the Greeks.

The angry Goddess

Blew therefore from the horn of the Trojan shore storm without
end, no slackening, no turn, no slumber

Of the eagle bound to break the oars of the fleet and split the
hulls venturing: you know what answer

Calchas the priest gave: his flesh must pay whose hand did the
evil—his flesh! mine also. His? My daughter.

They knew that of my three there was one that I loved.

Blameless white maid, my Iphigenia, whose throat the knife,

Whose delicate soft throat the thing that cuts sheep open was
drawn across by a priest's hand

93

And the soft-colored lips drained bloodless
That had clung here—here—Oh!

(*Drawing the robe from her breasts.*)

These feel soft, townsmen; these are red at the tips, they have
neither blackened nor turned marble.

King Agamemnon hoped to pillow his black-haired breast upon
them, my husband, that mighty conqueror,

Come home with glory. He thought they were still a woman's,
they appear a woman's. I'll tell you something.

Since fawn slaughtered for slaughtered fawn evened the debt
these that feel soft and warm are wounding ice,

They ache with their hardness . . .

Shall I go on and count the other follies of the King? The
insolences to God and man

That brought down plague, and brought Achilles' anger against
the army? Yet God brought home a remnant

Against all hope: therefore rejoice.

But lest too much rejoicing slay us I have made sacrifice. A little
girl's brought you over the sea.

What could be great enough for safe return? A sheep's death?
A bull's? What thank-offering?

All these captives, battered from the ships, bruised with captivity,
damaged flesh and forlorn minds?

God requires wholeness in the victim. You dare not think what
he demands. I dared. I, I,

Dared.

Men of the Argolis, you that went over the sea and you that
guarded the home coasts

And high stone war-belts of the cities: remember how many
spearmen these twelve years have called me

Queen, and have loved me, and been faithful, and *remain* faithful.
What I bring you is accomplished.

VOICES

King Agamemnon. The King. We will hear the King.

CLYTEMNESTRA   What I bring you is accomplished.

Accept it, the cities are at peace, the ways are safe between
them, the Gods favor us. Refuse it . . .

You will not refuse it . . .

VOICES   The King. We will hear the King. Let
us see the King.

CLYTEMNESTRA

You will not refuse it; I have my faithful. They would run, the
red rivers,

From the gate and by the graves through every crooked street
of the great city, they would run in the pasture

Outside the walls: and on this stair: stemmed at this entrance—

CASSANDRA

Ah, sister, do you also behold visions? I was watching red
water—

CLYTEMNESTRA

Be wise, townsmen. As for the King: slaves will bring him to you
when he has bathed; you will see him.

The slaves will carry him on a litter, he has learned Asian ways in
Asia, too great a ruler

To walk, like common spearmen.

CASSANDRA   Who is that, standing behind
you, Clytemnestra? What God

Dark in the doorway?

CLYTEMNESTRA   Deal *you* with your own demons. You
know what I have done, captive. You know

I am holding lions with my two eyes: if I turn and loose
them . . .

CASSANDRA   It is . . . the King. There! There! Ah!

CLYTEMNESTRA

Or of I should make any move to increase confusion. If I should
say for example, Spearman

Kill that woman. I cannot say it this moment; so little as from
one spear wound in your body

A trickle would loose them on us.

CASSANDRA   Yet he stands behind you.
A-ah! I can bear it. I have seen much lately

Worse.

A CAPTAIN (*down the stair; standing forward from his men*)
O Queen, there is no man in the world, but one (if that one
lives), may ask you to speak

Otherwise than you will. You have spoken in riddles to the
people . . .

CASSANDRA   Not me! Why will you choose

Me! I submitted to you living, I was forced, you entered me . . .

THE CAPTAIN   Also there was a slave here,

Whose eyes stood out from his chalk face, came buzzing from
the palace postern gate, whimpering

A horrible thing. I killed him. But the men have heard it.

CASSANDRA   You were the king, I was your slave.

Here you see, here, I took the black-haired breast of the bull,
I endured it, I opened my thighs, I suffered

The other thing besides death that you Greeks have to give
us . . .

THE CAPTAIN   Though this one raves and you are silent,

O Queen, terrible-eyed . . .

CASSANDRA   That was the slave's part: but this
time . . . dead King . . .

I . . . will . . . not submit. Ah! Ah! No!

If you will steal the body of someone living take your wife's,
take that soldier's there—

THE CAPTAIN

I pray you Queen command the captive woman be quieted in a
stone chamber; she increases confusion,

The soldiers cannot know some terrible thing may not have
happened; your men and the King's grin

Like wolves over the kill, the whole city totters on a sword-
edge over sudden—

CASSANDRA (*screaming*)

Drive him off me! Pity, pity!

I have no power; I thought when he was dead another man would
use me, your Greek custom,

Not he, he, newly slain.

He is driving me out, he enters, he possesses, this is my last de-
filement. Ah . . . Greeks . . .

Pity Cassandra!

                With the voice the spirit seemed to fly out.
She upflung her shining

Arms with the dreadful and sweet gesture of a woman surrender-
 ing utterly to force and love,
She in the eyes of the people, like a shameless woman, and fell
 writhing, and the dead King's soul
Entered her body. In that respite the Queen:
                                              Captain: and you,
  soldiers, that shift unsoldierly
The weapons that should be upright, at attention, like stiff
 grass-blades: and you, people of Mycenæ:
While this one maddened, and you muttered, echoing together,
 and you, soldier, with anxious questions
Increased confusion: who was it that stood firm, who was it that
 stood silent, who was it that held
With her two eyes the whole city from splitting wide asunder?
 Your Queen was it? I am your Queen,
And now I will answer what you asked. . . . It is true. . . . He
 has died. . . . I am the Queen.
My little son Orestes will grow up and govern you.
                                              While she
  spoke the body of Cassandra
Arose among the shaken spears, taller than the spears, and stood
 among the waving spears
Stone-quiet, like a high war-tower in a windy pinewood, bu\
 deadly to look at, with blind and tyrannous
Eyes; and the Queen: All is accomplished; and if you are wise,
 people of Mycenæ: quietness is wisdom.
No tumult will call home a dead man out of judgment. The end
 is the end. Ah, soldiers! Down spears!
What, now Troy's fallen you think there's not a foreigner in
 the world bronze may quench thirst on? Lion-cubs,
If you will tear each other in the lair happy the wolves, happy
 the hook-nose vultures.
Call the eaters of carrion? I am your Queen, I am speaking to
 you, you will hear me out before you whistle
The foul beaks from the mountain nest. I tell you I will forget
 mercy if one man moves now.
I rule you, I.

The Gods have satisfied themselves in this man's death; there
    shall not one drop of the blood of the city
Be shed further. I say the high Gods are content; as for the
    lower,
And the great ghost of the King: my slaves will bring out the
    King's body decently before you
And set it here, in the eyes of the city: spices the ships bring from
    the south will comfort his spirit;
Mycenæ and Tiryns and the shores will mourn him aloud; sheep
    will be slain for him; a hundred beeves
Spill their thick blood into the trenches; captives and slaves go
    down to serve him, yes all these captives
Burn in the ten-day fire with him, unmeasured wine quench it,
    urned in pure gold the gathered ashes
Rest forever in the sacred rock; honored; a conqueror. . . .
    Slaves, bring the King out of the house.
Alas my husband! she cried, clutching the brown strands of her
    hair in both her hands, you have left me
A woman among lions! Ah, the King's power, ah the King's
    victories! Weep for me, Mycenæ!
Widowed of the King!
             The people stood amazed, like sheep that
    snuff at their dead shepherd, some hunter's
Ill-handled arrow having struck him from the covert, all by
    mischance; he is fallen on the hillside
Between the oak-shadow and the stream; the sun burns his dead
    face, his staff lies by him, his dog
Licks his hand, whining. So, like sheep, the people
Regarded that dead majesty whom the slaves brought out of the
    house on a gold bed, and set it
Between the pillars of the porch. His royal robe covered his
    wounds, there was no stain
Nor discomposure.
            Then that captain who had spoken before:
    O Queen, before the mourning
The punishment: tell us who has done this. She raised her head,
    and not a woman but a lioness

Blazed at him from her eyes: Dog, she answered, dog of the
army,

Who said Speak dog, and you dared speak? Justice is mine.
Then he was silent; but Cassandra's

Body standing tall among the spears, over the parapet, her body
but not her spirit

Cried with a man's voice: Shall not even the stones of the stair,
shall not the stones under the columns

Speak, and the towers of the great wall of my city come down
against the murderess? O Mycenæ

I yearned to night and day under the tents by Troy, O Tiryns,
O Mycenæ, the door

Of death, and the gate before the door!

CLYTEMNESTRA   That woman lies, or the
spirit of a lie cries from her. Spearman,

Kill that woman!

                    But Cassandra's body set its back against the
parapet, its face

Terribly fronting the raised knife; and called the soldier by his
name, in the King's voice, saying

Sheathe it; and the knife lowered, and the soldier

Fell on his knees before the King in the woman's body; and the
body of Cassandra cried from the parapet:

Horrible things, horrible things this house has witnessed: but here
is the most vile, that hundreds

Of spears are idle while the murderess, Clytemnestra the mur-
deress, the snake that came upon me

Naked and bathing, the death that lay with me in bed, the death
that has borne children to me,

Stands there unslain.

CLYTEMNESTRA   Cowards, if the bawling of that bewildered
heifer from Troy fields has frightened you

How did you bear the horns of her brothers? Bring her to me.

THE BODY OF CASSANDRA

                    Let no man doubt, men of Mycenæ,

She has yet the knife hid in her clothes, the very blade that
stabbed her husband and the blood is on it.

Look, she handles it now. Look, fellows. The hand under the
   robe. Slay her not easily, that she-wolf.
Do her no honor with a spear! Ah! If I could find the word, if
   I could find it,
The name of her, to say husband-slayer and bed-defiler, bitch
   and wolf-bitch, king's assassin
And beast, beast, beast, all in one breath, in one word: spearmen
You would heap your shields over this woman and crush her
   slowly, slowly, while she choked and screamed,
No, you would peel her bare and on the pavement for a bride-
   bed with a spear-butt for husband
Dig the lewd womb until it burst: this for Agamemnon, this for
   Ægisthus—Agh, cowards of the city
Do you stand quiet?
CLYTEMNESTRA   Truly, soldiers,
I think it is he verily. No one could invent the abominable voice,
   the unspeakable gesture,
The actual raging insolence of the tyrant. I am the hand ridded
   the Argolis of him.
I here, I killed him, I, justly.
THE BODY OF CASSANDRA   You have heard her, you have
   heard her, she has made confession.
Now if she'll show you the knife too—
CLYTEMNESTRA   Here. I kept it for safety.
And, as that beast said, his blood's yet on it.
Look at it, with so little a key I unlocked the kingdom of de-
   struction. Stand firm, till a God
Lead home this ghost to the dark country
So many Greeks have peopled, through his crimes, his violence,
   his insolence, stand firm till that moment
And through the act of this hand and of this point no man shall
   suffer anything again forever
Of Agamemnon.
THE BODY OF CASSANDRA
                    I say if you let this woman live, this crime go
   unpunished, what man among you
Will be safe in his bed? The woman ever envies the man, his
   strength, his freedom, his loves.

Her envy is like a snake beside him, all his life through, her envy
and hatred: law tames that viper:
Law dies if the Queen die not: the viper is free then,
It will be poison in your meat or a knife to bleed you sleeping.
They fawn and slaver over us
And then we are slain.

CLYTEMNESTRA (*to one of the slaves that carried the King's*
body)
Is my lord Ægisthus
Slain on the way? How long? How long?

(*To the people*) He
came, fat with his crimes.
Greek valor broke down Troy, your valor, soldiers, and the brain
of Odysseus, the battle-fury of Achilles,
The stubborn strength of Menelaus, the excellence of you all:
this dead man here, his pride
Ruined you a hundred times: he helped nowise, he brought bitter
destruction: but he gathered your glory
For the cloak of his shoulders. I saw him come up the stair, I saw
my child Iphigenia
Killed for his crime; I saw his harlot, the captive woman there,
crying out behind him, I saw . . .
I saw . . . I saw . . . how can I speak what crowd of the dead
faces of the faithful Greeks,
Your brothers, dead of his crimes; those that perished of plague
and those that died in the lost battles
After he had soured the help of Achilles—for another harlot—
those dead faces of your brothers,
Some black with the death-blood, many trampled under the
hooves of horses, many spotted with pestilence,
Flew all about him, all lamenting, all crying out against him,—
horrible—horrible—I gave them
Vengeance; and you freedom.

(*To the slave*) Go up and look,
for God's sake, go up to the parapets,
Look toward the mountain. Bring me word quickly, my strength
breaks,
How can I hold all the Argolis with my eyes forever? I alone?

Hell cannot hold her dead men,
Keep watch there—send me word by others—go, go!
                                        (*To the people*) He
    came triumphing.
Magnificent, abominable, all in bronze.
I brought him to the bath; my hands undid the armor;
My hands poured out the water;
Dead faces like flies buzzed all about us;
He stripped himself before me, loathsome, unclean, with laughter;
The labors of the Greeks had made him fat, the deaths of the
    faithful had swelled his belly;
I threw a cloak over him for a net and struck, struck, struck,
Blindly, in the steam of the bath; he bellowed, netted,
And bubbled in the water;
All the stone vault asweat with steam bellowed;
And I undid the net and the beast was dead, and the broad vessel
Stank with his blood.
THE BODY OF CASSANDRA
                    The word! The word! O burning mind of God,
If ever I gave you bulls teach me that word, the name for her,
    the name for her!
A SLAVE (*running from the door; to* CLYTEMNESTRA)
My lord .T;i-thi:s has come down the mountain, Queen, he
    approaches the Lion-gate.
CLYTEMNESTRA   It is time. I am tired now.
Meet him and tell him to come in the postern doorway.
THE CAPTAIN (*on the stair: addressing the soldiers and the people
    below*)
Companions: before God, hating the smell of crimes, crushes the
    city into gray ashes
We must make haste. Judge now and act. For the husband-slayer
I say she must die, let her pay forfeit. And for the great ghost
    of the King, let all these captives,
But chiefly the woman Cassandra, the crier in a man's voice there,
    be slain upon his pyre to quiet him.
He will go down to his dark place and God will spare the city.
            (*To the soldiers above, on the ramp and the porch*)
                    Comrades: Mycenæ is greater

Than the Queen of Mycenæ. The King is dead: let the Queen
    die: let the city live. Comrades,
We suffered something in Asia, on the stranger's coast, laboring
    for you. We dreamed of home there
In the bleak wind and drift of battle; we continued ten years,
    laboring and dying; we accomplished
The task set us; we gathered what will make all the Greek cities
    glorious, a name forever;
We shared the spoil, taking our share to enrich Mycenæ. O but
    our hearts burned then, O comrades
But our hearts melted when the great oars moved the ships, the
    water carried us, the blue sea-waves
Slid under the black keel; I could not see them, I was blind with
    tears, thinking of Mycenæ.
We have come home. Behold the dear streets of our longing,
The stones that we desired, the steep ways of the city and the
    sacred doorsteps
Reek and steam with pollution, the accursed vessel
Spills a red flood over the floors.
The fountain of it stands there and calls herself the Queen. No
    Queen, no Queen, that husband-slayer,
A common murderess. Comrades join us
We will make clean the city and sweeten it before God. We
    will mourn together at the King's burying,
And a good year will come, we will rejoice together.
CLYTEMNESTRA   Dog, you dare
    something. Fling no spear, soldiers,
He has a few fools back of him would attempt the stair if the
    dog were slain: I will have no one
Killed out of need.
ONE OF HER MEN ON THE PORCH (*flinging his spear*)
                 Not at him: at you
Murderess!
              But some God, no lover of justice, turned it; the
    great bronze tip grazing her shoulder
Clanged on the stones behind: the gong of a change in the dance:
    now Clytemnestra, none to help her,

One against all, swayed raging by the King's corpse, over the
    golden bed: it is said that a fire
Stood visibly over her head, mixed in the hair, pale flames and
    radiance.

CLYTEMNESTRA   Here am I, thieves, thieves,
Drunkards, here is my breast, a deep white mark for cowards to
    aim at: kings have lain on it.
No spear yet, heroes, heroes?
See, I have no blemish: the arms are white, the breasts are deep
    and white, the whole body is blemishless:
You are tired of your brown wives, draw lots for me, rabble,
    thieves, there is loot here, shake the dice, thieves, a game yet!
One of you will take the bronze and one the silver,
One the gold, and one me,
Me Clytemnestra a spoil worth having:
Kings have kissed me, this dead dog was a king, there is another
King at the gate: thieves, thieves, would not this shining
Breast brighten a sad thief's hut, roll in his bed's filth
Shiningly? You could teach me to draw water at the fountain,
A dirty child on the other hip: where are the dice? Let me
    throw first, if I throw sixes
I choose my masters: closer you rabble, let me smell you.
Don't fear the knife, it has king's blood on it, I keep it for an
    ornament,
It has shot its sting.

THE BODY OF CASSANDRA   Fools, fools, strike!
Are your hands dead?

CLYTEMNESTRA   You would see all of me
Before you choose whether to kill or dirtily cherish? If what
    the King's used needs commending
To the eyes of thieves for thieves' use: give me room, give me
    room, fellows, you'll see it is faultless.
The dress . . . there . . .

THE BODY OF CASSANDRA   Fools this wide whore played wife
When she was going about to murder me the King; you, will
    you let her trip you
With the harlot's trick? Strike! Make an end!

CLYTEMNESTRA   I have not my
    sister's, Troy's flame's beauty, but I have something.
This arm, round, firm, skin without hair, polished like marble:
    the supple-jointed shoulders:
Men have praised the smooth neck, too,
The strong clear throat over the deep wide breasts . . .
THE BODY OF CASSANDRA   She is
    buying an hour: sheep: it may be Ægisthus
Is at the Lion-gate.
CLYTEMNESTRA   If he were here, Ægisthus,
I'd not be the pedlar of what trifling charms I have for an
    hour of life yet. You have wolves' eyes:
Yet there is something kindly about the blue ones there—yours,
    young soldier, young soldier. . . . The last,
The under-garment? You won't buy me yet? This dead dog,
The King here, never saw me naked: I had the night for nurse:
    turn his head sideways, the eyes
Are only half shut. If I should touch him, and the blood came,
    you'd say I had killed him. Nobody, nobody,
Killed him: his pride burst.
Ah, no one has pity!
I can serve well, I have always envied your women, the public ones.
Who takes me first? Tip that burnt log onto the flagstones,
This will be in a king's bed then. Your eyes are wolves' eyes:
So many, so many, so famishing—
I will undo it, handle me not yet, I can undo it . . .
Or I will tear it.
And when it is off me then I will be delivered to you beasts . . .
THE BODY OF CASSANDRA
Then strip her and use her to the bones, wear her through, kill
    her with it.
CLYTEMNESTRA
       When it is torn
You'll say I am lovely: no one has seen before . . .
It won't tear: I'll slit it with this knife—
      (ÆGISTHUS, *with many spearmen, issues from the great door.*
      CLYTEMNESTRA *stabs right and left with the knife; the*
      men are too close to strike her with their long spears.)

CLYTEMNESTRA

It's time. Cowards, goats, goats. Here! Ægisthus!

ÆGISTHUS

I am here. What have they done?

CLYTEMNESTRA

Nothing: clear the porch: *I* have done something. Drive them on the stair!

Three of them I've scarred for life: a rough bridegroom, the rabble, met a fierce bride.

(*She catches up her robe.*)

I held them with my eyes, hours, hours. I am not tired. . . . My lord, my lover:

I have killed a twelve-point stag for a present for you: with my own hands: look, on the golden litter.

You arrive timely.

THE BODY OF CASSANDRA

Tricked, stabbed, shamed, mocked at, the spoil of a lewd woman, despised

I lie there ready for her back-stairs darling to spit on. Tricked, stabbed, sunk in the drain

And gutter of time. I that thundered the assault, I that mustered the Achæans. Cast out of my kingdom,

Cast out of time, out of the light.

CLYTEMNESTRA One of the captives, dear.

It left its poor wits

Over the sea. If it annoys you I'll quiet it. But post your sentinels.

All's not safe yet, though I am burning with joy now.

THE BODY OF CASSANDRA O single-eyed glare of the sky

Flying southwest to the mountain: sun, through a slave's eyes,

My own broken, I see you this last day; my own darkened, no dawn forever; the adulterers

Will swim in your warm gold, day after day; the eyes of the murderess will possess you;

And I have gone away down: knowing that no God in the earth nor sky loves justice; and having tasted

The toad that serves women for heart. From now on may all
    bridegrooms
Marry them with swords. Those that have borne children
Their sons rape them with spears.

CLYTEMNESTRA   More yet, more, more, more,
    while my hand's in? It's not a little
You easily living lords of the sky require of who'd be like you,
    who'd take time in the triumph,
Build joy solid. Do we have to do everything? I have killed
    what I hated:
Kill what I love? The prophetess said it, this dead man says it:
    my little son, the small soft image
That squirmed in my arms be an avenger?—Love, from your loins
Seed: I begin new, I will be childless for you. The child my son,
    the child my daughter!
Though I cry I feel nothing.

ÆGISTHUS   O strongest spirit in the world.
    We have dared enough, there is an end to it.
We may pass nature a little, an arrow-flight,
But two shots over the wall you come in a cloud upon the feast-
    ing Gods, lightning and madness.

CLYTEMNESTRA
Dear: make them safe. They may try to run away, the children.
    Set spears to watch them: no harm, no harm,
But stab the nurse if they go near a door. Watch them, keep the
    gates, order the sentinels,
While *I* make myself Queen over this people again. I can do it.

THE BODY OF CASSANDRA   The sun's gone; that glimmer's
The moon of the dead. The dark God calls me. Yes, God,
I'll come in a moment.

CLYTEMNESTRA (*at the head of the great stairs*)
Soldiers: townsmen: it seems
I am not at the end delivered to you: dogs, for the lion came:
    the poor brown and spotted women
Will have to suffice you. But is it nothing to have come within
    handling distance of the clear heaven
This dead man knew when he was young and God endured him?
    Is it nothing to you?

It is something to me to have felt the fury
And concentration of you: I will not say I am grateful: I am
    not angry: to be desired
Is wine even to a queen. You bathed me in it, from brow to foot-
    sole, I had nearly enough.
But now remember that the dream is over. I am the Queen:
    Mycenæ is my city. If you grin at me
I have spears: also Tiryns and all the country people of the
    Argolis will come against you and swallow you,
Empty out these ways and walls, stock them with better subjects.
    A rock nest for new birds here, townsfolk:
You are not essential.

THE BODY OF CASSANDRA.   I hear him calling through the she-
wolf's noise, Agamemnon, Agamemnon,
The dark God calls. Some old king in a fable is it?

CLYTEMNESTRA   So choose.
    What choices? To reënter my service
Unpunished, no thought of things past, free of conditions . . .
Or—dine at this man's table, have new mouths made in you to
    eat bronze with.

THE BODY OF CASSANDRA   Who is Agamemnon?

CLYTEMNESTRA
You letting go of the sun: is it dark the land you are running
    away to?

THE BODY OF CASSANDRA   It is dark.

CLYTEMNESTRA   Is it sorrowful?

THE BODY OF CASSANDRA
There is nothing but misery.

CLYTEMNESTRA   Has any man ever come back thence?
    Hear *me*, not the dark God.

THE BODY OF CASSANDRA   No man has ever.

CLYTEMNESTRA
Go then, go, go down. You will not choose to follow him, people
    of the rock-city? No one
Will choose to follow him. I have killed: it is easy: it may be
    I shall kill nearer than this yet:
But not you, townsfolk, you will give me no cause; I want
    security; I want service, not blood.

I have been desired of the whole city, publicly; I want service,
 not lust. You will make no sign
Of your submission; you will not give up your weapons; neither
 shall your leaders be slain;
And he that flung the spear, I have forgotten his face.

ÆGISTHUS (*entering*)   Dearest,
 they have gone, the nurse and the children,
No one knows where.

CLYTEMNESTRA   I am taming this people: send men after
 them. If any harm comes to the children
Bring me tokens. I will not be in doubt, I will not have the arch
 fall on us. I dare
What no one dares. I envy a little the dirty mothers of the city.
 O, O!
Nothing in me hurts. I have animal waters in my eyes, but the
 spirit is not wounded. Electra and Orestes
Are not to live when they are caught. Bring me sure tokens.

CASSANDRA   Who is this woman like a beacon
Lit on the stair, who are these men with dogs' heads?
I have ranged time and seen no sight like this one.

CLYTEMNESTRA
Have you returned, Cassandra? . . . The dead king has gone
 down to his place, we may bury his leavings.

CASSANDRA
I have witnessed all the wars to be; I am not sorrowful
For one drop from the pail of desolation
Spilt on my father's city; they were carrying it forward
To water the world under the latter starlight.

CLYTEMNESTRA (*to her slaves*)
Take up the poles of the bed; reverently; careful on the stair;
 give him to the people. (*To the people*) O soldiers
This was your leader; lay him with honor in the burial-chapel;
 guard him with the spears of victory;
Mourn him until to-morrow, when the pyre shall be built.
Ah, King of men, sleep, sleep, sleep!
. . . But when shall I? . . . They are after their corpse, like
 dogs after the butcher's cart. Cleomenes, that captain

With the big voice: Neobulus was the boy who flung the spear
and missed. *I* shall not miss

When spear-flinging-time comes. . . . Captive woman, you have
seen the future, tell me my fortune.

(ÆGISTHUS *comes from the doorway.*)

Ægisthus,

Have your hounds got them?

ÆGISTHUS   I've covered every escape with men,
they'll not slip through me. But commanded

To bring them here living.

CLYTEMNESTRA   That's hard: tigresses don't do it: I
have some strength yet: don't speak of it

And I shall do it.

ÆGISTHUS   It is a thing not to be done: we'll guard them
closely: but mere madness

Lies over the wall of too-much.

CLYTEMNESTRA   King of Mycenæ, new-crowned
king, who was your mother?

ÆGISTHUS   Pelopia.

What mark do you aim at?

CLYTEMNESTRA   And your father?

ÆGISTHUS   Thyestes.

CLYTEMNESTRA   And her father?

ÆGISTHUS   The
same man, Thyestes.

CLYTEMNESTRA

See, dearest, dearest? They love what men call crime, they have
taken her crime to be the king of Mycenæ.

Here is the stone garden of the plants that pass nature: there is
no too-much here: the monstrous

Old rocks want monstrous roots to serpent among them. I will
have security. I'd burn the standing world

Up to this hour and begin new. You think I am too much used
for a new brood? Ah, lover,

I have fountains in me. I had a fondness for the brown cheek
of that boy, the curl of his lip,

The widening blue of the doomed eyes . . . I will be spared
nothing. Come in, come in, they'll have news for us.

CASSANDRA

If anywhere in the world
Were a tower with foundations, or a treasure-chamber
With a firm vault, or a walled fortress
That stood on the years, not staggering, not moving
As the mortar were mixed with wine for water
And poppy for lime: they reel, they are all drunkards,
The piled strengths of the world: no pyramid
In bitter Egypt in the desert
But skips at moonrise; no mountain
Over the Black Sea in awful Caucasus
But whirls like a young kid, like a bud of the herd,
Under the hundredth star: I am sick after steadfastness
Watching the world cataractlike
Pour screaming onto steep ruins: for the wings of prophecy
God once my lover give me stone sandals
Planted on stone: he hates me, the God, he will never
Take home the gift of the bridleless horse
The stallion, the unbitted stallion: the bed
Naked to the sky on Mount Ida,
The soft clear grass there,
Be blackened forever, may vipers and Greeks
In that glen breed
Twisting together, where the God
Come golden from the sun
Gave me for a bride-gift prophecy and I took it for a treasure:
I a fool, I a maiden,
I would not let him touch me though love of him maddened me
Till he fed me that poison, till he planted that fire in me,
The girdle flew loose then.

The Queen considered this rock, she gazed on the great stone
    blocks of Mycenæ's acropolis;
Monstrous they seemed to her, solid they appeared to her, safe
    rootage for monstrous deeds: Ah fierce one
Who knows who laid them for a snare? What people in the
    world's dawn breathed on chill air and the vapor

Of their breath seemed stone and has stood and you dream it is
 established? These also are a foam on the stream
Of the falling of the world: there is nothing to lay hold on:
No crime is a crime, the slaying of the King was a meeting of
 two bubbles on the lip of the cataract,
One winked . . . and the killing of your children would be
 nothing: I tell you for a marvel that the earth is a dancer,
The grave dark earth is less quiet than a fool's fingers,
That old one, spinning in the emptiness, blown by no wind in
 vain circles, light-witted and a dancer.

CLYTEMNESTRA (*entering*)
You are prophesying: prophesy to a purpose, captive woman.
 My children, the boy and the girl,
Have wandered astray, no one can find them.

CASSANDRA   Shall I tell the lioness
Where meat is, or the she-wolf where the lambs wander astray?

CLYTEMNESTRA   But look into the darkness
And foam of the world: the boy has great tender blue eyes,
 brown hair, disdainful lips, you'll know him
By the gold stripe bordering his garments; the girl's eyes are
 my color, white her clothing—

CASSANDRA   Millions
Of shining bubbles burst and wander
On the stream of the world falling . . .

CLYTEMNESTRA   These are my children!

CASSANDRA   I see
 mountains, I see no faces.

CLYTEMNESTRA
Tell me and I make you free; conceal it from me and a soldier's
 spear finishes the matter.

CASSANDRA
I am the spear's bride, I have been waiting, waiting for that
 ecstasy—

CLYTEMNESTRA (*striking her*) Live then. It will not be unpainful.
                              (CLYTEMNESTRA *goes in.*)

CASSANDRA
O fair roads north where the land narrows
Over the mountains between the great gulfs,

O that I too with the King's children
Might wander northward hand in hand.
Mine are worse wanderings:
They will shelter on Mount Parnassus,
For me there is no mountain firm enough,
The storms of light beating on the headlands,
The storms of music undermine the mountains, they stumble
    and fall inward,
Such music the stars
Make in their courses, the vast vibration
Plucks the iron heart of the earth like a harp-string.
Iron and stone core, O stubborn axle of the earth, you also
Dissolving in a little time like salt in water,
What does it matter that I have seen Macedon
Roll all the Greek cities into one billow and strand in Asia
The anthers and bracts of the flower of the world?
That I have seen Egypt and Nineveh
Crumble, and a Latian village
Plant the earth with javelins? It made laws for all men, it dis-
    solved like a cloud.
I have also stood watching a storm of wild swans
Rise from one river-mouth . . . O force of the earth rising,
O fallings of the earth: forever no rest, not forever
From the wave and the trough, from the stream and the slack,
    from growth and decay: O vulture-
Pinioned, my spirit, one flight yet, last, longest, unguided,
Try into the gulf,
Over Greece, over Rome, you have space O my spirit for the
    years

II

Are not few of captivity: how many have I stood here
Among the great stones, while the Queen's people
Go in and out of the gate, wearing light linen
For summer and the wet spoils of wild beasts
In the season of storms: and the stars have changed, I have
    watched
The grievous and unprayed-to constellations

Pile steaming spring and patient autumn
Over the enduring walls: but you over the walls of the world,
Over the unquieted centuries, over the darkness-hearted
Millenniums wailing thinly to be born, O vulture-pinioned
Try into the dark,
Watch the north spawn white bodies and red-gold hair,
Race after race of beastlike warriors; and the cities
Burn, and the cities build, and new lands be uncovered
In the way of the sun to his setting . . . go on farther, what
     profit
In the wars and the toils? but I say
Where are prosperous people my enemies are, as you pass them
     O my spirit
Curse Athens for the joy and the marble, curse Corinth
For the wine and the purple, and Syracuse
For the gold and the ships; but Rome, Rome,
With many destructions for the corn and the laws and the jave-
     lins, the insolence, the threefold
Abominable power: pass the humble
And the lordships of darkness, but far down
Smite Spain for the blood on the sunset gold, curse France
For the fields abounding and the running rivers, the lights in the
     cities, the laughter, curse England
For the meat on the tables and the terrible gray ships, for old
     laws, far dominions, there remains
A mightier to be cursed and a higher for malediction
When America has eaten Europe and takes tribute of Asia, when
     the ends of the world grow aware of each other
And are dogs in one kennel, they will tear
The master of the hunt with the mouths of the pack: new fall-
     ings, new risings, O winged one
No end of the fallings and risings? An end shall be surely,
Though unnatural things are accomplished, they breathe in the
     sea's depth,
They swim in the air, they bridle the cloud-leaper lightning to
     carry their messages:
Though the eagles of the east and the west and the falcons of
     the north were not quieted, you have seen a white cloth

Cover the lands from the north and the eyes of the lands and the
claws of the hunters,
The mouths of the hungry with snow
Were filled, and their claws
Took hold upon ice in the pasture, a morsel of ice was their
catch in the rivers,
That pure white quietness
Waits on the heads of the mountains, not sleep but death, will
the fire
Of burnt cities and ships in that year warm you my enemies?
The frost, the old frost,
Like a cat with a broken-winged bird it will play with you,
It will nip and let go; you will say it is gone, but the next
Season it increases: O clean, clean,
White and most clean, colorless quietness,
Without trace, without trail, without stain in the garment, drawn
down
From the poles to the girdle. . . . I have known one Godhead
To my sore hurt: I am growing to come to another: O grave
and kindly
Last of the lords of the earth, I pray you lead my substance
Speedily into another shape, make me grass, Death, make me
stone,
Make me air to wander free between the stars and the peaks;
but cut humanity
Out of my being, that is the wound that festers in me,
Not captivity, not my enemies: you will heal the earth also,
Death, in your time; but speedily Cassandra.
You rock-fleas hopping in the clefts of Mycenæ,
Suckers of blood, you carrying the scepter farther, Persian,
Emathian,
Roman and Mongol and American, and you half-gods
Indian and Syrian and the third, emperors of peace, I have seen
on what stage
You sing the little tragedy; the column of the ice that was before
on one side flanks it,
The column of the ice to come closes it up on the other: audience
nor author

I have never seen yet: I have heard the silence: it is I Cassandra,
Eight years the bitter watchdog of these doors,
Have watched a vision
And now approach to my end. Eight years I have seen the
    phantoms
Walk up and down this stair; and the rocks groan in the night,
    the great stones move when no man sees them.
And I have forgotten the fine ashlar masonry of the courts of my
    father. I am not Cassandra
But a counter of sunrises, permitted to live because I am crying
    to die; three thousand,
Pale and red, have flowed over the towers in the wall since I was
    here watching; the deep east widens,
The cold wind blows, the deep earth sighs, the dim gray finger
    of light crooks at the morning star.
The palace feasted late and sleeps with its locked doors; the last
    drunkard from the alleys of the city
Long has reeled home. Whose foot is this then, what phantom
Toils on the stair?
A VOICE BELOW   Is someone watching above? Good sentinel I
    am only a girl beggar.
I would sit on the stair and hold my bowl.
CASSANDRA   I here eight years have
    begged for a thing and not received it.
THE VOICE
You are not a sentinel? You have been asking some great boon,
    out of all reason.
CASSANDRA   No: what the meanest
Beggar disdains to take.
THE GIRL BEGGAR   Beggars disdain nothing: what is it that
    they refuse you?
CASSANDRA   What's given
Even to the sheep and to the bullock.
THE GIRL   Men give them salt, grass
    they find out for themselves.
CASSANDRA   Men give them
The gift that you though a beggar have brought down from the
    north to give my mistress.

THE GIRL   You speak riddles.
I am starving, a crust is my desire.

CASSANDRA   Your voice is young though
  winds have hoarsened it, your body appears
Flexible under the rags: have you some hidden sickness, the
  young men will not give you silver?

THE GIRL
I have a sickness: I will hide it until I am cured. You are not
  a Greek woman?

CASSANDRA   But you
Born in Mycenæ return home. And you bring gifts from Phocis:
  for my once master who's dead
Vengeance; and for my mistress peace, for my master the King
  peace, and, by-shot of the doom's day,
Peace for me also. But I have prayed for it.

THE GIRL   I know you, I knew
  you before you spoke to me, captive woman,
And I unarmed will kill you with my hands if you babble
  prophecies.
That peace you have prayed for, I will bring it to you
If you utter warnings.

CASSANDRA   To-day I shall have peace, you cannot
  tempt me, daughter of the Queen, Electra.
Eight years ago I watched you and your brother going north
  to Phocis: the Queen saw knowledge of you
Move in my eyes: I would not tell her where you were when
  she commanded me: I will not betray you
To-day either: it is not doleful to me
To see before I die generations of destruction enter the doors
  of Agamemnon.
Where is your brother?

ELECTRA   Prophetess: you see all: I will tell you
  nothing.

CASSANDRA   He has well chosen his ambush,
It is true Ægisthus passes under that house to-day, to hunt in
  the mountain.

ELECTRA   Now I remember
Your name. Cassandra.

CASSANDRA Hush: the gray has turned yellow, the standing beacons
Stream up from the east; they stir there in the palace; strange, is it not, the dawn of one's last day's
Like all the others? Your brother would be fortunate if to-day were also
The last of his.

ELECTRA He will endure his destinies; and Cassandra hers; and Electra mine.
He has been for years like one tortured with fire: this day will quench it.

CASSANDRA They are opening the gates: beg now.
To your trade, beggar-woman.

THE PORTER (*coming out*) Eh, pillar of miseries,
You still on guard there? Like a mare in a tight stall, never lying down. What's this then?
A second ragged one? This at least can bend in the middle and sit on a stone.

ELECTRA Dear gentleman
I am not used to it, my father is dead and hunger forces me to beg, a crust or a penny.

THE PORTER
This tall one's licensed in a manner. I think they'll not let two bundles of rag
Camp on the stair: but if you'd come to the back door and please me nicely: with a little washing
It'd do for pastime.

ELECTRA I was reared gently: I will sit here, the King will see me,
And none mishandle me.

THE PORTER I bear no blame for you.
I have not seen you: you came after the gates were opened.
(*He goes in.*)

CASSANDRA
O blossom of fire, bitter to men,
Watchdog of the woeful days,
How many sleepers
Bathing in peace, dreaming themselves delight,

All over the city, all over the Argolid plain, all over the dark
  earth,
(Not me, a deeper draught of peace
And darker waters alone may wash me)
Do you, terrible star, star without pity,
Wolf of the east, waken to misery.
To the wants unaccomplished, to the eating desires,
To unanswered love, to hunger, to the hard edges
And mold of reality, to the whips of their masters.
They had flown away home to the happy darkness,
They were safe until sunrise.

> (King Ægisthus, with his retinue, comes from the great
> door.)

ÆGISTHUS

Even here, in the midst of the city, the early day
Has a clear savor. (To ELECTRA) What, are you miserable, hold-
  ing the bowl out?
We'll hear the lark to-day in the wide hills and smell the moun-
  tain. I'd share happiness with you.
What's your best wish, girl beggar?

ELECTRA   It is covered, my lord, how
  should a beggar
Know what to wish for beyond a crust and a dark corner and a
  little kindness?

ÆGISTHUS   Why do you tremble?

ELECTRA

I was reared gently; my father is dead.

ÆGISTHUS   Stand up: will you take
  service here in the house? What country
Bred you gently and proved ungentle to you?

ELECTRA   I have wandered
  north from the Eurotas, my lord,
Begging at farmsteads.

ÆGISTHUS   The Queen's countrywoman then, she'll
  use you kindly. She'll be coming
In a moment, then I'll speak for you.—Did you bid them yoke
  the roans into my chariot, Menalcas,
The two from Orchomenus?

ONE OF THE RETINUE   Yesterday evening, my lord,
I sent to the stable.

ÆGISTHUS   They cost a pretty penny, we'll see how they
carry it.—She's coming: hold up your head, girl.

     (CLYTEMNESTRA, *with two serving-women, comes from
the door.*)

CLYTEMNESTRA
Good hunt, dearest. Here's a long idle day for me to look to.
Kill early, come home early.

ÆGISTHUS
There's a poor creature on the step who's been reared nicely
and slipped into misery. I said you'd feed her,
And maybe find her a service. Farewell, sweet one.

CLYTEMNESTRA   Where did she come from? How long have you
been here?

ÆGISTHUS   She says she has begged her way up from Sparta.
The horses are stamping on the cobbles, good-by, good-by.

     (*He goes down the stair with his huntsmen.*)

CLYTEMNESTRA   Good-by, dearest. Well. Let me see your face.

ELECTRA   It is filthy to look at. I am ashamed.

CLYTEMNESTRA (*to one of her serving-women*) Leucippe do
you think this is a gayety of my lord's, he's not used to be
so kindly to beggars?
—Let me see your face.

LEUCIPPE   She is very dirty, my lady. It is possible one of the
house-boys . . .

CLYTEMNESTRA   I say draw that rag back, let me see your face.
I'd have him whipped then.

ELECTRA   It was only in hope that someone would put a crust
in the bowl, your majesty, for I am starving. I didn't think
your majesty would see me.

CLYTEMNESTRA   Draw back the rag.

ELECTRA   I am very faint and starving but I will go down; I am
ashamed.

CLYTEMNESTRA   Stop her, Corinna. Fetch the porter, Leucippe.
You will not go so easily. (ELECTRA *sinks down on the steps
and lies prone, her head covered.*) I am aging out of queen-
ship indeed, when even the beggars refuse my bidding.

(LEUCIPPE *comes in with the porter*.) You have a dirty stair, porter. How long has this been here?

THE PORTER O my lady it has crept up since I opened the doors, it was not here when I opened the doors.

CLYTEMNESTRA Lift it up and uncover its face. What is that cry in the city? Stop: silent: I heard a cry . . .
Prophetess, your nostrils move like a dog's, what is that shouting? . . .
I have grown weak, I am exhausted, things frighten me . . .
Tell her to be gone, Leucippe, I don't wish to see her, I don't wish to see her.

(ELECTRA *rises*.)

ELECTRA Ah, Queen, I will show you my face.

CLYTEMNESTRA No . . . no . . . be gone.

ELECTRA (*uncovering her face*)
Mother: I have come home: I am humbled. This house keeps a dark welcome
For those coming home out of far countries.

CLYTEMNESTRA   I won't look: how could I know anyone? I am old and shaking.
He said, Over the wall beyond nature
Lightning, and the laughter of the Gods. I did not cross it, I will not kill what I gave life to.
Whoever you are, go, go, let me grow downward to the grave quietly now.

ELECTRA   I cannot
Go: I have no other refuge. Mother! Will you not kiss me, will you not take me into the house,
Your child once, long a wanderer? Electra my name. I have begged my way from Phocis, my brother is dead there,
Who used to care for me.

CLYTEMNESTRA   Who is dead, who?

ELECTRA   My brother Orestes,
Killed in a court quarrel.

CLYTEMNESTRA (*weeping*) Oh, you lie! The widening blue blue eyes,
The little voice of the child . . . Liar.

ELECTRA   It is true. I have wept
long, on every mountain. You, mother,
Have only begun weeping. Far off, in a far country, no fit
burial . . .

CLYTEMNESTRA   And do you bringing
Bitterness . . . or lies . . . look for a welcome? I have only
loved two:
The priest killed my daughter for a lamb on a stone and now
you say the boy too . . . dead, dead?
The world's full of it, a shoreless lake of lies and floating rumors
. . . pack up your wares, peddler,
Too false for a queen. Why, no, if I believed you . . . Beast,
treacherous beast, that shouting comes nearer,
What's in the city?

ELECTRA   I am a stranger, I know nothing of the city,
I know only
My mother hates me, and Orestes my brother
Died pitifully, far off.

CLYTEMNESTRA   Too many things, too many things call
me, what shall I do? Electra,
Electra help me. This comes of living softly, I had a lion's
strength
Once.

ELECTRA   Me for help? I am utterly helpless, I had help in my
brother and he is dead in Phocis.
Give me refuge: but each of us two must weep for herself, one
sorrow. An end of the world were on us
What would it matter to us weeping? Do you remember him,
Mother, mother?

CLYTEMNESTRA   I have dared too much: never dare anything,
Electra, the ache is afterward,
At the hour it hurts nothing. Prophetess, you lied.
You said he would come with vengeance on me: but now he is
dead, this girl says: and because he was lovely, blue-eyed,
And born in a most unhappy house I will believe it. But the
world's fogged with the breath of liars,
And if she has laid a net for me . . .

I'll call up the old lioness lives yet in my body, I have dared,
    I have dared, and tooth and talon
Carve a way through. Lie to me?

ELECTRA   Have I endured for months,
    with feet bleeding, among the mountains,
Between the great gulfs alone and starving, to bring you a lie
    now? I know the worst of you, I looked for the worst,
Mother, mother, and have expected nothing but to die of this
    home-coming: but Orestes
Has entered the cave before; he is gathered up in a lonely moun-
    tain quietness, he is guarded from angers
In the tough cloud that spears fall back from.

CLYTEMNESTRA   Was he still beau-
    tiful? The brown mothers down in the city
Keep their brats about them; what it is to live high! Oh!
Tell them down there, tell them in Tiryns,
Tell them in Sparta,
That water drips through the Queen's fingers and trickles down
    her wrists, for the boy, for the boy
Born of her body, whom she, fool, fool, fool,
Drove out of the world. Electra,
Make peace with me.
Oh, Oh, Oh!
I have labored violently all the days of my life for nothing—
    nothing—worse than anything—this death
Was a thing I wished. See how they make fools of us.
Amusement for them, to watch us labor after the thing that will
    tear us in pieces. . . . Well, strength's good.
I am the Queen; I will gather up my fragments
And not go mad now.

ELECTRA   Mother, what are the men
With spears gathering at the stair's foot? Not of Mycenæ by
    their armor, have you mercenaries
Wanting pay? Do they serve . . . Ægisthus?

CLYTEMNESTRA   What men? I seem
    not to know . . .
Who has laid a net for me, what fool
For me, me? Porter, by me.

Leucippe, my guards; into the house, rouse them. I am sorry for him,
I am best in storm. You, Electra?
The death you'll die, my daughter. Guards, out! Was it a lie?
No matter, no matter, no matter,
Here's peace. Spears, out, out! They bungled the job making me a woman. Here's youth come back to me,
And all the days of gladness.

LEUCIPPE (*running back from the door*) O, Queen, strangers . . .

ORESTES (*a sword in his hand, with spearmen following, comes from the door*) Where is that woman
The Gods utterly hate?

ELECTRA   Brother: let her not speak, kill quickly.
Is the other one safe now?

ORESTES   That dog
Fell under his chariot, we made sure of him between the wheels and the hooves, squealing. Now for this one.

CLYTEMNESTRA
Wait. I was weeping, Electra will tell you, my hands are wet still,
For your blue eyes that death had closed she said away up in Phocis. I die now, justly or not
Is out of the story, before I die I'd tell you—wait, child, wait. Did I quiver
Or pale at the blade? I say, caught in a net, netted in by my enemies, my husband murdered,
Myself to die, I am joyful knowing she lied, you live, the only creature
Under all the spread and arch of daylight
That I love, lives.

ELECTRA   The great fangs drawn fear craftiness now, kill quickly.

CLYTEMNESTRA As for her, the wife of a shepherd
Suckled her, but you
These very breasts nourished: rather one of your northern spearmen do what's needful; not you

Draw blood where you drew milk. The Gods endure much, but beware them.

ORESTES   This, a God in his temple
Openly commanded.

CLYTEMNESTRA   Ah, child, child, who has mistaught you and who has betrayed you? What voice had the God?

How was it different from a man's and did you see him? Who sent the priest presents? They fool us,

And the Gods let them. No doubt also the envious King of Phocis has lent you counsel as he lent you

Men: let one of them do it. Life's not jewel enough

That I should plead for it: this much I pray, for your sake, not with your hand, not with your hand, or the memory

Will so mother you, so glue to you, so embracing you,

Not the deep sea's green day, no cleft of a rock in the bed of the deep sea, no ocean of darkness

Outside the stars, will hide nor wash you. What is it to me that I have rejoiced knowing you alive,

O child, O precious to me, O alone loved, if now dying by my manner of death

I make nightmare the heir, nightmare, horror, in all I have of you;

And you haunted forever, never to sleep dreamless again, never to see blue cloth

But the red runs over it; fugitive of dreams, madman at length, the memory of a scream following you houndlike,

Inherit Mycenæ? Child, for this has not been done before, there is no old fable, no whisper

Out of the foundation, among the people that were before our people, no echo has ever

Moved among these most ancient stones, the monsters here, nor stirred under any mountain, nor fluttered

Under any sky, of a man slaying his mother. Sons have killed fathers—

ORESTES   And a woman her son's father—

CLYTEMNESTRA

O many times: and these old stones have seen horrors: a house of madness and blood

I married into: and worse was done on this rock among the older
    people before: but not this,
Not the son his mother; this the silent ones,
The old hard ones, the great bearers of burden have not seen yet,
Nor shall, to-day nor yet to-morrow, nor ever in the world.
    Let her do it, it is not unnatural,
The daughter the mother; the little liar there,
Electra do it. Lend her the blade.

ELECTRA   Brother though the great house
    is silent hark the city,
That buzzes like the hive one has dipped a wand in. End this.
    Then look to our safety.

ORESTES   Dip in my sword
Into my fountain? Did I truly, little and helpless,
Lie in the arms, feed on the breast there?

ELECTRA   Another, a greater, lay
    in them, another kissed the breast there,
You forget easily, the breaker of Asia, the over-shadower, the
    great memory, under whose greatness
We have hung like hawks under a storm, from the beginning,—
    and he when this poison destroyed him
Was given no room to plead in.

ORESTES   Dip my wand into my fountain?

CLYTEMNESTRA Men do not kill the meanest
Without defence heard—

ELECTRA   Him—Agamemnon?

CLYTEMNESTRA   But you, O my son, my son,
Moulded in me, made of me, made of my flesh, built with my
    blood, fed with my milk, my child
I here, I and no other, labored to bear, groaning—

ELECTRA   This that
    makes beastlike lamentation
Hunted us to slay us, we starving in the thicket above the stream
    three days and nights watched always
Her hunters with spears beating the field: prophetess was it for
    love that she looked after us?

CASSANDRA   That love

The King had tasted; that was her love.

ELECTRA   And mourning for our
father on the mountain we judged her;

And the God condemned her, what more, what more? Strike.

ORESTES   If they'd give me time, the pack there—how can I
think,

And all the whelps of Mycenæ yelling at the stair-foot? De-
cision: a thing to be decided:

The arm's lame, dip in, dip in? Shut your mouths, rabble.

CLYTEMNESTRA   There is one thing no man can do.

ORESTES   What, enter
his fountain?

ELECTRA

O coward!

ORESTES   I will be passive, I'm blunted. She's not this fellow's
mother.

ELECTRA   O spearman, spearman, do it!
One stroke: it is just.

THE SPEARMAN   As for me, my lord . . .

CLYTEMNESTRA (calling loudly)   Help, help, men
of Mycenæ, to your Queen. Break them.

Rush the stair, there are only ten hold it. Up, up, kill.

ORESTES   I will kill.

CLYTEMNESTRA (falling on her knees)   Child,
Spare me, let me live! Child! Ai! . . .

ELECTRA   You have done well.

ORESTES   I have done . . . I have done . . .

Who ever saw such a flow . . . was I made out of this, I'm not
red, am I?

See, father?

It was someone else did it but I told him to. Drink, drink, dog.
Drink dog.

He reaches up a tongue between the stones, lapping it. So thirsty
old dog, uh?

Rich and sticky.

CLYTEMNESTRA (raising herself a little)   Sleep . . . for me . . .
yes.

Not you . . . any more . . . Orestes . . . I shall be there. You
will beg death . . . vainly as I have begged . . . life. Ah
. . . beast that I unkennelled! (*She dies.*)

ORESTES (*crouching by her*) Ooh . . . Ooh . . .

ELECTRA
The face is lean and terrible. Orestes!
They are fighting on the stair. Man yourself. Come. Pick up the
sword.
Let her be, two of ours are down, they yield on the stair. Stand
up, speak or fight, speak to the people
Or we go where she is.

ORESTES There's a red and sticky sky that you
can touch here.
And though it's unpleasant we are at peace.

ELECTRA (*catching up the sword*) Agamemnon failed
here. Not in me. Hear, Mycenæans.
I am Agamemnon's daughter, we have avenged him, the crime's
paid utterly.
You have not forgotten the great King—what, in eight years?
I am Electra, I am his daughter.
My brother is Orestes. My brother is your King and has killed
his murderers. The dog Ægisthus is dead,
And the Queen is dead: the city is at peace.

ORESTES (*standing up*) Must I dip my wand
into my fountain, give it to me.
The male plaything. (*He catches* ELECTRA'S *arm, snatching at
the sword.*)

ELECTRA For what? Be quiet, they have heard me.

ORESTES You said I must do it, I will do it.

ELECTRA It is done!
Brother, brother? (ORESTES *takes the sword from her by force.*)
O Mycenæ
With this sword he did justice, he let it fall, he has retaken it,
He is your King.

ORESTES Whom must I pierce, the girl that plotted with
me in the mountain? There was someone to kill . . .
Sweet Electra?

ELECTRA It is done, it is finished!

CASSANDRA The nearest, the most
loved, her, truly. Strike!—Electra,
My father has wanted vengeance longer.

THE PEOPLE BELOW Orestes, Orestes!

ELECTRA (*pointing to* CASSANDRA) Her—
your mother—she killed him.

ORESTES (*turning and striking*) How tall you have grown,
mother.

CASSANDRA (*falling*) I . . . waited long for it . . .

ORESTES

I have killed my mother and my mother—two mothers—see,
there they lie—I have gone home twice. You put it in

And the flesh yields to it . . . (*He goes down the stair.*) Now,
to find her again

All through the forest . . .

ELECTRA Let him pass, Mycenæans. Avoid his
sword. Let him pass, pass. The madness of the house
Perches on him.

A LEADER OF THE MYCENÆANS Daughter of Agamemnon,
You with constancy and force

In the issueless thing have found an issue. Now it is for us the
kingless city

To find a ruler. Rest in the house. As for the young man,

Though he has done justice, and no hand in Mycenæ is raised
against him, for him there is no issue.

We let him go on; and if he does not slay himself with the red
sword he will die in the mountain.

With us be peace. Rest in the house, daughter of Agamemnon.
The old madness, with your brother,

Go out of our gates.

ELECTRA A house to rest in! . . . Gather up the
dead: I will go in; I have learned strength.

III

They carried the dead down the great stair; the slaves with pails
of water and sand scoured the dark stains.

The people meeting in another place to settle the troubled city
the stair was left vacant,

The porch untrampled, and about twilight one of the great
    stones: the world is younger than we are,
Yet now drawing to an end, now that the seasons falter. Then
    another, that had been spared the blood-bath:
What way do they falter?—There fell warm rain, the first an-
    swered, in the midst of summer. A little afterward
Cold rain came down; and sand was rubbed over me as when the
    winds blow. This in the midst of summer.
—I did not feel it, said the second sleepily. And a third: The
    noisy and very mobile creatures
Will be quieted long before the world's end.—What creatures?
    —The active ones, that have two ends let downward,
A mongrel race, mixed of soft stone with fugitive water. The
    night deepened, the dull old stones
Droned at each other, the summer stars wheeled over above them.
    Before dawn the son of Agamemnon
Came to the stair-foot in the darkness.

ORESTES   O stones of the house:
    I entreat hardness: I did not live with you
Long enough in my youth. . . . I will go up to where I killed
    her. . . . We must face things down, mother,
Or they'd devour us. . . . Nobody? . . . Even the stones have
    been scrubbed. A keen housekeeper, sweet Electra.
. . . It would be childish to forget it; the woman has certainly
    been killed, and I think it was I
Her son did it. Something not done before in the world. Here is
    the penalty:
You gather up all your forces to the act, and afterward
Silence, no voice, no ghost, vacancy, but all's not expended.
    Those powers want bitter action. No object.
Deeds are too easy. Our victims are too fragile, they ought to have
    thousands of lives, you strike out once only
The sky breaks like a bubble. . . . No, wife of Ægisthus,—why
    should I mask it?—mother, my mother,
The one soft fiber that went mad yesterday's
Burnt out of me now, there is nothing you could touch if you
    should come; but you have no power, you dead

Are a weak people. This is the very spot: I was here, she here:
and I walk over it not trembling,

Over the scrubbed stones to the door. (*He knocks with the
sword-hilt.*) They sleep well. But my sister having all her
desire

Better than any. (*He knocks again.*)

THE PORTER (*through the door*) Who is there?

ORESTES The owner of the house. Orestes.

THE PORTER Go away, drunkard.

ORESTES Shall I tell my servants to break in the door and whip
the porter?

THE PORTER Oh, Oh! You men from Phocis, stand by me while
I speak to the door. (*Having opened the door, holding a
torch.*) Is it you truly, my lord? We thought, we thought
. . . we pray you to enter the house, my lord Orestes.

ORESTES You are to waken my sister.

I'll speak with her here.

ELECTRA (*at the door*) Oh! You are safe, you are well! Did you
think I could be sleeping? But it is true,

I have slept soundly. Come, come.

ORESTES   A fellow in the forest

Told me you'd had the stone scrubbed . . . I mean, that you'd
entered the house, received as Agamemnon's daughter

In the honor of the city. So I free to go traveling have come with
—what's the word, Electra?—farewell.

Have come to bid you farewell.

ELECTRA   It means—you are going some-
where? Come into the house, Orestes, tell me . . .

ORESTES

The cape's rounded. I have not shipwrecked.

ELECTRA   Around the rock
we have passed safely is the hall of this house,

The throne in the hall, the shining lordship of Mycenæ.

ORESTES   No:

the open world, the sea and its wonders.

You thought the oars raked the headland in the great storm—
what, for Mycenæ?

ELECTRA   Not meanest of the Greek cities:

Whose king captained the world into Asia. Have you suddenly
    become . . . a God, brother, to over-vault
Agamemnon's royalty? O come in, come in. I am cold, cold.
    I pray you.

ORESTES   Fetch a cloak, porter.

If I have outgrown the city a little—I have earned it. Did you
    notice, Electra, she caught at the sword
As the point entered: the palm of her right hand was slashed to
    the bone before the mercy of the point
Slept in her breast: the laid-open palm it was that undermined
    me . . . Oh, the cloak. It's a blond night,
We'll walk on the stones: no chill, the stars are mellow. If I dare
    remember
Yesterday . . . because I have conquered, the soft fiber's burnt
    out.

ELECTRA You have conquered: possess: enter the house,
Take up the royalty.

ORESTES   You were in my vision to-night in the
    forest, Electra, I thought I embraced you
More than brotherwise . . . possessed, you call it . . . entered
    the fountain—

ELECTRA   Oh, hush. *Therefore* you would not kill her!

ORESTES

I killed. It is foolish to darken things with words. I was here, she
    there, screaming. Who if not I?

ELECTRA

The hidden reason: the bitter kernel of your mind that has made
    you mad: I that learned strength
Yesterday, I have no fear.

ORESTES   Fear? The city is friendly and took
    you home with honor, they'll pay
Phocis his wage, you will be quiet.

ELECTRA   Are you resolved to under-
    stand nothing, Orestes?

I am not Agamemnon, only his daughter. You are Agamemnon.
    Beggars and the sons of beggars
May wander at will over the world, but Agamemnon has his
    honor and high Mycenæ
Is not to be cast.

ORESTES   Mycenæ for a ship: who will buy kingdom
And sell me a ship with oars?

ELECTRA   Dear: listen. Come to the parapet
    where it hangs over the night:
The ears at the door hinder me. Now, let the arrow-eyed stars
    hear, the night, not men, as for the Gods
No one can know them, whether they be angry or pleased, tall
    and terrible, standing apart,
When they make signs out of the darkness. . . . I cannot tell you.
    . . . You will stay here, brother?

ORESTES   I'll go
To the edge and over it. Sweet sister, if you've got a message for
    them, the dark ones?

ELECTRA   You do not mean
Death; but a wandering; what does it matter what you mean?
    I know two ways and one will quiet you.
You shall choose either.

ORESTES   But I am quiet. It is more regular than
    a sleeping child's: be untroubled,
Yours burns, it is you trembling.

ELECTRA   Should I not tremble? It is only
    a little to offer,
But all that I have.

ORESTES   Offer?

ELECTRA   It is accomplished: my father is
    avenged: the fates and the body of Electra
Are nothing. But for Agamemnon to rule in Mycenæ: that is not
    nothing. O my brother
You are Agamemnon: rule: take all you will: nothing is denied
    you. The Gods have redressed evil
And clamped the balance.

ORESTES   No doubt they have done what they desired.

ELECTRA   And yours,
    yours? I will not suffer her
Justly punished to dog you over the end of the world. Your de-
    sire? Speak it openly, Orestes.
She is to be conquered: if her ghost were present on the stones
    —let it hear you. I will make war on her
With my life, or with my body.

ORESTES What strange martyrdom, Electra, what madness for sacrifice
Makes your eyes burn like two fires on a watch-tower, though the night darkens?

ELECTRA What you want you shall have:
And rule in Mycenæ. Nothing, nothing is denied you. If I knew which of the two choices
Would quiet you, I would do and not speak, not ask you. Tell me, tell me. Must I bear all the burden,
I weaker, and a woman? You and I were two hawks quartering the field for living flesh Orestes
Under the storm of the memory
Of Agamemnon: we struck: we tore the prey, that dog and that woman. Suddenly since yesterday
You have shot up over me and left me,
You are Agamemnon, you are the storm of the living presence, the very King, and I, lost wings
Under the storm, would die for you. . . . You do not speak yet?
. . . Mine to say it all? . . . You know me a maiden, Orestes,
You have always been with me, no man has even touched my cheek. It is not easy for one unmarried
And chaste, to name both choices. The first is easy. That terrible dream in the forest: if fear of desire
Drives you away: it is easy for me not to be. I never have known
Sweetness in life: all my young days were given—

ORESTES I thought to
be silent was better,
And understand you: afterwards I'll speak.

ELECTRA —to the noise of
blood crying for blood, a crime to be punished,
A house to be emptied: these things are done: and now I am lonely, and what becomes of me is not important.
There's water, and there are points and edges, pain's only a moment: I'd do it and not speak, but nobody knows
Whether it would give you peace or madden you again, I'd not be leagued with that bad woman against you,
And these great walls sit by the crater, terrible desires blow through them. O brother I'll never blame you,

I share the motherhood and the fatherhood, I can conceive the
madness, if you desire too near

The fountain: tell me: I also love *you*: not that way, but enough
to suffer. What needs to be done

To make peace for you, tell me. I shall so gladly die to make it
for you: or so gladly yield you

What you know is maiden. You are the King; have all your will:
only remain in steep Mycenæ,

In the honor of our father. Not yet: do not speak yet. You have
said it is not

Remorse drives you away: monsters require monsters, to have
let her live a moment longer

Would have been the crime: therefore it cannot be but desire
drives you: or the fear of desire: dearest,

It is known horror unlocks the heart, a shower of things hidden:
if that which happened yesterday unmasked

A beautiful brother's love and showed more awful eyes in it: all
that our Gods require is courage.

Let me see the face, let the eyes pierce me. What, dearest? Here
in the stiff cloth of the sacred darkness

Fold over fold hidden, above the sleeping city,

By the great stones of the door, under the little golden falcons
that swarm before dawn up yonder,

In the silence . . . must I dare to woo you,

I whom man never wooed? to let my hand glide under the cloak.
. . . O you will stay! these arms

Making so soft and white a bond around you . . . I also begin
to love—that way, Orestes,

Feeling the hot hard flesh move under the loose cloth, shudder
against me. . . . Ah, your mouth, Ah,

The burning—kiss me—

ORESTES   We shall never ascend this mountain.
So it might come true: we have to be tough against them,

Our dreams and visions, or they true themselves into flesh. It is
sweet: I faint for it: the old stones here

Have seen more and not moved. A custom of the house. To
accept you, little Electra, and go my journey

To-morrow: you'd call cheating. Therefore: we shall not go up
  this mountain dearest, dearest,
To-night nor ever. It's Clytemnestra in you. But the dead are a
  weak tribe. If I had Agamemnon's
We'd live happily sister and lord it in Mycenæ—be a king like
  the others—royalty and incest
Run both in the stream of the blood. Who scrubbed the stones
  there?
ELECTRA   Slaves. O fire burn me! Enter and lay waste,
Deflower, trample, break down, pillage the little city,
Make what breach you will, with flesh or a spear, give it to the
  spoiler. See, as I tear the garment.
What if I called it cheating? Be cruel and treacherous: I'll run
  my chances
On the bitter mercies of to-morrow.
ORESTES   Bitter they would be. No.
ELECTRA   It's clear
  that for this reason
You'd sneak out of Mycenæ and be lost outward. Taste first, bite
  the apple, once dared and tried
Desire will be not terrible. It's doglike to run off whining. Re-
  member it was I that urged
Yesterday's triumph. You: life was enough: let them live. I drove
  on, burning; your mind, reluctant metal,
I dipped it in fire and forged it sharp, day after day I beat and
  burned against you, and forged
A sword: I the arm. Are you sorry it's done? Now again with
  hammer and burning heat I beat against you,
You will not be sorry. We two of all the world, we alone,
Are fit for each other, we have so wrought . . . O eyes scorning
  the world, storm-feathered hawk my hands
Caught out of the air and made you a king over this rock, O axe
  with the gold helve, O star
Alone over the storm, beacon to men over blown seas, you will
  not flee fate, you will take
What the Gods give. What is a man not ruling? An ant in the hill:
  ruler or slave the choice is,

—Or a runaway slave, your pilgrim portion, buffeted over the
    borders of the lands, publicly

Whipped in the cities. But you, you will bind the north-star on
    your forehead, you will stand up in Mycenæ

Stone, and a king.

ORESTES   I am stone enough not to be changed by
    words, nor by the sweet and burning flame of you,

Beautiful Electra.

ELECTRA   Well then: we've wasted our night. See, there's
    the morning star

I might have draggled into a metaphor of you. A fool: a boy:
    no king.

ORESTES   It would have been better

To have parted kindlier, for it is likely

We shall have no future meeting.

ELECTRA   You will let this crime (the
    God commanded) that dirtied the old stones here

Make division forever?

ORESTES   Not the crime, the wakening. That deed is
    past, it is finished, things past

Make no division afterward, they have no power, they have be-
    come nothing at all: this much

I have learned at a crime's knees.

ELECTRA   Yet we are divided.

ORESTES   Because I
    have suddenly awakened, I will not waste inward

Upon humanity, having found a fairer object.

ELECTRA   Some nymph of
    the field? I knew this coldness

Had a sick root: a girl in the north told me about the hill-shep-
    herds who living in solitude

Turn beast with the ewes, their oreads baa to them through the
    matted fleece and they run mad, what madness

Met you in the night and sticks to you?

ORESTES   I left the madness of the
    house, to-night in the dark, with you it walks yet.

How shall I tell you what I have learned? Your mind is like a
    hawk's or like a lion's, this knowledge

Is out of the order of your mind, a stranger language. To wild
beasts and the blood of kings
A verse blind in the book.

ELECTRA   At least my eyes can see dawn gray-
ing: tell and not mock me, our moment
Dies in a moment.

ORESTES   Here is the last labor
To spend on humanity. I saw a vision of us move in the dark:
all that we did or dreamed of
Regarded each other, the man pursued the woman, the woman
clung to the man, warriors and kings
Strained at each other in the darkness, all loved or fought inward,
each one of the lost people
Sought the eyes of another that another should praise him; sought
never his own but another's; the net of desire
Had every nerve drawn to the center, so that they writhed like a
full draught of fishes, all matted
In the one mesh; when they look backward they see only a man
standing at the beginning,
Or forward, a man at the end; or if upward, men in the shining
bitter sky striding and feasting,
Whom you call Gods . . .
It is all turned inward, all your desires incestuous, the woman the
serpent, the man the rose-red cavern,
Both human, worship forever . . .

ELECTRA   You have dreamed wretchedly.

ORESTES   I have
seen the dreams of the people and not dreamed them.
As for me, I have slain my mother.

ELECTRA   No more?

ORESTES   And the gate's open,
the gray boils over the mountain, I have greater
Kindred than dwell under a roof. Didn't I say this would be dark
to you? I have cut the meshes
And fly like a freed falcon. To-night, lying on the hillside, sick
with those visions, I remembered
The knife in the stalk of my humanity; I drew and it broke;
I entered the life of the brown forest

And the great life of the ancient peaks, the patience of stone,
    I felt the changes in the veins
In the throat of the mountain, a grain in many centuries, we have
    our own time, not yours; and I was the stream
Draining the mountain wood; and I the stag drinking; and I was
    the stars,
Boiling with light, wandering alone, each one the lord of his own
    summit; and I was the darkness
Outside the stars, I included them, they were a part of me. I was
    mankind also, a moving lichen
On the cheek of the round stone . . . they have not made words
    for it, to go behind things, beyond hours and ages,
And be all things in all time, in their returns and passages, in the
    motionless and timeless center,
In the white of the fire . . . how can I express the excellence
    I have found, that has no color but clearness;
No honey but ecstasy; nothing wrought nor remembered; no
    undertone nor silver second murmur
That rings in love's voice, I and my loved are one; no desire but
    fulfilled; no passion but peace,
The pure flame and the white, fiercer than any passion; no time
    but spheral eternity: Electra,
Was that your name before this life dawned—

ELECTRA   Here is mere death.
    Death like a triumph I'd have paid to keep you
A king in high Mycenæ: but here is shameful death, to die because
    I have lost you. They'll say
*Having done justice Agamemnon's son ran mad and was lost in
    the mountain; but Agamemnon's daughter*
*Hanged herself from a beam of the house: O bountiful hands of
    justice!* This horror draws upon me
Like stone walking.

ORESTES   What fills men's mouths is nothing; and your
    threat is nothing; I have fallen in love outward.
If I believed you—it is I that am like stone walking.

ELECTRA   I can endure
    even to hate you,

But that's no matter. Strength's good. You are lost. I here remem-
    ber the honor of the house, and Agamemnon's.

She turned and entered the ancient house. Orestes walked in the
    clear dawn; men say that a serpent
Killed him in high Arcadia. But young or old, few years or many,
    signified less than nothing
To him who had climbed the tower beyond time, consciously,
    and cast humanity, entered the earlier fountain.

The dog barked; then the woman stood in the doorway, and hear-
ing iron strike stone down the steep road
Covered her head with a black shawl and entered the light rain;
she stood at the turn of the road.
A nobly formed woman; erect and strong as a new tower; the
features stolid and dark
But sculptured into a strong grace; straight nose with a high bridge,
firm and wide eyes, full chin,
Red lips; she was only a fourth part Indian; a Scottish sailor had
planted her in young native earth,
Spanish and Indian, twenty-one years before. He had named her
California when she was born;
That was her name; and had gone north.

> She heard the hooves and
wheels come nearer, up the steep road.
The buckskin mare, leaning against the breastpiece, plodded into
sight round the wet bank.
The pale face of the driver followed; the burnt-out eyes; they had
fortune in them. He sat twisted
On the seat of the old buggy, leading a second horse by a long
halter, a roan, a big one,
That stepped daintily; by the swell of the neck, a stallion. "What
have you got, Johnny?" "Maskerel's stallion.
Mine now. I won him last night, I had very good luck." He was
quite drunk. "They bring their mares up here now.
I keep this fellow. I got money besides, but I'll not show you."
"Did you buy something, Johnny,
For our Christine? Christmas comes in two days, Johnny." "By
God, forgot," he answered laughing.
"Don't tell Christine it's Christmas; after while I get her something,
maybe." But California:
"I shared your luck when you lost: you lost *me* once, Johnny, re-
member? Tom Dell had me two nights

Here in the house: other times we've gone hungry: now that
you've won, Christine will have her Christmas.
We share your luck, Johnny. You give me money, I go down to
Monterey to-morrow,
Buy presents for Christine, come back in the evening. Next day
Christmas." "You have wet ride," he answered
Giggling. "Here money. Five dollar; ten; twelve dollar. You
buy two bottles of rye whiskey for Johnny."
"All right. I go to-morrow."
                                        He was an outcast Hollander; not
old, but shriveled with bad living.
The child Christine inherited from his race blue eyes, from his
life a wizened forehead; she watched
From the house-door her father lurch out of the buggy and lead
with due respect the stallion
To the new corral, the strong one; leaving the wearily breathing
buckskin mare to his wife to unharness.

Storm in the night; the rain on the thin shakes of the roof like
the ocean on rock streamed battering; once thunder
Walked down the narrow canyon into Carmel valley and wore
away westward; Christine was wakeful
With fears and wonders; her father lay too deep for storm to
touch him.
                    Dawn comes late in the year's dark,
Later into the crack of a canyon under redwoods; and California
slipped from bed
An hour before it; the buckskin would be tired; there was a little
barley, and why should Johnny
Feed all the barley to his stallion? That is what he would do. She
tip-toed out of the room.
Leaving her clothes, he'd waken if she waited to put them on,
and passed from the door of the house
Into the dark of the rain; the big black drops were cold through
the thin shift, but the wet earth
Pleasant under her naked feet. There was a pleasant smell in the
stable; and moving softly,

Touching things gently with the supple bend of the unclothed
    body, was pleasant. She found a box,
Filled it with sweet dry barley and took it down to the old
    corral. The little mare sighed deeply
At the rail in the wet darkness; and California returning between
    two redwoods up to the house
Heard the happy jaws grinding the grain. Johnny could mind
    the pigs and chickens. Christine called to her
When she entered the house, but slept again under her hand. She
    laid the wet night-dress on a chair-back
And stole into the bedroom to get her clothes. A plank creaked,
    and he wakened. She stood motionless
Hearing him stir in the bed. When he was quiet she stooped after
    her shoes, and he said softly,
"What are you doing? Come back to bed." "It's late, I'm going
    to Monterey, I must hitch up."
"You come to bed first. I been away three days. I give you money,
    I take back the money
And what you do in town then?" she sighed sharply and came to
    the bed.
            He reaching his hands from it
Felt the cool curve and firmness of her flank, and half rising
    caught her by the long wet hair.
She endured, and to hasten the act she feigned desire; she had not
    for long, except in dream, felt it.
Yesterday's drunkenness made him sluggish and exacting; she
    saw, turning her head sadly,
The windows were bright gray with dawn; he embraced her still,
    stopping to talk about the stallion.
At length she was permitted to put on her clothes. Clear daylight
    over the steep hills;
Gray-shining cloud over the tops of the redwoods; the winter
    stream sang loud; the wheels of the buggy
Slipped in deep slime, ground on washed stones at the road-edge.
    Down the hill the wrinkled river smothered the ford.
You must keep to the bed of stones: she knew the way by willow
    and alder: the buckskin halted mid-stream,

Shuddering, the water her own color washing up to the traces;
    but California, drawing up
Her feet out of the whirl onto the seat of the buggy swung the
    whip over the yellow water
And drove to the road.
                All morning the clouds were racing north-
ward like a river. At noon they thickened.
When California faced the southwind home from Monterey it
    was heavy with level rainfall.
She looked seaward from the foot of the valley; red rays cried
    sunset from a trumpet of streaming
Cloud over Lobos, the southwest occident of the solstice. Twi-
    light came soon, but the tired mare
Feared the road more than the whip. Mile after mile of slow
    gray twilight.
              Then, quite suddenly, darkness.
"Christine will be asleep. It is Christmas Eve. The ford. That hour
    of daylight wasted this morning!"
She could see nothing; she let the reins lie on the dashboard and
    knew at length by the cramp of the wheels
And the pitch down, they had reached it. Noise of wheels on
    stones, plashing of hooves in water; a world
Of sounds; no sight; the gentle thunder of water; the mare snort-
    ing, dipping her head, one knew,
To look for footing, in the blackness, under the stream. The
    hushing and creaking of the sea-wind
In the passion of invisible willows.
              The mare stood still; the woman
shouted to her; spared whip,
For a false leap would lose the track of the ford. She stood.
    "The baby's things," thought California,
"Under the seat: the water will come over the floor"; and rising
    in the midst of the water
She tilted the seat; fetched up the doll, the painted wooden chick-
    ens, the woolly bear, the book
Of many pictures, the box of sweets: she brought them all from
    under the seat and stored them, trembling,

Under her clothes, about the breasts, under the arms; the corners
  of the cardboard boxes
Cut into the soft flesh; but with a piece of rope for a girdle and
  wound about the shoulders
All was made fast. The mare stood still as if asleep in the midst
  of the water. Then California
Reached out a hand over the stream and fingered her rump; the
  solid wet convexity of it
Shook like the beat of a great heart. "What are you waiting
  for?" But the feel of the animal surface
Had wakened a dream, obscured real danger with a dream of
  danger. "What for? For the water-stallion
To break out of the stream, that is what the rump strains for,
  him to come up flinging foam sidewise,
Fore-hooves in air, crush me and the rig and curl over his
  woman." She flung out with the whip then,
The mare plunged forward. The buggy drifted sidelong: was
  she off ground? Swimming? No: by the splashes.
The driver, a mere prehensile instinct, clung to the side-irons
  of the seat and felt the force
But not the coldness of the water, curling over her knees, break-
  ing up to the waist
Over her body. They'd turned. The mare had turned up stream
  and was wallowing back into shoal water.
Then California dropped her forehead to her knees, having seen
  nothing, feeling a danger,
And felt the brute weight of a branch of alder, the pendulous
  light leaves brush her bent neck
Like a child's fingers. The mare burst out of water and stopped
  on the slope to the ford. The woman climbed down
Between the wheels and went to her head. "Poor Dora," she
  called her by her name, "there, Dora. Quietly,"
And led her around, there was room to turn on the margin, the
  head to the gentle thunder of the water.
She crawled on hands and knees, felt for the ruts, and shifted
  the wheels into them. "You can see, Dora.
I can't. But this time you'll go through it." She climbed into the
  seat and shouted angrily. The mare

Stopped, her two forefeet in the water. She touched with the
  whip. The mare plodded ahead and halted.
Then California thought of prayer: "Dear little Jesus,
Dear baby Jesus born to-night, your head was shining
Like silver candles. I've got a baby too, only a girl. You had light
  wherever you walked.
Dear baby Jesus give me light." Light streamed: rose, gold, rich
  purple, hiding the ford like a curtain.
The gentle thunder of water was a noise of wing-feathers, the
  fans of paradise lifting softly.
The child afloat on radiance had a baby face, but the angels had
  birds' heads, hawks' heads,
Bending over the baby, weaving a web of wings about him. He
  held in the small fat hand
A little snake with golden eyes, and California could see clearly
  on the under radiance
The mare's pricked ears, a sharp black fork against the shining
  light-fall. But it dropped; the light of heaven
Frightened poor Dora. She backed; swung up the water,
And nearly oversetting the buggy turned and scrambled back-
  ward; the iron wheel-tires rang on boulders.

Then California weeping climbed between the wheels. Her wet
  clothes and the toys packed under
Dragged her down with their weight; she stripped off cloak and
  dress and laid the baby's things in the buggy;
Brought Johnny's whiskey out from under the seat; wrapped all
  in the dress, bottles and toys, and tied them
Into a bundle that would sling over her back. She unharnessed
  the mare, hurting her fingers
Against the swollen straps and the wet buckles. She tied the pack
  over her shoulders, the cords
Crossing her breasts, and mounted. She drew up her shift about
  her waist and knotted it, naked thighs
Clutching the sides of the mare, bare flesh to the wet withers, and
  caught the mane with her right hand,
The looped-up bridle-reins in the other. "Dora, the baby gives
  you light." The blinding radiance

Hovered the ford. "Sweet baby Jesus give us light." Cataracts of
    light and Latin singing
Fell through the willows; the mare snorted and reared: the roar
    and thunder of the invisible water;
The night shaking open like a flag, shot with the flashes; the
    baby face hovering; the water
Beating over her shoes and stockings up to the bare thighs; and
    over them, like a beast
Lapping her belly; the wriggle and pitch of the mare swimming;
    the drift, the sucking water; the blinding
Light above and behind with not a gleam before, in the throat
    of darkness; the shock of the fore-hooves
Striking bottom, the struggle and surging lift of the haunches.
    She felt the water streaming off her
From the shoulders down; heard the great strain and sob of the
    mare's breathing, heard the horseshoes grind on gravel.
When California came home the dog at the door snuffed at her
    without barking; Christine and Johnny
Both were asleep; she did not sleep for hours, but kindled fire
    and knelt patiently over it,
Shaping and drying the dear-bought gifts for Christmas morning.

    She hated (she thought) the proud-necked stallion.
He'd lean the big twin masses of his breast on the rail, his red-
    brown eyes flash the white crescents,
She admired him then, she hated him for his uselessness, serving
    nothing
But Johnny's vanity. Horses were too cheap to breed. She thought,
    if he could range in freedom,
Shaking the red-roan mane for a flag on the bare hills.

                                   A man
    brought up a mare in April;
Then California, though she wanted to watch, stayed with Chris-
    tine indoors. When the child fretted
The mother told her once more about the miracle of the ford;
    her prayer to the little Jesus
The Christmas Eve when she was bringing the gifts home; the
    appearance, the lights, the Latin singing,

The thunder of wing-feathers and water, the shining child, the
cataracts of splendor down the darkness.
"A little baby," Christine asked, "the God is a baby?" "The child
of God. That was his birthday.
His mother was named Mary: we pray to her too: God came to
her. He was not the child of a man
Like you or me. God was his father: she was the stallion's wife—
what did I say—God's wife,"
She said with a cry, lifting Christine aside, pacing the planks of
the floor. "She is called more blessed
Than any woman. She was so good, she was more loved." "Did
God live near her house?" "He lives
Up high, over the stars; he ranges on the bare blue hill of the
sky." In her mind a picture
Flashed, of the red-roan mane shaken out for a flag on the bare
hills, and she said quickly, "He's more
Like a great man holding the sun in his hand." Her mind giving
her words the lie, "But no one
Knows, only the shining and the power. The power, the terror,
the burning fire covered her over . . ."
"Was she burnt up, mother?" "She was so good and lovely, she
was the mother of the little Jesus.
If you are good nothing will hurt you." "What did she think?"
"She loved, she was not afraid of the hooves—
Hands that had made the hills and sun and moon, and the sea
and the great redwoods, the terrible strength,
She gave herself without thinking." "You only saw the baby,
mother?" "Yes, and the angels about him,
The great wild shining over the black river." Three times she
had walked to the door, three times returned,
And now the hand that had thrice hung on the knob, full of
prevented action, twisted the cloth
Of the child's dress that she had been mending. "Oh, oh, I've
torn it." She struck at the child and then embraced her
Fiercely, the small blonde sickly body.
                    Johnny came in, his face
reddened as if he had stood

Near fire, his eyes triumphing. "Finished," he said, and looked
  with malice at Christine. "I go
Down valley with Jim Carrier; owes me five dollar, fifteen I
  charge him, he brought ten in his pocket.
Has grapes on the ranch, maybe I take a barrel red wine instead
  of money. Be back to-morrow.
To-morrow night I tell you— Eh, Jim," he laughed over his
  shoulder, "I say to-morrow evening
I show her how the red fellow act, the big fellow. When I come
  home." She answered nothing, but stood
In front of the door, holding the little hand of her daughter, in the
  path of sun between the redwoods,
While Johnny tied the buckskin mare behind Carrier's buggy,
  and bringing saddle and bridle tossed them
Under the seat. Jim Carrier's mare, the bay, stood with drooped
  head and started slowly, the men
Laughing and shouting at her; their voices could be heard down
  the steep road, after the noise
Of the iron-hooped wheels died from the stone. Then one might
  hear the hush of the wind in the tall redwoods,
The tinkle of the April brook, deep in its hollow.

> Humanity is
  the start of the race; I say
Humanity is the mould to break away from, the crust to break
  through, the coal to break into fire,
The atom to be split.

> Tragedy that breaks man's face and a white
  fire flies out of it; vision that fools him
Out of his limits, desire that fools him out of his limits, unnatural
  crime, inhuman science,
Slit eyes in the mask; wild loves that leap over the walls of nature,
  the wild fence-vaulter science,
Useless intelligence of far stars, dim knowledge of the spinning
  demons that make an atom,
These break, these pierce, these deify, praising their God shrilly
  with fierce voices: not in a man's shape
He approves the praise, he that walks lightning-naked on the
  Pacific, that laces the suns with planets,

The heart of the atom with electrons: what is humanity in this
    cosmos? For him, the last
Least taint of a trace in the dregs of the solution; for itself, the
    mould to break away from, the coal
To break into fire, the atom to be split.

                               After the child slept, after
    the leopard-footed evening
Had glided oceanward, California turned the lamp to its least
    flame and glided from the house.
She moved sighing, like a loose fire, backward and forward on
    the smooth ground by the door.
She heard the night-wind that draws down the valley like the
    draught in a flue under clear weather
Whisper and toss in the tall redwoods; she heard the tinkle of
    the April brook deep in its hollow.
Cooled by the night the odors that the horses had left behind
    were in her nostrils; the night
Whitened up the bare hill; a drift of coyotes by the river cried
    bitterly against moonrise;
Then California ran to the old corral, the empty one where they
    kept the buckskin mare,
And leaned, and bruised her breasts on the rail, feeling the sky
    whiten. When the moon stood over the hill
She stole to the house. The child breathed quietly. Herself: to
    sleep? She had seen Christ in the night at Christmas.
The hills were shining open to the enormous night of the April
    moon: empty and empty,
The vast round backs of the bare hills? If one should ride up
    high might not the Father himself
Be seen brooding His night, cross-legged, chin in hand, squatting
    on the last dome? More likely
Leaping the hills, shaking the red-roan mane for a flag on the
    bare hills. She blew out the lamp.
Every fiber of flesh trembled with faintness when she came to
    the door; strength lacked, to wander
Afoot into the shining of the hill, high enough, high enough . . .
    the hateful face of a man had taken

The strength that might have served her, the corral was empty.
    The dog followed her, she caught him by the collar,
Dragged him in fierce silence back to the door of the house,
    latched him inside.

It was like daylight

Outdoors and she hastened without faltering down the foot-
    path, through the dark fringe of twisted oak-brush,
To the open place in a bay of the hill. The dark strength of the
    stallion had heard her coming; she heard him
Blow the shining air out of his nostrils, she saw him in the white
    lake of moonlight
Move like a lion along the timbers of the fence, shaking the
    nightfall
Of the great mane; his fragrance came to her; she leaned on the
    fence;
He drew away from it, the hooves making soft thunder in the
    trodden soil.
Wild love had trodden it, his wrestling with the stranger, the
    shame of the day
Had stamped it into mire and powder when the heavy fetlocks
Strained the soft flanks. "Oh, if I could bear you!
If I had the strength. O great God that came down to Mary,
    gently you came. But I will ride him
Up into the hill, if he throws me, if he tramples me, is it not
    my desire
To endure death?" She climbed the fence, pressing her body
    against the rail, shaking like fever,
And dropped inside to the soft ground. He neither threatened
    her with his teeth nor fled from her coming,
And lifting her hand gently to the upflung head she caught
    the strap of the headstall,
That hung under the quivering chin. She unlooped the halter
    from the high strength of the neck
And the arch the storm-cloud mane hung with live darkness. He
    stood; she crushed her breasts
On the hard shoulder, an arm over the withers, the other under
    the mass of his throat, and murmuring

Like a mountain dove, "If I could bear you." No way, no help,
a gulf in nature. She murmured, "Come,
We will run on the hill. O beautiful, O beautiful," and led him
To the gate and flung the bars on the ground. He threw his head
downward
To snuff at the bars; and while he stood, she catching mane and
withers with all sudden contracture
And strength of her lithe body, leaped, clung hard, and was
mounted. He had been ridden before; he did not
Fight the weight but ran like a stone falling;
Broke down the slope into the moon-glass of the stream, and
flattened to his neck
She felt the branches of a buckeye tree fly over her, saw the
wall of the oak-scrub
End her world: but he turned there, the matted branches
Scraped her right knee, the great slant shoulders
Laboring the hill-slope, up, up, the clear hill. Desire had died
in her
At the first rush, the falling like death, but now it revived,
She feeling between her thighs the labor of the great engine, the
running muscles, the hard swiftness,
She riding the savage and exultant strength of the world. Having
topped the thicket he turned eastward,
Running less wildly; and now at length he felt the halter when
she drew on it; she guided him upward;
He stopped and grazed on the great arch and pride of the hill,
the silent calvary. A dwarfish oakwood
Climbed the other slope out of the dark of the unknown canyon
beyond; the last wind-beaten bush of it
Crawled up to the height, and California slipping from her mount
tethered him to it. She stood then,
Shaking. Enormous films of moonlight
Trailed down from the height. Space, anxious whiteness, vastness.
Distant beyond conception the shining ocean
Lay light like a haze along the ledge and doubtful world's end.
Little vapors gleaming, and little
Darknesses on the far chart underfoot symbolized wood and
valley; but the air was the element, the moon-

Saturate arcs and spires of the air.

Here is solitude, here on the
calvary, nothing conscious
But the possible God and the cropped grass, no witness, no eye
but that misformed one, the moon's past fullness.
Two figures on the shining hill, woman and stallion, she kneeling
to him, brokenly adoring.
He cropping the grass, shifting his hooves, or lifting the long
head to gaze over the world,
Tranquil and powerful. She prayed aloud, "O God, I am not
good enough, O fear, O strength, I am draggled.
Johnny and other men have had me, and O clean power! Here
am I," she said, falling before him,
And crawled to his hooves. She lay a long while, as if asleep, in
reach of the fore-hooves, weeping. He avoided
Her head and the prone body. He backed at first; but later
plucked the grass that grew by her shoulder.
The small dark head under his nostrils: a small round stone, that
smelt human, black hair growing from it:
The skull shut the light in: it was not possible for any eyes
To know what throbbed and shone under the sutures of the
skull, or a shell full of lightning
Had scared the roan strength, and he'd have broken tether,
screaming, and run for the valley.

The atom bounds-breaking,
Nucleus to sun, electrons to planets, with recognition
Not praying, self-equaling, the whole to the whole, the microcosm
Not entering nor accepting entrance, more equally, more utterly,
more incredibly conjugate
With the other extreme and greatness; passionately perceptive of
identity. . . .
The fire threw up figures
And symbols meanwhile, racial myths formed and dissolved in
it, the phantom rulers of humanity
That without being are yet more real than what they are born of,
and without shape, shape that which makes them:
The nerves and the flesh go by shadowlike, the limbs and the lives
shadowlike, these shadows remain, these shadows

To whom temples, to whom churches, to whom labors and wars,
  visions and dreams are dedicate:
Out of the fire in the small round stone that black moss covered,
  a crucified man writhed up in anguish;
A woman covered by a huge beast in whose mane the stars were
  netted, sun and moon were his eyeballs,
Smiled under the unendurable violation, her throat swollen with
  the storm and blood-flecks gleaming
On the stretched lips; a woman—no, a dark water, split by jets
  of lightning, and after a season
What floated up out of the furrowed water, a boat, a fish, a fire-
  globe?
              It had wings, the creature,
And flew against the fountain of lightning, fell burnt out of the
  cloud back to the bottomless water . . .
Figures and symbols, castlings of the fire, played in her brain;
  but the white fire was the essence,
The burning in the small round shell of bone that black hair
  covered, that lay by the hooves on the hilltop.

She rose at length, she unknotted the halter; she walked and led
  the stallion; two figures, woman and stallion,
Came down the silent emptiness of the dome of the hill, under
  the cataract of the moonlight.

The next night there was moon through cloud. Johnny had re-
  turned half drunk toward evening, and California
Who had known him for years with neither love nor loathing
  to-night hating him had let the child Christine
Play in the light of the lamp for hours after her bedtime; who
  fell asleep at length on the floor
Beside the dog; then Johnny: "Put her to bed." She gathered the
  child against her breasts, she laid her
In the next room, and covered her with a blanket. The window
  was white, the moon had risen. The mother
Lay down by the child, but after a moment Johnny stood in
  the doorway. "Come drink." He had brought home
Two jugs of wine slung from the saddle, part payment for the
  stallion's service; a pitcher of it

Was on the table, and California sadly came and emptied her
   glass. Whiskey, she thought,
Would have erased him till to-morrow; the thin red wine. . . .
   "We have a good evening," he laughed, pouring it.
"One glass yet then I show you what the red fellow did." She
   moving toward the house-door his eyes
Followed her, the glass filled and the red juice ran over the table.
   When it struck the floor-planks
He heard and looked. "Who stuck the pig?" he muttered stupidly,
   "here's blood, here's blood," and trailed his fingers
In the red lake under the lamplight. While he was looking down
   the door creaked, she had slipped outdoors,
And he, his mouth curving like a faun's imagined the chase under
   the solemn redwoods, the panting
And unresistant victim caught in a dark corner. He emptied the
   glass and went outdoors
Into the dappled lanes of moonlight. No sound but the April
   brook's. "Hey Bruno," he called, "find her.
Bruno, go find her." The dog after a little understood and quested,
   the man following.
When California crouching by an oak-bush above the house
   heard them come near she darted
To the open slope and ran down hill. The dog barked at her
   heels, pleased with the game, and Johnny
Followed in silence. She ran down to the new corral, she saw
   the stallion
Move like a lion along the timbers of the fence, the dark arched
   neck shaking the nightfall
Of the great mane; she threw herself prone and writhed under
   the bars, his hooves backing away from her
Made muffled thunder in the soft soil. She stood in the midst of
   the corral, panting, but Johnny
Paused at the fence. The dog ran under it, and seeing the stallion
   move, the woman standing quiet,
Danced after the beast, with white-tooth feints and dashes. When
   Johnny saw the formidable dark strength
Recoil from the dog, he climbed up over the fence.

The child Christine waked when her mother left her
And lay half dreaming, in the half-waking dream she saw the
    ocean come up out of the west
And cover the world, she looked up through clear water at the
    tops of the redwoods. She heard the door creak
And the house empty; her heart shook her body, sitting up on the
    bed, and she heard the dog
And crept toward light, where it gleamed under the crack of the
    door. She opened the door, the room was empty,
The table-top was a red lake under the lamplight. The color of
    it was terrible to her;
She had seen the red juice drip from a coyote's muzzle her father
    had shot one day in the hills
And carried him home over the saddle: she looked at the rifle on
    the wall-rack: it was not moved:
She ran to the door, the dog was barking and the moon was
    shining: she knew wine by the odor
But the color frightened her, the empty house frightened her,
    she followed down hill in the white lane of moonlight
The friendly noise of the dog. She saw in the big horse's corral,
    on the level shoulder of the hill,
Black on white, the dark strength of the beast, the dancing fury
    of the dog, and the two others.
One fled, one followed; the big one charged, rearing; one fell
    under his fore-hooves. She heard her mother
Scream: without thought she ran to the house, she dragged a
    chair past the red pool and climbed to the rifle,
Got it down from the wall and lugged it somehow through the
    door and down the hillside, under the hard weight
Sobbing. Her mother stood by the rails of the corral, she gave
    it to her. On the far side
The dog flashed at the plunging stallion; in the midst of the space
    the man, slow-moving, like a hurt worm
Crawling, dragged his body by inches toward the fence-line. Then
    California, resting the rifle
On the top rail, without doubting, without hesitance,
Aimed for the leaping body of the dog, and when it stood, fired.
    It snapped, rolled over, lay quiet.

"O mother you've hit Bruno!" "I couldn't see the sights in the
    moonlight," she answered quietly. She stood
And watched, resting the rifle-butt on the ground. The stallion
    wheeled, freed from his torment, the man
Lurched up to his knees, wailing a thin and bitter bird's cry, and
    the roan thunder
Struck; hooves left nothing alive but teeth tore up the remnant.
    "O mother, shoot, shoot!" Yet California
Stood carefully watching, till the beast having fed all his fury
    stretched neck to utmost, head high,
And wrinkled back the upper lip from the teeth, yawning obscene
    disgust over—not a man—
A smear on the moon-like earth: then California moved by some
    obscure human fidelity
Lifted the rifle. Each separate nerve-cell of her brain flaming the
    stars fell from their places
Crying in her mind: she fired three times before the haunches
    crumpled sidewise, the forelegs stiffening,
And the beautiful strength settled to earth: she turned then on
    her little daughter the mask of a woman
Who has killed God. The night-wind veering, the smell of the
    spilt wine drifted down hill from the house.

NIGHT

The ebb slips from the rock, the sunken
Tide-rocks lift streaming shoulders
Out of the slack, the slow west
Sombering its torch; a ship's light
Shows faintly, far out,
Over the weight of the prone ocean
On the low cloud.

Over the dark mountain, over the dark pinewood,
Down the long dark valley along the shrunken river,
Returns the splendor without rays, the shining of shadow,
Peace-bringer, the matrix of all shining and quieter of shining.
Where the shore widens on the bay she opens dark wings
And the ocean accepts her glory. O soul worshipful of her
You like the ocean have grave depths where she dwells always,
And the film of waves above that takes the sun takes also
Her, with more love. The sun-lovers have a blond favorite,
A father of lights and noises, wars, weeping and laughter,
Hot labor, lust and delight and the other blemishes. Quietness
Flows from her deeper fountain; and he will die; and she is
    immortal.

Far off from here the slender
Flocks of the mountain forest
Move among stems like towers
Of the old redwoods to the stream,
No twig crackling; dip shy
Wild muzzles into the mountain water
Among the dark ferns.

NIGHT

O passionately at peace you being secure will pardon
The blasphemies of glowworms, the lamp in my tower, the
    fretfulness
Of cities, the cressets of the planets, the pride of the stars.
This August night in a rift of cloud Antares reddens,
The great one, the ancient torch, a lord among lost children,
The earth's orbit doubled would not girdle his greatness, one fire
Globed, out of grasp of the mind enormous; but to you O Night
What? Not a spark? What flicker of a spark in the faint far
    glimmer
Of a lost fire dying in the desert, dim coals of a sand-pit the
    Bedouins
Wandered from at dawn . . . Ah singing prayer to what gulfs
    tempted
Suddenly are you more lost? To us the near-hand mountain
Be a measure of height, the tide-worn cliff at the sea-gate a
    measure of continuance.

The tide, moving the night's
Vastness with lonely voices,
Turns, the deep dark-shining
Pacific leans on the land,
Feeling his cold strength
To the outmost margins: you Night will resume
The stars in your time.

O passionately at peace when will that tide draw shoreward?
Truly the spouting fountains of light, Antares, Arcturus,
Tire of their flow, they sing one song but they think silence.
The striding winter giant Orion shines, and dreams darkness.
And life, the flicker of men and moths and the wolf on the hill,
Though furious for continuance, passionately feeding, passionately
Remaking itself upon its mates, remembers deep inward
The calm mother, the quietness of the womb and the egg,
The primal and the latter silences: dear Night it is memory
Prophesies, prophecy that remembers, the charm of the dark.
And I and my people, we are willing to love the four-score years
Heartily; but as a sailor loves the sea, when the helm is for harbor.

Have men's minds changed,
Or the rock hidden in the deep of the waters of the soul
Broken the surface? A few centuries
Gone by, was none dared not to people
The darkness beyond the stars with harps and habitations.
But now, dear is the truth. Life is grown sweeter and lonelier,
And death is no evil.

BIRDS

The fierce musical cries of a couple of sparrowhawks hunting
  on the headland,
Hovering and darting, their heads northwestward,
Prick like silver arrows shot through a curtain the noise of the
  ocean
Trampling its granite; their red backs gleam
Under my window around the stone corners; nothing gracefuller,
  nothing
Nimbler in the wind. Westward the wave-gleaners,
The old gray sea-going gulls are gathered together, the north-
  west wind wakening
Their wings to the wild spirals of the wind-dance.
Fresh as the air, salt as the foam, play birds in the bright wind,
  fly falcons
Forgetting the oak and the pinewood, come gulls
From the Carmel sands and the sands at the river-mouth, from
  Lobos and out of the limitless
Power of the mass of the sea, for a poem
Needs multitude, multitudes of thoughts, all fierce, all flesh-eaters,
  musically clamorous
Bright hawks that hover and dart headlong, and ungainly
Gray hungers fledged with desire of transgression, salt slimed
  beaks, from the sharp
Rock-shores of the world and the secret waters.

FOG

Invisible gulls with human voices cry in the sea-cloud
"There is room, wild minds,
Up high in the cloud; the web and the feather remember
Three elements, but here
Is but one, and the webs and the feathers
Subduing but the one
Are the greater, with strength and to spare." You dream, wild
    criers,
The peace that all life
Dreams gluttonously, the infinite self that has eaten
Environment, and lives
Alone, unencroached on, perfectly gorged, one God.
Cæsar and Napoleon
Visibly acting their dream of that solitude, Christ and Gautama,
Being God, devouring
The world with atonement for God's sake . . . ah sacred hungers,
The conqueror's, the prophet's,
The lover's, the hunger of the sea-beaks, slaves of the last peace,
Worshippers of oneness.

BOATS IN A FOG

Sports and gallantries, the stage, the arts, the antics of dancers,
The exuberant voices of music,
Have charm for children but lack nobility; it is bitter earnestness
That makes beauty; the mind
Knows, grown adult.

     A sudden fog-drift muffled the ocean,
A throbbing of engines moved in it,
At length, a stone's throw out, between the rocks and the vapor,
One by one moved shadows
Out of the mystery, shadows, fishing-boats, trailing each other
Following the cliff for guidance,
Holding a difficult path between the peril of the sea-fog
And the foam on the shore granite.
One by one, trailing their leader, six crept by me,
Out of the vapor and into it,
The throb of their engines subdued by the fog, patient and
  cautious,
Coasting all round the peninsula
Back to the buoys in Monterey harbor. A flight of pelicans
Is nothing lovelier to look at;
The flight of the planets is nothing nobler; all the arts lose virtue
Against the essential reality
Of creatures going about their business among the equally
Earnest elements of nature.

GRANITE AND CYPRESS

White-maned, wide-throated, the heavy-shouldered children of
   the wind leap at the sea-cliff.
The invisible falcon
Brooded on water and bred them in wide waste places, in a bride-
   chamber wide to the stars' eyes
In the center of the ocean,
Where no prows pass nor island is lifted . . . the sea beyond
   Lobos is whitened with the falcon's
Passage, he is here now,
The sky is one cloud, his wing-feathers hiss in the white grass,
   my sapling cypresses writhing
In the fury of his passage
Dare not dream of their centuries of future endurance of tempest.
   (I have granite and cypress,
Both long-lasting,
Planted in the earth; but the granite sea-boulders are prey to no
   hawk's wing, they have taken worse pounding,
Like me they remember
Old wars and are quiet; for we think that the future is one piece
   with the past, we wonder why tree-tops
And people are so shaken.)

Great-enough both accepts and subdues; the great frame takes
all creatures;
From the greatness of their element they all take beauty.
Gulls; and the dingy freightship lurching south in the eye of a
rain-wind;
The airplane dipping over the hill; hawks hovering
The white grass of the headland; cormorants roosting upon the
guano-
Whitened skerries; pelicans awind; sea-slime
Shining at night in the wave-stir like drowned men's lanterns;
smugglers signaling
A cargo to land; or the old Point Pinos lighthouse
Lawfully winking over dark water; the flight of the twilight
herons,
Lonely wings and a cry; or with motor-vibrations
That hum in the rock like a new storm-tone of the ocean's to
turn eyes westward
The navy's new-bought Zeppelin going by in the twilight,
Far out seaward; relative only to the evening star and the ocean
It slides into a cloud over Point Lobos.

PEOPLE AND A HERON

A desert of weed and water-darkened stone under my western
    windows
The ebb lasted all afternoon,
And many pieces of humanity, men, women, and children, gath-
    ering shellfish,
Swarmed with voices of gulls the sea-breach.
At twilight they went off together, the verge was left vacant, an
    evening heron
Bent broad wings over the black ebb,
And left me wondering why a lone bird was dearer to me than
    many people.
Well: rare is dear: but also I suppose
Well reconciled with the world but not with our own natures
    we grudge to see them
Reflected on the world for a mirror.

AUTUMN EVENING

Though the little clouds ran southward still, the quiet autumnal
Cool of the late September evening
Seemed promising rain, rain, the change of the year, the angel
Of the sad forest. A heron flew over
With that remote ridiculous cry, "Quawk," the cry
That seems to make silence more silent. A dozen
Flops of the wing, a drooping glide, at the end of the glide
The cry, and a dozen flops of the wing.
I watched him pass on the autumn-colored sky; beyond him
Jupiter shone for evening star.
The sea's voice worked into my mood, I thought "No matter
What happens to men . . . the world's well made though."

SHINE, PERISHING REPUBLIC

While this America settles in the mould of its vulgarity, heav-
    ily thickening to empire,
And protest, only a bubble in the molten mass, pops and sighs out,
    and the mass hardens,

I sadly smiling remember that the flower fades to make fruit, the
    fruit rots to make earth.
Out of the mother; and through the spring exultances, ripeness
    and decadence; and home to the mother.

You making haste haste on decay: not blameworthy; life is good,
    be it stubbornly long or suddenly
A mortal splendor: meteors are not needed less than mountains:
    shine, perishing republic.

But for my children, I would have them keep their distance from
    the thickening center; corruption
Never has been compulsory, when the cities lie at the monster's
    feet there are left the mountains.

And boys, be in nothing so moderate as in love of man, a clever
    servant, insufferable master.
There is the trap that catches noblest spirits, that caught—they
    say—God, when he walked on earth.

THE TREASURE

Mountains, a moment's earth-waves rising and hollowing; the
earth too's an ephemerid; the stars—
Short-lived as grass the stars quicken in the nebula and dry in their
summer, they spiral
Blind up space, scattered black seeds of a future; nothing lives
long, the whole sky's
Recurrences tick the seconds of the hours of the ages of the gulf
before birth, and the gulf
After death is like dated: to labor eighty years in a notch of
eternity is nothing too tiresome,
Enormous repose after, enormous repose before, the flash of
activity.
Surely you never have dreamed the incredible depths were pro-
logue and epilogue merely
To the surface play in the sun, the instant of life, what is called
life? I fancy
That silence is the thing, this noise a found word for it; inter-
jection, a jump of the breath at that silence;
Stars burn, grass grows, men breathe: as a man finding treasure
says "Ah!" but the treasure's the essence;
Before the man spoke it was there, and after he has spoken he
gathers it, inexhaustible treasure.

JOY

Though joy is better than sorrow joy is not great;
Peace is great, strength is great.
Not for joy the stars burn, not for joy the vulture
Spreads her gray sails on the air
Over the mountain; not for joy the worn mountain
Stands, while years like water
Trench his long sides. "I am neither mountain nor bird
Nor star; and I seek joy."
The weakness of your breed: yet at length quietness
Will cover those wistful eyes.

WOODROW WILSON

(february, 1924)

It said "Come home, here is an end, a goal,
Not the one raced for, is it not better indeed? Victory you know
    requires
Force to sustain victory, the burden is never lightened, but final
    defeat
Buys peace: you have praised peace, peace without victory."

He said "It seems I am traveling no new way,
But leaving my great work unfinished how can I rest? I enjoyed
    a vision,
Endured betrayal, you must not ask me to endure final defeat,
Visionless men, blind hearts, blind mouths, live still."

It said "Yet perhaps your vision was less great
Than some you scorned, it has not proved even so practicable;
    Lenin
Enters this pass with less reluctance. As to betrayals: there are so
    many
Betrayals, the Russians and the Germans know."

He said "I knew I have enemies, I had not thought
To meet one at this brink: shall not the mocking voices die in
    the grave?"
It said "They shall. Soon there is silence." "I dreamed this end,"
    he said, "when the prow
Of the long ship leaned against dawn, my people

Applauded me, and the world watched me. Again
I dreamed it at Versailles, the time I sent for the ship, and the
    obstinate foreheads
That shared with me the settlement of the world flinched at my
    threat and yielded.
That is all gone. . . . Do I remember this darkness?"

It said "No man forgets it but a moment.
The darkness before the mother, the depth of the return." "I
    thought," he answered,
"That I was drawn out of this depth to establish the earth on
    peace. My labor
Dies with me, why was I drawn out of this depth?"

It said "Loyal to your highest, sensitive, brave,
Sanguine, some few ways wise, you and all men are drawn out of
    this depth
Only to be these things you are, as flowers for color, falcons for
    swiftness,
Mountains for mass and quiet. Each for its quality

Is drawn out of this depth. Your tragic quality
Required the huge delusion of some major purpose to produce it.
What, that the God of the stars needed your help?" He said
    "This is my last
Worst pain, the bitter enlightenment that buys peace."

SCIENCE

Man, introverted man, having crossed
In passage and but a little with the nature of things this latter
century
Has begot giants; but being taken up
Like a maniac with self-love and inward conflicts cannot manage
his hybrids.
Being used to deal with edgeless dreams,
Now he's bred knives on nature turns them also inward: they
have thirsty points though.
His mind forebodes his own destruction;
Actæon who saw the goddess naked among leaves and his hounds
tore him.
A little knowledge, a pebble from the shingle,
A drop from the oceans: who would have dreamed this infinitely
little too much?

APOLOGY FOR BAD DREAMS

I

In the purple light, heavy with redwood, the slopes drop seaward,
Headlong convexities of forest, drawn in together to the steep
ravine. Below, on the sea-cliff,
A lonely clearing; a little field of corn by the streamside; a roof
under spared trees. Then the ocean
Like a great stone someone has cut to a sharp edge and polished
to shining. Beyond it, the fountain
And furnace of incredible light flowing up from the sunk sun.
In the little clearing a woman
Is punishing a horse; she had tied the halter to a sapling at the
edge of the wood, but when the great whip
Clung to the flanks the creature kicked so hard she feared he
would snap the halter; she called from the house
The young man her son; who fetched a chain tie-rope, they
working together
Noosed the small rusty links round the horse's tongue
And tied him by the swollen tongue to the tree.
Seen from this height they are shrunk to insect size.
Out of all human relation. You cannot distinguish
The blood dripping from where the chain is fastened,
The beast shuddering; but the thrust neck and the legs
Far apart. You can see the whip fall on the flanks . . .
The gesture of the arm. You cannot see the face of the woman.
The enormous light beats up out of the west across the cloud-
bars of the trade-wind. The ocean
Darkens, the high clouds brighten, the hills darken together.
Unbridled and unbelievable beauty
Covers the evening world . . . not covers, grows apparent out
of it, as Venus down there grows out
From the lit sky. What said the prophet? "I create good: and
I create evil: I am the Lord."

II

This coast crying out for tragedy like all beautiful places,
(The quiet ones ask for quieter suffering: but here the granite cliff
    the gaunt cypresses crown
Demands what victim? The dykes of red lava and black what
    Titan? The hills like pointed flames
Beyond Soberanes, the terrible peaks of the bare hills under the
    sun, what immolation?)
This coast crying out for tragedy like all beautiful places: and
    like the passionate spirit of humanity
Pain for its bread: God's, many victims', the painful deaths, the
    horrible transfigurations: I said in my heart,
"Better invent than suffer: imagine victims
Lest your own flesh be chosen the agonist, or you
Martyr some creature to the beauty of the place." And I said,
"Burn sacrifices once a year to magic
Horror away from the house, this little house here
You have built over the ocean with your own hands
Beside the standing boulders: for what are we,
The beast that walks upright, with speaking lips
And little hair, to think we should always be fed,
Sheltered, intact, and self-controlled? We sooner more liable
Than the other animals. Pain and terror, the insanities of desire;
    not accidents but essential,
And crowd up from the core:" I imagined victims for those
    wolves, I made them phantoms to follow,
They have hunted the phantoms and missed the house. It is not
    good to forget over what gulfs the spirit
Of the beauty of humanity, the petal of a lost flower blown
    seaward by the night-wind, floats to its quietness.

III

Boulders blunted like an old bear's teeth break up from the
    headland; below them
All the soil is thick with shells, the tide-rock feasts of a dead
    people.

Here the granite flanks are scarred with ancient fire, the ghosts
of the tribe
Crouch in the nights beside the ghost of a fire, they try to re-
member the sunlight,
Light has died out of their skies. These have paid something for
the future
Luck of the country, while we living keep old griefs in memory:
though God's
Envy is not a likely fountain of ruin, to forget evils calls down
Sudden reminders from the cloud: remembered deaths be our
redeemers;
Imagined victims our salvation: white as the half moon at mid-
night
Someone flamelike passed me, saying, "I am Tamar Cauldwell,
I have my desire,"
Then the voice of the sea returned, when she had gone by, the
stars to their towers.
. . . Beautiful country burn again, Point Pinos down to the
Sur Rivers
Burn as before with bitter wonders, land and ocean and the
Carmel water.

IV

He brays humanity in a mortar to bring the savor
From the bruised root: a man having bad dreams, who invents
victims, is only the ape of that God.
He washes it out with tears and many waters, calcines it with
fire in the red crucible,
Deforms it, makes it horrible to itself: the spirit flies out and
stands naked, he sees the spirit,
He takes it in the naked ecstasy; it breaks in his hand, the atom
is broken, the power that massed it
Cries to the power that moves the stars, "I have come home to
myself, behold me.
I bruised myself in the flint mortar and burnt me
In the red shell, I tortured myself, I flew forth,
Stood naked of myself and broke me in fragments,
And here am I moving the stars that are me."

APOLOGY FOR BAD DREAMS

I have seen these ways of God: I know of no reason
For fire and change and torture and the old returnings.
He being sufficient might be still. I think they admit no reason;
  they are the ways of my love.
Unmeasured power, incredible passion, enormous craft: no
  thought apparent but burns darkly
Smothered with its own smoke in the human brain-vault: no
  thought outside: a certain measure in phenomena:
The fountains of the boiling stars, the flowers on the foreland,
  the ever-returning roses of dawn.

ANTE MORTEM

It is likely enough that lions and scorpions
Guard the end; life never was bonded to be endurable nor the
    act of dying
Unpainful; the brain burning too often
Earns, though it held itself detached from the object, often a
    burnt age.
No matter, I shall not shorten it by hand.
Incapable of body or unmoved of brain is no evil, one always
    went envying
The quietness of stones. But if the striped blossom
Insanity spread lewd splendors and lightning terrors at the end
    of the forest;
Or intolerable pain work its known miracle,
Exile the monarch soul, set a sick monkey in the office . . .
    remember me
Entire and balanced when I was younger,
And could lift stones, and comprehend in the praises the cruelties
    of life.

POST MORTEM

Happy people die whole, they are all dissolved in a moment,
   they have had what they wanted,
No hard gifts; the unhappy
Linger a space, but pain is a thing that is glad to be forgotten;
   but one who has given
His heart to a cause or a country,
His ghost may spaniel it a while, disconsolate to watch it. I was
   wondering how long the spirit
That sheds this verse will remain
When the nostrils are nipped, when the brain rots in its vault
   or bubbles in the violence of fire
To be ash in metal. I was thinking
Some stalks of the wood whose roots I married to the earth of
   this place will stand five centuries;
I held the roots in my hand,
The stems of the trees between two fingers: how many remote
   generations of women
Will drink joy from men's loins,
And dragged from between the thighs of what mothers will
   giggle at my ghost when it curses the axemen,
Gray impotent voice on the sea-wind,
When the last trunk falls? The women's abundance will have
   built roofs over all this foreland;
Will have buried the rock foundations
I laid here: the women's exuberance will canker and fail in its
   time and like clouds the houses
Unframe, the granite of the prime
Stand from the heaps: come storm and wash clean: the plaster
   is all run to the sea and the steel
All rusted; the foreland resumes
The form we loved when we saw it. Though one at the end of
   the age and far off from this place

POST MORTEM

Should meet my presence in a poem,
The ghost would not care but be here, long sunset shadow in the
    seams of the granite, and forgotten
The flesh, a spirit for the stone.

SUMMER HOLIDAY

When the sun shouts and people abound
One thinks there were the ages of stone and the age of bronze
And the iron age; iron the unstable metal;
Steel made of iron, unstable as his mother; the towered-up cities
Will be stains of rust on mounds of plaster.
Roots will not pierce the heaps for a time, kind rains will cure
  them,
Then nothing will remain of the iron age
And all these people but a thigh-bone or so, a poem
Stuck in the world's thought, splinters of glass
In the rubbish dumps, a concrete dam far off in the mountain . . .

from THE WOMEN AT POINT SUR

Here were new idols again to praise him;
I made them alive; but when they looked up at the face before
 they had seen it they were drunken and fell down.
I have seen and not fallen, I am stronger than the idols,
But my tongue is stone how could I speak him? My blood in my
 veins is seawater how could it catch fire?
The rock shining dark rays and the rounded
Crystal the ocean his beam of blackness and silence
Edged with azure, bordered with voices;
The moon her brittle tranquillity; the great phantoms, the foun-
 tains of light, the seed of the sky,
Their plaintive splendors whistling to each other:
There is nothing but shines though it shine darkness; nothing but
 answers; they are caught in the net of their voices
Though the voices be silence; they are woven in the nerve-warp.
One people, the stars and the people, one structure; the voids
 between stars, the voids between atoms, and the vacancy
In the atom in the rings of the spinning demons,
Are full of that weaving; one emptiness, one presence: who had
 watched all his splendor
Had known but a little: all his night, but a little.
I made glass puppets to speak of him, they splintered in my hand
 and have cut me, they are heavy with my blood.
But the jewel-eyed herons have never beheld him
Nor heard; nor the tall owl with cat's ears, the bittern in the
 willows, the squid in the rock in the silence of the ocean,
The vulture that broods in the pitch of the blue
And sees the earth globed, her edges dripping into rainbow twi-
 lights: eyed hungers, blind fragments: I sometime
Shall fashion images great enough to face him
A moment and speak while they die. These here have gone mad:
 but stammer the tragedy you crackled vessels.

THE OLD MAN'S DREAM AFTER HE DIED

from CAWDOR

Gently with delicate mindless fingers
Decomposition began to pick and caress the unstable chemistry
Of the cells of the brain; Oh very gently, as the first weak breath
    of wind in a wood: the storm is still far,
The leaves are stirred faintly to a gentle whispering: the nerve-
    cells, by what would soon destroy them, were stirred
To a gentle whispering. Or one might say the brain began to
    glow, with its own light, in the starless
Darkness under the dead bone sky; like bits of rotting wood on
    the floor of the night forest
Warm rains have soaked, you see them beside the path shine like
    vague eyes. So gently the dead man's brain
Glowing by itself made and enjoyed its dream.

                                The nights of many
    years before this time
He had been dreaming the sweetness of death, as a starved man
    dreams bread, but now decomposition
Reversed the chemistry; who had adored in sleep under so many
    disguises the dark redeemer
In death across a thousand metaphors of form and action cele-
    brated life. Whatever he had wanted
To do or become was now accomplished, each bud that had been
    nipped and fallen grew out to a branch,
Sparks of desire forty years quenched flamed up fulfilment.
Out of time, undistracted by the nudging pulse-beat, perfectly
    real to itself being insulated
From all touch of reality the dream triumphed, building from
    past experience present paradise
More intense as the decay quickened, but ever more primitive
    as it proceeded, until the ecstasy

Soared through a flighty carnival of wines and women to the
  simple delight of eating flesh, and tended
Even higher, to an unconditional delight. But then the intercon-
  nections between the groups of the brain
Failing, the dreamer and the dream split into multitude. Soon the
  altered cells became unfit to express
Any human or at all describable form of consciousness.

                                              Pain and
  pleasure are not to be thought
Important enough to require balancing: these flashes of post-
  mortal felicity by mindless decay
Played on the breaking harp by no means countervalued the ex-
  cess of previous pain. Such discords
In the passionate terms of human experience are not resolved,
  nor worth it.

THE CAGED EAGLE'S DEATH DREAM

from CAWDOR

While George went to the house
For his revolver, Michal climbed up the hill
Weeping; but when he came with death in his hand
She'd not go away, but watched. At the one shot
The great dark bird leaped at the roof of the cage
In silence and struck the wood; it fell, then suddenly
Looked small and soft, muffled in its folded wings.

The nerves of men after they die dream dimly
And dwindle into their peace; they are not very passionate,
And what they had was mostly spent while they lived.
They are sieves for leaking desire; they have many pleasures
And conversations; their dreams too are like that.
The unsocial birds are a greater race;
Cold-eyed, and their blood burns. What leaped up to death,
The extension of one storm-dark wing filling its world,
Was more than the soft garment that fell. Something had flown
    away. Oh cage-hoarded desire,
Like the blade of a breaking wave reaped by the wind, or flame
    rising from fire, or cloud-coiled lightning
Suddenly unfurled in the cave of heaven: I that am stationed,
    and cold at heart, incapable of burning,
My blood like standing sea-water lapped in a stone pool, my de-
    sire to the rock, how can I speak of you?
Mine will go down to the deep rock.
                    This rose,
Possessing the air over its emptied prison,
The eager powers at its shoulders waving shadowless
Unwound the ever-widened spirals of flight
As a star light, it spins the night-stabbing threads
From its own strength and substance: so the aquiline desire
Burned itself into meteor freedom and spired

Higher still, and saw the mountain-dividing
Canyon of its captivity (that was to Cawdor
Almost his world) like an old crack in a wall,
Violet-shadowed and gold-lighted; the little stain
Spilt on the floor of the crack was the strong forest;
The grain of sand was the Rock. A speck, an atomic
Center of power clouded in its own smoke
Ran and cried in the crack; it was Cawdor; the other
Points of humanity had neither weight nor shining
To prick the eyes of even an eagle's passion.

This burned and soared. The shining ocean below lay on the
    shore
Like the great shield of the moon come down, rolling bright rim
    to rim with the earth. Against it the multiform
And many-canyoned coast-range hills were gathered into one
    carven mountain, one modulated
Eagle's cry made stone, stopping the strength of the sea. The
    beaked and winged effluence
Felt the air foam under its throat and saw
The mountain sun-cup Tassajara, where fawns
Dance in the steam of the hot fountains at dawn,
Smoothed out, and the high strained ridges beyond Cachagua,
Where the rivers are born and the last condor is dead,
Flatten, and a hundred miles toward morning the Sierras
Dawn with their peaks of snow, and dwindle and smooth down
On the globed earth.

                        It saw from the height and desert space of
        unbreathable air
Where meteors make green fire and die, the ocean dropping
    westward to the girdle of the pearls of dawn
And the hinder edge of the night sliding toward Asia; it saw
    far under eastward the April-delighted
Continent; and time relaxing about it now, abstracted from being,
    it saw the eagles destroyed,
Mean generations of gulls and crows taking their world: turn
    for turn in the air, as on earth

THE CAGED EAGLE'S DEATH DREAM

The white faces drove out the brown. It saw the white decayed
    and the brown from Asia returning;
It saw men learn to outfly the hawk's brood and forget it again;
    it saw men cover the earth and again
Devour each other and hide in caverns, be scarce as wolves. It
    neither wondered nor cared, and it saw
Growth and decay alternate forever, and the tides returning.

It saw, according to the sight of its kind, the archetype
Body of life a beaked carnivorous desire
Self-upheld on storm-broad wings: but the eyes
Were spouts of blood; the eyes were gashed out; dark blood
Ran from the ruinous eye-pits to the hook of the beak
And rained on the waste spaces of empty heaven.
Yet the great Life continued; yet the great Life
Was beautiful, and she drank her defeat, and devoured
Her famine for food.
               There the eagle's phantom perceived
Its prison and its wound were not its peculiar wretchedness,
All that lives was maimed and bleeding, caged or in blindness,
Lopped at the ends with death and conception, and shrewd
Cautery of pain on the stumps to stifle the blood, but not
Refrains for all that; life was more than its functions
And accidents, more important than its pains and pleasures,
A torch to burn in with pride, a necessary
Ecstasy in the run of the cold substance,
And scape-goat of the greater world. (But as for me,
I have heard the summer dust crying to be born
As much as ever flesh cried to be quiet.)
Pouring itself on fulfilment the eagle's passion
Left life behind and flew at the sun, its father.
The great unreal talons took peace for prey
Exultantly, their death beyond death; stooped upward, and struck
Peace like a white fawn in a dell of fire.

The old woman sits on a bench before the door and quarrels
With her meager pale demoralized daughter.
Once when I passed I found her alone, laughing in the sun
And saying that when she was first married
She lived in the old farmhouse up Garapatas Canyon.
(It is empty now, the roof has fallen
But the log walls hang on the stone foundation; the redwoods
Have all been cut down, the oaks are standing;
The place is now more solitary than ever before.)
"When I was nursing my second baby
My husband found a day-old fawn hid in a fern-brake
And brought it; I put its mouth to the breast
Rather than let it starve, I had milk enough for three babies.
Hey, how it sucked, the little nuzzler,
Digging its little hoofs like quills into my stomach.
I had more joy from that than from the others."
Her face is deformed with age, furrowed like a bad road
With market-wagons, mean cares and decay.
She is thrown up to the surface of things, a cell of dry skin
Soon to be shed from the earth's old eyebrows,
I see that once in her spring she lived in the streaming arteries,
The stir of the world, the music of the mountain.

A REDEEMER

The road had steepened and the sun sharpened on the high
  ridges; the stream probably was dry,
Certainly not to be come to down the pit of the canyon. We
  stopped for water at the one farm
In all that mountain. The trough was cracked with drought, the
  moss on the boards dead, but an old dog
Rose like a wooden toy at the house-door silently. I said "There
  will be water somewhere about,"
And when I knocked a man showed us a spring of water. Though
  his hair was nearly white I judged him
Forty years old at most. His eyes and voice were muted. It is
  likely he kept his hands hidden,
I failed to see them until we had dipped the spring. He stood then
  on the lip of the great slope
And looked westward over an incredible country to the far hills
  that dammed the sea-fog: it billowed
Above them, cascaded over them, it never crossed them, gray
  standing flood. He stood gazing, his hands
Were clasped behind him; I caught a glimpse of serous red under
  the fingers, and looking sharply
When they drew apart saw that both hands were wounded. I said
  "Your hands are hurt." He twitched them from sight,
But after a moment having earnestly eyed me displayed them.
  The wounds were in the hearts of the palms,
Pierced to the backs like stigmata of crucifixion. The horrible
  raw flesh protruded, glistening
And granular, not scabbed, nor a sign of infection. "These are
  old wounds." He answered, "Yes. They don't heal." He stood
Moving his lips in silence, his back against that fabulous basin
  of mountains, fold beyond fold,
Patches of forest and scarps of rock, high domes of dead gray
  pasture and gray beds of dry rivers,
Clear and particular in the burning air, too bright to appear real,
  to the last range

A REDEEMER

The fog from the ocean like a stretched compacted thunder-
storm overhung; and he said gravely:
"I pick them open. I made them long ago with a clean steel. It
is only a little to pay—"
He stretched and flexed the fingers, I saw his sunburnt lips whiten
in a line, compressed together,
"If only it proves enough for a time—to save so many." I
searched his face for madness but that
Is often invisible, a subtle spirit. "There never," he said, "was
any people earned so much ruin.
I love them, I am trying to suffer for them. It would be bad if
I should die, I am careful
Against excess." "You think of the wounds," I said, "of Jesus?"
He laughed angrily and frowned, stroking
The fingers of one hand with the other. "Religion is the people's
opium. Your little Jew-God?
My pain," he said with pride, "is voluntary.
They have done what never was done before. Not as a people
takes a land to love it and be fed,
A little, according to need and love, and again a little; sparing
the country tribes, mixing
Their blood with theirs, their minds with all the rocks and rivers,
their flesh with the soil: no, without hunger
Wasting the world and your own labor, without love possessing,
not even your hands to the dirt but plows
Like blades of knives; heartless machines; houses of steel: using
and despising the patient earth . . .
Oh, as a rich man eats a forest for profit and a field for vanity,
so you came west and raped
The continent and brushed its people to death. Without need,
the weak skirmishing hunters, and without mercy.
Well, God's a scarecrow; no vengeance out of old rags. But
there are acts breeding their own reversals
In their own bellies from the first day. I am here" he said—and
broke off suddenly and said "They take horses
And give them sicknesses through hollow needles, their blood
saves babies: I am here on the mountain making

Antitoxin for all the happy towns and farms, the lovely blameless
    children, the terrible
Arrogant cities. I used to think them terrible: their gray pros-
    perity, their pride: from up here
Specks of mildew.

              But when I am dead and all you with whole
    hands think of nothing but happiness,
Will you go mad and kill each other? Or horror come over
    the ocean on wings and cover your sun?
I wish," he said trembling, "I had never been born."

His wife came from the door while he was talking. Mine asked
    her quietly, "Do you live all alone here,
Are you not afraid?" "Certainly not," she answered, "he is
    always gentle and loving. I have no complaint
Except his groans in the night keep me awake often. But when
    I think of other women's
Troubles: my own daughter's: I'm older than my husband, I
    have been married before: deep is my peace."

AN ARTIST

That sculptor we knew, the passionate-eyed son of a quarry-
man,
Who astonished Rome and Paris in his meteor youth, and then
was gone, at his high tide of triumphs,
Without reason or good-bye; I have seen him again lately, after
twenty years, but not in Europe.

In desert hills I rode a horse slack-kneed with thirst. Down a
steep slope a dancing swarm
Of yellow butterflies over a shining rock made me hope water.
We slid down to the place,
The spring was bitter but the horse drank. I imagined wearings
of an old path from that wet rock
Ran down the canyon; I followed, soon they were lost, I came
to a stone valley in which it seemed
No man nor his mount had ever ventured, you wondered
whether even a vulture'd ever spread sail there.
There were stones of strange form under a cleft in the far hill;
I tethered the horse to a rock
And scrambled over. A heap like a stone torrent, a moraine,
But monstrously formed limbs of broken carving appeared in
the rock-fall, enormous breasts, defaced heads
Of giants, the eyes calm through the brute veils of fracture. It
was natural then to climb higher and go in
Up the cleft gate. The canyon was a sheer-walled crack wind-
ing at the entrance, but around its bend
The walls grew dreadful with stone giants, presences growing
out of the rigid precipice, that strove
In dream between stone and life, intense to cast their chaos . . .
or to enter and return . . . stone-fleshed, nerve-stretched
Great bodies ever more beautiful and more heavy with pain,
they seemed leading to some unbearable
Consummation of the ecstasy . . . but there, troll among
Titans, the bearded master of the place accosted me

In a cold anger, a mallet in his hand, filthy and ragged. There
　　was no kindness in that man's mind,
But after he had driven me down to the entrance he spoke a
　　little.

　　　　The merciless sun had found the slot now
To hide in, and lit for the wick of that stone lamp-bowl a sky
　　almost, I thought, abominably beautiful;
While our lost artist we used to admire: for now I knew him:
　　spoke of his passion.

　　　　　　He said, "Marble?
White marble is fit to model a snow-mountain: let man be
　　modest. Nor bronze: I am bound to have my tool
In my material, no irrelevances. I found this pit of dark-gray
　　freestone, fine-grained, and tough enough
To make sketches that under any weathering will last my life-
　　time. . . .

The town is eight miles off, I can fetch food and no one follows
　　me home. I have water and a cave
Here; and no possible lack of material. I need, therefore, nothing.
　　As to companions, I make them.
And models? They are seldom wanted; I know a Basque shepherd
　　I sometimes use; and a woman of the town.
What more? Sympathy? Praise? I have never desired them and
　　also I have never deserved them. I will not show you
More than the spalls you saw by accident.

　　　　　　　　What I see is the enor-
　　mous beauty of things, but what I attempt
Is nothing to that. I am helpless toward that.
It is only to form in stone the mould of some ideal humanity
　　that might be worthy to *be*
Under that lightning. Animalcules that God (if he were given
　　to laughter) might omit to laugh at.

Those children of my hands are tortured, because they feel,"
    he said, "the storm of the outer magnificence.
They are giants in agony. They have seen from my eyes
The man-destroying beauty of the dawns over their notch
    yonder, and all the obliterating stars.
But in their eyes they have peace. I have lived a little and I
    think
Peace marrying pain alone can breed that excellence in the
    luckless race, might make it decent
To exist at all on the star-lit stone breast.

                        I hope," he said, "that
    when I grow old and the chisel drops,
I may crawl out on a ledge of the rock and die like a wolf."

                                 These
    fragments are all I can remember,
These in the flare of the desert evening. Having been driven
    so brutally forth I never returned;
Yet I respect him enough to keep his name and the place secret.
    I hope that some other traveller
May stumble on that ravine of Titans after their maker has
    died. While he lives, let him alone.

SOLILOQUY

August and laurelled have been content to speak for an age, and the ages that follow
Respect them for that pious fidelity;
But you have disfeatured time for timelessness.
They had heroes for companions, beautiful youths to dream of, rose-marble-fingered
Women shed light down the great lines;
But you have invoked the slime in the skull,
The lymph in the vessels. They have shown men Gods like racial dreams, the woman's desire,
The man's fear, the hawk-faced prophet's; but nothing
Human seems happy at the feet of yours.
Therefore though not forgotten, not loved, in gray old years in the evening leaning
Over the gray stones of the tower-top,
You shall be called heartless and blind;
And watch new time answer old thought, not a face strange nor a pain astonishing;
But you living be laired in the rock
That sheds pleasure and pain like hailstones.

THE BIRD WITH THE
DARK PLUMES

The bird with the dark plumes in my blood,
That never for one moment, however I patched my truces,
Consented to make peace with the people,
It is pitiful now to watch her pleasure in a breath of tempest
Breaking the sad promise of spring.
Are these that morose hawk's wings, vaulting, a mere mad
    swallow's,
The snow-shed peak, the violent precipice?
Poor outlaw that would not value their praise do you prize
    their blame?
"Their liking," she said, "was a long creance,
But let them be kind enough to hate me, that opens the sky."
It is almost as foolish my poor falcon
To want hatred as to want love; and harder to win.

TOR HOUSE

If you should look for this place after a handful of lifetimes:
Perhaps of my planted forest a few
May stand yet, dark-leaved Australians or the coast cypress, haggard
With storm-drift; but fire and the axe are devils.
Look for foundations of sea-worn granite, my fingers had the art
To make stone love stone, you will find some remnant.
But if you should look in your idleness after ten thousand years:
It is the granite knoll on the granite
And lava tongue in the midst of the bay, by the mouth of the Carmel
River-valley, these four will remain
In the change of names. You will know it by the wild sea-fragrance of wind
Though the ocean may have climbed or retired a little;
You will know it by the valley inland that our sun and our moon were born from
Before the poles changed; and Orion in December
Evenings was strung in the throat of the valley like a lamp-lighted bridge.
Come in the morning you will see white gulls
Weaving a dance over blue water, the wane of the moon
Their dance-companion, a ghost walking
By daylight, but wider and whiter than any bird in the world.
My ghost you needn't look for; it is probably
Here, but a dark one, deep in the granite, not dancing on wind
With the mad wings and the day moon.

HURT HAWKS

I

The broken pillar of the wing jags from the clotted shoulder,
The wing trails like a banner in defeat,
No more to use the sky forever but live with famine
And pain a few days: cat nor coyote
Will shorten the week of waiting for death, there is game without talons.
He stands under the oak-bush and waits
The lame feet of salvation; at night he remembers freedom
And flies in a dream, the dawns ruin it.
He is strong and pain is worse to the strong, incapacity is worse.
The curs of the day come and torment him
At distance, no one but death the redeemer will humble that head,
The intrepid readiness, the terrible eyes.
The wild God of the world is sometimes merciful to those
That ask mercy, not often to the arrogant.
You do not know him, you communal people, or you have forgotten him;
Intemperate and savage, the hawk remembers him;
Beautiful and wild, the hawks, and men that are dying, remember him.

II

I'd sooner, except the penalties, kill a man than a hawk; but the great redtail
Had nothing left but unable misery
From the bone too shattered for mending, the wing that trailed under his talons when he moved.
We had fed him six weeks, I gave him freedom,
He wandered over the foreland hill and returned in the evening, asking for death,
Not like a beggar, still eyed with the old

HURT HAWKS

Implacable arrogance. I gave him the lead gift in the twilight.
    What fell was relaxed,
Owl-downy, soft feminine feathers; but what
Soared: the fierce rush: the night-herons by the flooded river
    cried fear at its rising
Before it was quite unsheathed from reality.

MEDITATION ON SAVIORS

I

When I considered it too closely, when I wore it like an
element and smelt it like water,
Life is become less lovely, the net nearer than the skin, a little
troublesome, a little terrible.

I pledged myself awhile ago not to seek refuge, neither in death
nor in a walled garden,
In lies nor gated loyalties, nor in the gates of contempt, that
easily lock the world out of doors.

Here on the rock it is great and beautiful, here on the foam-wet
granite sea-fang it is easy to praise
Life and water and the shining stones: but whose cattle are the
herds of the people that one should love them?

If they were yours, then you might take a cattle-breeder's de-
light in the herds of the future. Not yours.
Where the power ends let love, before it sours to jealousy. Leave
the joys of government to Caesar.

Who is born when the world wanes, when the brave soul of
the world falls on decay in the flesh increasing
Comes one with a great level mind, sufficient vision, sufficient
blindness, and clemency for love.

This is the breath of rottenness I smelt; from the world waiting,
stalled between storms, decaying a little,
Bitterly afraid to be hurt, but knowing it cannot draw the savior
Caesar but out of the blood-bath.

The apes of Christ lift up their hands to praise love: but wisdom
without love is the present savior,
Power without hatred, mind like a many-bladed machine sub-
duing the world with deep indifference.

MEDITATION ON SAVIORS

The apes of Christ itch for a sickness they have never known;
   words and the little envies will hardly
Measure against that blinding fire behind the tragic eyes they
   have never dared to confront.

II

Point Lobos lies over the hollowed water like a humped whale
   swimming to shoal; Point Lobos
Was wounded with that fire; the hills at Point Sur endured it;
   the palace at Thebes; the hill Calvary.

Out of incestuous love power and then ruin. A man forcing the
   imaginations of men,
Possessing with love and power the people: a man defiling his
   own household with impious desire.

King Oedipus reeling blinded from the palace doorway, red
   tears pouring from the torn pits
Under the forehead; and the young Jew writhing on the domed
   hill in the earthquake, against the eclipse

Frightfully uplifted for having turned inward to love the peo-
   ple:—that root was so sweet Oh, dreadful agonist?—
I saw the same pierced feet, that walked in the same crime to its
   expiation; I heard the same cry.

A bad mountain to build your world on. Am I another keeper
   of the people, that on my own shore,
On the gray rock, by the grooved mass of the ocean, the sick-
   nesses I left behind me concern me?

Here where the surf has come incredible ways out of the splendid
   west, over the deeps
Light nor life sounds forever; here where enormous sundowns
   flower and burn through color to quietness;

Then the ecstasy of the stars is present? As for the people, I
   have found my rock, let them find theirs.
Let them lie down at Caesar's feet and be saved; and he in his
   time reap their daggers of gratitude.

III

Yet I am the one made pledges against the refuge contempt, that
easily locks the world out of doors.
This people as much as the sea-granite is part of the God from
whom I desire not to be fugitive.

I see them: they are always crying. The shored Pacific makes
perpetual music, and the stone mountains
Their music of silence, the stars blow long pipings of light:
the people are always crying in their hearts.

One need not pity; certainly one must not love. But who has
seen peace, if he should tell them where peace
Lives in the world . . . they would be powerless to understand;
and he is not willing to be reinvolved.

IV

How should one caught in the stone of his own person dare tell
the people anything but relative to that?
But if a man could hold in his mind all the conditions at once,
of man and woman, of civilized

And barbarous, of sick and well, of happy and under torture,
of living and dead, of human and not
Human, and dimly all the human future:—what should persuade
him to speak? And what could his words change?

The mountain ahead of the world is not forming but fixed. But
the man's words would be fixed also,
Part of that mountain, under equal compulsion; under the same
present compulsion in the iron consistency.

And nobody sees good or evil but out of a brain a hundred cen-
turies quieted, some desert
Prophet's, a man humped like a camel, gone mad between the
mud-walled village and the mountain sepulchres.

V

Broad wagons before sunrise bring food into the city from the
open farms, and the people are fed.
They import and they consume reality. Before sunrise a hawk
in the desert made them their thoughts.

VI

Here is an anxious people, rank with suppressed blood-thirstiness.
Among the mild and unwarlike
Gautama needed but live greatly and be heard, Confucius needed
but live greatly and be heard.

This people has not outgrown blood-sacrifice, one must writhe
on the high cross to catch at their memories;
The price is known. I have quieted love; for love of the people
I would not do it. For power I would do it.

—But that stands against reason: what is power to a dead man,
dead under torture?—What is power to a man
Living, after the flesh is content? Reason is never a root, neither
of act nor desire.

For power living I would never do it; they are not delightful to
touch, one wants to be separate. For power
After the nerves are put away underground, to lighten the ab-
stract unborn children toward peace . . .

A man might have paid anguish indeed. Except he had found
the standing sea-rock that even this last
Temptation breaks on; quieter than death but lovelier; peace
that quiets the desire even of praising it.

VII

Yet look: are they not pitiable? No: if they lived forever they
would be pitiable:
But a huge gift reserved quite overwhelms them at the end;
they are able then to be still and not cry.

MEDITATION ON SAVIORS

And having touched a little of the beauty and seen a little of the
    beauty of things, magically grow
Across the funeral fire or the hidden stench of burial themselves
    into the beauty they admired,

Themselves into the God, themselves into the sacred steep un-
    consciousness they used to mimic
Asleep between lamp's death and dawn, while the last drunkard
    stumbled homeward down the dark street.

They are not to be pitied but very fortunate; they need no savior,
    salvation comes and takes them by force,
It gathers them into the great kingdoms of dust and stone, the
    blown storms, the stream's-end ocean.

With this advantage over their granite grave-marks, of having
    realized the petulant human consciousness
Before, and then the greatness, the peace: drunk from both
    pitchers: these to be pitied? These not fortunate?

But while he lives let each man make his health in his mind,
    to love the coast opposite humanity
And so be freed of love, laying it like bread on the waters; it is
    worst turned inward, it is best shot farthest.

Love, the mad wine of good and evil, the saint's and murderer's,
    the mote in the eye that makes its object
Shine the sun black; the trap in which it is better to catch the
    inhuman God than the hunter's own image.

THE LOVING SHEPHERDESS

The little one-room schoolhouse among the redwoods
Opened its door, a dozen children ran out
And saw on the narrow road between the dense trees
A person—a girl by the long light-colored hair:
The torn brown cloak that she wore might be a man's
Or woman's either—walking hastily northward
Among a huddle of sheep. Her thin young face
Seemed joyful, and lighted from inside, and formed
Too finely to be so wind-burnt. As she went forward
One or another of the trotting sheep would turn
Its head to look at her face, and one would press
Its matted shoulder against her moving thigh.
The schoolchildren stood laughing and shouting together.
"Who's that?" "Clare Walker," they said, "down from the hill.
She'd fifty sheep and now she's got eight, nine,
Ten: what have you done with all the others, Clare Walker?"
The joy that had lived in her face died, she yet
Went on as if she were deaf, with forward eyes
And lifted head, but the delicate lips moving.
The jeering children ran in behind her, and the sheep
Drew nervously on before, except the old ram,
That close at her side dipped his coiled horns a little
But neither looked back nor edged forward. An urchin shouted
"You killed your daddy, why don't you kill your sheep?"
And a fat girl, "Oh where's your lover, Clare Walker?
He didn't want you after all."
                              The patriarch ram
That walked beside her wore a greasy brown bundle
Tied on his back with cords in the felt of wool,
And one of the little boys, running by, snatched at it
So that it fell. Clare bent to gather it fallen,
And tears dropped from her eyes. She offered no threat
With the bent staff of rosy-barked madrone-wood

That lay in her hand, but said "Oh please, Oh please,"
As meek as one of her ewes. An eight-year-old girl
Shrilled, "Whistle for the dogs, make her run like a cat,
Call your dog, Charlie Geary!" But a brown-skinned
Spanish-Indian boy came forward and said,
"You let her alone. They'll not hurt you, Clare Walker.
Don't cry, I'll walk beside you." She thanked him, still crying.
Four of the children, who lived southward, turned back;
The rest followed more quietly.
　　　　　　　　　The black-haired boy
Said gently, "Remember to keep in the road, Clare Walker.
There's enough grass. The ranchers will sick their dogs on you
If you go into the pastures, because their cows
Won't eat where the sheep have passed; but you can walk
Into the woods." She answered, "You're kind, you're kind.
Oh yes, I always remember." The small road dipped
Under the river when they'd come down the hill,
A shallow mountain river that Clare skipped over
By stone after stone, the sheep wading beside her.
The friendly boy went south to the farm on the hill, "good-by,
　　　good-by," and Clare with her little flock
Kept northward among great trees like towers in the river-valley.
　　　Her sheep sidled the path, sniffing
The bitter sorrel, lavender-flowering in shade, and the withered
　　　ferns. Toward evening they found a hollow
Of autumn grass.

II

　　　Clare laughed and was glad, she undid the bundle
　　　from the ram's back
And found in the folds a battered metal cup and a broken loaf.
　　　She shared her bread with the sheep,
A morsel for each, and prettily laughing
Pushed down the reaching faces. "Piggies, eat grass. Leave me the
　　　crust, Tiny, I can't eat grass.
Nosie, keep off. Here Frannie, here Frannie." One of the ewes
　　　came close and stood to be milked, Clare stroked

The little udders and drank when the cup filled, and filled it again
    and drank, dividing her crust
With the milch ewe; the flock wandered the glade, nibbling white
    grass. There was only one lamb among them,
The others had died in the spring storm.

                        The light in the glade
    suddenly increased and changed, the hill
High eastward began to shine and be rosy-colored, and bathed
    in so clear a light that up the bare hill
Each clump of yucca stood like a star, bristling sharp rays; while
    westward the spires of the giant wood
Were strangely tall and intensely dark on the layered colors of
    the winter sundown; their blunt points touched
The high tender blue, their heads were backed by the amber, the
    thick-branched columns
Crossed flaming rose. Then Clare with the flush
Of the solemn and glad sky on her face went lightly down to
    the river to wash her cup; and the flock
Fed on a moment before they looked up and missed her. The
    ewe called Frannie had gone with Clare, and the others
Heard Frannie's hooves on the crisp oak-leaves at the edge of the
    glade. They followed, bleating, and found their mistress
On the brink of the stream, in the clear gloom of the wood, and
    nipped the cresses from the water. Thence all returning
Lay down together in the glade, but Clare among them
Sat combing her hair, with a gap-toothed comb brought from
    the bundle. The evening deepened, the thick blonde strands
Hissed in the comb and glimmered in the brown twilight, Clare
    began weeping, full of sorrow for no reason
As she had been full of happiness before. She braided her hair
    and pillowed her head on the bundle; she heard
The sheep breathing about her and felt the warmth of their
    bodies, through the heavy fleeces.

                      In the night she moaned
And bolted upright. "Oh come, come,
Come Fern, come Frannie, Leader and Saul and Tiny,

We have to go on," she whispered, sobbing with fear, and stood
With a glimmer in her hair among the sheep rising. The halved
    moon had arisen clear of the hill,
And touched her hair, and the hollow, in the mist from the river,
    was a lake of whiteness. Clare stood wreathed with her
    flock
And stared at the dark towers of the wood, the dream faded
    away from her mind, she sighed and fondled
The frightened foreheads. "Lie down, lie down darlings, we
    can't escape it." But after that they were restless
And heard noises in the night till dawn.

                                        They rose in the quivering
Pale clearness before daylight, Clare milked her ewe,
The others feeding drifted across the glade
Like little clouds at sunrise wandering apart;
She lifted up the madrone-wood staff and called them.
"Fay, Fern, Oh Frannie. Come Saul.
Leader and Tiny and Nosie, we have to go on."
They went to the stream and then returned to the road
And very slowly went north, nibbling the margin
Bushes and grass, tracking the tender dust
With numberless prints of oblique crossings and driftings.
They came to Fogler's place and two ruffian dogs
Flew over the fence: Clare screaming "Oh, Oh, Oh, Oh,"
An inarticulate wildbird cry, brandishing
The staff but never striking, stood out against them,
That dashed by her, and the packed and trembling ball
Of fleeces rolling into the wood was broken.
The sheep might have been torn there, some ewe or the lamb
Against the great foundations of the trees, but Fogler
Ran shouting over the road after his dogs
And drove them home. Clare gathered her flock, the sobbing
Throats and the tired eyes, "Fay, Fern, Oh Frannie,
Come Leader, come little Hornie, come Saul"; and Fogler:
"You ought to get a good dog to help take care of them."
He eyed curiously her thin young face,
Pale parted lips cracked by the sun and wind,

And then the thin bare ankles and broken shoes.
"Are you Clare Walker? I heard that you'd gone away:
But you're Clare Walker, aren't you?" "We had a dog,"
She said, "a long time ago but he went away.
There, Nosie. Poor Frannie. There. These poor things
Can find their food, but what could I keep a dog with?
But that was some years ago." He said, "Are these all?
They're all gathered? I heard you'd thirty or forty."
Then hastily, for he saw the long hazel eyes
Filling with tears, "Where are you going, Clare Walker?
Because I think it will rain in a week or two,
You can't sleep out then." She answered with a little shudder,
"Wherever I go this winter will be all right.
I'm going somewhere next April." Fogler stood rubbing
His short black beard, then dropped his hand to scratch
The ram's forehead by the horns but Saul drew away.
And Fogler said: "You're too young and too pretty
To wander around the country like this.
I'd ask you to come here when it rains, but my wife . . .
And how could I keep the sheep here?" "Ah, no," she answered,
"I couldn't come back." "Well, wait," he said, "for a minute,
Until I go to the house. Will you wait, Clare?
I'll tie up the dogs. I've got some biscuit and things . . ."
He returned with a sack of food, and two old shoes
A little better than Clare's. She sat on a root;
He knelt before her, fumbling the knotted laces
Of those she had on, and she felt his hands tremble.
His wife's shoes were too short for the slender feet. When the
    others
Had been replaced, Fogler bent suddenly and kissed
Clare's knee, where the coat had slipped back. He looked at her
    face,
His own burning, but in hers nor fear nor laughter,
Nor desire nor aversion showed. He said "good-by,"
And hurried away.

          Clare travelled northward, and sometimes
Half running, more often loitering, and the sheep fed.

In the afternoon she led them into the willows,
And choosing a green pool of the shallow stream
Bathed, while the sheep bleated to her from the shoals.
They made a pleasant picture, the girl and her friends, in the
    green shade
Shafted with golden light falling through the alder branches.
Her body, the scarecrow garments laid by,
Though hermit-ribbed and with boyishly flattened flanks hardly
    a woman's,
Was smooth and flowing, glazed with bright water, the shoulders
    and breasts beautiful, and moved with a rapid confidence
That contradicted her mind's abstractions. She laughed aloud
    and jetted handfuls of shining water
At the sheep on the bank; the old ram stood blinking with pleas-
    ure, shaking his horns. But after a time Clare's mood
Was changed, as if she thought happiness must end.
She shivered and moved heavily out of the stream
And wept on the shore, her hands clasping her ankles,
Her face bowed on her knees, her knotted-up coils
Of citron-colored hair loosening. The ewe
That she called Nosie approached behind her and pressed
Her chin on the wet shoulder; Clare turned then, moaning,
And drew the bony head against the soft breasts.
"Oh what will you do," she whispered laughing and sobbing,
"When all this comes to an end?"

                        She stood and stroked off
The drops of water, and dressed hastily. They went
On farther; now there was no more forest by the road,
But open fields. The river bent suddenly westward
And made a pond that shone like a red coal
Against the shore of the ocean, under the sundown
Sky, with a skeleton of sandbar
Between the pond and the sea.

                  When deepening twilight
Made all things gray and made trespass safe, Clare entered
The seaward fields with her flock. They had fed scantly

In the redwood forest, and here on the dead grass
The cattle had cropped all summer they could not sleep.
She led them hour after hour under the still stars.
Once they ran down to the glimmering beach to avoid
The herd and the range bull; they returned, and wandered
The low last bluff, where sparse grass labors to live in the wind-
    heaped sand. Silently they pastured northward,
Gray file of shadows, between the glimmer and hushing moan
    of the ocean and the dark silence of the hills.
The erect one wore a pallor of starlight woven in her hair. Be-
    fore moonrise they huddled together
In a hollow cup of old dune that opened seaward, but sheltered
    them from the nightwind and from morning eyes.

III

The bleating of sheep answered the barking of sea-lions and Clare
    awoke
Dazzled in the broad dawn. The land-wind lifted the light-spun
    manes of the waves, a drift of sea-lions
Swung in the surf and looked at the shore, sleek heads uplifted
    and great brown eyes with a glaze of blind
Blue sea-light in them. "You lovely creatures," she whispered.
She went to the verge and felt the foam at her ankles. "You lovely
    creatures come closer." The sheep followed her
And stopped in the sand with lonesome cries. Clare stood and
    trembled at the simple morning of the world; there was
    nothing
But hills and sea, not a tree on the shore nor a ship on the sea;
    an edge of the hill kindled with gold,
And the sun rose. Then Clare took home her soul from the world
    and went on. When she was wandering the flats
Of open pasture between the Sur Hill sea-face and the great
    separate sea-dome rock at Point Sur,
Forgetting, as often before, that she and her flock were tres-
    passers
In cattle country: she looked and a young cowboy rode down
    from the east. "You'll have to get off this range.
Get out of this field," he said, "your tallow-hoofed mutton."

"Oh," she answered trembling, "I'm going. I got lost in the
   night.
Don't drive them." "A woman?" he said. He jerked the reins and
   sat staring. "Where did *you* drop from?" She answered
   faintly,
With a favor-making smile, "From the south." "Who's with
   you?" "Nobody."
"Keep going, and get behind the hill if you can
Before Nick Miles the foreman looks down this way."
She said to the ram, "Oh Saul, Oh hurry. Come Leader.
Tiny and Frannie and Nosie, we have to go on.
Oh, hurry, Fern." They huddled bleating about her,
And she in the midst made haste; they pressed against her
And moved in silence. The young cowboy rode on the east
As hoping to hide the flock from Nick Miles his foreman,
Sidelong in the saddle, and gazed at Clare, at the twisting
Ripple of pale bright hair from her brown skin
Behind the temples. She felt that his looks were friendly,
She turned and timidly smiled. Then she could see
That he was not a man but a boy, sixteen
Or seventeen; she felt more courage. "What would your foreman
Do if he saw us?" "He'd be rough. But," he said,
"You'll soon be behind the hill. Where are you going?"
She made no answer. "To Monterey?" "Oh . . . to nowhere!"
She shivered and sought his face with her eyes. "To nowhere,
   I mean."
"Well," he said sulkily, "where did you sleep last night?
Somewhere?" She said with eagerness, "Ah, two miles back,
On the edge of the sand; we weren't really in the field."
He stared. "You're a queer one. Is that old coat
All you've got on?" "No, no, there's a dress under it.
But scrubbed so often," she said, "with sand and water
Because I had no soap, it's nothing but rags."
"You needn't hurry, no one can see you now.
 . . . My name's Will Brighton," he said. "Well, mine is Clare."
"Where do you live when you're at home, Clare?" "I haven't
   any."

They rounded the second spur of the hill. Gray lupine clothed
    the north flank, a herd of cattle stared down
From the pale slope of dead grass above the gray thicket. Rumps
    high, low quarters, they were part of the world's end sag,
The inverted arch from the Sur Hill height to the flat foreland
    and up the black lava rock of Point Sur;
In the open gap the mountain sea-wall of the world foam-
    footed went northward. Beyond the third spur Clare saw
A barn and a house up the wrinkled hill, oak-scrub and sycamores.
    The house built of squared logs, time-blackened,
Striped with white plaster between the black logs, a tall dead
    cube with a broken chimney, made her afraid;
Its indestructible crystalline shape. "Oh! There's a house.
They'll see us from there. I'll go back . . ." "Don't be afraid,"
He answered smiling, "that place has no eyes.
There you can turn your sheep in the old corral,
Or graze them under the buckeyes until evening.
No one will come." She sighed, and then faintly:
"Nobody ever lives there, you're sure?" "Not for eight years.
You can go in," he said nervously: "maybe
You haven't been inside a house a good while?"
She looked up at his pleasant unformed young face,
It was blushing hot. "Oh, what's the matter with the house?"
"Nothing. Our owner bought the ranch, and the house
Stands empty, he didn't want it. They tell me an old man
Claiming to be God . . . a kind of a preacher boarded there,
And the family busted up." She said "I don't believe
Any such story." "Well, he was kind of a preacher.
They say his girl killed herself; he washed his hands
With fire and vanished." "Then she was crazy. What, spill
Her own one precious life," she said trembling,
"She'd nothing but that? Ah! no!
No matter how miserable, what goes in a moment,
You know . . . out . . ." Her head bowed, and her hand
Dug anxiously in the deep pads of wool
On the shoulder of the ram walking against her side;
When her face lifted again even the unwatchful boy

Took notice of tears.

They approached the house; the fence in
front was broken but the windows and doors were whole,
The rose that grew over the rotted porch steps was dead; yet
the sleep of the house seemed incorruptible,
It made Clare and the boy talk low. He dropped out of the
saddle and made the bridle hang down
To serve for tether. "Come round by the back," he whispered,
"this door is locked." "What for?" "To go in," he whispered.
"Ah no, I have to stay with my sheep. Why in the world should
I go in to your dirty old house?"
His face now he'd dismounted was level with hers; she saw the
straw-colored hairs on his lip, and freckles,
For he'd grown pale. "Hell," he said, narrowing his eyes, hoping
to be manly and bully her: but the heart failed him,
He said sadly, "I hoped you'd come in." She breathed, "Oh," her
mouth twitching,
But whether with fear or laughter no one could tell,
And said, "You've been kind. Does nobody ever come here?
Because I'd have to leave my poor friends outdoors,
Someone might come and hurt them." "The sheep?
Oh, nobody
No one can see them. Oh, Clare, come on. Look here,"
He ran and opened a gate, "the corral fence
Is good as new and the grass hasn't been touched."
The small flock entered gladly and found green weeds
In the matted gray. Clare slowly returned. The boy
Catching her by the hand to draw her toward the house,
She saw his young strained face, and wondered. "Have you ever
Been, with a woman?" "Ah," he said proudly, "yes."
But the honesty of her gaze dissolving his confidence
He looked at the ground and said mournfully, "She wasn't white.
And I think she was quite old . . ." Clare in her turn
Reddened. "If it would make you happy," she said.
"I want to leave glad memories. And you'll not be sorry
After I'm gone?"

The sheep, missing their mistress,

Bleated and moved uneasily, forgetting to feed,
While Clare walked in the house. She said, "Oh, not yet.
Let's look at the house. What was the man's name
Whose daughter . . . he said he was God and suddenly van-
    ished?"
"A man named Barclay," he said, "kind of a preacher."
They spoke in whispers, peering about. At length Clare sighed,
And stripped off the long brown coat.

                        When they returned outdoors,
Blinking in the sun, the boy bent his flushed face
Toward Clare's pale one and said, "Dear, you can stay here
As long as you want, but I must go back to work."
She heard the sheep bleating, and said, "Good-by.
Good luck, Will Brighton." She hurried to her flock, while he
Mounted, but when he had ridden three strides of a canter
Clare was crying, "Oh help. Oh help. Oo! Oo!" He returned,
And found her in the near corner of the corral
On hands and knees, her flock huddling about her,
Peering down a pit in the earth. Oak-scrub and leafless
Buckeyes made a dark screen toward the hill, and Clare
Stood up against it, her white face and light hair
Shining against it, and cried, "Oh, help me, they've fallen,
Two have fallen." The pit was an old well;
The hand-pump had fallen in, and the timbers
That closed the mouth had crumbled to yellow meal.
Clare lay and moaned on the brink among the dark nettles,
Will Brighton brought the braided line that hung at his saddle
And made it fast and went down.

                        The well-shaft was so filled up
With earth-fall and stones and rotting timbers, it was possible
    for the boy and girl to hoist up the fallen
Without other contrivance than the looped rope. The one came
    struggling and sobbing, Clare cried her name,
"Oh, Fern, Fern, Fern." She stood and fell, and scrambled up to
    her feet, and plunged on three legs. The other

Came flaccid, it slipped in the rope and hung head downward,
  Clare made no cry. When it was laid by the well-brink
A slime of half-chewed leaves fell from its mouth. The boy
  climbed up. "While I was making your pleasure,"
Clare said, "this came. While I was lying there. What's punished
  is kindness." He touched the lifeless ewe with his foot,
Clare knelt against her and pushed him away. He said, "It fell the
  first and its neck was broken." And Clare:
"This was the one that would nudge my hands
When I was quiet, she'd come behind me and touch me, I called
  her Nosie. One night we were all near frozen
And starved, I felt her friendly touches all night." She lifted the
  head. "Oh, Nosie, I loved you best.
Fern's leg is broken. We'll all be like you in a little while." The
  boy ran and caught Fern, and said
"The bones are all right. A sprain I guess, a bad sprain. I'll come
  in the evening, Clare, if you're still here.
I'm sorry." She sat with the head on her lap, and he rode away.
  After a time she laid it on the earth.
She went and felt Fern's foreleg and went slowly up the hill; her
  small flock followed.

IV

Fern lagged and lagged,
Dibbling the dust with the mere points of the hoof
Of the hurt foreleg, and rolling up to her shepherdess
The ache of reproachful eyes. "Oh, Fern, Oh, Fern,
What can I do? I'm not a man, to be able to carry you.
My father, he could have carried you." Tears from Clare's eyes
Fell in the roadway; she was always either joyful or weeping.
They climbed for half the day, only a steep mile
With many rests, and lay on the Sur Hill summit.
The sun and the ocean were far down below, like fire in a bowl;
The shadow of the hills lay slanting up a thin mist
Into the eastern sky, dark immense lines
Going out of the world.

          Clare slept wretchedly, for thirst
And anxious dreams and sorrow. She saw the lighthouse
Glow and flash all night under the hill;
The wind turned south, she smelled the river they had left,
Small flying clouds from the south crossed the weak stars.
In the morning Fern would not walk.

                  Between noon and morning
A dark-skinned man on a tall hammer-headed
Flea-bitten gray horse rode north on the hill-crest.
Clare ran to meet him. "Please help me. One of my sheep
Has hurt her leg and can't walk. . . . Entiendes inglés?"
She faltered, seeing him Indian-Spanish, and the dark eyes
Gave no sign whether they understood, gazing through her with
    a blue light across them
Like the sea-lions' eyes. He answered easily in English, "What can
    I do?" in the gentle voice of his people;
And Clare: "I thought you might carry her down. We are very
    thirsty, the feed is all dry, here is no water,
And I've been gathering the withered grasses to feed her." He
    said, "We could tie her onto the horse." "Ah, no,
She'd be worse hurt. . . . She's light and little, she was born in
    the hills." The other sheep had followed their shepherdess
Into the road and sadly looked up, the man smiled and dis-
    mounted among them. "Where are you going?"
She answered, "North. Oh, come and see her. Unless you carry
    her
I don't know what we can do." "But it's two miles
Down to the river." The lame ewe, whether frightened
By the stranger and his horse, or rested at length,
Now rose and went quietly to Clare, the hurt foreleg
Limping but serving. Clare laughed with pleasure. "Oh, now,
We can go down by ourselves. Come Fern, come Saul,
Fay, Frannie, Leader . . ." She was about to have called
The name of the one that died yesterday; her face
Changed and she walked in silence, Fern at her thigh.
The friendly stranger walked on the other side,
And his horse followed the sheep. He said: "I have seen
Many things, of this world and the others, but what are you?"

"My name's Clare Walker." "Well, I am Onorio Vasquez.
I meant, what are you doing? I think that I'd have seen you or
    heard of you
If you live near." "I'm doing? I'm taking care of my sheep." She
    looked at his face to be sure of kindness,
And said, "I'm doing like most other people; take care of those
    that need me and go on till I die.
But *I* know when it will be; that's the only . . . I'm often
    afraid." Her look went westward to the day moon,
Faint white shot bird in her wane, the wings bent downward,
    falling in the clear over the ocean cloud-bank.
"Most people will see hundreds of moons: I shall see five.
When this one's finished." Vasquez looked intently at her thin
    young face, turned sideways from him, the parted
Sun-scarred lips, the high bridge of the nose, dark eyes and light
    hair; she was thin, but no sign of sickness; her eyes
Met his and he looked down and said nothing. When he looked
    down he remembered chiefly the smooth brown throat
And the little hollow over the notch of the breast-bone. He said
    at length, carefully, "You needn't be afraid.
I often," he murmured shyly, "have visions. I used to think they
    taught me something, but I was a fool.
If you saw a vision, or you heard a voice from heaven, it is noth-
    ing." She answered, "What I fear really's the pain.
The rest is only a kind of strangeness." Her eyes were full of tears
    and he said anxiously, "Oh, never
Let visions nor voices fool you.
They are wonderful but we see them by chance; I think they
    mean something in their own country but they mean
Nothing in this; they have nothing to do with our lives and
    deaths." She answered in so changed a voice that Vasquez
Stared; the tears were gone and her eyes were laughing. "Oh,
    no, it was nothing," she said, "in the way of that.
Visions? My trouble is a natural thing.
But tell me about those visions." He muttered to himself
With a shamed face and answered, "Not now." The south wind
That drove the dust of the little troop before them
Now increased and struck hard, where the road gained

A look-out point over the fork of the canyon
And the redwood forest below. The sheep were coughing
In the whirl of wind. At this point the lame ewe
Lay down and refused to rise, "Oh, now, now, now,"
Clare wrung her hands, "we're near the water too. We're all so
    thirsty.
Oh, Fern!" Vasquez said sadly, "If she'd be quiet
Over my shoulders, but she won't." He heard a hoarse voice
Cry in the canyon, and Clare softly cried answer
And ran to the brink of the road. She stood there panting
Above the pitch and hollow of the gorge, her grotesque cloak
Blown up to her shoulders, flapping like wings
About the half nakedness of the slender body.
Vasquez looked down the way of her gaze, expecting
To see some tragical thing; he saw nothing but a wide heron
Laboring thwart wind from the shore over the heads of the red-
    woods. A heavy dark hawk balanced in the storm
And suddenly darted; the heron, the wings and long legs waver-
    ing in terror, fell, screaming, the long throat
Twisted under the body; Clare screamed in answer. The pirate
    death drove by and had missed, and circled
For a new strike, the poor frightened fisherman
Beat the air over the heads of the redwoods and labored upward.
    Again and again death struck, and the heron
Fell, with the same lost cry, and escaped; but the last fall
Was into the wood, the hawk followed, both passed from sight
Under the waving spires of the wood.

                    Clare Walker
Turned, striving with the gesture of a terrified child
To be quiet, her clenched fist pressed on her mouth,
Her teeth against the knuckles, and her blonde hair
Wild on the wind. "Oh, what can save him, can save him?
Oh, how he cried at each fall!" She crouched in the wind
At the edge of the road, trembling; the ewe called Tiny
Crossed over and touched her, the others turned anxious looks
From sniffing the autumn-pinched leaves of the groundling black-
    berries.

When she was quieted Vasquez said, "You love
All creatures alike." She looked at his face inquiringly
With wide candid brown eyes, either not knowing
Or not thinking. He said, "It is now not far
Down to the running water; we'd better stretch her
Across the saddle"—he nodded toward the lame ewe—
"You hold her by the forelegs and I by the hind ones,
She'll not be hurt." Clare's voice quieted the sheep
And Vasquez' the indignant horse. They came down at length
To dark water under gigantic trees.

V

She helped Fern drink before herself drooped eagerly
Her breast against the brown stones and kissed the cold stream.
She brought from the bundle what food remained, and shared it
With Vasquez and the munching sheep. There were three apples
From Fogler's trees, and a little jar of honey
And crumbled comb from his hives, and Clare drew a net
Of water-cress from the autumn-hushed water to freshen
The old bread and the broken biscuits. She was gay with delight
At having something to give. They sat on the bank, where
  century
After century of drooping redwood needles had made the earth,
  as if the dark trees were older
Than their own mother.

Clare answered Vasquez' question and
    said she had come from the coast mountains in the south;
She'd left her home a long time ago; and Fogler, the farmer by
    the Big Sur, had given her this food
Because he was sorry his dogs had worried the sheep. But yes-
    terday she was passing Point Sur, and Fern
Had fallen into a well by the house. She said nothing of the other
    ewe, that had died; and Vasquez
Seemed to clench himself tight: "What were you doing at Point
    Sur, it's not on the road?" "The sheep were hungry,
And I wandered off the road in the dark. It was wicked of me
    to walk in the pasture, but a young cowboy

Helped me on the right way. We looked into the house." He
  said, "Let no one go back there, let its mice have it.
God lived there once and tried to make peace with the people;
  no peace was made." She stared in silence, and Vasquez:
"After that time I bawled for death, like a calf for the cow. There
  were no visions. My brothers watched me,
And held me under the hammers of food and sleep."
He ceased; then Clare in a troubled silence
Thought he was lying, for she thought certainly that no one
Ever had desired death. But, for he looked unhappy
And said nothing, she said Will Brighton had told her
Something about a man who claimed to be God,
"Whose daughter," she said, "died." Vasquez stood up
And said trembling, "In the ruin of San Antonio church
I saw an owl as big as one of your sheep
Sleeping above the little gilt Virgin above the altar.
That was no vision. I want to hear nothing
Of what there was at Point Sur." He went to his horse
That stood drooping against the stream-bank, and rode
The steep soft slope between the broad butts of trees.
But, leaving the undisturbed air of the wood
For the rough wind of the roadway, he stopped and went back.
"It will rain," he said. "You ought to think of yourself.
The wind is digging water since we came down.
My father's place is too far. There's an old empty cabin
A short ways on." She had been crouching again
Over the stream to drink, and rose with wet lips
But answered nothing. Vasquez felt inwardly dizzy
For no reason he knew, as if a gray bird
Turned in his breast and flirted half-open wings
Like a wild pigeon bathing. He said, "You'll see it
Above the creek on the right hand of the road
Only a little way north." He turned and rode back,
Hearing her call "Good-by," into the wind on the road.

This man was that Onorio Vasquez
Who used to live on Palo Corona mountain

With his father and his six brothers, but now they lived
Up Mill Creek Canyon beside the abandoned lime-kiln
On land that was not their own. For yearly on this coast
Taxes increase, land grows harder to hold,
Poor people must move their places. Onorio had wealth
Of visions, but those are not coinable. A power in his mind
Was more than equal to the life he was born to,
But fear, or narrowing fortune, had kept it shut
From a larger life; the power wasted itself
In making purposeless visions, himself perceived them
To have no meaning relative to any known thing: but always
They made him different from his brothers; they gave him
A kind of freedom; they were the jewels and value of his life.
So that when once, at a critical time, they failed
And were not seen for a year, he'd hungered to die.
That was nine years ago; his mind was now quieter,
But still it found all its value in visions.
Between them, he hired out his hands to the coast farms,
Or delved the garden at home.

Clare Walker, when he was gone, forgot him at once.
She drank a third draught, then she dropped off her shoes
And washed the dust from her feet. Poor Fern was now hobbling
Among the others, and they'd found vines to feed on
At the near edge of the wood, so that Clare felt
Her shepherdess mind at peace, to throw off
The coat and the rags and bathe in the slender stream,
Flattening herself to find the finger's depth water.
The water and the air were cold now, she rubbed her body
Hastily dry with the bleached rags of her dress
And huddled the cloak about her, but hung the other
Over a branch to dry. Sadly she studied
The broken shoes and found them useless at last,
And flung them into the bushes. An hour later
She resumed the dress, she called her flock to go on
Northward. "Come Fern, come Frannie. Oh, Saul.
Leader and Hoinie and Tiny, we have to go on."

VI

The sky had blackened and the wind raised a dust
When they came up to the road from the closed quiet of the
wood,
The sun was behind the hill but not down yet. Clare passed the
lichen-plated abandoned cabin that Vasquez
Had wished her to use, because there was not a blade of pasture
about it, nothing but the shafted jealousy.
And foodless possession of the great redwoods. She saw the gray
bed of the Little Sur like a dry bone
Through its winter willows, and on the left in the sudden
Sea-opening V of the canyon the sun streaming through a cloud,
the lank striped ocean, and an arched film
Of sand blown from a dune at the stream's foot. The road ahead
went over a bridge and up the bare hill
In lightning zigzags; a small black bead came down the lightning,
flashing at the turns in the strained light,
A motor-car driven fast, Clare urged her flock into the ditch by
the road, but the car turned
This side the bridge and glided down a steep driveway.
When Clare came and looked down she saw the farmhouse
Beside the creek, and a hundred bee-hives and a leafless orchard,
Crossed by the wheeling swords of the sun.
A man with a gray mustache covering his mouth
Stood by the road, Clare felt him stare at the sheep
And stare at her bare feet, though his eyes were hidden
In the dark of his face in the shadow of the turbid light.
She smiled and murmured, "Good evening." He giggled to him-
self
Like a half-witted person and stared at her feet
She passed, in the swirls of light and dust, the old man
Followed and called, "Hey: Missy: where will you sleep?"
"Why, somewhere up there," she answered. He giggled, "Eh,
Eh!
If I were you. Ho," he said joyfully,
"If I were in your *shoes*, I'd look for a roof.
It's big and bare, Serra Hill. You from the south?"

"I've been in the rain before," she answered. She laid
Her hand on a matted fleece. "I've got to find them
Some feeding-place, they're hungry, they've been in the hungry
Redwoods." He stopped and peered and giggled: "One's lame.
But," he said chuckling, "you could go on all night
And never muddy your shoes. Ho, ho! Listen, Missy.
You ain't a Mexican, I guess you've had bad luck.
I'll fix you up in the hay-shed and you'll sleep dry,
These fellows can feed all night." "The owner," she said,
"Wouldn't let me. They'd spoil the hay." "The owner.
Bless you, the poor old man's too busy to notice.
Paying his debts. That was his sharp son
Drove in just now. They hated the old man
But now they come like turkey-buzzards to watch him die."
"Oh! Is he dying?" "Why, fairly comfortable.
As well as you can expect." "I think, we'll go on,"
She murmured faintly. "Just as you like, Missy.
But nobody cares whether you spoil the hay.
There's plenty more in the barn, and all the stock
'll soon be cleared out. I don't work for his boys.
Ho, it's begun already." Some drops were flying, and the sun
Drowned in a cloud, or had set, suddenly the light was twilight.
The old man waved his hand in the wind
Over the hives and the orchard. "This place," he giggled, "meant
    the world to old Warfield: Hey, watch them sell.
It means a shiny new car to each of the boys." He shot up the
    collar of his coat, and the huddling sheep
Tucked in their rumps; the rain on a burst of wind, small drops
    but many. The sheep looked up at their mistress,
Who said, feeling the drift like needles on her cheek, and cold
    drops
Run down by her shoulder, "If nobody minds, you think, about
    our lying in the hay." "Hell no, come in.
Only you'll have to be out in the gray to-morrow, before the
    sharp sons get up." He led her about
By the bridge, through the gapped fence, not to be seen from the
    house.
The hay-shed was well roofed, and walled southward

Against the usual drive of the rain. Clare saw in the twilight
Wealth of fodder and litter, and was glad, and the sheep
Entered and fed.

> After an hour the old man
Returned, with a smell of fried grease in the gray darkness.
Clare rose to meet him, she thought he was bringing food,
But the odor was but a relic of his own supper.
"It's raining," he said; as if she could fail to hear
The hissing drift on the roof; "you'd be cosy now
On Serra Hill." He paused and seemed deeply thoughtful,
And said, "But still you could walk all night and never
Get your shoes wet. Ho, ho! You're a fine girl,
How do you come to be on the road? Eh? Trouble?"
"I'm going north. You're kind," she said, "people are kind."
"Why, yes, I'm a kind man. Well, now, sleep cosy."
He reached into the dark and touched her, she stood
Quietly and felt his hand. A dog was heard barking
Through the hiss of rain. He said, "There's that damn' dog.
I tied him up after I let you in,
Now he'll be yelling all night." The old man stumped off
Into the rain, then Clare went back to her sheep
And burrowed in the hay amongst them.

> The old man returned
A second time; Clare was asleep and she felt
The sheep lifting their heads to stare at his lantern.
"Oh! What do you want?" "Company, company," he muttered.
"They've got an old hatchet-faced nurse in the house . . .
But he's been dying for a month, he makes me nervous.
The boys don't mind, but *I'm* nervous." He kicked
One of the sheep to make it rise and make room,
Clare murmured sadly, "Don't hurt them." He sat in the hay
In heavy silence, holding the lantern on knee
As if it were a fretful baby. The fulvous glimmer
Through one of his hands showed the flesh red, and seemed
To etch the bones in it, the gnarled shafts of the fingers
And scaly lumps in the skin. Clare heard the chained dog howling,

And the rain had ceased. She reached in pitying tenderness
And touched the old man's illuminated hand and said
"How hard you have worked." "Akh," he groaned, "so has he.
And gets . . ." He moved his hand to let the warm light
Lie on her face, so that her face and his own were planets
To the lantern sun; hers smooth except the wind-blistered lips,
    pure-featured, pitying, with large dark eyes
The little sparkles of the reflected lantern had room to swim in;
    his bristly and wrinkled, and the eyes
Like sparks in a bush; the sheep uneasily below the faces moved
    formless, only Saul's watchful head
With the curled horns in the halo of light. The faint and farther
    rays of that sun touched falling spheres
Of water from the eaves at the open side of the shed, or lost
    themselves at the other in cobwebbed corners
And the dust of space. In the darkness beyond all stars the little
    river made a noise. The old man muttered,
"I heard him choking night before last and still he goes on.
It's a hell of a long ways to nothing . . .
You know the best thing to do? Tip this in the straw,"
He tilted the lantern a little, "end in a minute,
In a blaze and yell." She said, "No! no!" and he felt
The hay trembling beside him. The unconscious motion of her
    fear
Was not inward but toward the sheep. He observed
Nothing of that, but giggled to himself to feel
The hay trembling beside him. He dipped his hand
And caught her bare foot; clutching it with his fingers
He scratched the sole with his thumb, but Clare sat quiet
In pale terror of tipping the lantern. The old man
Groaned and stood up. "You wouldn't sit like a stone
If I were twenty years younger. Oh, damn you," he said,
"You think we get old? I'm the same fresh flame of youth still,
Stuck in an old wrinkled filthy rawhide
That soon'll rot and lie choking." She stammered, "Ah, no, no,
You oughtn't to think so. You're well and strong. Or maybe
At last it'll come suddenly or while you sleep,
Never a pain." He swung up the lantern

Before his hairy and age-deformed face. "Look at me. Pfah!
And still it's April inside." He turned to go out,
Clare whispered, "Oh! Wait." She stood wringing her hands,
Warm light and darkness in waves flushing and veiling
Her perplexed face, the lantern in the old man's fist
Swinging beyond his body. "Oh, how can I tell?"
She said trembling. "You see: I'll never come back:
If anything I could do would give you some pleasure;
And you wouldn't be sorry after I'm gone." He turned,
Stamping his feet. "Heh?" He held up the lantern
And stared at her face and giggled. She heard the sheep
Nestling behind her and saw the old man's mouth
Open to speak, a black hole under the grizzled thatch,
And close again on round silence. "I'd like to make you
Happier," she faltered. "Heh?" He seemed to be trembling
Even more than Clare had trembled; he said at length,
"Was you in earnest?" "I had a great trouble,
So that now nothing seems hard . . .
That a shell broke and truly I love all people.
I'll . . . it's a little thing . . . my time is short."
He stood giggling and fidgeting. "Heh, heh? You be good.
I've got to get my sleep. I was just making the rounds.
He makes me nervous, that old man. It's his stomach
Won't hold nothing. You wouldn't play tricks to-night
And the old man puking his last? Now, you lie down.
Sleep cosy," he said. The lantern went slowly winking away,
And she was left among the warm sheep, and thoughts
Of death, and to hear the stream; and again the wind
Raved in the dark.

    She dreamed that a two-legged whiff of flame
Rose up from the house gable-peak crying, "Oh! Oh!"
And doubled in the middle and fled away on the wind
Like music above the bee-hives.

    At dawn a fresh burst of rain
Delayed her, and two of the sheep were coughing. She thought
that no unfriendly person would come in the rain,

And hoped the old man might think to bring her some food, she
    was very hungry. The house-dog that all night long
Had yapped his chain's length, suddenly ran into the shed, then
    Clare leaped up in fear for the sheep, but this
Was a friendly dog, loving to fondle and be fondled, he shook his
    sides like a mill-wheel and remained amongst them.
The rain paused and returned, the sheep fed so contentedly
Clare let them rest all morning in the happy shelter, she dulled her
    own hunger with sleep. About noon
She lifted her long staff from the hay and stood up. "Come Saul,
    come little Hornie,
Fay, Fern and Frannie and Leader, we have to go on.
Tiny, Tiny, get up. Butt and Ben, come on":
These were the two old wethers: and she bade the dog
"Good-by, good-by." He followed however; but at length
Turned back from the crooked road up the open hill
When cold rain fell. Clare was glad of that, yet she wished
She'd had something to give him.

VII

                She gained the blasty hill-top,
The unhappy sheep huddling against her thighs,
And so went northward barefoot in the gray rain,
Abstractedly, like a sleepwalker on the ridge
Of his inner necessity, or like
Some random immortal wish of the solitary hills.
If you had seen her you'd have thought that she always
Walked north in the rain on the ridge with the sheep about her.
Yet sometimes in the need of a little pleasure
To star the gray, she'd stop in the road and kiss
One of the wet foreheads: but then run quickly
A few steps on, as if loitering were dangerous,
You'd have pitied her to see her.

                  Over Mescal Creek
High on the hill, a brook in a rocky gulch, with no canyon,
Light-headed hunger and cold and the loneliness unlocked

Her troubled mind, she talked and sang as she went. "I can't eat
    the cold cress, but if there were acorns,
Bitter acorns. Ai chinita que si,
Ai que tu dami tu amor. Why did you
Have to go dry at the pinch, Frannie? Poor thing, no matter.
    Que venga con migo chinita
A donde vivo yo.
I gave them all my bread, the poor shipwrecked people, and they
    wanted more." She trembled and said, "They're cruel,
But they were hungry. They'll never catch us I think.
Oh, hurry, hurry." With songs learned from the shepherd she
    came to the fall of the road into Mill Creek Canyon.
Two of the sheep were sick and coughing, and Clare looked
    down. Flying bodies of fog, an unending fleet
Of formless gray ships in a file fled down the great canyon
Tearing their keels over the redwoods; Clare watched them and
    sang, "Oh, golondrina, oh, darting swallow,"
And heard the ocean like the blood in her ears. The west-covered
    sun stared a wan light up-canyon
Against the cataract of little clouds.

                    The two coughing sheep
Brought her to a stand; then she opened their mouths and found
Their throats full of barbed seeds from the bad hay
Greedily eaten; and the gums about their teeth
Were quilled with the wicked spikes; which drawn, thin blood
Dripped from the jaw. The folds of the throat her fingers
Could not reach nor relieve; thereafter, when they coughed,
Clare shook with pain. Her pity poisoned her strength.

                    Unhappy shepherdess,
Numbed feet and hands and the face
Turbid with fever:
You love, and that is no unhappy fate.
Not one person but all, does it warm your winter?
Walking with numbed and cut feet
Along the last ridge of migration
On the last coast above the not-to-be-colonized

Ocean, across the streams of the people
Drawing a faint pilgrimage
As if you were drawing a line at the end of the world
Under the columns of ancestral figures:
So many generations in Asia,
So many in Europe, so many in America:
To sum the whole. Poor Clare Walker, she already
Imagines what sum she will cast in April.

                                She came by the farmhouse
At Mill Creek, then she wavered in the road and went to the door,
Leaving her sheep in the road; the day was draining
Toward twilight. Clare began to go around the house,
Then stopped and returned and knocked faintly at the door.
No answer; but when she was turning back to the road
The door was opened, by a pale slight young man
With no more chin than a bird, and Mongol-slanted
Eyes; he peered out, saying, "What do you want?" Clare stood
Wringing the rain from her fingers. "Oh, oh," she stammered,
"I don't know what. I have some sheep with me.
I don't know where we can stay." He stood in the door
And looked afraid. The sheep came stringing down
Through the gate Clare had left open. A gray-eyed man
With a white beard pushed by the boy and said
"What does she want? What, are you hungry? Take out your
      beasts,
We can't have sheep in the yard." Clare ran to the gate,
"Come Leader, come Saul." The old man returned indoors,
Saying, "Wait outside, I'll get you some bread." Clare waited,
Leaning against the gate, it seemed a long while;
The old man came back with changed eyes and changed voice:
"We can't do anything for you. There isn't any bread.
Move on from here." She said through her chattering teeth,
"Come Saul, come Leader, come Frannie. We have to go on.
Poor Fern, come on." They drifted across the Mill Creek bridge
And up the road in the twilight. "The ground-squirrels," she said,
      "hide in their holes

All winter long, and the birds have perches but we have no place."
   They tried to huddle in the heart of a bush
Under a redwood, Clare crouched with the sheep about her, her
   thighs against her belly, her face on her knees,
Not sleeping, but in a twilight consciousness, while the night
   darkened. In an hour she thought she must move or die.
"Ah little Hornie," she said, feeling with shrivelled fingers the
   sprouts of the horns in the small arched forehead,
"Come Fern: are you there, Leader? Come Saul, come Nosie . . .
Ah, no, I was dreaming. Oh, dear," she whispered, "we're very
Miserable now." She crept out of the bush and the sheep fol-
   lowed; she couldn't count them, she heard them
Plunge in the bush and heard them coughing behind her. They
   came on the road
In the gray dark; there, though she'd meant to go north
She went back toward the farmhouse. Crossing the bridge
She smelled oak-smoke and thought of warmth. Grown reckless
Clare entered the farmhouse yard with her fleeced following,
But not daring enough to summon the door
Peered in a window. What she saw within
Mixed with her fever seemed fantastic and dreadful. It was
   nothing strange:
The weak-faced youth, the bearded old man, and two old women
Idle around a lamp on a table. They sat on their chairs in the
   warmth and streaming light and nothing
Moved their faces. But Clare felt dizzy at heart, she thought they
   were waiting for death: how could they sit
And not run and not cry? Perhaps they were dead already? Then,
   the old man's head
Turned, and the youth's fingers drummed on his chair.
One of the blank old women was sewing and the other
Frowned and breathed. She lifted and spoke to white-beard, then
   the first old woman
Flashed eyes like rusty knives and sheathed them again
And sewed the cloth; they grew terribly quiet;
Only the white beard quivered. The young man stood up
And moved his mouth for a good while but no one
Of those in the room regarded him. He sighed and saw

Clare's face at the window. She leaped backward; the lamplight
Had fed her eyes with blindness toward the gray night,
She ran in a panic about the barren garden,
Unable to find the gate; the sheep catching her fear
Huddled and plunged, pricking the empty wet earth with num-
    berless hoof-prints. But no one came out pursuing them,
The doors were not opened, the house was quiet. Clare found
    the gate
And stood by it, whispering, "Dear Tiny. Ah, Fern, that's you.
    Come Saul," she fumbled each head as it passed the gate-post,
To count the flock.

               But all had not passed, a man on a horse
Came plodding the puddled road. Clare thought the world
Was all friendly except in that house, and she ran
To the road's crown. "Oh, Oh," she called; and Onorio
Vasquez answered, "I rode early in the morning
To find you and couldn't find you. I've been north and south.
I thought I could find the track of the sheep." She answered
Through chattering teeth, "I thought I could stand the rain.
I'm sick and the sheep are sick." He said gravely
"There's hardly a man on the coast wouldn't have helped you
Except in that house. There, I think they *need* help.
Well, come and we'll live the night." "How far?" she sighed
Faintly, and he said "Our place is away up-canyon,
You'll find it stiff traveling by daylight even.
To-night's a camp."

              He led her to the bridge, and there
Found dry sticks up the bank, leavings of an old flood, under
    the spring of the timbers,
And made a fire against the creekside under the road for a roof.
    He stripped her of the dripping cloak
And clothed her in his, the oil-skin had kept it dry, and spread her
    the blanket from under his saddle to lie on.
The bridge with the tarred road-bed on it was a roof
Over their heads; the sheep, when Clare commanded them, lay
    down like dogs by the fire. The horse was tethered
To a clump of willow in the night outside.

When her feet and her
hands began to be warm he offered her food,
She ate three ravenous mouthfuls and ran from the fire and
vomited. He heard her gasping in the night thicket
And a new rain. He went after while and dragged her
Back to the frugal fire and shelter of the bridge.

VIII

She lay and looked up at the great black timbers, the flapping fire-
shadows,
And draggled cobwebs heavy with dirt and water;
While Vasquez watched the artery in the lit edge
Of her lean throat jiggle with its jet of blood
Like a slack harp-string plucked: a toneless trembling:
It made him grieve.

After a time she exclaimed
"My sheep. My sheep. Count them." "What," he said, "they all
Are here beside you." "I never dreamed," she answered,
"That any were lost, Oh no! But my sight swam
When I looked at them in the bad light." He looked
And said "Are there not . . . ten?" "No, nine," she answered.
"Nosie has died. Count them and tell me the truth."
He stood, bowing down his head under the timbers,
And counted seven, then hastily the first two
A second time, and said "Nine." "I'm glad of that,"
She sighed, and was quiet, but her quill fingers working
The border of the saddle blanket. He hoped she would soon
Sleep.

The horse tethered outside the firelight
Snorted, and the sheep lifted their heads, a spot of white
Came down the dark slope. Vasquez laid his brown palm
Over Clare's wrists, "Lie still and rest. The old fellow from the
house is coming.
Sleep if you can, I'll talk to him." "Is there a dog?" she whispered
trembling. "No, no, the old man is alone."

Who peered under the heavy stringer of the bridge, his beard
    shone in the firelight. "Here," he shouted, "Hey!
Burn the road, would you? You want to make people stay home
And suck the sour bones in their own houses? Come out of that
    hole." But Vasquez: "Now, easy, old neighbor. She wanted
Fire and a roof, she's found what you wouldn't give." "By God,
    and a man to sleep with," he said, "that's lucky,
But the bridge, the bridge." "Don't trouble, I'm watching the
    fire. Fire's tame, this weather." The old man stood twitching
    and peering,
And heard the sheep coughing in their cave
Under the road. He squinted toward Clare, and muttered at
    length meekly, "Let me stay a few minutes.
To sit by the little road-fire of freedom. My wife and my sister
    have hated each other for thirty years,
And I between them. It makes the air of the house. I sometimes
    think I can see it boil up like smoke
When I look back at the house from the hill above." Vasquez said
    gravely
"I have often watched that." He answered "You haven't lived in
    it. They sit in the house and feed on their own poison
And live forever. I am now too feeble with age to escape." Clare
    Walker lifted her head, and faintly:
"Oh stay," she said, "I wish I could gather all that are unhappy
Before I die. But why do they hate each other?"
"Their nature," he answered, "old women." She sighed and lay
    down.
"I shan't grow old." "Young fellow," the old man said wearily
To Vasquez, "they all make that promise, they never keep it.
Life glides by and the bright loving creatures
Eat us in the evening. I'd have given this girl bread
And meat, but my hawks were watching me." He'd found a stone
On the edge of the creek, the other side of the fire, and squatted
    there, his two fists
Closing his eyes, the beard shimmering between the bent wrists.
    His voice being silent they heard the fire
Burst the tough bark of a wet branch; the wind turned north,
    then a gust of hail spattered in the willows

And checked at once, the air became suddenly cold. The old man
lifted his face: "Ah can't you talk?
I thought you'd be gay or I'd not have stayed here, you too've
grown old? I wish that a Power went through the world
And killed people at thirty when the ashes crust them. You,
cowboy, die, your joints will begin to crackle,
You've had the best. Young bank-clerk, you've had the best,
grow fat and sorry and more dollars? Here farmer, die,
You've spent the money: will you bleed the mortgage
Fifty years more? You, cunning pussy of the world, you've had
the fun and the kissing, skip the diseases.
Oh you, you're an honest wife and you've made a baby: why
should you watch him
Grow up and spoil, and dull like cut lead? I see, my dear, you'll
never be filled till you grow poisonous,
With eyes like rusty knives under the gray eyebrows. God bless
you, die." He had risen from the stone, and trampled,
Each condemnation, some rosy coal fallen out at the fire's edge
Under his foot as if it had been a life. "Sharp at thirty," he said.
    Clare vaguely moaned
And turned her face to the outer darkness, then Vasquez,
Misunderstanding her pain, thinking it stemmed
From the old man's folly: "Don't mind him, he's not in earnest.
These nothing-wishers of life are never in earnest;
Make mouths to scare you: if they meant it they'd do it
And not be alive to make mouths." She made no answer,
But lay and listened to her own rustling pulse-beat,
Her knees drawn up to her breast. White-beard knelt down and
mended the fire,
And brushed his knees. "There's another law that I'd make: to
burn the houses. Turn out the people on the roads,
And neither homes nor old women we'd be well off. All young,
all gay, all moving, free larks and foolery
By gipsy fires." His voice fell sad: "It's bitter to be a reformer:
with two commandments
I'd polish the world a-shining, make the sun ashamed."
Clare Walker stood up, then suddenly sought the dark night
To hide herself in the bushes; her bowels were loosened

With cold and fever. Vasquez half rose to follow her,
And he understood, and stayed by the fire. Then white-beard
Winking and nodding whispered: "Is she a good piece?
Hey, is she sick? I have to protect my son.
Where in hell did she get the sheep?" Vasquez said fiercely,
"You'd better get home, your wife'll be watching for you.
This girl is sick and half starved, I was unwilling
To let her die in the road." The old man stood up
As pricked with a pin at the thought of home. "What? We're
    free men,"
He said, lifting his feet in an anxious dance
About the low fire: "but it's devilish hard
To be the earthly jewel of two jealous women."
"Look," Vasquez said, "it seems to me that your house is afire.
I see rolls of tall smoke . . ." "By God," he answered,
"I wish it were," he trotted up to the road
While a new drift of hail hissed in the willows,
Softening to rain.

                    When he was gone, Vasquez
Repaired the fire, and called "Clare! Come in to shelter.
Clare, come! The rain is dangerous for you. The old fool's gone
    home."
He stumbled in the dark along the strand of the creek,
Calling "Clare, Clare!" then looking backward he saw
The huddle of firelit fleeces moving and rising,
And said "The sheep are scattering away to find you.
You ought to call them." She came then, and stood by the fire.
He heard the bleating cease, and looked back to see her
Quieting her friends, wringing the rain from her hair,
The fire had leaped up to a blaze. Vasquez returned
Under the bridge, then Clare with her lips flushed
And eyes brilliant with fever: "That poor old man, has he gone?
I'm sorry if he's gone.
My father was old, but after he'd plowed the hilltop I've seen
    him ride
The furrows at a dead run, sowing the grain with both hands,
    while he controlled the colt with his knees.

The time it fell at the furrow's end
In the fat clay, he was up first and laughing. He was kind and
cruel." "Your father?" he said. She answered
"I can't remember my mother, she died to bear me, as I . . . We
kept her picture, she looked like me,
And often my father said I was like her.—Oh what's become of the
poor old man, has he gone home?
Here he was happy." "Yes, had to go home," he answered. "But
you must sleep. I'll leave you alone if you like,
You promise to stay by the fire and sleep." "Oh I couldn't, truly.
My mind's throwing all its wrecks on the shore
And I can't sleep. That was a shipwreck that drove us wander-
ing. I remember all things. Your name's Onorio Vasquez:
I wish you had been my brother." He smiled and touched her
cold hand. "For then," she said, "we could talk
Old troubles asleep: I haven't thought, thought,
For a long while, to-night I can't stop my thoughts. But we all
must die?" "Spread out your hands to the fire,
Warm yourself, Clare." "No, no," she answered, her teeth chat-
tering, "I'm hot.
My throat aches, yet you see I don't cough, it was Frannie cough-
ing.—It was almost as if I killed my father,
To swear to the lies I told after he was killed, all to save Charlie.
Do you think he'd care, after . . .
He was surely dead? You don't believe we have spirits? Nobody
believes we have spirits." He began to answer,
And changed his words for caution. "Clare: all you are saying
Is hidden from me. It's like the visions I have,
That go from unknown to unknown." He said proudly,
"I've watched, the whole night of a full moon, an army of
centaurs
Come out of the ocean, plunging on Sovranes reef
In wide splendors of silver water,
And swim with their broad hooves between the reef and the
shore and go up
Over the mountain—I never knew why.
What you are saying is like that." "Oh, I'll tell you . . ." "To-
morrow,"

He pleaded, remembering she'd eaten nothing and seeing
The pulse like a plucked harp-string jiggle in her throat;
He felt like a pain of his own the frail reserves of her body
Burn unreplenished. "Oh, but I'll tell you: so then
You'll know me, as if we'd been born in the same house,
You'll tell me not to be afraid: maybe I'll sleep
At the turn of night. Onorio—that's really your name?
How stately a name you have—lie down beside me.
I am now so changed: every one's lovely in my eyes
Whether he's brown or white or that poor old man:
In those days nobody but Charlie Maurice
Seemed very dear, as if I'd been blind to all the others.
He lived on the next hill, two miles across a deep valley, and then
    it was five to the next neighbor
At Vicente Springs; people are so few there. We lived a long way
    south, where the hills fall straight to the sea,
And higher than these. He lived with his people. We used to meet
    near a madrone-tree, Charlie would kiss me
And put his hands on my breasts under my clothes. It was quite
    long before we learned the sweet way
That brings much joy to most living creatures, but brought us
    misery at last.

IX

    "My father," she said,
"Had lived there for thirty years, but after he sold his cattle
And pastured sheep, to make more money, the neighbors
Were never our friends. Oh, they all feared my father;
Sometimes they threatened our shepherd, a Spanish man
Who looked like you, but was always laughing. He'd laugh
And say 'Guarda a Walker!' so then they'd leave him.
But we lived lonely.

        "One morning of great white clouds gliding
    from the sea,
When I was with Charlie in the hollow near the madrones, I felt
    a pleasure like a sweet fire: for all

My joy before had been in *his* pleasure: but this was my own, it
　　frightened me." She stopped speaking, for Vasquez
Stood up and left her: he went and sat by the fire. Then Clare:
"Why do you leave me, Onorio? Are you angry now?"
"I am afraid," he answered, "of this love.
My visions are the life of my life: if I let the pitcher
Break on the rock and the sun kill the stars,
Life would be emptier than death." Her mind went its own way,
Not understanding so strange a fear: "The clouds were as bright
　　as stars and I could feel them," she said,
"Through the shut lids of my eyes while the sweet fire
Poured through my body: I knew that some dreadful pain would
　　pay for such joy. I never slept after that
But dreamed of a laughing child and wakened with running tears.
　　After I had trembled for days and nights
I asked Tia Livia—that was our shepherd's cousin, she helped me
　　keep house—what sign tells women
When they have conceived: she told me the moon then ceases
To rule our blood. I counted the days then,
Not dreaming that Tia Livia would spy and talk.
Was that not strange? I think that she told the shepherd too,
And the shepherd had warned my lover: for Charlie failed
Our meeting time, but my father was there with a gray face.
In silence, he didn't accuse me, we went home together.

"I met my lover in another place. 'Oh Charlie,
Why do you wear a revolver?' He said the mountain
Was full of rattlers, 'We've killed twenty in a week.
There never have been so many, step carefully sweetheart.'
Sweetheart he called me: you're listening Onorio?
'Step carefully by the loose stones.' We were too frightened that
　　day
To play together the lovely way we had learned.

"The next time that I saw him, he and my father
Met on a bare hilltop against a gray cloud.
I saw him turn back, but then I saw that he was ashamed
To seem afraid of a man on the ridge of earth,

With the hills and the ocean under his feet: and my father called
    him.—What was that moan?" She stopped, and Vasquez
Heard it far off, and heard the sap of a stick whistle in the fire.
    "Nothing," he said, "low thunder
Far out the ocean, or the surf in the creek-mouth." "—I was run-
    ning up the steep slope to reach them, the breath in my heart
Like saw-grass cut me, I had no power to cry out, the stones and
    the broken stubble flaked under my feet
So that I seemed running in one place, unable to go up. It was not
    because he hated my father,
But he was so frightened. They stood as if they were talking, a
    noise of smoke
Blew from between them, my father turned then and walked
Slowly along the cloud and sat on the hilltop
As if he were tired.
I said after a time, without thinking,
'Go home, Charlie. I'll say that he killed himself.
And give me the revolver, I'll say it was his.'
So Charlie did.
But when the men came up from Salinas I told my lie
So badly that they believed I was the murderer.
I smelled the jail a long while. I saw the day moon
Down the long street the morning I was taken to court,
As weary-looking and stained as if it were something of mine.
I remembered then, that since I came there my blood
Had never been moved when the moon filled: what Livia'd told
    me.
So then I told them my father took his own life
Because the sheep had a sickness and I was pregnant.
The shepherd and Livia swore that they saw him do it.
I'd have been let home:
But the fever I'd caught gathered to a bursting pain,
I had to be carried from the courthouse to the hospital
And for a time knew nothing.
When I began to see with my eyes again
The doctor said: 'The influenza that takes
Many lives has saved yours, you'll not have a child.
Listen,' he said, 'my girl, if you're wise.

Your miscarriage is your luck. Your pelvis—the bones down there
Are so deformed that it's not possible for you
To bear a living baby: no life can pass there:
And yours would be lost. You'd better remember,
And try not to be reckless.' I remember so well, Onorio.
I have good reason to remember. You never could guess
What a good reason.

My little king was dead
And I was too weak to care. I have a new king.

"When I got home," she said patiently,
"Everybody believed that I was a murderer;
And Charlie was gone. They left me so much alone
That often I myself believed it. I'd lead the sheep to that hill,
There were fifty left out of three hundred,
And pray for pardon."

Sleep and her fever confused her brain,
One heard phrases in the running babble, across a new burst of
    hail. "Forgive me, father, for I didn't
Know what I was doing." And, "Why have you forsaken me,
    father?" Her mind was living again the bare south hilltop
And the bitter penitence among the sheep. "The two men that
    I loved and the baby that I never saw,
All taken away."

Then Vasquez was calling her name to break
    the black memories; she turned on her side, the flame-light
Leaped, and he saw her face puckering with puzzled wonder. "Not
    all alone? But how can that be?"
She sighed and said, "Oh Leader, don't stray for a while. Dear
    Saul: can you keep them here on the hill around me
Without my watching? No one else helps me. I'll lie down here
    on the little grass in the windy sun
And think whether I can live. I have *you*, dear stragglers.
    Thoughts come and go back as lightly as deer on the hill,
But as hard to catch . . . Not *all* alone. Oh.

Not alone at *all*.
Indeed it is even stranger than I thought."

She laughed and sat up.
"Oh sweet warm sun . . .
Are you there, Onorio? But where's the poor old man
Who seemed to be so unhappy? I wish he hadn't gone home,
For now I remember what I ought to tell him. I'm sadly changed
Since that trouble and sickness, and though I'm happy
I hardly ever remember in the nick o' time
What ought to be said. You must tell him
That all our pain comes from restraint of love."
The hail had suddenly hushed, and all her words
Were clear but hurried. "I learned it easily, Onorio,
And never have thought about it again till now. The only
    wonder's
Not to've known always. The beetle beside my hand in the grass
    and the little brown bird tilted on a stone,
The short sad grass, burnt on the gable of the world with near
    sun and all winds: there was nothing there that I didn't
Love with my heart, yes the hill though drunk with dear blood:
    I looked far over the valley at the patch of oaks
At the head of a field, where Charlie's people had lived (they had
    moved away) and loved them, although they'd been
Always unfriendly I never thought of it." Then Vasquez, for the
    first time forgetting the person a moment
To regard the idea: "You were cut off from the natural objects
    of love, you turned toward others." "Ah," she answered
Eagerly, "I'd always been turned to all others,
And tired my poor strength confining the joy to few. But now
    I'd no more reason to confine it, I'd nothing
Left to lose nor keep back.—Has the poor old man gone?
He seemed to be truly unhappy.
Wasn't he afraid we'd burn the bridge; we ought surely
To have drowned our fire. I was sick, or I'd have done . . .
    anything.
But old men are so strange, to want and not want,
And then be angry."

"He has gone," he answered.
"Now, Clare, if you could eat something, then sleep,
To fill the cup for to-morrow."
"I have to tell you the rest.—Why did he go?
Was he angry at me?—Oh, I feel better, Onorio,
But never more open-eyed.

          "There was one of those great owly hawks
That soar for hours, turning and turning below me along the
    bottom of the slope: I so loved it
I thought if it were hungry I'd give it my hand for meat.

          "Then winter came.
Then about Christmas time (because I'd counted the months and
    remembered Christmas) storm followed storm
Like frightened horses tethered to a tree, around and around.
    Three men came in the door without knocking,
Wherever they moved, water and black oil ran down. There'd
    been a shipwreck. I gave them the house, then one of them
Found the axe and began chopping firewood, another went back
    across wild rain to the fall of the hill
And shouted. He was so big, like a barrel walking, I ran in his
    shelter
And saw the great, black, masted thing almost on shore, lying on
    its side in the shadow of the hill,
And the flying steam of a fire they'd built on the beach. All that
    morning the people came up like ants,
Poor souls they were all so tired and cold, some hurt and some
    crying. I'd only," she said, "a few handfuls of flour
Left in the house." She trembled and lay down. "I can't remem-
    ber any more."

          Vasquez made up the fire,
And went and drew up the blanket over Clare's shoulder.
He found her shuddering. "Now sleep. Now rest." She answered:
"They killed a sheep. They were hungry.
I'd grown to love so much the flock that was left.

Our shepherd, I think, had taken them away mostly
While I was kept in Salinas.
I heard her crying when they threw her down, she thought I
    could save her.
Her soft white throat.

'That night I crept out in the thin rain at moonrise
And led them so far away, all that were left,
The house and the barn might hold a hundred hungry mouths
To hunt us all night and day and could never find us.
We hid in oak-woods. There was nothing to eat,
And never any dry place. We walked in the gray rain in the flow-
    ing gorges of canyons that no one
But the hawks have seen, and climbed wet stone and saw the
    storms racing below us, but still the thin rain
Sifted through the air as if it fell from the stars. I was then much
    stronger
Than ever since then.

                        "A man caught me at last, when I was too
    weak to run, and conquered my fear.
He was kind, he promised me not to hurt the poor flock,
But the half of them had been lost, I never could remember how.
He lived alone; I was sick in his cabin
For many days, dreaming that a monkey nursed me: he looked
    so funny, he'd a frill of red hair
All around his face.

                        "When I grew better, he wanted to do like
    Charlie. I knew what the doctor had said,
But I was ashamed to speak of death: I was often ashamed in
    those days: he'd been so kind. Yet terror
Would come and cover my head like a cold wave.
I watched the moon, but at the full moon my fear
Flowed quietly away in the night.

"The spring and summer were full of pleasure and happiness.
I'd no more fear of my friend, but we met seldom. I went in
    freedom
From mountain to mountain, wherever good pasture grew,
Watching the creeks grow quiet and color themselves
With cool green moss, and the green hills turn white.
The people at the few farms all knew me, and now
Their minds changed; they were kind. All the deer knew me;
They'd walk in my flock.

                    "In the midst of summer,
When the moon filled my blood failed to be moved,
The life that will make death began in my body.
I'd seen that moon when it was little as a chip
Over my left shoulder, from Palos ridge
By a purple cloud.

                           X
            "Oh, not till April," she said.
"All's quiet now, the bitterness is past, I have made peace
With death except in my dreams, those can't be ruled. But then,
    when I first
Began to believe and knew it had happened . . . I felt badly.
    I went back to my father's house,
Much was broken and chopped down, but I found
Little things that I'd loved when I was a child, hidden in corners.
    When I was drunk with crying
We hurried away. The lambs never seemed able to live, the
    mothers were glad to give me their milk,
We hid in the secret hills till it seemed desolate to die there.—
    Tell me, Onorio,
What month is this?"

                           He answered, "Clare, Clare, fear nothing.
Death is as far away from you as from any one.
There was a girl (I've heard my brothers talking:
The road-overseer's daughter) was four or five months along
And went to a doctor: she had no trouble:

She's like a virgin again." Clare struck the earth with her hands
And raised her body, she stared through the red of the fire
With brilliant confused eyes. "Your face was like a devil's in the
steamy glimmer:
But only because you don't understand. Why, Tia Livia herself
. . . you are too innocent, Onorio,
Has done so . . . but women often have small round stones
Instead of hearts." "But," he answered, "if you're not able to
bear it. Not even a priest would bid you die
For a child that couldn't be born alive. You've lived too much
alone, bodiless fears have become
Giants in secret. I too am not able to think clearly tonight, in
the stinging drift of the fire
And the strange place, to-morrow I'll tell you plainly. My mind
is confused
As I have sometimes felt it before the clouds of the world
Were opened: but I know: for disease to refuse cure
Is self-murder, not virtue." She squatted upright,
Wrapping the coat about her shoulders and knees,
And said, "Have you never seen in your visions
The golden country that our souls came from,
Before we looked at the moon and stars and knew
They are not perfect? We came from a purer peace
In a more perfect heaven; where there was nothing
But calm delight, no cold, no sickness, no sharp hail,
The haven of neither hunger nor sorrow,
But all-enfolding love and unchangeable joy
Near the heart of life." Vasquez turned from the fire
And stared at her lit face. "How did you learn
This wonder? It is true." "I remembered it,"
She answered, "when I was in trouble." "This is the bitter-sweet
memory,"
He said, "that makes the breast of the earth bitter
After we are born and the dear sun ridiculous. We shall return
there, we homesick."
"No," she answered. "The place was my mother's body before
I was born. You may remember it a little but I've

Remembered plainly: and the wailing pain of entering this air.
I've thought and thought and remembered. I found
A cave in a high cliff of white stone, when I was hiding from
people: it was there I had the first memory.
There I'd have stayed in the safe darkness forever; the sheep
were hungry and strayed out, so I couldn't stay.
I remembered again when I went home to our house and the
door hung crazy
On a snapped hinge. You don't believe me, Onorio,
But after while you'll remember plainly, if some long trouble
Makes you want peace; or being handled has broken your shame.
I have no shame now." He answered nothing
Because she seemed to speak from a frantic mind.
After a moment, "No matter," she said. "When I was in my worst
trouble
I knew that the child was feeding on peace and happiness. I had
happiness here in my body. It is not mine,
But I am its world and the sky around it, its loving God. It is
having the prime and perfect of life,
The nine months that are better than the ninety years. I'd not
steal one of its days to save my life.
I am like its God, how could I betray it? It has not moved yet
But feels its blessedness in its quietness; but soon I shall feel it
move, Tia Livia said it will nestle
Down the warm nest and flutter like a winged creature. It shook
her body, she said." But Vasquez, loathing
To hear these things, labored with the sick fire
In the steam of the wet wood, not listening, then Clare
Sighed and lay down. He heard her in a moment
Miserably sobbing, he went and touched her. "What is it?
Clare? Clare?" "Ai, when will morning come?
It is horrible to lie still," she said, "feeling
The black of April . . . it's nothing, it's nothing . . . like a cat
Tick tick on padded feet. Ah let me alone, will you?
Lying quiet does it: I'll have courage in my time."

A little later she asked for food, she ate,
And drank from the stream, and slept. She moved in her sleep

And tossed her arms, Vasquez would cover them again,
But the fever seemed quieted. He crossed the stream by the
stones in the dull fire-glimmer
And fetched armfuls of flood-wood from under the opposite
bridge-head. The fire revived; the earth turned past mid-
night;
Far eastward beyond the coasts of the continent morning troubled
the Atlantic.

XI

Vasquez crouched by the fire
And felt one of those revelations that were in his own regard
the jewels and value of his life
Approach and begin. First passed—as always
Since Barclay was gone, whom he had taken for incarnate God
—ancestral forms against the white cloud,
The high dark heads of Indian migrations, going south along the
coast, drawn down from the hungry straits and from Asia,
The heads like worn coins and the high shoulders,
The brown-lipped patient mouths below vulture beaks, and bur-
nished fall of black hair over slant foreheads,
Going up to the Mayan and the Aztec mountains, and sowing
the coast. They swept the way and the cloud cleared,
The vision would come: came instead a strong pause.
                                        A part of his mind
Wished to remember what the rest had forgotten,
And groping for it in the dark withstood the prepared
Pageant of dreams. He'd read in his curious boyhood
Of the child the mother is found incapable of bearing
Cut from the mother's belly. Both live: the wound
Heals: it was called the Cæsarean section. But he, fearing
Whatever thought might threaten to infringe his careful
Chastity of mind, had quickly canceled the memory;
That now sought a new birth; it might save Clare
If he could think of it.

THE LOVING SHEPHERDESS

That revived part
Made itself into the vision, all to no purpose,
His precious dreams were never to the point of life.
Only the imperial name, and the world's
Two-thousand-year and ten-thousand-miles-traveled
Cæsarean memory appeared. He imagined at first that the voice
Cried "Ave Maria," but it cried "Ave Cæsar."

He saw the firelight-gilded
Timbers of the bridge above; and one of the ewes lifted her head
      in the light beside Clare sleeping;
The smoke gathered its cloud into a floating globe and these were
      forgotten. On the globe of the earth
The aquiline-headed Roman, who summed in his one person the
      powers and ordered science of humanity,
Stood and possessed his orb of empire, and looked at the stars.
      Then the voice cried
"The pride of the earth."

But Vasquez laughed aloud, for the
      earth was a grain of dust circling the fire,
And the fire itself but a spark, among innumerable sparks. The
      swarm of the points of light drifting
No path down darkness merged its pin-prick eyelets into one
      misty glimmer, a millstone in shape,
A coin in shape, a mere coin, a flipped luckpenny: but again
      Vasquez
Laughed out, for who was the spendthrift sowed them all over
      the sky, indistinguishable innumerable
Fish-scales of light? They drew together as they drifted away
      no path down the wild darkness; he saw
The webs of their rays made them one tissue, their rays that
      were their very substance and power filled wholly
The space they were in, so that each one touched all, there was
      no division between them, no emptiness, and each
Changed substance with all the others and became the others.
      It was dreadful to see

No space between them, no cave of peace nor no night of quiet-
    ness, no blind spot nor no deaf heart, but the tides
Of power and substance flood every cranny; no annihilation, no
    escape but change: it must endure itself
Forever. It has the strength to endure itself. We others, being
    faintly made of the dust of a grain of dust
Have been permitted to fool our patience asleep by inventing
    death. A poor comfort, he thought,
Yet better than none, the imaginary cavern, how we all come
    clamoring
To the gates of our great invention after few years.
Though a cheat, it works.

　　　　　　　　　The speckled tissue of universes
Drew into one formed and rounded light, and Vasquez
Worshiped the one light. One eye . . . what, an eye?
A dark mountain with an eye in its cliff? A coal-black stallion
Eyed with one burning eye in the mid brow?
Night has an eye. The poor little vision-seer
Groaned, that he never had wit to understand visions.
See all and know nothing. The eye that makes its own light
And sees nothing but itself. "I am seeing Barclay again,"
He marveled, as who should say "I am seeing God:
But what is God?" He continued gazing,
And beads of sweat spilled from his forehead into the fire-edge
Ashes. He saw at last, neither the eyed mountain
Nor the stallion, nor Barclay, but his own eye
In the darkness of his own face.

　　　　　　　　　The circuit was closed:
"I can endure all things," he thought, "forever. I am he
Whom I have sought.

　　　　　　　　　"And Clare loves all things
Because all things are herself. She has killed her father
And inherited. Her old enormous father
Who rode the furrows full tilt, sowing with both hands

The high field above the hills and the ocean. We kill steers for
   meat, and God
To be atoned with him. But I remain from myself divided, gazing
   beyond the flaming walls,
Not fortunate enough, and too faint-hearted."

                                                    He continued gaz-
   ing across the wane of the fire at the dark
Vision of his own face turned sideways, the light of one eye.
   Clare turned in her place and awoke and said,
"How awfully little. Ooh, Ooh," in a dove's voice,
And then, "I forgot I wasn't alone, Onorio:
And here are the sheep. Have I slept a moment?
I did have a strange dream. I went out across the starlight
Knocking through flight after flight of the shiny balls
And got so far away that the sun and the great earth
And beautiful moon and all the stars were blended
Into one tiny light, Oh terribly little,
The flame of a pitiful little candle blown over
In the wind of darkness, in the fear of the night. It was so tiny
I wanted to be its comfort
And hold it and rock it on my breast. One wee flicker
In all the wild dark. What a dream." She turned anxiously
To touch the sheep, fondling their heads and naming them.
"Dear Fay, dear Fern. And here's Captain Saul. Ah bad little
   Hornie
Who taught you to be so bold?" Suddenly she cried
"Did Leader and Frannie go out—did two of the sheep
Go out lately?" But Vasquez, caught in his vision,
Answered "You also have broken
The fire-studded egg of heaven and we're together
In the world outside." "Ah Ah," she cried desolately,
"Did you lie when you counted them? When I was sick
And my eyes failed?" She ran into the darkness outside, calling
   their names;
The flock that remained stood up, in the edge of firelight, tremu-
   lously crying. Then Vasquez: "I hear a multitude

Of people crying, but why do you lament and cry? You particles
    of the eye of light, if some of you
Endure evil, the others endure good, the balance is perfect. The
    eye lives on mixed light and darkness,
Not either alone. And you are not many but one, the eye is not
    glad nor sorry, nor the dark face
Disquieted: be quiet, voices, and hear the real voice." Clare
    Walker came in from the dark with wide strained eyes,
In each iris the fire reflected made a red stain, and she cried:
"Onorio, for Christ's sake tell me, were they not with me?
Or have they slipped out?" He turned slowly an unanswering
    face
Of cool, dark and deaf stone, tempered to the mood
Of what he imagined . . . or perhaps perceived. And Clare:
"If I have slept and been dreaming while they're in danger
Or die in the dark: and they cried for me
In the dead night, while I slept and ate: I hope that all the
    miseries I ever feared for myself
Will come doubled, the rain on my hair be knives of ice, the sun
    whips of fire, the death I must die
Drawn out and dreadful like the dream of hell: Onorio, Oh come,
Help me to find them!" He rose, passively under command in
    the shrill of her voice, muttering: "I can't
Imagine what further's to find: yet I'll go along.
Is there another light or another darkness?"
"Oh," she answered, "it's black," and snatched the most eager
    brands
Out of the fire for a torch. He with deft fingers
Mimicking her act, but with a sleepwalker mindlessness,
Bound fire into a bundle of sallow twigs,
And calmly, twirling his torch to flame, followed
The red glow of her rod-ends. They ran on the bridge and
    wandered
Up the wet road, Clare calling her flock around her
And sobbing the names of the lost. The useless torches
Flared in the puddles and ruts of water, and ruddied
The plump backs of the sheep; so sanguine-outlined
The little ridiculous procession strayed up the road

In the lane of the trees, the great-trunked wood like storms
Of darkness on either hand. The torches died soon,
Then Clare stood still, desolately calling; weak dawn
Had washed all the world gray.

                       The heads of the little flock
Suddenly and all together were turned one way, then a limping
    ewe
Came out of the wood. Clare screamed with joy, and ran and
    dropped on her knees to embrace the lean neck. "Oh Leader!
Leader! She's safe, Onorio. Oh Leader where's Frannie?" But
    then the wound was discovered, the flap torn back
Red from the flank and hanging from the rump, and the blood-
    caked wool. Clare moaned awhile with no words, and said,
"When I forgot you because I was sick, when I forgot to call
    you and count you in the rain in the night:
I wish I had died. I have nothing but these,
Onorio, to take care of, and lose and lose. She used to go first
    always, I called her Leader:
And now she's hurt." Onorio heard Clare's teeth clacking to-
    gether in the thin cheeks, and her breath
Hissing between them, he answered calmly, still caught in his
    vision: "The five claws of a lion. Look, Clare.
But don't grieve, the great river of the blood of life is always
    bursting its banks, never runs dry,
Secret inexhaustible fountains feed it." She stared at his face and
    turned on the forest her desert eyes
And wrung her hands. "Leader is hurt; and Frannie I think has
    died."

             They searched long; the fourth hour
Of daylight they found the half consumed body. The head was
    not mangled, Clare fell beside it
On the wet earth and kissed the half open eyes,
Weeping and self-reproachful, but yet she lamented
Less violently than Vasquez had feared. At length
He said, "If you wish, Clare, I will fetch tools
And bury it here." She answered faintly, "No matter.

She feels nothing to-day, darkness nor light,
Teeth nor the grave. Oh, I loved her well: but now, see,
She's not living any more, Onorio . . . isn't that your name?
What a stately name! . . . this is the one that fed me with milk
Long after the others were dry, she was like a mother to me,
    when I might have starved.
She loved me, I know.
But even the udders are torn. Her name, Onorio, was Frannie."
She turned and said, "Poor Leader. Can you come now?
Come Fern, come Fay, come Tiny, we have to go on.
Come Saul."

       Vasquez begged her to turn again
And stay at his father's place in the canyon
Until she was well. She had to go on, she answered.
And Vasquez: "My father is withered up with old age but he'd
    be kind; and my brothers
Would be your brothers. There's pasture for the sheep. We're
    only a sort of Indians but we can be kind. Come, Clare.
The place is pleasant and alone, up the deep canyon, beside the
    old quarry and the kilns where they burnt the lime.
A hundred laborers used to live there, but now the woods have
    grown back, the cabins are standing empty,
The roads are gone. I think the old masonry kilns are beautiful,
    standing like towers in the deep forest,
But cracked and leaning, and maidenhair fern grows from the
    cracks. The creek makes music below. Come, Clare.
It is deep with peace. When I have to go about and work on
    men's farms for wages I long for that place
Like some one thinking of water in deserts. Sometimes we hear
    the sea's thunder, far down the deep gorge.
The darkness under the trees in spring is starry with flowers,
    with redwood sorrel, colt's foot, wakerobin,
The slender-stemmed pale yellow violets,
And Solomon's seal that makes intense islands of fragrance in
    April." "Oh, April," she said trembling,
"How exactly it follows. How could I rest? Ah, no,

Good-by, good-by, Onorio. Poor Leader, I am sure
We can go a little way before dark. Come, Saul, Saul."
She ran a few steps, panting hard.
                    Vasquez perceived
No hope of staying her: "Then I'll go back to the bridge
And fetch my horse and my coat. I'll not leave you, Clare."
He went slowly, heavy and amazed. His horse
Had broken tether in the night, stung by the hailstones.
Then Vasquez, still drunken with the dregs of his vision
To fatalist indifference, went hunting the horse
And found it late. He followed Clare the next morning,
But met another vision on the road, that waved
Impatient white hands against his passage, saying
"If I go up to Calvary ten million times: what is that to you?
Let me go up." Vasquez drew rein and sat staring.
He saw beyond the vision in the yellow mud
Prints of bare feet, dibbled about with many
Little crowding hoof-marks; he marveled, feeling no sadness
But lonely thoughts.

XII

                Clare Walker had crossed the ridge and
   gone down
To the mouth of Cawdor's Canyon. Japanese tenants
Now kept the house; short broad-faced men who planted
Lettuces in the garden against the creek-side
And beans on the hill. The barns were vacant, the cattle
Were vanished from the high pastures. The men were friendly,
Clare begged at their hands a little oil to soften
The bandage on Leader's wound; she'd torn her spent dress
In strips to bind it, and went now without clothing
But the long brown cloak.

                She went northward, and on a foreland
Found vacant cabins around a ruined saw-mill;
And finding sacks of dry straw with a worn blanket
In one of the cabins, slept well and awoke refreshed

To travel on slowly northward in the glad sunlight
And sparkle of the sea. But the next day was dark,
And one of the wethers died, she never knew why,
She wept and went on.

                    Near Point Lobos, by a gate
Where Tamar Cauldwell used to lean from her white pony
To swing the bars, the lion-stricken ewe, Leader,
Groaned and lay down and died. Clare met much kindness there;
She was nursed in the house, helpless, for many days,
And the sheep were guarded and fed. The people clothed her
And calmed her wild mind; but she was not willing to tell them
Her griefs nor her cause of fear. They kept her by watchful
     force
Until she escaped, a great night of moonlight, and fled
With her small flock.

                    Far up the Carmel Valley
The river became a brook, she watched a salmon
Row its worn body up-stream over the stones
And struck by a thwart current expose the bruised
White belly to the white of the sky, gashed with red wounds,
     but right itself
And wriggle up-stream, having that within it, spirit or desire,
Will spend all its dear flesh and all the power it has gathered, in
     the sweet salt pastures and fostering ocean,
To find the appointed high-place and perish. Clare Walker, in
     a bright moment's passage of anxious feeling,
Knowing nothing of its fate saw her own fate reflected. She
     drank, and the sheep drank; they went up the valley
And crossed, the next day, among the long-needled pines, the
     great thirsty sky-ridge.
                    In the valley beyond
Clare journeyed northward again, anxiously avoiding
The traveled roads and hiding herself from people
In fear that some one's force or kindness might steal her
From the helpless flock; and later in habitual fear.

THE LOVING SHEPHERDESS

She was seen much later, heavily swollen
Toward child-birth, cowering from a thin April rain
By a little fire on the San Joaquin river-bank,
Sharing a camp of outcast men; no sheep
Remained with her, but when she moved in the morning
She called the names of many, Fern, Fay and Leader,
Nosie and Saul and little Hornie and the others,
"Dear Tiny, dear Frannie, come on, we have to go on."
The toothless tramp bandaging his foot by the fire
Looked up with a flicker of light in his slack face,
And the sickly sullen boy on the other side
Smiled without mockery. Clare had gone half a mile
And felt a grinding pang in her back, she clung to the fence
And saw the poplars planted along the road
Reach dreadfully away northward. When the pain ended
She went on northward; but after the second pain
She crept down to the river and hid her body
In a willow thicket. In the evening, between the rapid
Summits of agony before exhaustion, she called
The sheep about her and perceived that none came.

THE BROKEN BALANCE

I · REFERENCE TO A PASSAGE IN PLUTARCH'S LIFE OF SULLA

The people buying and selling, consuming pleasures, talking in
the archways,
Were all suddenly struck quiet
And ran from under stone to look up at the sky: so shrill and
mournful,
So fierce and final, a brazen
Pealing of trumpets high up in the air, in the summer blue over
Tuscany.
They marveled; the soothsayers answered:
"Although the Gods are little troubled toward men, at the end
of each period
A sign is declared in heaven
Indicating new times, new customs, a changed people; the Romans
Rule, and Etruria is finished;
A wise mariner will trim the sails to the wind."

                          I heard yesterday
So shrill and mournful a trumpet-blast,
It was hard to be wise. . . . You must eat change and endure;
not be much troubled
For the people; they will have their happiness.
When the republic grows too heavy to endure, then Cæsar will
carry it;
When life grows hateful, there's power . . .

II · TO THE CHILDREN

Power's good; life is not always good but power's good.
So you must think when abundance
Makes pawns of people and all the loaves are one dough.
The steep singleness of passion
Dies; they will say, "What was that?" but the power triumphs.

THE BROKEN BALANCE

Loveliness will live under glass
And beauty will go savage in the secret mountains.
There is beauty in power also.
You children must widen your minds' eyes to take mountains
Instead of faces, and millions
Instead of persons; not to hate life; and massed power
After the lone hawk's dead.

III

That light blood-loving weasel, a tongue of yellow
Fire licking the sides of the gray stones,
Has a more passionate and more pure heart
In the snake-slender flanks than man can imagine;
But he is betrayed by his own courage,
The man who kills him is like a cloud hiding a star.

Then praise the jewel-eyed hawk and the tall blue heron;
The black cormorants that fatten their sea-rock
With shining slime; even that ruiner of anthills
The red-shafted woodpecker flying,
A white star between blood-color wing-clouds,
Across the glades of the wood and the green lakes of shade.

These live their felt natures; they know their norm
And live it to the brim; they understand life.
While men moulding themselves to the anthill have choked
Their natures until the souls die in them;
They have sold themselves for toys and protection:
No, but consider awhile: what else? Men sold for toys.

Uneasy and fractional people, having no center
But in the eyes and mouths that surround them,
Having no function but to serve and support
Civilization, the enemy of man,
No wonder they live insanely, and desire
With their tongues, progress; with their eyes, pleasure; with
    their hearts, death.

Their ancestors were good hunters, good herdsmen and swords-
    men,
But now the world is turned upside down;
The good do evil, the hope's in criminals; in vice
That dissolves the cities and war to destroy them.
Through wars and corruptions the house will fall.
Mourn whom it falls on. Be glad: the house is mined, it will
    fall.

IV

Rain, hail and brutal sun, the plow in the roots,
The pitiless pruning-iron in the branches,
Strengthen the vines, they are all feeding friends
Or powerless foes until the grapes purple.
But when you have ripened your berries it is time to begin to
    perish.

The world sickens with change, rain becomes poison,
The earth is a pit, it is time to perish.
The vines are fey, the very kindness of nature
Corrupts what her cruelty before strengthened.
When you stand on the peak of time it is time to begin to perish.

Reach down the long morbid roots that forget the plow,
Discover the depths; let the long pale tendrils
Spend all to discover the sky, now nothing is good
But only the steel mirrors of discovery . . .
And the beautiful enormous dawns of time, after we perish.

V

Mourning the broken balance, the hopeless prostration of the
    earth
Under men's hands and their minds,
The beautiful places killed like rabbits to make a city,
The spreading fungus, the slime-threads
And spores; my own coast's obscene future: I remember the
    farther
Future, and the last man dying

Without succession under the confident eyes of the stars.
It was only a moment's accident,
The race that plagued us; the world resumes the old lonely im-
mortal
Splendor; from here I can even
Perceive that that snuffed candle had something . . . a fantastic
virtue,
A faint and unshapely pathos . . .
So death will flatter them at last: what, even the bald ape's by-
shot
Was moderately admirable?

VI · PALINODE

All summer neither rain nor wave washes the cormorants'
Perch, and their droppings have painted it shining white.
If the excrement of fish-eaters makes the brown rock a snow-
mountain
At noon, a rose in the morning, a beacon at moonrise
On the black water: it is barely possible that even men's present
Lives are something; their arts and sciences (by moonlight)
Not wholly ridiculous, nor their cities merely an offense.

VII

Under my windows, between the road and the sea-cliff, bitter
wild grass
Stands narrowed between the people and the storm.
The ocean winter after winter gnaws at its earth, the wheels
and the feet
Summer after summer encroach and destroy.
Stubborn green life, for the cliff-eater I cannot comfort you,
ignorant which color,
Gray-blue or pale-green, will please the late stars;
But laugh at the other, your seed shall enjoy wonderful venge-
ances and suck
The arteries and walk in triumph on the faces.

BIRTH-DUES

Joy is a trick in the air; pleasure is merely contemptible, the
    dangled
Carrot the ass follows to market or precipice;
But limitary pain—the rock under the tower and the hewn
    coping
That takes thunder at the head of the turret—
Terrible and real. Therefore a mindless dervish carving himself
With knives will seem to have conquered the world.

The world's God is treacherous and full of unreason; a torturer,
    but also
The only foundation and the only fountain.
Who fights him eats his own flesh and perishes of hunger; who
    hides in the grave
To escape him is dead; who enters the Indian
Recession to escape him is dead; who falls in love with the God
    is washed clean
Of death desired and of death dreaded.

He has joy, but joy is a trick in the air; and pleasure, but pleasure
    is contemptible;
And peace; and is based on solider than pain.
He has broken boundaries a little and that will estrange him;
    he is monstrous, but not
To the measure of the God. . . . But I having told you—
However I suppose that few in the world have energy to hear
    effectively—
Have paid my birth-dues; am quits with the people.

EVENING EBB

The ocean has not been so quiet for a long while; five night-
     herons
Fly shorelong voiceless in the hush of the air
Over the calm of an ebb that almost mirrors their wings.
The sun has gone down, and the water has gone down
From the weed-clad rock, but the distant cloud-wall rises. The
     ebb whispers.
Great cloud-shadows float in the opal water.
Through rifts in the screen of the world pale gold gleams, and the
     evening
Star suddenly glides like a flying torch.
As if we had not been meant to see her; rehearsing behind
The screen of the world for another audience.

HANDS

Inside a cave in a narrow canyon near Tassajara
The vault of rock is painted with hands,
A multitude of hands in the twilight, a cloud of men's palms, no
    more,
No other picture. There's no one to say
Whether the brown shy quiet people who are dead intended
Religion or magic, or made their tracings
In the idleness of art; but over the division of years these careful
Signs-manual are now like a sealed message
Saying: "Look: we also were human; we had hands, not paws.
    All hail
You people with the cleverer hands, our supplanters
In the beautiful country; enjoy her a season, her beauty, and
    come down
And be supplanted; for you also are human."

HOODED NIGHT

At night, toward dawn, all the lights of the shore have died,
And the wind moves. Moves in the dark
The sleeping power of the ocean, no more beastlike than man-
   like,
Not to be compared; itself and itself.
Its breath blown shoreward huddles the world with a fog; no
   stars
Dance in heaven; no ship's light glances.
I see the heavy granite bodies of the rocks of the headland,
That were ancient here before Egypt had pyramids,
Bulk on the gray of the sky, and beyond them the jets of young
   trees
I planted the year of the Versailles peace.
But here is the final unridiculous peace. Before the first man
Here were the stones, the ocean, the cypresses,
And the pallid region in the stone-rough dome of fog where the
   moon
Falls on the west. Here is reality.
The other is a spectral episode: after the inquisitive animal's
Amusements are quiet: the dark glory.

THURSO'S LANDING

The coast-road was being straightened and repaired again,
A group of men labored at the steep curve
Where it falls from the north to Mill Creek. They scattered and
   hid
Behind cut banks, except one blond young man
Who stooped over the rock and strolled away smiling
As if he shared a secret joke with the dynamite;
It waited until he had passed back of a boulder,
Then split its rock cage; a yellowish torrent
Of fragments rose up the air and the echoes bumped
From mountain to mountain. The men returned slowly
And took up their dropped tools, while a banner of dust
Waved over the gorge on the northwest wind, very high
Above the heads of the forest.
                    Some distance west of the road,
On the promontory above the triangle
Of glittering ocean that fills the gorge-mouth,
A woman and a lame man from the farm below
Had been watching, and turned to go down the hill. The young
   woman looked back,
Widening her violet eyes under the shade of her hand. "I think
   they'll blast again in a minute."
And the man: "I wish they'd let the poor old road be. I don't
   like improvements." "Why not?" "They bring in the world;
We're well without it." His lameness gave him some look of age
   but he was young too; tall and thin-faced,
With a high wavering nose. "Isn't he amusing," she said, "that
   boy Rick Armstrong, the dynamite man,
How slowly he walks away after he lights the fuse. He loves to
   show off. Reave likes him, too,"
She added; and they clambered down the path in the rock-face,
   little dark specks
Between the great headland rock and the bright blue sea.

11

The road-workers had made their camp
North of this headland, where the sea-cliff was broken down and
    sloped to a cove. The violet-eyed woman's husband,
Reave Thurso, rode down the slope to the camp in the gorgeous
    autumn sundown, his hired man Johnny Luna
Riding behind him. The road-men had just quit work and four
    or five were bathing in the purple surf-edge,
The others talked by the tents; blue smoke fragrant with food
    and oak-wood drifted from the cabin stove-pipe
And slowly went fainting up the vast hill.
                                    Thurso drew rein by
    a group of men at a tent door
And frowned at them without speaking, square-shouldered and
    heavy-jawed, too heavy with strength for so young a man,
He chose one of the men with his eyes. "You're Danny Wood-
    ruff, aren't you, that drives the tractor?" Who smiled
And answered "Maybe. What then?" "Why, nothing, except you
    broke my fence and you've got to fix it." "You don't say,"
He said laughing. "Did somebody break your fence? Well, that's
    too bad." "My man here saw you do it.
He warned you out of the field." "Oh, was I warned?" He turned
    to Luna: "What did I say to you, cowboy?"
"You say, you say," Luna's dark face flushed black, "you say
    'Go to hell.'" Woodruff gravely, to Thurso:
"That's what I say." The farmer had a whip in his hand, a hot-
    ter man might have struck, but he carefully
Hung it on the saddle-horn by the thong at the butt, dismounted,
    and said, "You'll fix it though." He was somewhat
Short-coupled, but so broad in the chest and throat, and ob-
    viously all oak, that Woodruff recoiled a step,
Saying "If you've got a claim for damages, take it to the county."
    "I'm taking it nearer hand.
You'll fix the fence." Woodruff's companions
Began to come in between, and one said "Wait for him
Until he fixes it, your cows will be down the road."
Thurso shook his head slightly and bored forward

267

Toward his one object; who felt the persecuting
Pale eyes under dark brows dazzle resistance.
He was glad the bathers came up the shore, to ask
What the dispute was, their presence released his mind
A moment from the obstinate eyes. The blithe young firer
Of dynamite blasts, Rick Armstrong, came in foremost,
Naked and very beautiful, all his blond body
Gleaming from the sea; he'd been one or two evenings
A guest at the farmhouse, and now took Thurso's part
So gracefully that the tractor-driver, already
Unnerved by that leaden doggedness, was glad to yield.
He'd mend the fence in the morning: Oh, sure, he wanted
To do the right thing: but Thurso's manner
Had put him off.

        The group dissolved apart, having made for
   a moment its unconscious beauty
In the vast landscape above the ocean in the colored evening;
   the naked bodies of the young bathers
Polished with light, against the brown and blue denim core of
   the rest; and the ponies, one brown, one piebald,
Compacted into the group, the Spanish-Indian horseman dark
   bronze above them, under broad red
Heavens leaning to the lonely mountain.

III

In the moonlight two hours before Sunday dawn
Rick Armstrong went on foot over the hill
Toward the farmhouse in the deep gorge, where it was dark,
And he smelled the stream. Thurso had invited him
To go deer-hunting with them, seeing lights in the house
He hurried down, not to make his friends wait.
He passed under a lonely noise in the sky
And wondered at it, and remembered the great cable
That spanned the gorge from the hill, with a rusted iron skip
Hanging from it like a stuck black moon; relics,
With other engines on the headland, of ancient lime-kilns
High up the canyon, from which they shot the lime
To the promontory along the airy cable-way

To be shipped by sea. The works had failed; the iron skip
Stuck on its rusted pulleys would never move again
Until it fell, but to make a desolate creaking
In the mountain east-wind that poured down the gorge
Every clear night. He looked for it and could not find it
Against the white sky, but stumbled over a root
And hurried down to the house.

There were layered smells of
   horses and leather
About the porch; the door stood half open, in the yellow slot
Of lamplight appeared two faces, Johnny Luna's dark hollow
   Egyptian profile and Helen Thurso's
Very white beyond, her wide-parted violet eyes looked black
   and her lips moved. Her husband's wide chest
Eclipsed the doorway. "Here you are. I was afraid you wouldn't
   wake up. Come in," Thurso said,
"Coffee and bacon, it will be long to lunch." A fourth in the
   room was the lame man, Reave Thurso's brother,
Who said at parting, "Take care of Helen, won't you, Reave,
Don't tire her out." He was not of the party but had risen to see
   them off. She answered from the porch, laughing,
The light from the door gilding her cheek, "I'll not be the tired
   one, Mark, by evening. Pity the others."
"Let the men do the shooting, Helen, spare yourself. Killing's
   against your nature, it would hurt with unhappy thought
Some later time." "Ah," she answered, "not so gentle as you
   think. Good-bye, brother."
They mounted the drooping horses and rode up canyon
Between black trees, under that lonely creaking in the sky, and
   turned southward
Along the coast-road to enter a darker canyon.
The horses jerked at the bridle-hands,
Nosing out a way for the stammering hooves
Along the rocks of a ribbed creek-bed; thence a path upward
To the height of a ridge; in that clear the red moonset
Appeared between murky hills, like a burning ship
On the world's verge.

Thurso and Luna stealthily dismounted.

They stole two ways down the starry-glimmering slope like
    assassins, above the black fur of forest, and vanished
In the shifty gray. The two others remained, Armstrong looked
    wistfully
Toward his companion through the high reddish gloom, and
    saw the swell of her breast and droop of her throat
Darkling against the low moon-scarred west. She whispered and
    said, "The poor thing may drive up hill toward us:
And I'll not fire, do you want to trade rifles with me? The old
    one that Reave has lent you is little use."
He answered, "I guess one gun's as good as another, you can't
    see the bead, you can't see the notch." "Oh: well.
The light will grow." They were silent a time, sitting and hold-
    ing the horses, the red moon on the sea-line
Suddenly foundered; still the east had nothing.

                      "We'd better take ourselves
Out of the sky, and tie up the horses." She began to move, down
    the way lately climbed, the cowboy's
Pony trailing behind her, Armstrong led Reave's. He saw her
    white shirt below him gleam in the starlight
Like bare shoulders above the shadow. They unbridled the horses
    and tethered them to buckthorn bushes, and went back
Into the sky; but lay close against the ridge to be hidden, for a
    cloud whitened. Orion and Sirius
Stood southward in the mid heaven, and Armstrong said,
"They're strange at dawn, see, they're not autumn stars,
They belong to last March." "Maybe next March," she answered
Without looking. "Tell me how you've charmed Reave
To make him love you? He never has cared for a friend before,
Cold and lonely by nature. He seems to love you."
"Why: nothing. If he lacks friends perhaps it's only
Because this country has been too vacant for him
To make choices from." "No," she answered, "he's cold,
And all alone in himself. Well. His goodness is strength.
He's never set his mind on anything yet
But got it with a strong hand. His brother, you met this morning,
Is very different, a weak man of course,

But kindly and full of pity toward every creature, but really at
   heart
As cold as Reave. I never loved hunting, and he's
Persuaded me to hate it. Let him persuade
Reave if he could!" Armstrong said, "Why did you come then?"
"Ah? To watch things be killed."

                    They heard the wind
Flustering below, and felt the sallow increase of clearness
On grass-blades, and the girl's face, and the far sea,
A light of visions, faint and a virgin. One rifle-shot
Snapped the still dawn; Armstrong cradled his gun
But nothing came up the hill. The cloud-line eastward
Suddenly flushed with rose-color flame, and standing
Rays of transparent purple shadow appeared
Behind the fired fleece. Helen Thurso sighed and stood up,
"Let's see if we can't lead one of the horses down,
Now light has come, to bring up the corpse." "The . . . fo.
   what?"
"The meat," she said impatiently, "the killed thing. It's a hard
   climb."
"You think they got it?" "Couldn't fail; but other years
They've taken two in that trap." Nearly straight down,
At the edge of the wood, in the pool of blue shade in the cleft
   hill,
The two men were seen, one burdened, like mites in a bowl; and
   Helen with a kind of triumph: "Look down there:
What size Reave Thurso is really: one of those little dirty black
   ants that come to dead things could carry him
With the deer added."

                  They drove a horse down the headlong
   pitch; the sun came up like a man shouting
While they climbed back, then Helen halted for breath. Thurso
   tightened the lashings under the saddle,
That held his booty on the pony's back, and said to Armstrong,
   "That tree that stands alone on the spur,

It looks like a match: its trunk's twenty feet through. The biggest
   redwoods left on the coast are there,
The lumbermen couldn't reach them."
                                   Johnny Luna, when they
   reached the ridge,
Was sent home leading his horse, with the buck mounted. The
   others rode east, the two men ahead, and Helen
Regarding their heads and shoulders against the sharp sky or
   the sides of hills; they left the redwood canyons
And rode a long while among interminable gray ranges bushed
   on the north with oak and lupin;
Farther they wandered among flayed bison-shaped hills, and rode
   at noon under sparse bull-pines,
And so returned, having seen no life at all
Except high up the sun the black vultures,
Some hawks hunting the gorges, and a far coyote.
In the afternoon, nearing toward home, it was Helen
Who saw five deer strung on a ridge. "Oh. Look.
So I've betrayed them," she said bitterly. Reave said to Arm-
   strong,
"Your shot: the buck to the north," and while he spoke fired, but
   the other
Had raised his cheek from the rifle-stock to look
At Helen angrily laughing, her face brilliant
In the hard sunlight, with lakes of deep shade
Under the brows and the chin; when he looked back
The ridge was cleared. "Why didn't you let him have it?
You'd such an easy shot," Thurso said,
"Against the cloud, mine was among the bushes,
I saw him fall and roll over." "Be very happy,"
Helen said. "He was hard hit, for he ran down hill.
That makes you shine."
                       They labored across the gorge
And climbed up to the ridge. A spongy scarlet thing
Was found at the foot of a green oak-bush and Helen
Came and saw it. "He was hit in the lung," Reave said,
"Coughed up a froth of blood and ran down hill.

I have to get him." "It looks like a red toadstool:
Red scum on rotten wood. Does it make you sick?
Not a bit: it makes you happy." "Why do you come hunting,
Helen,
If you hate hunting? Keep still at least. As for being happy:
Look where I have to go down." He showed her the foamy spots
of blood, on the earth and the small leaves,
Going down a steep thicket that seemed impassable. She an-
swered, "Let the poor thing die in peace." "It would seem
a pity,"
He answered, "to let him suffer; besides the waste." Armstrong
looked down and said, "He'll be in the creek-bed.
I'll go down there and work up the gulch, if you go down here."
"You'd never find him without the blood-trail,"
Reave answered. Then Helen suddenly went back and touched
the foam of blood on the ground, dipping four fingers,
And returned and said, "I was afraid to do it, so I did it. Now
I'm no better than you. Don't go down.
Please, Reave. Let's hurry and go home. I'm tired." Reave said
to Armstrong, "That would be best, if you'd take her home.
It's only a mile and a half, help her with the horses, won't you?
Take mine too. I'll hang the buck in a tree
Near where I find him, and come fetch him to-morrow." "If you
want," Armstrong said. Helen clenched
Her blood-tipped fingers and felt them stick to the palm. "All
right. I'll do
What you've chosen," she said with smoothed lips. "Mark wins,
he said I'd be tired. But he was wrong,"
Opening her hand, regarding the red-lined nails,
"To think me all milk and kindness." Thurso went down
The thicket; and Helen: "Nothing could turn him back.
He's never set his mind on anything yet
But snuffled like a bloodhound to the bitter end." They heard
the branches
Breaking below, and returned by the open slope
To the horses across the creek.

They rode softly
Down the canyon; Helen said, "I'm not tired.
Do you ever think about death? I've seen you play with it,
Strolling away while the fuse fizzed in the rock."
"Hell no, that was all settled when they made the hills."
"Did you notice how high he held his bright head
And the branched horns, keen with happiness?
Nothing told him
That all would break in a moment and the blood choke his throat.
I hope that poor stag
Had many loves in his life." He looked curiously,
A little moved, at her face; too pale, like a white flame
That has form but no brilliance in the light of day;
The wide violet eyes hollowed with points of craving darkness
Under the long dark lashes; and the charcoal mark
Across her slightly hollowed cheek, where a twig had crossed it
When they rode the burnt hillside. He said: "I ought
To've gone with Reave, it doesn't seem fair to let him
Sweat alone in that jungle." "He *enjoys* toil.
You don't know him yet. Give him a blood-trail to follow,
That's all he wants for Christmas. What he's got's nothing to
    him,
His game's the getting. But slow, slow: be hours yet.
From here we can choose ways, and though it's a good deal
    longer,
There's daylight left, we'll go by the head of the hill: up there
    you can see the whole coast
And a thousand hills. Look," she said laughing,
"What the crooked bushes have done," showing her light shirt
Torn at the breast, and a long red scratch
Under the bright smooth breast. He felt in his mind
A moving dizziness, and shifted his body backward
From the saddle-horn.

A curl of sea-cloud stood on the head of the hill
Like a wave breaking against the wind; but when they reached
    it, windows of clearness in it were passing

From the northwest, through which the mountain sea-wall looked
    abrupt as dreams, from Lobos like a hand on the sea
To the offshore giant at Point Sur southward. Straight down
    through the coursing mists like a crack in the mountain sea-
    root,
Mill Creek Canyon, like a crack in the naked root of a dead pine
    when the bark peels off. The bottom
Of the fissure was black with redwood, and lower
Green with alders; between the black and the green the painted
    roof of the farmhouse, like a dropped seed,
Thurso's house, like a grain of corn in the crack of a plank, where
    the hens can't reach it.

                      Cloud steered between;
Helen Thurso said "What if the rut is a rock canyon,
Look how I'm stuck in a rut: do I have to live there?
And Reave's old mother's like a white-headed hawk.
Your job here's nearly finished, where will you go?"
"I haven't thought: all places are like each other:
Maybe Nevada in the spring.
There's work all over." "I," she said, trembling; "it seems cold
    up here.
I hate the sea-fog. Now let's look east." They had tied
The horses to the highest bushes on the north slope,
And walked on the open dome of the hill, they crossed it
And the east was clear; the beautiful desolate inhuman range
    beyond range of summits all seen at once,
Dry bright and quiet and their huge blue shadows. Helen said
    faintly,
"He's down there somewhere. It's that deer's blood.
It made me drunk, it was too red I thought.
Life is so tiny little, and if it shoots
Into the darkness without ever once flashing?"
They turned back to the dome-top under the cloud.
"You're tired, Helen." "I'll not let the days of my life
Hang like a string of naughts between two nothings.
Wear a necklace of round zeros for pearls;

I'm not made that way. Think what you please. Shall we go down
    now?"
"The cloud has come all around us," he answered, seeing the dis-
    tilled drops of the cloud like seed-pearls
Hung in her hair and on the dark lashes. He turned to go down
    to the horses, she said "I have seen dawn with you,
The red moonset and white dawn,
And starlight on the mountain, and noon on burnt hills where
    there was no shadow but a vulture's, and that stag's blood:
    I've lived with you
A long day like a lifetime, at last I've drawn something
In the string of blanks." She lifted her face against his shoulder
    and said "Good-bye." He said "I'm Reave's friend,"
And kissed her good-bye seeing she desired it, her breasts bur-
    rowed against him and friendship forgot his mind,
With such brief wooing they stirred the deep wells of pleasure.

                She lay but half quieted, still hotly longing,
Her eyes morbidly shuttered like the sleep of fever showed
    threads of the white and faint arcs of the crystalline
Violet irises, barred across by the strong dark lashes; the night
    of the lids covered the pupils,
Behind them, and under the thick brown hair and under the
    cunning sutures of the hollow bone the nerve-cells
With locking fibrils made their own world and light, the multi-
    tude of small rayed animals of one descent.
That make one mind, imagined a mountain
Higher than the scope of nature, predominant over all these edges
    of the earth, on its head a sacrifice
Half naked, all flaming, her hair blown like a fire through the
    level skies; for she had to believe this passion
Not the wild heat of nature, but the superstitiously worshipped
    spirit of love, that is thought to burn
All its acts righteous.

While Helen adorned the deed with the
dream it needed, her lover meanwhile
Explored with hands and eyes the moulded smoothness through
the open clothing, reviving his spent desire
Until they were joined in longer-lasting delight; her nerve-cells
intermitted their human dream;
The happy automatism of life, inhuman as the sucking heart of
the whirlwind, usurped the whole person,
Aping pain, crying out and writhing like torture.

They rose and
went down to the horses;
The light had changed in the sea-cloud, the sun must be near
setting. When they were halfway down the mountain
The whole cloud began to glow with color like a huge rose, a
forest of transparent pale crimson petals
Blowing all about them; slowly the glory
Flared up the slope and faded in the high air.

IV

They rode
through pale twilight
And whispered at the farmhouse door inarticulate leave-takings.
Helen went in; Armstrong unsaddled the horses
And walked heavily up canyon and crossed the hill.

Helen said, "Reave went after a wounded deer
And sent me home. He hasn't come home yet?"
Reave's mother said "We've not seen him," steadily watching her
Across the lamplight with eyes like an old hawk's,
Red-brown and indomitable, and tired. But if she was hawk-like
As Helen fancied, it was not in the snatching look
But the alienation and tamelessness and sullied splendor
Of a crippled hawk in a cage. She was worn at fifty
To thin old age; the attritions of time and toil and arthritis
That wear old women to likeness had whetted this one
To difference, as if they had bitten on a bronze hawk
Under the eroded flesh.

Helen avoided her eyes
And said to the other in the room, "Ah, Mark, you guessed right.
I'm tired to death, must creep up to bed now." The old woman:
"So you came home alone? That young Armstrong
Stayed with Reave." Helen faltered an instant and said,
"No, for Reave sent him with me, wishing his horse
To be taken home. Mr. Armstrong stopped
By the corral, he was unsaddling the horses I think,
But I was too tired to help him. My rifle, Mark,
Is clean: I minded your words."

An hour later the heavy tread
of a man was heard on the steps
And the fall of a fleshy bulk by the door, crossed by the click of
hooves or antlers, and Reave came in,
His shirt blood-stained on the breast and shoulders. "I got him,"
he said. "It seemed for awhile I'd be out all night.
By luck I found him, at twilight in a buckeye bush. Where's
Helen, gone to bed?" "She seemed flurried with thoughts,"
His mother answered, and going to the door that led to the
kitchen she called, "Olvidia,"
Bring in the supper." "Well, yes," Reave said. "I must first hang
up the carcass and wash my hands." "Olvidia,"
His mother called to the kitchen, "will you tell Johnny: is Johnny
there? Tell him to fetch the meat
From the door-step and hang it up with the other." Mark said,
"How far, Reave, did you carry it?" "Two miles or so.
Rough country at first; I held it in front of me to butt the brush
with." "Why, what does it weigh?" "Oh," he said, "a young
buck.
About Helen's weight." "You are strong," his mother said, "that's
good: but a fool." "Well, mother, I might have hung it
In a tree and gone up with a horse to-morrow; I shouldered it
to save time."

Mark, enviously:
"You've seen many green canyons and the clouds on a hundred
hills.

278

My mind has better mountains than these in it,
And bloodless ones." The dark Spanish-Indian woman
Olvidia took Reave's empty plate and the dish,
And Mrs. Thurso said, "Reave, you've big arms,
And ribs like a rain-barrel, what do they amount to
If the mind inside is a baby? Our white-face bull's
Bigger and wiser." "What have I done?" "I'll never say
Your young Helen's worth keeping, but while you have her
Don't turn her out to pasture on the mountain
With the yellow-haired young man. Those heavy blue eyes
Came home all enriched." Reave laughed and Mark said bitterly,
   "Mother, that's mean.
You know her too well for that. Helen is as clear as the crystal
   sky, don't breathe on her." "You," she answered fondly.
Reave smiled, "I trust Rick Armstrong as I do my own hand."
   "It shames my time of life,"
She answered, "to have milky-new sons. What has he done for
   you
To be your angel?" "Why," he said, "I like him." "That's gen-
   erous,
And rare in you. How old is he?" "My age. Twenty-four."
"Oh, that's a better reason to trust him." "Hm?" "You're the
   same age."
"That's no reason." "No," she answered.

v

                       Toward noon the next day
Helen was ironing linen by the kitchen stove,
A gun-shot was heard quite near the house, she dropped the iron
And ran outdoors and met Mark. "What was that shot?" "Don't
   go up there, Helen." "Why not, why not," she stammered,
"Why not," the flush of the stove-heat graying on her cheek.
   "Reave has put poor old Bones out of pain." "Oh, that!"
Laughing and trembling, "Your funeral face. I thought some-
   thing had happened to someone. Let the old dog sleep."
She went up hill to the screen of seawind-stunted laurel and oak,
   where Reave was already spading

279

Dust into the gape of a small grave. "You've done for poor old
  Bones, have you? You knew I loved him,
So you took him off." "A pity you came just now, Helen. He
  died in a moment. If we'd used this mercy
Two or three months ago we'd have saved pain." She answered,
  quivering with anger, "You do it on the sly
And call it mercy. Ah, killing's your pleasure, your secret vice."
  "I'll wish you sunnier pleasures: and a little
Sense in your head: he was made of miseries: you've seen him
  plead
To be helped, and wonder at us when the pain stayed.
I've helped him now." "Will you do as much for yourself
When life dirties and darkens? Your father did."
"No, I will not," he said, shovelling the dust.
"What's that said for? For spite?" "No, Reave.
I was wondering. For I think it's reasonable.
When the flower and fruit are gone, nothing but sour rind,
Why suck the shell? I think your father was right."
"Drop a little silence on him," Reave answered.
"We may help out the beasts, but a man mustn't be beaten.
That was a little too easy, to pop himself off because he went
  broke.
I was ten years old, I tried not to despise the soft stuff
That ran away to the dark from a touch of trouble:
Because the lime-kilns failed and the lumber mill
Ran out of redwood.
My mother took up his ruins and made a farm;
She wouldn't run away, to death or charity. Mark and I helped.
We lost most of the land but we saved enough."
"Think of one man owning so many canyons:
Sovranes, Granite," she counted on her fingers, "Garapatas, Palo
  Colorado,
Rocky Creek, and this Mill Creek." "Oh, that was nothing, the
  land was worth nothing
In those days, only for lime and redwood." She answered,
"You needn't despise him, Reave. *My* dad never owned any-
  thing.
While I worked in a laundry and while I crated fruit

He ate my wages and lived as long as he could
And died crying." "We're proud of our fathers, hm?
Well, he was sick a long time," Reave said, patting
The back of the spade on the filled grave; "but courage might
    live
While the lungs rot. I think it might. You never
Saw him again, did you?" "How saw him?" "We used to see
    mine
Often in the evenings." "What do you mean, Reave?"
    "Why: in the evenings.
Coming back to stare at his unfinished things.
Mother still often sees him." Helen's face brightening
With happy interest, "Oh where?" she said. "On the paths;
Looking up at that thing, with his mouth open."
Reave waved his hand toward the great brown iron skip
Hanging on its cable in the canyon sky,
That used to carry the lime from the hill, but now
Stuck on dead pulleys in the sky. "It ought to be taken down
Before it falls. I'll do it when we've done the plowing."
Helen said, "Does he ever speak?" "Too ashamed of himself.
    I spoke to him once:
I was carrying firewood into the house, my arms were full. He
    worked a smile on his face and pointed
At the trolley up there." "Do you really believe," she said, "that
    your father's ghost?" "Certainly not. Some stain
Stagnates here in the hollow canyon air, or sticks in our minds.
    How could too weak to live
Show after it died?" "I knew," she answered, blanching again
    with capricious anger, "you'd no mercy in you,
But only sudden judgment for any weak thing;
And neither loving nor passionate; dull, cold and scornful. I used
    to keep a gay heart in my worst days
And laugh a little: how can I live
Where nothing except poor Mark is even half human, you like
    a stone, hard and joyless, dark inside,
And your mother like an old hawk, and even dirty Olvidia and
    Johnny Luna, dark and hollow

As the hearts of jugs. The dog here in the ground—Oh but how
    carefully you scrape the blood-lake—
Had loving brown eyes: so you killed him: he was sometimes
    joyful: it wouldn't do. You killed him for that." He an-
    swered,
Staring, "Were you born a fool? What's the matter, Helen?"
    "If I had to stay here
I'd turn stone too: cold and dark: I'd give a dollar
For a mirror now, and show you that square face of yours
Taken to pieces with amazement: you never guessed
Helen's a shrew. Oh, what do you want her for?
Let her go." She left him; and when he came in at noon
Spoke meekly, she seemed to have wept.

V I

                               In the evening, in
    Helen's presence,
Reave's mother said, "Did that sand-haired young man
Find you, Reave, when he came this afternoon?
He didn't come to the house." "Who?" "That road-worker,
Arnfield." "Rick Armstrong?" "Most likely: the one I warned
    you
Not to pasture your heifer with." "He was here?" "No,
Not here. I saw him come down the hill, and Helen
Went out to meet him." Mark Thurso looked up
From the book he'd been reading, and watched his mother
As a pigeon on a rock watches a falcon quartering
The field beyond the next fence; but Helen suddenly:
"Now listen, Mark. I'm to be framed, ah?
I think so. I never liked her." The old woman said,
"Did you say something?" "Not yet," she answered. Reave made
    a mocking
Noise in his throat and said, "Let them alone.
No peace between women.
This morning I sent Luna over the hill
With one of the bucks we killed, no doubt my friend came over
At quitting-time to say thank-you: why he didn't find me's
Less clear, but watch the women build it between them

282

To a big darkness." "Not I," Helen said,
And dipped her needle two or three careful stitches
In the cloth she was mending, then looked up suddenly
To see who watched her. "If I'd seen him," she said, "I'd have
    spoken to him.
I am not sick with jealousy of your new friend. But he was
    probably not here; the old eyes that make
A dead man's phantom can imagine a live one's." The old woman:
    "When you saw him you ran to meet him; I sent Olvidia
To see if the speckled hen had stolen a nest in the willows. She
    walked down there, what she saw amazed her.
I've not allowed her to tell me though she bubbles with it. Your
    business, Reave: ask her. Not mine: I'm only
The slow man's mother." Helen stood up, trembling a little and
    smiling, she held the needle and the spool
And folded the cloth, saying "Your mother, Reave,
Loves you well: too well: you and I honor her for that. She has
    hated me from the day she heard of me,
But that was jealousy, the shadow that shows love's real: nothing
    to resent. But now you seem very friendly
With that young man too: she can't bear to yield you again, it
    cracks the string of her mind. No one can fancy
What she's plotted with the kitchen woman . . ." Mark Thurso
    said with lips that suddenly whitened: "*I* met Armstrong.
I told him you'd ridden up the high pasture, for so I believed.
    He asked me to thank you warmly
For the buck you sent: I forgot to tell you. I was with him while
    he was here, and when he went back I hobbled
Some ways up hill." The old woman moved her lips but said
    nothing; but Reave: "Here: what's the matter,
Brother? You were with me constantly all afternoon." "But an
    hour," Mark said. "Hm? Five minutes." Then Helen,
Looking from the one to the other: "If I am hated, I think I am
    loved too. I'd something to say . . .
Oh: yes: will you promise, Reave, promise Olvidia
You'll give her, for telling the perfect truth, whatever your
    mother has promised her for telling lies: then I'm safe.

Call her and ask her." He answered, "She'll sleep in hell first.
Here's enough stories
Without hers in the egg-basket. Do you think it was Armstrong
you saw, mother? I trust Rick Armstrong
From the bright point to the handle." Helen said, "Ah, Mark,
You'd never imagine I'd be satisfied with that.
I have to be satisfied with that." "Why not?" Reave said.
And she: "If it was nothing worse than killing to fear
I'd confess. All kinds of lies. I fear you so much
I'd confess . . . all kinds of lies . . . to get it over with,"
She said, making a clicking noise in her throat
Like one who has drunk too much and hiccoughs, "only
To get it over with: only, I haven't done anything.
This terror, Mark, has no reason,
Reave never struck nor threatened me, yet well I know
That while I've lived here I've always been sick with fear
As that woman is with jealousy. Deep in me, a black lake
His eyes drill to, it spurts. Sometime he'll drill to my heart
And that's the nut of courage hidden in the lake.
Then we'll see. I don't mean anything bad, you know: I'm very
innocent,
And wish to think high, like Mark. Olvidia of course is a hollow
liar. May I go now? I'm trembling-tired:
If you'll allow me to go up to bed? But indeed I dare not
While you sit judging." She looked at Mark and slightly
Reached both her hands toward him, smiled and went out.
But in the little dark hallway under the stair,
When she hastened through it in the sudden darkness,
The door being neither open nor shut passed edgewise
Between her two groping hands, her cheek and brow
Struck hard on the edge.

                  Her moan was heard in the room of
    lamplight;
Where they had been sitting silent while she went out,
And when she had gone Mark Thurso had said, "Mother:
You've done an infamous thing." "They might play Jack and
queen

All they please," she answered, "but not my son
For the fool card in the deck," the shock of struck wood was
    heard,
And Helen's hushed groan: Mark, dragging his lameness, reeled
Swiftly across the room saying "What has she done?"
He groped in the passage and spoke tenderly, then Reave
Went and brought Helen to the lamplight; a little blood
Ran through her left eye to her lips from the cut eyebrow.
The implacable old woman said "She's not hurt.
Will you make a fuss?" Helen said, "The wood of your house
Is like your mother, Reave, hits in the dark.
This will wash off." She went to the kitchen and met
Olvidia who'd been listening against the door,
Then Helen, moaning "I'm ringed with my enemies," turned
To flee, and turned back. "I will take it now. My husband, Olvidia,
Is ready to kill me, you see. I have been kind to you
Two or three times. Have you seen any unusual
Or wicked meeting to-day?" The Indian woman,
Dreading Reave's anger and seeing the blood, but hardly
Understanding the words, blanked her dark face
And wagged her head. "Don't know. What you mean, wicked?
I better keep out of this." "A dish of water, Olvidia.
Be near me, Mark. Reave: will you ask her now?"
He said "Wash and be quiet." Helen said, "Oh Olvidia,
Someone has made him angry at you and me.
Look in my eyes. Tell no bad stories . . . lies, that is . . .
Did you see anything when you looked for eggs
In the willows along the creek?" Olvidia folded
Her lips together and stepped backward, then Helen
Sighed, dabbling her cheek with water. "It hurts. I think
It will turn black." Reave suddenly shouted "Answer."
Olvidia, retreating farther: "What you want of me?
I find no eggs." Mark said, "Come, Helen, Oh come. I've watched
    innocence tormented
And can no more. Go up and sleep if you can, I'll speak for you,
    to-morrow all this black cloud of wrong
Will be melted quite away in the morning." Reave said, "Don't
    fawn on her, you make me mad. Women will do it.

But why praise 'em for it?" Helen, meekly: "I am very tired and
   helpless and driven to the edge. Think kindly of me,
Mark, I believe I shall be much hated. Your mother . . .
This is all. Light me a candle." At the foot of the stair
She closed the door, and silently tip-toed through
The passage and the other room to the door of the house,
There pinched the wick, and praying for no wind
To make a stir in the house, carefully opened
The outer door and latched it behind her.

                          She traversed the hill,
And at the road-men's camp, plucking at the fly
Of a lit tent, thought momently it was curious
She stood among so many unrestrained men
Without fear, yet feared Reave. "I must see Rick Armstrong
This moment: which tent?" They laid their hands of cards
Carefully face down on the packing-box.
"Why, ma'am, I can't say exactly," but she had run off
To another lamp of shining canvas and found him.
"Let me stand into the light." She showed her cut brow
A little bleeding again with hurry in the dark,
And the purpling bruise. "What Reave did. Your friend Reave.
His mother spied and told on us. What will you do?"
"By God!" "Oh," she said, "that's no good.
How could you keep me *here*? Borrow a car,
There are cars here." He said "I'll take care of you." She
   shuddered,
Beating her fists together, breathed long and said:
"If you choose to stand here and talk among the men listening
It is not my fault. I say if you and these men could stop him when
   he comes—
You can't—to-night, to-night, in an hour—nothing can stop him:
   he'd call the sheriff to-morrow and have me
Like a stolen cow, nothing but ridiculous, a mark for children to
   hoot at, crying in my hair, probably
Led on a rope. Don't you know him? *I* do. Oh my lover
Take me to the worst hut at the world's end and kill me there,
   but take me from here before Reave comes.

I'd go so gladly. And how could you bear to face him, he thought
    you his faithful friend, for shame even?
Oh hurry, hurry!"

VII

          In the desert at the foot of sun-rotted hills
A row of wooden cabins flanks a gaunt building
Squatted on marbly terraces of its own excrement,
Digested rock from which the metal has been sucked,
Drying in the rage of the sun. Reave Thurso stopped
At the first cabin, a woman came out and pointed;
He went to the farthest cabin, knocked, and went in.
"Well, Helen. You found a real sunny place." Opening the door
She'd been a violet-eyed girl, a little slatternly
But rich with life; she stood back from the door
Sallow, with pinched nostrils and dwindled eyes,
As if she had lost a fountain of blood, and faintly
Whispering "I knew you." Reave looked about him like one
Attentively learning the place, and Helen said
"I never hoped that you wouldn't come at last,
It seemed a kind of blood-trail for you to follow.
And then I knew you were tardy and cold of course and at last
You'd come at last, you never give up anything,
How did you track us at last?" "Oh," he laughed, "Time and I.
He's at work?" "Yes." "If you wanted to hide
You'd have got him to change his name." "I begged him to," she
    answered,
Suddenly weeping, "so many times." "Don't cry, don't cry.
You know that I'll never hurt you. Mark loves you too, he's been
    very lonely. He wanted me to let you go,
But that was nonsense. He's been sick since you went away. Do
    you remember the rose-bush you made me buy
That time in Salinas? Mark's watered it for you, sick or well,
Every day, limping around the house with a pail of water spilling
    on his poor ankle-joint,
He'll be glad to see you again. Well, pack your things." She
    gathered

Her blanked face to some show of life. "Look around at this
    country. Oh Reave. Reave. Look. I let him
Take me here at last. And he hasn't been always perfectly kind:
    but since I've been living with him I love him . . .
My heart would break if I tried to tell you how much. I'm not
    ashamed. There was something in me that didn't
Know about love until I was living with him. I kissed him, when
    he went back to work this noon.
I didn't know you were coming; forgot you were coming some-
    time. See how it is. No: I understand:
You won't take me." He, astonished: "Not take you? After hunt-
    ing you a whole year? You dream too much, Helen.
It makes you lovely in a way, but it clouds your mind. You must
    distinguish. All this misfortune of yours
Probably . . ." "Oh God," she said, shuddering,
"Will you preach too? First listen to me: I tell you all the other
    joys I've ever known in my life
Were dust to this . . . misfortune; the desert sun out there is a
    crow's wing against the brightness of this . . .
Misfortune: Oh I didn't mean, dear,
To make you angry." She was suddenly kneeling to him and
    pressed her face
On his hard thigh: "I know I've been wicked, Reave.
You must leave me in the dirt for a bad woman: the women here
See the marks of it, look sidelings at me.
I'll still believe you used to love me a little,
But now of course
You wouldn't want for a wife . . . a handkerchief
You lost and another man picked me up and
Wiped his mouth. Oh there may have been many
Other men. In a year: you can't tell.
Your mother is strong and always rightly despised me.
She'd spit on me if she saw me now. So now
You'll simply cast me off; you're strong, like your mother,
And when you see that a thing's perfectly worthless
You can pick it out of your thoughts. Don't forgive me. I only
Pray you to hate me. Say 'She's no good. To hell with her,'
That's the mercy I pray you for." He said hastily, "Get up,

This is no theater. I intend to take you back, Helen,
I never was very angry at you, remembering
That a woman's more like a child, besides you were muddled
With imaginations and foolish reading. So we'll shut this bad year
In a box of silence and drown it out of our minds." She stood
    away from him toward the farther wall
With a sharp white face, like a knife-blade worn thin and hollow
    with too much whetting, and said, turning her face
Toward the window, "How do I know that he can compel me?
    He can torment us, but there's no law
To give me to him. You can't take me against my will. No: I
    won't go. Do you think you're God,
And we have to do what you want?" He said, "You'll go all
    right." She, laughing, "At last you've struck something
Stiffer than you. Reave, that stubborn will
Is not strength but disease, I've always known it, like the slow
    limy sickness
You hear about, that turns a man's flesh to bone,
The willing muscles and fibers little by little
Grow hard and helpless, at last you can't dent them, nothing will
    move,
He lands in a tent beside the circus, with a painting of him
Over the door and people pay ten cents
To see the petrified man: that's your stubbornness,
Your mind sets and can't change, you don't go on
Because you want to but because you have to, I pity you,
But here you're stopped." Suddenly she trembled and shrank
    little again. "*If* you could take me
I'd stab you in bed sleeping." "You know," he answered,
"You're talking foolishness. I have to see Armstrong before we go,
When he quits work, I guess there's a couple of hours, but you'd
    best get ready." "Why must you see . . . Rick?"
Reave made no answer, Helen covertly watched him, slowly the
    metal temper failed from her face.
"I'll go," she said faintly, "and tell him." "You'll stay here."
"Reave?
Reave. You said you weren't angry." "Not at you. If I'd anyone
To help me, I'd send you off first. Walked around like a man,

Was a male bitch . . ." "I led him, I called him, I did it.
It's all mine." "What?" "The blame, the blame, the blame,
I planned it, all mine, I did it, Reave." A white speck glittered
At the commissure of his lips, he licked his lips
As if he were thirsty and said difficultly, "I've had a
Year to think about it: have to have relief, you're
Let off, keep still." She felt his eyes
Craftily avoiding hers, and something monstrous in him mould-
　　ing the mass of his body to a coarsened
More apelike form, that a moment appeared and then was
　　cramped back to human: her image-making mind beheld
Her lover go under the hammers of this coarse power, his face
　　running thick blood turn up at last
Like a drowning man's, before he went down the darkness, all his
　　gay bravery crushed made horrible submission:
With any warning or whatever weapons he'd be like a bird in a
　　dog's mouth, Reave had all the strength,
Would fight foul, with all means and no mercy: "Oh, Oh, take
　　me with you
If you want me, but now. Before he comes.
How could I look at him again if I'm going to leave him? You
　　understand
That's too much to ask me, to stand between you
Like a cow between the brown bull and the white one.
In spite of all I'm not so . . . shameless as . . .
You think." He made a questioning noise, "Hm?" and she
　　thinking
He'd failed to hear: "I'll go and live with you
If you'll take me now. I can't face Rick, not wait for Rick,"
She said, weaving and parting the fingers
Of her two supplicant hands. She essayed more words,
But only the lips and no voice made them, then again
Breath filled the words, "I've done wickedly, I'm sorry.
I will obey you now." His eyes were hidden
While he considered, all at once he said joyfully
"Pack then." "Me, not my things: there's nothing." "Then come."
She followed him; suddenly in the doorway she dropped
And kissed the threshold.

                              Thurso watched and said nothing;
She got up and walked at his side in the hot white dust by the
     row of small cabins,
The wood of their doors and walls was worn to the look of sea-
     drift by the desert sand-scour. Suddenly Helen
Laughed like the bitter crying of a killdeer when someone walks
     near the nest, "My God, Reave, have you come for me
In the old wreck of a farm-truck, will it still run?" "What else?
     We haven't got rich, we haven't bought cars
While I've been away from home hunting you." "The pigs and
     I," she cried shrilly. Reave nodded, and went to the door
Of the last cabin, and said to the woman to whom he had spoken
     before: "I'm taking my wife home.
This woman's my wife. When Armstrong comes, tell that bastard
We're going west. He's got a car." Helen cried, "Oh, cheat, cheat,
Will you tole him after you?" He said heavily. "What do you
     mean?
Come on," and so holding her wrist that the bones ached
Drew her to the car. She had yielded and was subject to him,
She could imagine no recourse, her mind palsied
Like the wrist-clenched hand.

                              VIII
                              After twenty miles he turned
The carbureter-connection, slyly regarding
His seat-mate, she fogged with misery observed nothing.
The engine went lame. "What's the matter?" he said, turning
The carbureter-connection; the engine stalled.
He lifted the hood and made the motions of helplessness,
Looking up sometimes at Helen, who sat in the dust on the high
     seat on the folded blanket,
Her face in her hands. "We're stuck here," Thurso said. "Well,
     we have water." She dropped her hands from her face
And stared at the road ahead; then she began to see the desert
     about them, the unending incandescent
Plain of white dust, stippled with exact placing of small gray
     plants, each tuft a painfully measured

Far distance from every other and so apparently forever, all
    wavering under the rage of the sun,
A perfect arena for the man's cruelty; but now she was helpless.
Still Armstrong failed to come; Helen awoke again
From blind misery, and watched Reave's nerves
Growing brittle while the sun sailed west. He babbled childlike
About cattle and pastures, things unreal, unimaginable,
In the white anguish here; his hands quivered,
And the sun sank.

            In the night Helen revived
Enough to make action appear possible again.
She crept stealthily away in the starry darkness
Thinking Reave slept; when he spoke she tried to run,
Her thighs and calves were like hollow water, he followed
And brought her back through the vast unnatural pallor of the
    night,
Rough-handed, but only saying "You're too restless." She writhed
    her hands together like bitter flames and lay down
On the spread blanket. After while she lay face upward. Those
    foam-bubbles on the stale water of night
Were floating stars, what did it matter, which of two men?
Yesterday the one had been lovely and the other
Came in like ugly death, but difference had died. Rick Armstrong
    must have made some ridiculous plan
For heading them off or else he'd have come. Perhaps he thought
    she went willingly. Why not? "I go with you willingly,"
She said aloud, "dear, do you hear me? I've shot my load of
    feeling, there's nothing left in the world
Worth thinking twice. We'll crawl home to our hole."
He answered, "I can't believe he's a coward: he'll come in the
    morning." "I dread death
More than your mother's eyes," she answered. "I'm the coward
    or I'd kill myself. Dear, I fear death
More than I hate this dishwater broth of life. A bowlful a day, O
    God! Do the stars look
Like lonely and pretty sparkles when you look up?
They look to me like bubbles of grease on cold

Dishwater." He said, "Sleep, you'll feel better." He heard her
 sighing
And twisting her body on the sand while the night waned.
He got up and stood beside her and said anxiously,
"I was to blame too, Helen. Part of the blame
Is mine, Helen. I didn't show enough love,
Nor do often enough
What women want. Maybe it made your life
Seem empty. It seems . . . it seems to me it wouldn't be decent
To do it just now: but I'll remember and be
Better when we get home." She said, "O God! Fool, fool,
A spoonful a night. Your mother was lying to you.
She knows better."

                    In the morning
Thurso waited two hours from sunrise;
They had nothing to eat; Helen endured her headache, and the
 shameless sun
Blared from the east. Reave greased the joints of the truck.
When one of those long gray desert lizards that run
With heads raised highly, scudded through the white sand,
He flung the wrench suddenly and broke its back
And said "He won't come then. My God, Helen,
Was he tired of you? He won't come." She watched her husband
Pick up the wrench and batter that broken life,
Still lifting up its head at him, into the sand. He saw the yellow
Grains of fat in the red flesh and said,
"Come here, Helen. Yellow you see, yellow you see.
Your friend makes us all vile." She understood
That "yellow" meant cowardly, and that this was Armstrong
Battered to a cake of blood.

                     IX
                 They drove west
Through the white land; the heat and the light increased,
At length around a ridge of ancient black lava
Appeared a place of dust where food could be bought, but Helen
Would eat nothing. In the evening they came

                     293

Among fantastic Joshua-trees to a neat
Framed square of cabins at the foot of a mountain
Like a skeleton; seeing Helen so white and sick,
And the motor misfiring, Reave chose to lodge at this camp.
He'd tinker the engine while there was daylight. He found the
    timer
Choked up with drift of the desert; having washed it with gaso-
    line and heard the cylinders
Roar cheerfully again, he returned to Helen.

                            She was not in the cabin,
But sat with chance companions on a painted bench under the
    boughs of one of those reptilian trees
Near the camp entrance; no longer white and morose, her face
    was flushed, her eyes sparkling with darkness
In the purple evening that washed the mountain. Before he came
    she was saying, "My husband just doesn't care
What anyone thinks: he said, all right, if I wanted to see the
    desert, but he wouldn't take either one
Of our new cars to be spoiled, he'd drive the old farmtruck . . ."
    Seeing Reave approaching, greased black to the elbows, "Oh,
    Oh,
What's he been doing? Oh: it's black, I think? Dear, I felt better
When the sun went down." He, staring at her companions:
"That's good." "They call it desert fever," she stammered.
"The heat's the cause." She stood up, giggling and swaying.
"Was nearly exhausted, they gave me a little medicine.
Nice people." "What did you give her?" "She begged for a table-
    spoonful," the old woman answered, "Texas corn-whiskey.
Are you going west?" Helen said gravely, "A spoonful a night:
    O God!" "She's eaten nothing," Reave said,
"Since yesterday. Come and lie down, Helen." She obeyed, walk-
    ing unsteadily beside him, with terrified eyes.
"Dear, please don't touch me, your hands are terrible," she said.
    "They think you killed him."
He made her lie down on the bed while he washed himself.
She wept and said, "I always make friends easily.
I used to be full of joy. Now my wishes

Or your own soul will destroy you when you get home.
I'd give my life to save you." He groaned angrily,
But she was unable to be silent and said:
"I think you're even worse hurt than I am. Were you ever on a
    ship?
This place is like a ship, everything smells
In spite of neatness, and I am desert-sick.
Oh, Reave, I never dreamed that you'd be deep-wounded.
Forgive me dear." He violently: "Lick your own sores.
The man was my friend and that degrades me: but you've
Slept with him. You couldn't help but have learned him
In a year's familiar life and I've been thinking
That whores you, because no woman can love a coward,
And still you stayed . . ." "For his money, for his money you
    know,"
She answered through chattering teeth, "and the fine house
You found me in among the rich gardens, the jewels and furs,
Necklaces of pearls like round zeroes, all these hangings of gold
That make me heavy . . ." "Ah," he said, "be quiet." He went
    out, and returning after a time with a tray of food
Lighted the lamp and cut meat in small bites and forced her to
    eat. "Dear," she mourned, "I can't swallow
Though I chew and chew. The rocking of the ship and the hot
    smell close up my throat. Oh be patient with me.
When we land I'll feel better," her deep-colored eyes moving in
    sickly rhythm to the roll of the ship,
He said "You're in the desert: an auto-camp by the road. Wake
    up and eat." She sat up on the bed
And looked anxiously about the bleak lamplight, then took the
    tray
And obeyed his will. "I thought you were my dad.
Once we travelled on a boat from the south
To San Francisco. I expect I saw from the deck the Mill Creek
    mountains and never
Guessed," she said, shuddering. While she ate she began to fear
That people who were going to die dreamed of a ship
The night before. The truck would be overturned
And crush her body in the sand like that lizard's,
A tire would have burst.

Against the black horror of death
All living miseries looked sweet; in a moment of aimless
Wild anguish she was unable not to cry out, and said:
"Ah, Ah, what have you done, tearing me from him? I love him,
    you know.
Maybe he's cowardly or maybe he's only tired of me, but if he's
    yellow to the bones, if he's yellower than gold,
I love him, you know.
If I were crushed in the sand like that lizard you killed, to a cake
    of blood—why not? for I think you'll
Do it sometime—the sun would dry me and my dust would blow
    to his feet: if I were dead in the desert
And he drowned in the middle ocean toward Asia, yet something
    and something from us would climb like white
Fires up the sky and twine high shining wings in the hollow sky:
    while you in your grave lie stuck
Like a stone in a ditch." He, frowning: "Have you finished?"
    He took the tray and said, "Have you had enough?"
"Never enough. Dear, give me back to him. I can't think yet
That you understand," she said slyly and trembling.
"Don't you care, that he and I have made love together
In the mountains and in the city and in the desert,
And once at a Navajo shepherd's camp in the desert in a storm of
    lightnings
Playing through the cracks of the shed: can you wink and
    swallow
All that?" "I can't help it. You've played the beast.
But you are my goods and you'll be guarded, your filthy time
Has closed. Now keep still."
                    She was silent and restless for a good while.
He said, "You'll be sleeping soon, and you need sleep.
I'll go outside while you get ready for bed."
"Let me speak, just a little," she said humbly.
"Please, Reave, won't you leave me here in the morning, I'll
    manage somehow.
You're too strong for us, but, dear, be merciful.
I think you don't greatly want me: what you love really

Is something to track down: your mountains are full of deer:
Oh, hunt some bleeding doe. I truly love you.
I always thought of you as a dear, dear friend
When even we were hiding from you." He was astonished
To see her undress while she was speaking to him,
She seemed to regard him as a mere object, a keeper,
But nothing human. "And Rick Armstrong," she said,
"I can't be sure that I love him: dear, I don't know
That I'll go back to him; but I must have freedom, I must have
    freedom
If only to die in, it comes too late . . ."
She turned her back and slipped off the undergarment
And glided into the bed. She was beautiful still,
The smooth fluted back and lovely long tapering legs not
    changed,
Nor the supple motions; nor that recklessness
Of what Thurso called modesty was any change;
She never tried to conceal her body from him
Since they were married, but always thoughtless and natural;
And nestled her head in the pillow when she lay down
With little nods, the tender way he remembered:
So that a wave of compassionate love
Dissolved his heart: he thought, "Dearest, I've done
Brutally: I'll not keep you against your will.
But you must promise to write to me for help
When you leave that cur." He made the words in his mind
And began to say: "Dearest . . ." but nothing further
Had meaning in it, mere jargon of mutterings, the mouth's refusal
Of the mind's surrender; and his mind flung up a memory
Of that poor dead man, his father, with the sad beaten face
When the lime-kilns failed: that man yielded and was beaten,
A man mustn't be beaten. But Helen hearing
The "dearest," and the changed voice, wishfully
Lifted her head, and the great violet eyes
Sucked at Reave's face. "No," he said. He blew out the lamp,
Resolved to make this night a new marriage night
And undo their separation. She bitterly submitted;
"I can bear this: it doesn't matter: I'll never tell him.

I feel the ship sailing to a bad place. Reave, I'm so tired
That I shall die. If my wrist were broken
You wouldn't take my hand and arm in your hands
And wriggle the bones for pleasure? You're doing that
With a worse wound." Her mind had many layers;
The vocal one was busy with anguish, and others
Finding a satisfaction in martyrdom
Enjoyed its outcry; the mass of her mind
Remained apparently quite neutral, under a familiar
Embrace without sting, without savor, without significance,
Except that this breast was hairier.

X

They drove through the two
deserts and arrived home. Helen went in
With whetted nerves for the war with Reave's mother, resolving
Not to be humble at least; but instead of the sharp old woman a
little creature
With yellow hair and pleated excess of clothing stood up in the
room; and blushed and whitened, anxiously
Gazing, clasping thin hands together. Reave said, "It's Hester
Clark." And to Hester Clark: "Tell Olvidia
To count two more for supper; my wife and I have come home."
She answered, "Oh yes," fleeing. Then Helen:
"What's this little thing? Why does it wear my dress?" "She's
only hemmed it over," he said, "at the edges.
Have it again if you want, I had to find something for her." His
mother was heard on the stair, and entering
Looked hard at Helen and went and kissed Reave. Who said, "I
shall stay at home now, mother: Helen's come home."
"Yes. How do you do." Her red-brown eyes brushed Helen's
body from the neck to the ankles, "I'll have them heat
Bathwater." Helen trembled and said, "How kind. There are
showers in all the camps: if you mean anything else:
Reave seems content." "Very well. He's easily of course con-
tented. He picks up things by the road: one of them
I've allowed to live here: to speak honestly

In hope to keep his mind off another woman: but that cramps
and can't change." "If I knew what I want!"
Helen cried suddenly. "The girl is a servant here," Reave said.
"I hate the spitefulness of women. The housework
Needed help when you were not here." Then Helen: "She's quite
sick I think: she'll have to clear out I think.
Yet something in me felt kindly toward that little wax face
In my old clothes. I came home against my will. Why isn't Mark
here?" The far door opened for Olvidia,
Unable to imagine any pretext for entrance, but unable to bridle
her need
Of coming, to stare and smile from flat black eyes. Behind her
Johnny Luna was seen peering, but dared not enter.
Then Helen wondered, where was that thin little thing?
Crying somewhere? And Reave's mother said: "Now you'll cut
down
The old cable, as you promised, Reave. We're tired of seeing it.
You'll have time now." He answered, "Where's Mark, mother?
Helen just asked you." "I heard her.
Sitting under a bush on the hill, probably. Your wife's adventures
Stick in his throat." Then Helen, trembling, and the words marred
By sudden twitchings of her lips: "I'm not ashamed. No reason
to be. I tried to take myself out of here
And am brought back by threats and by force, to a gray place
like a jail, where the sea-fog blows up and down
From the hill to the rock, around a house where no one ever
loved or was glad. But your spite's nothing,
Pour it out, I'll swim in it: and fear Reave but not you, and maybe
after while . . . That's all. Reave, I'll go up
And change my dress before supper, if your . . . if little wax-
face you know . . . has left me any
Clothes in the closet."

                     She went upstairs; the others were silent,
Until the old woman: "Ah why, why," she said, "Reave,
Did you have to bring back . . . I know. You had to. Your mind
Sticks in its own iron: when you've said 'I will'
Then you're insane, the cold madness begins.
It's better than weakness."

He answered with shamefast look shunning her eyes, "I must tell
    you, mother,
Though it may seem strange: I love her, you know. Some acci-
    dent,
Or my neglect, changed her; I'll change her over
And bring the gold back." "You talk like poor Mark. Oh, worse.
Mark at least feels disgust. A woman that can't it seems
Even have babies. . . . About the old cable:
He's been seeing lately . . . your father: the man who's
    dead . . .
Pitifully staring up at it in the evenings.
He broods on that. The shock of your disgrace I believe
Started his mind swarming, and he hobbles out
In the starlight. I wish you to keep your promise
And cut that ruin from our sky. It's bad for Mark
To remember his father; and I've a feeling
The memory slacks us all, something unlucky will clear
When that cord's cut. Don't you hate seeing it?" "Oh, yes,
Like anything else that's no use. It'd fall by itself
Some winter. I'll cut it down. There are trees under it
That have to be saved. Mother, I won't ask you
To make friends with my wife: you're not to fuss either.
And don't prod her with Hester. We'll have some peace in the
    house,
Or I'll growl too."

XI

       Mark's lameness appeared more painful than
    formerly; Helen from the window seeing him
Limping across the dooryard, she went and followed. He stood
    by the sycamore, under great yellowing leaves,
And Helen: "You hardly spoke to me last night, though a year
    had passed. Have I lost your love, my brother? I valued it.
I need it more than in happier times." "That . . ." he answered,
"Oh Helen!" "Because I could hardly think how to live here,"
    she said, "without it." "I have no color of words
To say how dearly . . . When I seem dark: you must think of
    me as a foolish day-dreamer

Whose indulgence turns and clouds him, so that he sees a dead
man
Walk on the deck, and feels the ship sailing
Through darkness to a bad place." She, astonished with memory:
"The ship, the ship?" "You see. My foolish dreams
Twine into my common talk. Maybe it's my hearing at night
The watery noises and hoarse whisper of the shore that sets me
Into that dream, I feel the see-sawing keel, my mind tries darkly
ahead under the stars
What destiny we're driving toward. . . . Do you think, Helen,
a dead man's
Soul can flit back to his scene long afterwards?" "Your father,
you mean? But I was lying in the scrawny desert,
A thousand miles from any noise of the shore. It scared me be-
cause I seem to remember hearing
That to dream of a ship means death . . ." "If that's all," he
smiled meagerly:
"If we both dream it. I, for one, shan't trouble
My survivors with any starlight returns, but stick to peace
Like a hungry tick." "Oh," she said eagerly, "hush.
It's wicked to talk like that." He was silent, then said,
"Did you love him, Helen?" She clenched her hands, and turning
Her head from him, "I thought you'd ask that. What's love?"
And laid her hand on the leaning pillar of the tree
To turn herself back to his face, to study no higher
Than the lean jaw and strained mouth, lower than the eyes,
And carefully said, "Of course I loved him; but I believe
My shining terror of Reave was the cause.
For now that desert stalk's cut, the old root of fear
Seems aching to a new flowering. Why do I fear him? I know for
certain
He'll neither kill me nor beat me, I've proved it: and I even
tricked him out of his vengeance, you know, he came home
With nothing but me. . . . Where did he get that Hester? No,
tell me after while. . . . Listen. I used to think
That the only good thing is a good time: I've got past that . . .
Into the dark. I need something, I can't know what it is." She
thought in her heart: "I know.

To humble your strong man, that's what I need." And said: "To
be free. He called me a harlot, Mark. I am a
Harlot of a rare nature. The flesh is only a symbol. Oh, can't you
see me
Beaten back and forth between the two poles, between you and
Reave?"
She watched, that his lips moved like a plucked string,
So that she thought "It can be done," and said,
"The one pole's power, that I tried to escape: that strong man,
you know:
And have been . . . retrieved, and can't tell whether I hate him
Or what. The second, you can name better than I:
The power behind power, that *makes* what the other can only
Direct or destroy. See how wise I've grown. Dear: in the desert
I cried a good deal at night: it wasn't for Reave,
Nor for his mother! my eyelids rained in the dusty
Country where rain's not natural. I'd look up the night
And see the sharp dry stars like great bubbles
Blown up and swollen, full of most bitter rainbows,
Float on the wave of the world: it was for you
My tears ran down."

        She watched his mouth, in the thought
That if she stretched romance to laughter, or his doubting point,
She'd be warned by his lips: but Mark perhaps had not even
heard her; he said, "I used to thank God
Whatever it is that's coming, Helen's not here. If even she's crying
in the night somewhere: she's flown
Like a bird out of the hands of *our* catcher. Now you've come
home! . . . Oh, at better times
I think my fears are only a flaw of the mind;
Or else that the dark ship driving to its drowning
Is only my own poor life: *that* might go down
Without a bubble." She angrily: "Reave at least
Is something solid to fear . . . You and your shadows!
I was going to make love to you, Mark,
All to spite Reave and because he bores me, but your nonsense
Has run mine out of breath. You've missed something.

Tell me about this . . . what's her name? Reave's wisp,
All eyes and hair." Mark failed to answer; she looked
And saw his face fixed and anxious. "What's the matter now?"
"Is that Reave?" he whispered. "Exactly. What's in Reave
To make you dome out your eyes like a caught fish?"
"He's staring up at the cable, Helen! The old man stands in
That same place and stares up at the cable
Every night." "Soon to miss his amusement, poor ghost.
Reave's planning to take it down. Be sure when Reave looks up
He has a purpose."

              He approached and said, "To-morrow morning
We'll cut it down. But the best trees in the canyon
Stand in the shadow of its fall.
I've planned a way to tie the cut end with rope
And steer it west in its fall, and I hope clear them.
They must take their chance." He looked at Mark and said,
    "We'll feel better
After the old advertisement of failure's down.
It's cobwebbed the canyon for twenty years." He looked at
    Helen:
"We'll start a new life to-morrow." She marvelled secretly
At the reasonless anger that ran through her dry nerves like a
    summer grass-fire, and shrilly, "You and I?" she answered,
"Or you and your . . . little floozie, that whittled match?"
He frowned, his temples darkened with the heavy muscle
Setting the jaw, he said in a moment: "I've given Hester notice
    to go. She's going to-morrow.
You're staying. So rest your mind." "Ah, Ah," she said, "be
    proud of strength while you can. Cut the cable
And forget your father. Whatever fails, cut it down. Whatever
gets old or weakens. Send Hester packing
Because a bigger woman's brought home. If a dog or a horse
    have been faithful, kill them on the shore of age
Before they slacken. See to keep everything around you as strong
    and stupid
As Reave Thurso." And turning suddenly:

"Oh, Mark, tell me what's good, I don't know which way to
  turn. Is there anything good? Whisper, whisper.
That mould of hard beef and bone never asks,
He never wonders, took it ready-made when he was a baby,
  never changes, *can't* change. You and I
Have to wonder at the world and stand between choices. That's
  why we're weak and ruled. If we could ever
Find out what's good, we'd do it. He'd be surprised.
What a rebellion!" She changed and said, "Reave?
Let that girl stay a week; you might need her yet.
In any case I'd like to know her a little.
She keeps out of my way, I haven't had time.
A week or two." He, staring: "That's a sickly thing
For a man's wife to want. No. She's going
At the set time. If you can't tell what's good:
It's lucky I have a compass and can steer the ship."
"Oh, Oh. That ship again?" she cried laughing,
"Maybe there's something in it, if even Reave . . .
Can you feel it straining through the dark night? Mark: you heard
  him:
He's a dreamer too. You'd never imagine it,
To see him stand there so fleshy, shaking his head
Like a bull in fly-time: if he dreams he'll fall yet. We'll try."
She turned and went toward the house.

                        Reave said, "What was all that?
There was a time when I'd have stared at myself
For bringing home . . . and letting it talk and talk
As if it had rights in the world. It's her colored abounding life
That makes her lovely." "She's tied to you," Mark answered,
"Like a falcon tied up short to a stone, a fierce one,
Fluttering and striking in ten inches of air. I believe deeply
You're precious to each other." "Hm. I bear clawing
As well as anyone." Mark, earnestly: "Oh be good to her,
Not to let her be hurt in the coming time."
"No more of that, Mark. You know these forebodings
Date from our time in France and the muddy splinter
That wrecked your ankle. You must make allowances." He an-
  swered, "You'd think

This rocked-in gorge would be the last place in the world to bear
    the brunt: but it's not so: they told me
This is the prow and plunging cutwater,
This rock shore here, bound to strike first, and the world behind
    will watch us endure prophetical things
And learn its fate from our ends." "Booh. We'll end well," he an-
    swered, laughing, "the world won't watch.
When you and I toast long white beards and old freckled hands,
    and Helen
Like a little shrivelled apple by the fire between us
Still faintly glows, in the late evenings of life,
We'll have the fun that old people know, guessing
Which of us three will die first. I dare say the world
Will be quite changed then." "You're very hopeful. But even you
I think feel the steep time build like a wave, towering to break,
Higher and higher; and they've trimmed the ship top-heavy.
. . . Do you take it down to-morrow?" "Ah? The cable you
    mean?
I told you: in the morning. You must all come and watch.
The fall will be grand. Those things have weight."

XII

                      Helen had gone
As if she carried news in her mind through the house to the
    kitchen; there dark Olvidia
Stood big and ominous in a steam of beef boiling. "Where's your
    helper, Olvidia, the little mop
That pares potatoes?" She answered sadly, "Is cabbage too." "I
    say where's the elf-child,
The inch with the yellow hair? Ought to be helping you."
"Oh, that? She going away." "To-morrow, maybe.
Where is she now?" The Indian rolled her dun eyes
Toward the open door of the laundry, and Helen passing
Looked all about among piled tubs and behind
An old desk of Reave's father's; the girl she sought
Stood up in a corner. "What enormous eyes you have.
Why were you hiding?" Helen said. "Oh no. I'd done my work,"
She answered plaintively, "I was just thinking here.

I have to go away to-morrow." "Wearing my dress," Helen said.
"Did you come here without any clothes at all?" "He . . . Mr.
Thurso . . . mine were worn out,
He burned them up." "A handkerchief would cover you, though.
I don't believe you weigh ninety pounds
Without the weight of my clothes. Oh, you're welcome.
I think I'll take the prettiest one in the closet
And cut it to fit you like finch's feathers.
Is your name Hester? How can you bear Reave's weight,
Your body's the width of my arm?" The girl trembled
And twisted herself sidewise. "Aren't you angry at me?"
"Oh no," Helen said; and anxiously: "I don't know. I'm lost.
Oh why should I be angry, nothing is worth . . .
Nothing, I believe.
Do you want to stay here? Don't you hate Reave? *I* do.
Madly." The other with a begging whine: "I'd work.
You are so kind." And whispered, "I might do all
The old Spanish woman's work, you could let her go."
Then Helen suddenly, her lips withering
From the white teeth: "Olvidia, come here. This scrap
Wants us to fire you: she wants to be with my husband:
Take both our places, how's that for treachery? Because she's
  nothing earthly but a stack of hair and enormous
Gray eyes, thinks I'll stand anything. . . . Wives hate your
  trade, don't you know that?" "I . . . didn't understand. I
  thought you
Meant me to stay. I never felt safe before, but here I had my own
  room and was warm enough,
And Mr. Thurso was never drunk." "Oh, that was something.
Where did you come from?" She looked at Olvidia's dark ex-
  pressionless face, and sidling a little nearer
To Helen for shelter: "Hymettus, Nebraska: I lived with my
  aunt Margaret, she was always punishing me
Because my uncle wouldn't let me alone. She was big and thin.
I ran away with a boy but he soon left me.
I tried to get rides west, people would keep me awhile
And turn me out. I think I was going to die
When Mr. Thurso saw me beside the road."

"And loaded you into the farm-truck, ah?
Go on." "He gave me some bread and got some coffee
At the next place. I've been happy here. Oh,
What will become of me now?" "I can't guess," Helen said. "My
    husband
Can't change his mind: so you'll have to go, whatever you and
    I want. It jams in the slot; nothing
Will budge it after that, not with a crowbar. What will he be at
    fifty, ah? How old are you, Hester?"
"Eighteen . . . nineteen." "I expect it's true: that stack of hair,
    Olvidia, took time to grow." Olvidia
Scowled and said darkly to Hester: "You set the table.
It's time for dinner." The girl moved quickly to obey, but Helen:
"Stay here."

             She stood then in white anxiety
Between the two, and suddenly began to weep.
Helen went near her and said, "I want awfully
To know you, Hester. There's deep strangeness in your
Wanting to stay in this place. . . . Olvidia, I'm still your mis-
    tress:
Make us two sandwiches: set the table yourself.
Sandwiches: meat between bread." She said to Hester:
"You're not false, I think. Helpless; perfectly;
A person without any will: mine's only hiding.
If I could just imagine what's good, or even
What's bad, you'd see the machine move like a ship.
You mustn't fear Reave, either.
He has a great will, frittered away on trifles,
Farm things, and you and me. And unable to strike a woman:
So we needn't fear to take food in our hands
And go and play on the shore. Yes, I command you.
That makes it easy."

             They walked under the alders that pave the
    gorge, and Helen: "Does it taste mouldy,
The meat of this house? But you must eat and not waste it or
    you'll be sorry, for freedom, Hester, that's coming,

Is a hungry condition. . . . Where will you go to?" "He says
I must go to San Francisco." Helen looked, and laughed
To see tears in her eyes. "You're crazy to cry about that. You
wouldn't stay in this wretched crack
Between two rocks? Come along, walk faster. Hester: that first
time,
When you ran away with a boy: did you want a boy,
Or only you didn't dare go alone? Ah? I think that's
What makes you cry. It keeps grinding in my mind
That maybe I too . . . just to break jail . . .
It would be a dirty discovery."

                    The creek-bank path
Straightened a moment, so that a great aisle of bright breathing
ocean
Stood clear ahead, and Helen: "Hester: do you know what?
I'm going with you. I'll cut my hair to the bone
And borrow Johnny Luna's greasy black hat,
We'll fly away. I'll work for you, beg if we have to,
We'll try all the roads in America
And never quarrel; no disgust and no bullying. . . . Dear, it
won't do.
You'd obey orders, we know: but look at these hips
And breasts of mine: these bulges in a man's blue-jeans
Would bulge the laws of nature, ah? My affections
Go with my build, we're talking froth, dear,
Only to poultice the inner bitterness: taste me and you'd call
Quinine honey."

              Suddenly emerging at the creek-mouth beach
they breathed and stood still. The narrow crescent
Of dark gravel, sundered away from the world by its walls of
cliff, smoked in a burst of sun
And murmured in the high tide through its polished pebbles. The
surf broke dazzling on fins of rock far out,
And foam flowed on the ankles of the precipice. Helen looked
up, cliff over cliff, the great naked hill

All of one rifted rock covering the northwest sky; and said: "It's
    called Thurso's Landing. That's something,
To have the standing sea-cliffs named after you. His father used
    to swing down the barrels of lime
From the head of that to the hulls of ships. The old wrecks of
    rusting engines are still to be seen up there,
And the great concrete block that anchors the cable. I hope you'll
    stay
To see it come down. He said, in the morning. You'll ride the
    mail-stage, I think:
Passes at noon. . . . Will you have the willow or the rock,
    Hester,
To undress beside?" "What . . . what is it?" "For a swim.
Didn't they have a swimming-pool in Nebraska?
Here's ours." "I can't. Oh, Oh." "You can duck up and down
In the long waves," Helen said, laughing. "Undress.
What do you think we came down for, to see cormorants?"
"The cold will kill me." She answered, "You by this rock
And I by that one. I've been ruled with dull iron,
Now I'll rule *you* at least."

                                She went, and returned
In a moment, clean of clothing, but her small companion
Stood shivering in a worn cotton under-shift
And quavered, "I'll go down like this." Helen suddenly
Anxious and haggard, standing far off, with a screaming voice:
"I told you I want to see you: if I die of it.
Nothing can be worse than what I imagine.
Take off that rag." She sobbing and obedient
Dropped it to the ankles and stepped out and stood
Furled like a sail to the mast, the straw-thin arms
Crossed on her breast, the hands hugging the tiny
Bones of her crooked shoulders in the golden under-spray
Of coiled-up hair. Helen stared and sighed, "Nothing
But a white bony doll"; and turning to the sea: "We're all mon-
    strous
Under the skins, but nothing is real I think

Even if you *can't* **see it. Come on, poor thing, let's be launched;** the foam-ripple's
Like running cream and the clouds gather."

She went down and
Hester followed helplessly a few sad steps,
But when the steel chill of the wave ached in her feet stood still,
whining between hammering teeth, then Helen
Caught her by the hand and dragged her thigh-deep, still keeping
her face averse from her victim, like one compelled
To handle a loathsome thing she made her dance in the waves.
"Don't you love it, Hester, isn't this cold
More noble than the heat of a sleeping man? Here comes a foam-
head. I hate the man, yet I can hardly
Keep back my hands from holding you down and drowning
you; why's that, why's that?" while Hester childlike lament-
ing
Danced up and down as the seas deepened. Helen said, "He killed
my friend
In the bitter desert, a beautiful youth
Yellow-haired like you, like you a wanderer. He flung a hammer,"
She said, seeing in her mind the running lizard
That Reave had killed, "My dear friend fell, and that man
Who seems so quiet and controlled wallowed like a boar
Gnashing and trampling. There was no help anywhere
In all the abominable flat lifeless plain. When Reave stood up
A crooked red stump that had no eyes was dying in the sand,
instead of the blond beautiful body
I had often hugged in my arms. I heard it die. We travelled on,
blinded with thirst and sun,
And left it blackening; there are no tears in the desert,
Water's too precious there."

A greater wave came, gathering
The mottled lit blue water in a bladed heap, then Helen braced
well apart
Her straight white legs, and lifted her little nearly fainting com-
panion over the comb of the wave,

So that the face was clear and the yellow hair felt but the spray.
    In the trough behind the white wave
Helen shook her dark head, the water sluiced from her shoulders
And rose-tipped breasts. "Fear nothing, Hester, I'm strong
    enough.
That deadly secret I told you: if you should dare
To tell it again, think what might happen: a hanging.
I might be freed. . . . Look up: there he comes now: can't live
    without us." She jeered, "Look at him,
Stolid on the wild colt." They were looking shoreward and a
    wave covered them,
Then Helen drew her companion from the roaring foam and
    carried her ashore.

                    Thurso's half-broken mount
Danced on the sea's edge in beaten terror, the thin black whip
    streaked the brown flanks; and Helen Thurso
Like a myth of dawn born in the west for once, glowing rose
    through white all her smooth streaming body
Came through the foam, and dragged beside her for a morning
    star fainting and dull in the rose of dawn
That wisp of silver flesh and the water-darkened burden of hair;
She stood panting, unable to speak, and Thurso
Felt through his underconsciousness something morbid and men-
    acing
In blue-shadowed silver foiled upon glowing rose, against the
    livid
Foam, the tongues of cobalt water, and the shark-fin gray
Rocks of the inlet, for now the sun was clouded,
All colors found their significance; then Helen wrestling for
    breath:
"Ah, Reave. Here, Reave.
I knew you'd come, I left word with Olvidia.
Here's your wet honey: without my dress to pad her life-size
Compare us two." His face wried and dark red,
He twitched the whip in his hand, choking with anger, and
    Helen:

"That's for your colt: not me you daren't. You haven't the
  courage, simply you haven't the courage. This peeled thing—"
She held Hester by the wrist not to escape—"this peeled and
  breastless willow-twig here feared you
Until I told her . . . Strike, strike. Let her see you." He shud-
  dered and blackened, laboring for words, and groaned, "Go
  home.
Get on your clothes." "Now I've learned something," she an-
  swered, "that even a thin slip like this is a better lover
Than any . . . strike *me*, not her!" She let Hester go, who van-
  ished instantly, and Helen raised both round arms
To unguard her smooth flanks and said writhing, "That whip of
  yours
Might do what no love nor strength . . . you've never let your-
  self go,
You've never . . . I always bitterly feared you:
Give me cause. I could bear much. I'd not move nor scream
While you wrote the red stripes:
But there's no nature in you, nothing but . . . noble . . .
Nothing but . . . one of those predestined stone men
For women to respect and cheat . . ." She was suddenly weeping
And shivering; she leaned her face toward his knee
And the horse danced sidewise, with a dull clashing sound
Of unshod hooves in the pebbles, curving its body
Away from her and against the whip; she stood back,
Saying, "He thinks I'm a monster out of the sea.
I'm not like . . . what you think. I'd have kissed your stirrup:
But that's not sense either." She limped like an old woman
Across the gravel toward her clothing, bent over,
Stroking the sea-water off.

XIII

It is certain that too violent
Self-control is unlucky, it attracts hard events
As height does lightning; so Thurso rode up the canyon with a
  little death in himself,
Seeing in his mind Helen's naked body like a red bird-cage
Welted with whip-stripes; and having refused the precious relief
  of brutality, and being by chance or trick

Cheated of revenge on her desert lover, he endured small deaths
    in his mind, atrophied spots, like mouse-holes
For the casual malice of things to creep in uncountered: so
    shortened by refusal of a fair act, Thurso
Rode up from the shore in the frown of fortune. The cress-paved
    pools of the stream, the fortifying beauty on the north
Of the rock rampart, and toward the south of the forested slope,
    and the brave clouds with flashing bellies
Crossing the gorge like a fleet of salmon, were as nothing to him.
    Once he jerked back the colt's
Bit-spread jaws to its breast and half turned back
To the shore again, but sat bewildered a moment
And snapped his teeth together and rode on, imagining
Some work to do.

              He tied the colt by the house-door
And went through the house to a closet where hunting-gear,
Guns, traps and vermin-poisons were kept, he fetched some
    pounds of bitter barley in the butt of a sack
To abate the pest of ground-squirrels. Returning through the
    still rooms
He met his mother and said, "I've been to the beach, where they
    were bathing. I'm going to the upper field
With squirrel-poison." She said, "In October?" "Nobody else
Seems to have kept them down, in my absences.
Without some killing they'll breed armies in spring."
"Mark isn't able to kill, Luna's too lazy:
I ought to have driven him: I didn't think of it, Reave,
Not being often in the fields." He sighed and said,
"I wish it would rain. Mother, you have been right
To dislike that woman. I guess you're right." She turned
Her reddish flint eyes from his face to the window,
Thinking "What now has she done?" and saying, "Nobody
Can praise your choices. Soft pliable men have the luck in love.
Maybe you can get rid of her without much trouble."
He answered fiercely, "Why did you let Luna
Bridle the brown colt while I was away?
He broke it with a whip: it was gentle-natured.

Don't speak, mother, of Helen.
I never will let her go until she is dead."
The old woman, sharply eyeing him again: "If you could stand
her
Under the iron skip when you cut the cable
To-morrow morning." He looked down at the flat
White hair on the gray forehead and laughed doubtfully
Without knowing why. "Our ship sails when I cut the cable.
He ought to be whipped himself: Johnny a horse-breaker!
The colt is spoilt. . . . I must ask you, mother,
Not to interfere between mine and me.
Whatever you say about the stock or the fields
I'll see to very patiently: my wife is my own concern,
You must not meddle." "I have no desire to: as you know clearly,
Reave,
In your mind's quiet time." "What does that mean, that I seem
excited: drunk, hm? Wrong, mother, quite wrong.
I've noticed in other autumns, when the earth bakes brittle and
the rains lag, I become gloomy and quarrelsome,
But not this year. Cheerful. Squirrel-poison's
What I came in for,
To sow it in the fields above: they increased out of all bounds in
my absences."

He left the house
And rode up the hill to the gray stubble-field, where many
ground-squirrels scampered away before him, or erected
Like pegs on mounds of dug earth before their house-doors
barked shrill warning to each other in the sunny air,
While Thurso, leading his horse about the borders of the field,
laid at the mouth of each burrow and carefully
In the little trackways light treacherous gifts; he mounted and
rode to the lower plowland. From thence returning
Above the path of dazzle on the burnished sea, he heard one of
his vermin singing its terror
In the first pain of death; its chirping voice was muffled in the
earth; and Thurso likewise went down

Out of the tension of the sun to the shadowed canyon. Where the
    path from the hill
Joined one that wound into the redwoods, he saw his brother
Cross hastily and glance toward him, and labor down
Like a hobbled horse, the plunge and drag of lame haste.
Reave overtook him. Mark said, "Look. Now he stands.
I was talking to him until he drifted away
As if a wind had come up. Reave, I beg you
Ride some way around, or he'll glide off again
And never tell me the rest." Reave leaned in the saddle
And took his brother by the shoulder: "Come up from dreams,
    old fellow.
This won't do, you'll be sick again. These fancies
Are nothing if you don't yield." "Keep your hand off me,"
He said angrily. "If you can't see him clear
Against the dark leaves of laurel: blindness is all.
He's wearing a different coat, and his tie-pin's
A small jade mask I never noticed before.
Ss: quiet; he's coming towards us. . . . You told me, father . . .
Ah, Ah." The deranged man's trembling excitement
Infected the ill-tamed colt, it sweated and shuddered
Between Reave's knees, with hard breathings
Cupping its ears toward the image that Mark imagined,
But the bit and the knees held it.

                              Mark, mournfully: "Then death's
No nearer peace. No dreamlessness. That's bad." He listened
    again,
And shrewdly answered, "Harmonized: happier, happier?
I do wish to have faith: but your voice, father,
Sounds flat of happiness, and all the woes of the world
Seem hosting behind your smile. For God's sake tell me
The honest truth." He listened, and said painfully,
"Make me sure of it. For if the blind tugging here
And self-contempt continue, and death's no peace,
It would be better to live forever . . . but best, best,
Never've been born." He listened again and said,

"I'll try . . ." Then turning to Reave; who sat like bronze,
Half his mind grieving to hear his brother's madness, and half
Busied with its own bitterness: "He says to warn you,
Let his work stand. He says *honor your father*
That your days may . . . I have it wrong. Shortened?
Shortened? Because death's better, I suppose.
. . . Not to pull down his work." Reave laughed impatiently,
Saying, "Tell that imagination I honor as much
As I can see of him: that's nothing. A perfect ground-squirrel,
Pop out of life for the first dog that barked
Into the shady earth. Come down to the house
And rest, brother. We owe him no duties
If he were really in the wind here." He laid his hand again on
     Mark's shoulder,
Whose loaded nerves suddenly discharging at the touch of re-
     straint struck his clenched bony fist
To the neck of the colt; that flew a leap sidewise and three
     forward in the crackling brushwood, then breathed itself
With vertical flights and humped bone-rigid landings. Reave
     hurt it with whip and bridle, he squeezed it tame
Between his two knees and angrily returned.

                                        Mark meanwhile,
     following his vision,
With no mind for this world, questioned it hard
About that other, he ate its fallacious answers
Together with his own doubts, like a starved man gulping
The meal with the weevils. "Life's all a dream," it said,
"And death is a better more vivid immortal dream
But love is real; both are made out of love,
That's never perfect in life, and the voids in it
Are the pains of life; but when our ungainly loads
Of blood and bone are thrown down, then the voids close,
Love becomes perfect, all's favor and immediate joy,
For then we are what we love." So the false prophet
Sang sweetly, Mark was drunken with the easy ecstasy,
But while he listened his eyes kept wavering down

From the face to the throat of his vision, to that tie-pin
Tipped with white jade: that also had a face, carved
In the bright waxy stone, and was grown bigger,
The face was Helen's. The spectre sang that love
Must become conscious of itself and claim its own,
Mark's gaze drifting again to the stone at its throat
Found a cleft whiteness, for the carving reversed
Was now the beautiful fork of female thighs,
And the little hill: because the seer was virgin,
Knowing only pictures of women, he saw smooth white
What's rough in nature; but very smooth was too rough
For that intolerant sick mind. He fled back in terror,
Crying shrilly, "I can't. I can't. Oh, Reave, the cunning devil
Was making traps to take me, and I have conceived
A monstrous thing, poisoning the soul with flesh.
Either our dead hate us or the living devil
Was here instead." Reave followed him and coaxed him home,
Where Helen stood in the room. They nodded to her
Like two effigies.

                 In the night Reave dreamed that Helen
Lay with him in the deep grave, he awoke loathing her,
But when the weak moment between sleep and waking
Was past, his need of her and his judgment of her
Knew their suspended duel; and he heard her breathing,
Irregularly, gently in the dark.

XIV

To save the redwoods under it, a rope was drawn
From the old cable, near the end to be cut,
To an oak a little higher than the cable-anchorage
And fifty yards to the west; so in their falling
The heavy steel serpent and the hanging iron skip
Should be deflected enough to miss those highest
And best-grown trees; the cable would be swung west
Before the inch rope should take the whole weight and snap,
Or, holding, be cut at leisure.

                                    Reave had brought up a hack-saw,
But the blades broke on the strained steel; he wedged a wood
    block
In the rusty angle between the black cable and the brown con-
    crete, and worked against it with a slim file
Until four strands were gored through and his palm bleeding; he
    pried the wires back and put Luna to work,
Himself walking aside, testing the guide-rope's tautness, and
    somewhat wondering
What engines his father used to sling so great weight so high:
    a man capable of that, blow out
In the first draught of bad luck like a poor candle!
In the open, in the fresh morning, high up the precipitous hill, his
    spirit mounted to a kind of cheerfulness;
He had work to do; and now the sea-wind began, the wool-
    white fog on the ocean detached clouds
Flying up the gorge of the gulf underfoot, so Thurso felt for a
    moment a little laughably godlike,
Above the cloud-stream, hewing an old failure from the face of
    nature. Down in the gorge, from the house dooryard
The cable and the skip could be seen high up the east, the rapid
    mist-wreaths flowing in the sky below them
Like ice-cakes under a spidery bridge. Mark and his mother stood
    on the path to the porch, she'd brought him
Out of his bedroom to watch the cable go down, hoping it might
    cure sick thoughts. Hester and Olvidia
Stood, each alone, at some distance; but Helen came down from
    among the trees. Then Mark remembering
His lawless vision trembled at her approach.
She came and said, "Reave left the gate open,
And the horses were coming out when I happened past.
I never knew him to be forgetful before.
What was he thinking of?" They looked at her, Mark with eyes
That mutely implored pardon and fled away,
His mother made a carefully disinterested
Stare, and no answer. Helen stood wilfully near them,
And said, "How long has it hung?" After a moment
Mark answered hoarsely. And Helen: "Not more? Eighteen?

I thought it had always hung on these hills. I've seen it myself
Through an earthquake and some big winds, and that brush-fire
Three years ago. When *Reave* tackles it,
Down it shall come. Not the mountain-backed earth bucking like
    a bad horse, nor fire's
Red fox-tail on the hills at midnight, nor the mad southeasters:
    nothing can do it
But Reave Thurso, ah? That's the man we're measured against."
The old woman considered her once more, smiled, and to Mark:
"An inch to the mile. Dear, are you tired standing?
Surely it will not be long now." Mark whispered to her,
"Do you think he cares?" "Who?" "Father: his old work
Falling from the air at last." "We'll credit the dead
With a little more intelligence than to be troubled
About old iron." Helen overheard her,
And out of the uneasy malice of unhappiness: "Why credit them?
Very likely their minds like their spoiled bodies
Decay and go down the scale, through childish mutterings
To poisonous imbecility, and things that seem
Worthless to us might be to them like playthings
Precious to children, worth spite, all they've got left . . ."
    "You—"
The old woman felt Mark's anguish, and pushing by him
Stood against Helen—"weren't asked. When we're dull and want
    laughter
We'll ask you to tell us your thoughts." Helen retreated
With looks of startled innocence, "Oh, how have I made you
    angry? I was praising your son, the other one,
A man who masters earthquake, storm and bad horses, and has no
    fear of the dead, and can drive a truck
With his wife in it; never reached out his hand for anything yet
    but down it came. Look up: he's there
By the oak-tree, your strong man of this hollow, his feet on a
    cloud. He'd never falter if a thousand ghosts
Were camped against him: but look at the size of the man: one
    of those tiny
Black ants that come to dead things could carry him

With the oak too. Mark, you hate cruelty and killers: do you
    know that he spent yesterday
Poisoning squirrels? Olvidia told me.
Poor little dusty monkeys whipped for my sins,
Dying in agony." Mark answered hollow and slow,
"It has to be done, I suppose. Once he told me,
No poison no farms. He said that strychnin's
What civilized California: there'd still be grizzlies
And timber-wolves." "So all your sweet starts of mercy
Tune down to that meek end. Well, Mark: some time
San Francisco and New York and Chicago will fall
On the heads of their ghosts, so will that cable."

                    A small bright falcon,
Invisible from the floor of the gorge, but Reave saw it
Above the cloud-stream, shot down the shiny sky
And lighted on the long cable above the skip,
Folded its wings, and veered its vizarded face
With sharp looks north and south. Reave thought, "All the birds
Count on this ironware for as fixed as mountains,
It was here before they were hatched in the high nests,
Now I'll surprise him." He said, "Hand me the axe,"
For all the weight was hanging on a few cords
Of twisted wire. He lifted the dinted axe,
An old one for rough work. "Stand clear, Johnny," but the wires
Were not chewed deep enough yet; the edge nicked and bent
    them
Into the block, the whole cable like a hive of bees
Hummed over the gulf in the hanging air, and the hawk flew,
But the wires held. Reave looked at the bright crescent
Chipped in the brown axe-edge. "The old man's tough;
But wait a minute." An instant thought of Helen
Ran like a string of ants over his mind,
No danger of Helen standing under the skip
As his mother wished in her spite, but Mark's mind
Was not secure, better look down. The trees in the canyon
Hid the dooryard from here, and Reave went seaward
Some twenty paces along the steep of the hill

Through pale oak-leaves and russet ferns to see Mark standing
By his mother, Helen beside them, foreshortened specks
On the foot-worn patch of earth from the dark redwoods
And the globular golden puff of the sycamore
To the painted roofs of the house. Light mist flew over them,
Helen lifted the pin-point white of her face,
She looked like an incredibly small flower-stock
Suddenly flowering.

     Johnny Luna
Stood by the cable with a file, and looking down
Saw the wires move like a scarred twist of worms
In the wood they were dented into, the all but invisible
Kinks printed in them by the steel edge straightening,
A nicked strand broke, then all parted at once
Very smoothly and instantly. He saw the scything rope
That ran from the cable to the oak-tree go west
And strike Reave standing, he was bent at the loins backward
And flung on the face of the hill.

        Helen also saw,
But the others watched the great cable and the skip fall,
Obliquely in the draw of the rope, and the high oak-tree
Rush down the hill, the arched balks and crooked thighs
Of root in the scant soil on the near rock
Channeled with dry-rot, proving less masterful
Than one inch twist of hemp: so avalanchelike
The whole tree went down to the gorge, from its great yellow
  furrow on the face of the hill
A long track of dust blew east, above and below
The racing clouds.

      Thus the long trough and the covering sky
Of Mill Creek Canyon were cleared of that old cobweb,
The black moon over the gorge was down, and the mountain lips
Wiped clean. Helen Thurso ran up
Under the trees, through the oak-thicket, up the glacis
Of gray dead grass to the wreck of the oak-tree,

And up by the long furrow of the slide to Reave's
Body on its edge, dragged down and flung aside,
Like a red root cut by the plow and pitched
Forth of the furrow. He was not dead but crawling,
His belly and legs flat to the ground, his head
Lifted, like that lizard in the desert, and Helen saw the red ropes
   of muscle
Labor in his great shoulder, the shirt and the skin flayed off them.

               Luna came down from above, then Helen's
Face frightened him more than his master's body, it was white as
   lightning, eyed and mouthed with darkness, and the strained
   breath
Whined from the pit of her lungs like a bat's cries. She stood
Wavering, Reave crawled at her feet, the gorge glimmered below.
"God evens things. My lover in the desert,"
She gasped, "crawled in the sand like that after Reave struck him.
A bushel for a bushel says God exactly.
What can we do?" Luna stood mute and helpless, the color of
   his Indian skin like pale blue slate.
Reave crawled down hill between them; they watched the corded
   strips of flesh in his shoulder reddening and paling,
And when he began to speak they were terrified. "Must 'a' been
   holes in my mind. Everything wrong. Won't die."
Helen cried shrilly, "How can we get you down, where can I
   touch you?" "Hell," he said, "you'll wash." "For your pain!"
She cried shrilly. He raised up his gray face, fantastically grown
   smaller, hewn thin and focussed
On resistance, like a flint chip: "Can't worsen it, fool. I don't die.
   Drag." They dragged him a little way
Down the hill and his mother came; in a flash Helen understood
   whose face it was
That Reave's in pain resembled identically, and felt toward his old
   mother
Her heart move in a jet of loving compassion
Wild and lost like peering down a precipice,
She cried "O mother!" The old woman went to Reave's head
And carried it against her breast. Helen and Luna

Carried his body, so they went tottering down;
His legs dragged in the feather-gray sage until Olvidia
And Hester came. On the steep of the slope came Mark
Hitching up on hands and knees for his lameness.
Helen thought, "Both her sons crawling!" and cried shrilly,
"Get out of the way, will you. He's met somebody
Stronger than himself. Now I forgive him, now I forgive him.
I'd die for him." The old woman glanced at her
With astonished hatred across Reave's head. "You forgive him!"

X V

Winter had begun and Reave was brought home from the
    hospital
In Monterey. Luna drove and Helen crouched
Beside Reave's mattress in the open body of the farm-truck.
She thought they all came by turns to ride in it: pigs and calves
    to the butcher, Hester Clark from Nevada,
Herself from her lover and the desert mine, and again Reave
    Thurso. All compelled; all unhappy; all helpless.
Clouds with dragging keels came in from the ocean, over Mal
    Paso bridge a thin rain began,
Helen drew up the oil-skin over the blanket and said, "I know
    that you suffer pain day and night,
And now the jolting of the road is torture." He was silent a time;
    his face looked like his mother's. "What of it?"
He said suddenly. "Not to hide it from me, hidden pain's worse.
    If you trusted me . . ." "Do you think rat-gnawings
Mean much to a man who never any more . . . all the endless
    rest of his life lie flat like a cut tree . . .
Something to think about, ah? Have food brought and be wiped,
    grow fat between a tray and a bed-pan,
While every shiftless and wavering fool in the world
Has walking legs. Never waste pity: the cramps and the stabbing
    are my best diversion: if they ever ended
I'd have to lie and burn my fingers with matches. Well: day by
    day." She watched the small raindrops
Beading his rough eyebrows and hair, and said "I'd willingly die
    for you; I have not one grain of comfort
To answer with."

323

At Sovranes Creek he began to peer about and
look up the mountain, but dimly
To be seen through leaning pillars of rain. "You throw off the
oilcloth. What are you looking at, dear?" "Pasture.
Pasture for cows." Helen saw mist-green veils tapering up the
iron folds to the mountain-head,
The noble slopes and the crowning pyramid, and suddenly began
to weep aloud. He said, "I can't help it.
You promised lightly to take the worse with the better. This is
the worse.
I never will let you go until you are dead.
When you played the chippy I went and fetched you back;
You'll never try it again." His focussed will
Forgot to control the outthrows of bodily pain,
He ended groaning, with convulsed lips. Helen answered,
"I wasn't crying. I wasn't crying for myself. I will not be
At last contemptible." And lifting her white throat
Against the blue hills and rain: "Nothing can break you,
It was only bones and nerves broke, nothing can change you.
Now I've begun to know good from bad
I can be straight too." "Hell," he said, "changed enough.
Dead legs and a back strapped in plaster. You'll never
Be as straight as this." Helen shivered in the rain and said,
"What kind of a doctor was that, who leaves you suffering."
"An honest old man. He told me plainly that the nerves of pain
Might live, and the nerves of motion were lost. He told me,
When I asked him, that I shall never ride, walk, nor even
Be able to stand." She answered suddenly, "I'll never leave you
In life or death." He smiled and his lips whitened with pain. He
said, "How's Mark?" "Stark mad: all his gentleness
Gone into vengeful broodings. He thinks a dead man tore up an
oak on the mountain . . ." Reave frowned and said,
"Exactly. With my imbecility to spring the trap. Our fathers
build and cowardly slip out and we
Catch the fall. Not so crazy as you think. Do you think there's
anything beyond death, Helen?" "Yes," she answered,
"Worms." "And sleep, without pain or waking. Don't worry, I'll
never ease myself out by hand. The old dog
Stinks in that alley."

Luna drove fast; Helen leaned on her hands
for balance in the swirling turn
Around the cape of the road over Garapatas and said, "How did
he kill himself? I never knew."
Reave sharply between tight lips of suffering: "Leave that." She
answered, "He acted cowardly and you despise him,
But perfect courage might call death like a servant at the proper
time, not shamefully but proudly." His mind
At civil war in the darkness forgot to control the animal tokens
of pain, he groaned and answered:
"Means your freedom, ah?" "You are right," Helen said, "to ex-
pect vileness in me: I will show you before the end
That I am changed." "I didn't mean that. Blind bitterness. But I
mean to stick it out, you know, and there's tempting
Too sweet to be patient with. I say damn quitters."

The little
farm-truck, with its dull-smoldering sparks of sad life,
Ran swiftly on south the wavering and twisted road on the steep
foot of the mountain sea-wall. No life
Ought to be thought important in the weave of the world, what-
ever it may show of courage or endured pain;
It owns no other manner of shining, in the broad gray eye of the
ocean, at the foot of the beauty of the mountains
And skies, but to bear pain; for pleasure is too little, our inhuman
God is too great, thought is too lost.
It drove above the long crescent beach toward Palo Colorado,
That is lined with lonely splendor of standing wind-carven rocks,
like a chariot-racetrack adorned with images,
Watched by the waving crowds and clamor of the sea, but there
are no chariots. Thurso's Landing
Stood heavy-shouldered in the south beyond.

XVI

After some days
and nights Reave called for Luna.
Helen fetched him, Reave instructed him to choose two fence-
rails
And whittle handles on the ends, and nail cross-pieces

To make a stretcher. An old tarpaulin was cut
For canvas, which Helen sewed over and bound with fishline
Between the two rails. Reave had thought carefully,
There was no reason for being jailed in the house,
There were things he was bound to bear, that was not one of
     them.
Helen and Olvidia each holding a handle,
And Luna at the other end, carried him forth
Heavily, of fantastic shape and weight
With the plaster girdle about his loins: like a stone man,
Petrified man, was echoing in Helen's mind
While she labored with the weight, "Does everything I dream
     come true?"
They laid him on a low bank near the corral,
Where he could turn his head and at times
See horses in the muddy enclosure. Or see tall redwoods,
And if he wished, the long narrow canyon sky,
Reminding him what its clearance had cost.

                                        One day that Helen
Was bringing his lunch from the house, she saw Mark
Waiting in her path; she went about him to avoid him,
Feeling unable at length to hear his troublesome
Mysteries with patience, and approached Reave
An unusual way, unseen and silently, on the new grass
Around a thicket. She saw the whitened knuckles
Of his heavy-boned hands over his breast,
One clutching the other, and then the fists beaten together
Like stones, and heard a high helpless moaning. She stole back
And broke through the branches into her accustomed path,
To go to him lying quiet and watching stolidly
While she came near. She trembled and set the tray on the
     ground,
And said, "May I shift the pillows under you?" He answered,
     rolling his head,
"I can shift them. Look here." The bluish bruised look of his
     face darkened, that the gray eyes

Looked white in it, his thick neck swelled; he was raising himself
    upward with prodigious pain and effort by the thrust
Of his elbows backward against the earth, saying harshly, "I am
    not helpless." He clutched his hands in the soil
And slowly with immobile face and no groan lay down. She felt
    in her breast like the rush of a big bird
Flying from a covert and the threshing wings: "If I'd never been
    here," she said, "nothing would have been the same."
She knew that she ought to be silent, she could not cease, crying
    uncontrollably,
"You'd not be hurt, you'd be riding on the hill. I wish I had died
    in misery before you saw me,
I wish you had seen me first lying five days dead in the jagged
    mountain, blackening on a white rock
In a dry place, the vultures had dipped their white beaks in my
    eyes, their red heads in my side,
You'd make them raise the great wings and soar, you'd see my
    bowels drawn out of my body and the rock stained under me
And the soil of death, I was lying black-mouthed in the filth of
    death. You'd not have wanted me then, and nothing
Would be as it is, but you'd be lucky and I quiet." He looked
    in her eyes and smiled, with that bruised look,
Not hearing, bent inward on his own pain; but after a time he
    seemed to remember that she spoke of death
And said angrily: "Have you death for sale, you talk like a sales-
    man.
Every fool knows it's pleasant to rot in peace
After long pain but that's not the question.
I saw a nigger boxer in Monterey one night,
Cut all to pieces,
Sail on up the wind of fists, beaten and blinded,
Vomiting blood: he needed only let down
His knees onto the canvas and be at peace,
He wouldn't do it. I say I cared for that man;
He was better than a better fighter."

XVII

Reave's doctor came to break the cast from his body; Helen
helped, and washed the ill-smelling
Long-enclosed flesh. Afterwards while Reave rested she spoke
with his mother in another room. "You saw him.
The giant shoulders and the pitiful part below. I know that he
has hoped secretly to live again . . .
Ride a horse . . . he'll never sit up in bed. What can we do?"
She answered with a like contorted face,
But not twitching like Helen's: "There were two oaks broken
that morning. What can you do? Run away.
Follow that Hester. You and she are out of employment
When a man's withered from the waist down." She answered,
"Yet I was thinking there's . . . another kindness
That I could do for him. Another that his mother can't." "What?"
she said fiercely. "Nothing, nothing, nothing,"
Helen faintly answered. "However, I'll never leave him. I prom-
ised him never to leave him and I've grown faithful
At last." She felt the old woman's eyes like flints press on her
own, she shuddered and said, "I know
You hate me: let our spites lie, we're both unhappy. Tell me
something, if you know, what's all this troublesome
Affair of living, and people being troubled and the sun rising
and setting: what's it all about, what's it for?
I've seen you go on bitterly year after year, living, planning,
working: do you know something
That's hidden from the weak like me? Or it's only
Gloomy stubbornness like Reave's blind . . . or else perhaps
we live for no other reason than because our parents
Enjoyed their pleasure and we dread to die? *I* dread it," she said
with her hands at her throat, "so . . . I can't bear it,
But Reave's too proud. I mean, if the pain ceases, if his pain ceases
at last . . . then I can't imagine.
But if the pain keeps up I must do it." "What can you do
But run away off? You're not the make. I wish
He could see your slobbered face, Helen, he'd hardly
Have hunted into Arizona to fetch it home,

Do what then?" Her mouth shuddered and tautened, she answered,
"I cannot tell." "I believe you," she answered scornfully.
Helen stood moving her sad lips in silence
Like one casting a sum of numbers, and said,
"I must have read it somewhere: a hundred and twenty-three
Millions in this one country of the world, besides the animals.
　Far more in Asia. How can it be sacred
Being so common? I've never hated you back for hating me;
　I've called you Mother; now if you'd help me
To know what's right I'd be grateful." The old woman with
　eyes like a hawk's watching
A bush of sparrows: "Tell me then." "For now it seems to me
　that all the billion and a half of our lives on earth,
And the more that died long ago, and the things that happened
　and will happen again, and all the beacons of time
Up to this time look very senseless, a roadless forest full of cries
　and ignorance. But is life precious
At the worst you know? I used to wish for round jewels and a
　fur cloak: I could love opals,
Born in October: and a set of gay laughing friends to fool with,
　and one of those long low stream-lined cars
That glide quietly and shine like satin: so I can't say, whether
　life maybe might 'a' been precious
At the best. And death's awful. . . . We're too closed-in here."
　"If you think of killing yourself": she laughed,
Lifting her shoulders. Helen looked down and said,
"How did . . . Reave's dad do it?" "In the forehead, poor fool,
And was long dying." "In the heart would have been better?"
"You must find out for yourself." "I wasn't thinking of myself;
I'm faithful now." "To the death? Ah?
A new color for you, worn strangely."

　　　　　　　　　　　　　　　　　　She went through the house
To her son's room. Helen followed, saying, "Go quietly,
And listen." They tip-toed down to hear a thin moaning
Increase and break off; then hands beat on the bed
In the room behind the shut door; a silence followed,
And again the moaning. The old woman rolled her gray head

And whispered, "I'll not awake him." But Helen: "If that is
    sleep,
Then life's a dream." She touched the door-handle
And the room was full of silence; they entered, Reave lay
Stolid and strong, meeting them with calm eyes
Blood-shot around the gray-blue. Helen said faintly,
"May I turn you now?" He said "What meanness in you
Is always making me out worse than I am? Helpless enough,
But not to that point." The old woman went to the window
    and looked down the canyon; then turning: "Helen talks
    strangely.
She says that she's now faithful. What does that mean, do you
    think?" Reave answered, "I know she is, and I pay it
With cross impatiences: I'm sorry, Helen." "Oh, but you'd never
    guess," the mother said furiously,
"How far that reaches, this kind of faithfulness. She's likely had
    word
From the yellow-haired man, because . . ." Helen said sharply,
"That man is dead." Reave strained up his head, groaning,
"Who told you? Everything slips away. I was hopeful still
To touch him with my hands. He might have come near me
Sometime to mock my ruin. . . ." The old woman said,
"How could she hear? She's lying, I watched her mouth." "Reave
    killed him,"
Helen said patiently; "only by waiting for him and he didn't
    come, beat him to corrupt earth,
Dust and a wind. Oh Reave, be at peace
For anything you owed there." "She was lying again,"
The mother said, "but a moment ago in the other room
Her truth came out. This white, violet-eyed thing
Would if she dared murder you: Oh, from high motives,
All mercy and good will like a lamp in a window, but mostly
    wondering
Whether a dutiful wife will shoot her man
In the head or the heart." Helen had cried out to speak,
But checked herself and watched Reave; he answered heavily,
His light eyes withstanding his mother's dark ones: "We've talked
    it over.

But I have forbidden her." Then Helen cried, "Don't send me
away.
I believe you will never need me: but God's not moderate enough
to trust, and when he turns bad, no one
Can bear him to the end." He answered, "That's cowardly said;
there's nothing a man can't bear. Push my bed
To the window and let me look out westward." They moved
his bed; in the mouth of the gorge the evening sea-cloud
Hung heavy black, leoparded all over with sanguine fire-spots;
he muttered wearily, "We're too closed-in here.
I lie like a felled log in a gully and women wrangle above me.
I have no power and no use
And no comfort left and I cannot sleep. I have my own law
That I will keep, and not die despising myself."

The stormy twi-
light closed over and filled the canyon
And drowned the house, and the ocean made a great noise in
the dark, crying up the canyon; with between the cries
Noises like trespassers breaking fences, or the cattle running.

Helen slept in a room by herself,
For Thurso wanted no witness to hear his nights of endured
pain, and had sent her from the low couch
Beside his bed, to use the little room that Hester Clark had
been glad of.
She fell asleep for a moment and lay an hour
Terribly awake, and went down the stair, having a candle
In both her hands, the right hooding the flame
That etched red lines between the dark fingers,
The left holding the shaft, and the white grease
Dripped hot films on it. She went barefoot and silently
With the one piece of linen about her, hearing
The stairs groan like a man, and stole through the house
To a distant closet where vermin-traps and squirrel-poison,
Hunting-gear and a smell of leather were kept. She sought her
own rifle
In that close place, meaning to hide it in her bed

Between the springs and the mattress, knowing that no one
Commands life without the tools of death
Readily hid in the background. She loaded in
New cartridges with glittering brass jackets, for oil
Or time might have damped the old; and turned to the door.
Mark stood in the door.
But Helen thought that the strain in her mind had bred a
    phantom,
And waited for it to fade.

                             He said, "A thready light
Pricked into my room through the cracked panel.
I think my mind has been roiled, when I lie wakeful
Blades of strange light. Are you going hunting?
Dear Helen let the deer feed. Life's bad for people,
But the clean deer, that leap on the high hills
And feed by the hollow streams, there's not one of them
Lame nor a fool." She answered in her mind, "Nothing
Is very serious," and said, "Ah, there's one hurt one,
Would thank me kindly, if it had a man's brain,
For death, that great fallen stag." "Where is it? I'll feed it
With tender grass." "It fell on the mountain and its broken bones
Have caught the nerves in their hard lumps of healing,
So that it's in pain forever: I hate . . . love him too.
Love him, I said." "If you kill any living
Creature, the happiness of your heart is troubled
In quiet times afterwards." "What's that to me?
I shall have no quiet time after this hunting;
But brief and violent. Let me go now." He answered,
"I know what love is, I saw it in the devil's tie-pin.
How dared you come down undressed?" She saw him shaking
In the candle-light, and thought with a thread ravelled
From her mind's gathering fire-mist, "You poor good fool,
Is it there with you?" He said, "Horrible dreams of love
Like splintered glass in my bed cut me all night, like a splintered
    mirror.
Reave betrayed you with that pale bright doll." He came from
    the doorway toward her, then Helen laughed and dipped

Her hand in a half sack of barley on the shelf, and felt the kernels
    light and luxuriously
Lie in her fingers, and said through white lips: "Is this the poison-
    soaked grain? that makes the squirrels cry
In the quiet of their little caves, that bitter death?" "Let it alone.
    Oh, this place crawls with death,
Traps, guns, knives, poisons: but no one sleeps near, no one can
    bear us. There's a bright wanting beast in me:
Hunt that, Helen. Kill that. I thought love
Was kindness, it's a blind burning beast. Oh, wait: because I
    heard voices and answered them, saw spirits and feared
    them,
You and the rest were whispering that I was crazy. Why, that
    was nothing. But now, when I burn to tear
That last white rag from you, and do—how can I say it?—striking
    the obscene parts of our flesh together—
This is the real thing, this is the madness." She laughed and ran
    her fingers through the deadly barley and answered:
"Yours is a common trouble, we'd manage you a kind cure
If I were liberal; but you'd loathe me for it, and my winter's come.
    I wish to leave my poor spotted memory
A little lonely and distinct at this bitter end. Is it nearly morn-
    ing?" "Do you think . . ." he answered, and suddenly
The pallor of his face gleamed with a film of sweat, he said "I've
    fooled myself out of life for fancy
Feelings and second-hand noble dreams. Kill all the deer on the
    mountain, what's that to me? I've seen them
Go to it like dogs in the bushes outside the cantonment: wise
    soldiers: did you think you could come naked
And not be mauled?" She said furiously,
"You fool," and heard him hiss when he touched her breast and
    cry:
"The lids of your eyes are swollen, your eyes are knives.
This is it. Yes." His teeth clattered together so that she thought
    of a crooked stone the returning
Wave sucks, and the stone rolls over and over, clashing on the
    pebbles. He wiped his forehead with his hand and shook

The fingers as if blood hung on them, saying, "That Hester's
    gone. I might have had a second-hand . . .
Noble thought very likely.
Tell the audience for all those cat-calls there's not one of them
But's more or less in my manner
Done out of his dear life by scrupulous cowardices.
Men ought to ravage: then down comes the black curtain,
We died like old empty priests." But Helen seeing him
All shrunken again, "Believe me," she said in pity,
"These rosy toys you've missed make a bad bargain
At the time of the end. I could be very envious
Of virgins and a quiet life." "The two you've had
Are nothing," he answered, "take two hundred. But only
Beware not to make a baby, we know what life is:
That mercy's weakness, and honesty
The simple fear of detection; and beauty, paint;
And love, a furious longing to join the sewers of two bodies.
That's how God made us and the next wars
Will swallow up all. . . . Helen, I'm very tired
With cloudy thoughts, and have been fearful at times
Of falling into some unclearness of mind.
That would be bad: lunacy's worse than death.
If I should consider taking a certain remedy
While I'm still sane, to scour the rancid bowl
Back to its first brightness, who could be blamed?
You've always been kind beyond words."

                      He went, and Helen
At once forgot him, all her energy reverting
To its old preoccupation like a freed spring,
She took the rifle to hide it below her mattress
And barefoot stilly went up through the house.

                    She passed Reave's door,
And returned again to listen whether he moaned
Or slept. No sound appeared, but wind or the ocean
Whispering high over the house. In that silence
Her intention flowered; she became calm, convinced

That time had come to cut all the knots at once
And lead the agonies of strain to a sharp end.
Mark's outcry, though she forgot him, had tired her,
The resistances of a drained spirit faint
Before the power does, she had lost the strength not to act
And stealthily unlatched the door. It seemed clear, plain
And reasonable, to seal that heavy sleep
From ever waking to worse; but having planted
The candle upon the chest by the door, and drawing
Down the steel barrel the three points to one line,
She met his eyes wide open, broad and inhuman, like the uni-
versal eyes of night, judging
And damning her act, with remote absolute merciless compre-
hension. She was like a touched sleepwalker,
Unnerved and annihilated: what contemptible
Distraction had made the reasons of her dream? and **Reave:**
"Come closer. You'd botch it from there, and I'd be days
Dying or not, cursing you for a fool."
She leaned and shuffled toward him.

She felt her neck
Wrenched by the buffet, and lukewarm blood wandering
From her mouth down the left side of her throat and tasted
The thick salt sweetness, and Reave saying furiously, "Sneak in
behind me
Fighting on my last inch? I never struck you before, you earned
it enough." She mumbled,
"It doesn't hurt . . ." "Trust you," he said, "to side with my
enemy." His great hands, and the white knuckles
Like peaks among the black hairs, blazed in the lit center of
the orbital darknesses that hooded her eyes.
His hands had her little rifle and were strained to break it, but the
great strength that she believed could do anything
Failed after all. Snapping and whining with pain like a wounded
dog he shifted over on his elbows
And thrust the barrel under the board of the bedside, drew up
against his own weight, and the splitting stock

Ripped from the steel. "That's yours," he said gasping. "Go call
Luna." She felt the pain of her lips swelling,
Cut on the dog-tooth edge, and the blood on her throat, and
muttered, "It doesn't hurt." "You red and white
Barber's-pole," he said, "fetch Johnny Luna.
We'll have a disarmament here." "What?" "Light the lamp and
take
Your light and fetch him." "What? Oh, oh!" she cowered and
knelt down against the bedside, "don't send me away.
I'll promise never . . . I promise . . ." "You'll not be sent away,
I'll not let you go." "How could I sleep,"
She prayed, not hearing him, "or lie down, or *live*, in another
place, not knowing
How you were, and never see you nor touch you?" "You lie,"
he groaned, "or you're changed.
Be sure I'll not let you go. I am not changed."
She clenched a fold of the coverlet and stammered, "*I* am not
changed.
I was only ignorant. When the idiot body and perverse
Imagination went whoring . . . then still whatever it is
That loves was weeping here."

                              Reave's old mother
Stood in the door, her corded bare throat thrust
From the fold of a brown cloak, and dull-white wisps
Starring her head; the noise of the broken gun-stock
Had beckoned her from a dream. "Praying is she? Religion's
Their last trick . . ." She saw the blood-streak, and blazing
Went and dragged up Helen's face, one hand in the hair,
One at her throat, saying "What have you done, you . . .
It's your own, is it? That's better." Reave said, "Let her alone.
I called and she came running asleep, in the dark,
She struck her face." The old woman looked down the candle-
light
At the rifle-barrel and the splintered stock, and said,
"You are still strong." "But can't run my own errands.
Wash yourself," he said to Helen; "light the lamp;
Go and call Johnny."

When Helen was gone, the old mother:
"Tell me what she was doing." He rolled his shoulders
And groaned, striking his hand down at his thigh.
"Would you believe this fixed and passive flesh
Has red hot wire in it? What nights." "Why have you sent for
   Luna
At midnight?" "To amuse me awhile. Get to bed, mother,
Before the aching night strikes to your bones.
I had an inflamed throat
After that fall of rain, all my discomforts
Turned fiery then. . . . Oh, if you need, I'll tell you.
We've rifles and a shotgun, but nobody
Will ever go hunting from here again, and to save oiling
He's to break the guns. They call it disarmament. I dreamed
The old dog that was your husband and my father
Stood in a cave-mouth calling; and, to speak exactly,
I'll not be tempted."

XVIII

The house in the deep gorge
Had been darkened again. One of those night-birds that cry in
   quickening rhythm like the rattle of a spun plate falling
Cried, then the silver streak southeast loosed a slight moon. A few
   of the house-windows feebly glittered
Back its horned light; the massed black obelisks of redwood
   utterly ignored it, but the leafless leaning sycamore
Shone like a trunked and branched moon on the dark wood,
   a tree made wholly of luminous lunar material,
Except one long hanging shadow. The clouds took the moon
   again, the sycamore vanished, the dream in the eyes
Of the house died; and imperceptibly a twilight began to exist,
   without wind or color, or foam
Of a formal cloud, but misty rain fell. A faintly more curded
   mist-wreath flowed from a chimney and down
The house-roof valleys, it spread earthling dissolving, and sensi-
   tive wild nostrils up the great gorge
Tasted the oak-smoke and coffee fragrance of a waking house.
The world lightened, the rain increased.

A broad brown face peered from a window, a woman whose
   blood had known this coast for ten thousand years
Perceived a strangeness of shape in that moony sycamore. She
   had work in hand, but an hour later she poured
Coffee for Mark Thurso, who'd not come down yet, and set it
   with his egg back of the stove and went
To empty the grounds into the willows. She hooded her head
   against the rain with an apron, but returning
Saw the sycamore framed in the apron-fold
And it looked dreadful. She approached and found Mark hanging
Long-necked, very wet with rain. She stood at some distance,
Mournfully, with the coffee-pot in her hand,
Thinking the grounds were bad for chickens, but this
Rainy morning she might have mixed them with the other
   leavings,
Not gone out, and seen nothing. She went and washed plates
   and cups,
Wishing for Johnny, but he was busy in the barn.
The rain fell on the barn roof, the rain fell . . . everywhere . . .
And no one could sleep: smashing rifles all night.
Old Mrs. Thurso went in and out; Olvidia
Trembled each time, but after going to the privy
Was more composed in her mind.

                       The soft beneficent rain hung
   on the hills without flowing down
And filled the soil to the rock, all it could hold; it lay on the
   shore, it sweetened the bitter sea,
It dripped from every bough of the forest, and from the feet of
   the dead man and his hands and his chin,
It glazed his pale-blue face, and glazed the great seaward rock-
   face of Thurso's Landing, and each green leaf
And grass-blade south by the coast to Point Conception; and
   north into Oregon; so long an island of cloud,
Blinding white above, dark and dove-purple below, rained on
   a thousand miles of the continent's edge;
The old savage brood-mare, the earth, drank strength and forgot
   her deserts. Helen Thurso

Walked in Reave's room and looked out the window, and the
    ivory tree
Seemed to have borne in the rain enormous fruit.
She covered her mouth, through incredulous fear feeling
The bulge of her bruised lip, and left the room
Silently; she met Reave's mother carrying a white
Bundle of linen that glimmered down the dark passage,
And said, "Have you seen Mark?" She answered jealously
"What do you want?" "Oh, oh. If he's in his room.
I was thinking about the rain, I haven't seen him this morn-
    ing . . .
My eyes are sick." She passed and felt the smell
Of the freshly ironed linen mix with her fear,
And came to Olvidia in the hot kitchen
Stroking the iron on the board. "Come to the door
For God's sake, for the windows are blind with rain.
In the sycamore tree?" The Indian hung back, mumbling
"Might 'a' been a mountain-lion or a big hawk," and Helen
Dragged her by the wrist, but the old mother
Had followed and heard, and when they came to the door
She was at the foot of the tree. They heard her cry
Three times, a dry scream more goshawk's than woman's.
Helen breathed and said "Reave has heard that. I . . .
Get a knife." She ran to the tree; where Mark's mother
Stood stiffly quiet by the grotesque legs
And said, "I can't reach. He is the one I loved."
Helen began to clamber at the tree, her knees
Slipping on the wet bark and her fingers
On the ivory bough, the old woman said harshly, "Make no
    show of yourself.
He's been long dead and will not admire you. This one is mine,
    my servants will help me. Stand off, you."
Helen looked back at her face and saw Olvidia and Luna coming;
    she looked at the dead man's face
And said, "Oh, good-bye," and looked down quickly. "I will go
    to Reave," she said trembling.

She went to his room.
The bed-covers were trailed on the floor and he at the window
Hung like a broken snake, his hands on the sill lifting his head
    to the glass. He turned toward her,
Wrinkled like a fighting mastiff with rage and pain, saying "That
    dead dog." She shivering and shrill cried out
"No!" but he said, "The dead dog that walks in the wood, that
    he used to talk to, has done this: too shot with cowardice
To live, and too envious to let his sons. Praising death. Oh my
    poor brother,
If you lived in the hell of pain and impotence
That I inhabit, yet you oughtn't to have yielded. It was some-
    thing to see the envy slaver with hunger
And not be fed." Then Helen said faintly, half borne into be-
    lief by Reave's passion, "Oh, have you seen him?"
The great strained shoulders began to fail, the hooked fingers to
    slip on the painted sill, "Felt him," he said,
Angularly falling.

Unable to lift his weight, she dragged it
To the side of the bed, and heaved up the dead half
Of his body, and he the living. She fell over against him
In the strain of lifting, his violent hands held her
Like a lover's, hurting her breasts against his ribs, she felt a
    ghastliness in him
But forced her charged nerves to make no resistance
And kissed his cheek with her bruised mouth, the hardening
Muscles of his jaw hurt that. "Fool," he said hoarsely.
"Have you forgotten? You'll have to learn to endure
A starved life for a hot woman." She stood up
And saw his lips bluish and compressed and his eyes blunted.
    "Our loves now,
Ah," he said, "a little too heavy. A wrench of pain
For the consummation.
Pain is the solidest thing in the world, it has hard edges,
I think it has a shape and might be handled,
Like a rock worn with flat sides and edges, harder than rock, but
Like love it can hardly last more than fifty years.

340

Mark is dead. He'd not have yielded in his right mind.
Go help my mother." Helen said, "She drove me away.
He was always faithful and kind. Oh, oh, what shore
Are we sailing toward, with such wrecks for the sea-marks?
Dear, you didn't dream I meant to outlive you? Our poor brother
Did very wisely though I wish . . . I can hardly remember
The time when death used to seem terrible to me:
I've worse fears now. But if the whole world should be burned
    alive.
Our brother, whom we loved well, is safe."

XIX

                          Reave sighed,
And said, "Go and tell her to send Luna.
He'll have to ride to Lobos, there's no telephone
Nearer. To let the coroner know. Oh God, why bother?
I used to have legs and do my own business.
Do you believe in a God?" "I didn't use to."
"Well? Now do you?" "We've less reason to. Yes.
There's not a tinge of goodness in the whole world,
But war in my mind and agony in yours, and darkness
Over the sea and the heights and all bright spirits
Forsake the earth. We've excellent cause
To know there's none: but there is." "Go to church then.
A torturer then." He wiped his forehead and said,
"Another dead dog to bite us. What, that sits calmly
Above the stars, and sees the old woman lose both her sons for
    nothing, one in a dirty noose
And the other like a broken stick on a dung-hill; then smiles over
    the sea to China on a million people
Dying of hunger, the lucky ones sold their children for tufts of
    grass and die with green teeth, God pats
His baby hands together and looks down pleasantly. No, the
    world's not so comic as that: I'll tell you
What the world's like: like a stone for no reason falling in the
    night from a cliff in the hills, that makes a lonely
Noise and a spark in the hollow darkness, and nobody sees and
    nobody cares. There's nothing good in it

Except the courage in us not to be beaten. It can't make us
Cringe or say please." "Dear," she answered,
"Where would the weakness be in kicking off a random and senseless
Darkness like that? Strength doesn't suffer for nothing,
Strength would refuse to suffer for nothing, but choose its times
To live or die." "Listen," he said; "there's a silver spoon
With my initials on it in a drawer somewhere.
When I was five years old I saw my father
Use it in his mouth: I never would touch it again.
No doubt it stinks." Tenderly she answered,
"You have great hands: I love you: kill me first,
And then eat with *my* spoon. It would be wine and honey,
Oh sweet, sweet, after this life." He laughed angrily
And moaned and said, "Let's talk sense if we talk.
I'll not have him buried here and put him forever
In the black dog's power: superstitious as you:
To Monterey, some old graveyard
Where decent people are lying beside each other
And a rose turns from the sea.

                              ". . . Mother," he said,
She entering the room, "your loss is hard.
There's nothing. We must take our pain and live in it." Her eyes
More like dry flints than ever, "Can you read this,"
She said, holding a rag of sodden paper,
"My sight fails, and the rain has washed it, pinned to his coat."
She gave it to Reave, he holding it against the light
Said wearily, "Read it, Helen." Sick pencil-marks
On death-cold paper: she read in a brittle voice:
"I fear insanity. Forgive this ugly sight,
Dribbling and screeching would be an uglier sight,
Or to do something worse. Oh, why did you go away,
Why did you come back?
My only cause for this act is fear of madness.
That must be stated clearly. No other cause. Dear love,

Come soon, this room is purer." Helen's voice fainted on the
final words.
She fixed her eyes on the old mother's and said,
"It was written to *you*." Who answered harshly, "*I* did not go
away nor come back. Her tricks of nature
Have made their misery again. I never hated her enough." Helen,
without moving: "How could I care
Who hates me or not, when I think about him writing that in
the night? He often made notes for thoughts
With a stub pencil," she bit her lip not to weep, and suddenly
the tears rained down. The old mother: "Ah, Reave?
We have to face it: she fished for *him* too. If I'd married a
stronger man my sons might have outlived me,
But a woman from nowhere comes and burns you like wax.
Give me that paper." Helen gave it and the wet slip
Tore in the taking. Reave said, "Snatch, sea-gull. Be a little quiet
over my head, pain's worn me thin,
And Mark's dead in the house. We're sorry for you,
Mother. As for that message, it has no meaning but the pity in
it." The old woman looked young, with the angry
Color on her cheek-bones; Helen looked aged and pale, saying,
"Very likely it is quite true that I brought
Misery in both my hands, unwillingly. I am much to be blamed
for all our miseries. I can bear it.
But while the night darkens, and God closes his hand on this
house, and there's no help, I might do well at last
What you can't do. After that I'll submit meekly, whether you
wish to punish me or please to say
Some merciful thing."

           Reave opened his eyes and said,
"Mark's not to be buried here, this is the dog's ditch.
He'd 'a' lived long if he hadn't walked in the woods.
If you have to sell horses to buy a grave to the north, there's a
little colt
That has no name, I'm fond of him, I rode him before the fall."
His mother stared, saying "Who buys horses?"

He answered, "He's not for sale, I'll not have it. I hunted the
   desert for him
When he strayed, and brought him back. Are you all ganged
   against me
With the devil in the woods?" The old woman touched him and
   said,
"Reave. Nobody will sell your horses. There's no buyer.
You're tired." He answered, "Not tired: but to say it plainly:
In hell, in hell. . . . I have talked foolishness.
I can bear twice as much. Go back to Mark, mother.
He needs . . . I remember." The women stood side by side
Gazing at his locked face, the mother weaving
Her thin hands together, having that rainy paper
Crushed between the two palms, but Helen stone still; then
   Reave
Drew down the lids over his staring eyes
And made a thin careful smile. The old woman suddenly
Sighed and went out.

> Reave drew loud breath and his eyes
Opened, fastened on Helen's: "Don't let her come in again.
I'd hate to tell her. She's much to be pitied too. Never let her
   know," he said craftily,
"That she's the cause. She lay with my enemy, all springs from
   that. I believe you'd never dream it, to look at her,
She'd do such things. Has it cleared?" She stammered "What—
   what?" "Go to the window," he said, "and look out, and see
Whether the rain has stopped yet." She went and said, "No."
   "It is clearing eastward?" "All dark. Some wind moves
The sky-ridge trees." "Rain or not"; and after a moment, "Did
   you notice anything," he said, "Helen, disordered
In what I said lately?" "I know you suffer
Overpowering pain at times." "Hm? Not a bit. Firm as a rock.
   . . . Listen, Helen:
My pride and I have agreed: I can bear this punishment,
But I don't have to." She thought he had yielded and was willing
   to die;

That he was beaten seemed to be breaking her heart, that he
    would die terrified her, that his useless pain
Would find its goal in peace was a great sheaf of good; so three
    ways stricken, white and faint: and the undertow
Unconscious enmity that never died from her mind tearing her
    too with its exultation: "Oh,"
She whispered, "what change?" "Why should I refuse the means
    to relieve it?"
He said defiantly. "I'm like in the sea's gut here,
Weighed down with tons of green thick water: while above the
    air's
Clean and alive. We're too closed-in here." He paused,
His eyes glassed and hands clenched. "A twinge. Don't imagine
I'm running from the dead dog: we'll make a bonfire
Of his platforms on the rock-head some night.
That's my one point in life now: to clean out
Trace and shape and smell of him and leave the canyon
Virgin if fire and dynamite can do it.
In summer when the ground hardens we'll slash
A driveway up to the kilns and blow them clean
By the foundations. Have you told him yet?" "What?" she
    asked.
"What!—bring it to the door." "Dear, I'm dull with sadness,
I can't see to your mind." "Have I not told you
Three times already? The truck, the truck, the motor-truck.
The thing that runs on four wheels. Tell him—tell Luna
To bring it to the door and help you load on your cripple,
So I'll taste air to-day." "Where?" "Where it's widest,
And the ocean and hills are clear to be seen,
On the Landing: the rock-head: up there." "Oh, Oh, that's in
    the sky.
That's well thought." She trembled violently and said,
"I'll do my part. It's noon:
First you must eat, though Mark's dead in the house.
Then we'll go up to the rock. It seems long
Since morning." He said, "To-morrow they'll need the motor
To take my brother . . . who has died, as you say. Akh, do
    quickly."

XX

"You'll need the jack and a shovel, Johnny Luna,
For the ground's rotten with rain; and an axe
For brushwood no doubt has grown up in the old road.
Yet another thing:
There was a man named Rick Armstrong: do you remember?
He's dead quite lately. *He* died too. The world's
Full of that kind of thing." She pressed her hand
On the reeling pulse in her throat and said, "I'll tell you.
He drove too fast at the Salinas River bridge,
Suddenly his sins came on him and swerved the wheel
Over the concrete, he rolled with his car
And got his life bumped out in the willow-bushes.
Do you understand? It will please my husband,
For he was his bitter enemy: but if *I* told him
I might not be believed.
I am very anxious to make him feel . . . contentment
Before he . . . sleeps, because he suffers great pain
And has no joy nor hope. Johnny, you'll help me
For love of him, and I'll give you this ring besides.
I wore it through all my ventures, bought long ago
With money I earned. I paid twelve dollars for it,
You can get three no doubt: the stone's nothing,
But the hoop's gold. Take it please.
I've nothing else of any priceable value
Except my marriage ring: I'll die in that,
Though stained, some acid. What you must do is, tell him
About Rick Armstrong's death, as I told it to you,
To make him happier; but say the Vasquez boys
Told you, not I. Everyone's talking about it,
He was well known on the coast; he worked, you know,
With the road-builders. Mind the jack and the spade,
And the hand-axe: he's half mad with pain
Or he'd not want to go up. Why, the rain's stopped,"
She said, and sobbed once and smiled. "That's a grand sign.
Ah don't forget how Rick Armstrong died."

XXI

Reave's mother heard
The motor stammer to the house-door, and spin and stop. She
stood up beside her own bed,
On which she had had her dearest laid down, and had never
ceased to arrange the body, to make it seem
Happily asleep if she could; having dried it with a warm towel
and washed the rain-stains, and dressed her son
In clean night-clothes, covering the throat: she looked at the
bed with unmoistened eyes like a mother falcon,
And went downstairs to the door; Luna was entering. "Who
ordered this? Take it back to the shed.
He will stay in my house with me to-night: if we go to-morrow
To another place, I will tell you, not that woman." Helen came
while she spoke, and Luna
Looked from her face to hers, as a boatman
From the rock shore to the driving sea. Helen said, "We must
take the bedding first, it is ready."
The old mother: "You're very confident suddenly. You think
you've made enough wretchedness to break my mind and
make you
Commander here." Helen, vaguely, in her own thought snared:
"What? No. Is a wind blowing, the trees on the cloud
Look hunched: and all my strength's gone: Oh mother,
Tell Reave to wait! Comfort him." "Reave?" She turned and
went toward his room, then Helen remembered that sud-
denly
He seemed to dislike his mother: "Don't go in to Reave:
Oh, I was wrong," and followed her; and Luna followed
The two women. Helen said to Luna: "Take out the mattress
and the covers: we'll have to go." The old mother
To Reave: "You called for that? Did you tell me you were going
somewhere,
And I missed hearing?" His eyes avoided her, he answered:
"I'm going to the head of the rock to smell the rain.
Why not? I can't make Mark live
By smothering here." "The rock?" "Uh, what y' call the Landing.

I believe the air's free there." He closed his eyes
And fists, and smiled. Helen said sharply to Luna:
"The little package is mine: let it lie, I'll take it.
Bread and meat." Reave's mother looked back and saw
Her throat shuddering and swallowing as strained with sickness
At the thought of food. "Why: how long are you staying up
    there?"
"While our . . . the light lasts," she answered, and swallowed,
    and said,
"Olvidia's here if you need anything." The mother:
"Reave. This is not in your line, to run off from trouble.
She leads you I think." "Run?" He rolled his head on the thick
    neck. "*Run*,
To a man with no legs. And *she leads me:* you are very greedy
    to make humiliation perfect, ah?
I might have a grudge too . . . wi' that dog . . . ugh. Mother,
    mother:
You endure something and so do I: but bodily pain is ignoble
    and soils the mind. If ever
I should talk wildly . . . no danger: I can bear much more than
    anything yet . . . you'll not take it to heart,
Put it aside as just foam and nothing. I love you and respect you,
    and when you are bitter with me I know
How life has used you.
About the other thing: have you ever known me to turn back
    from something begun? I've grown touchy,
But not all changed." "In this raw air," she answered,
"In the likely rain to go up: you told me your trouble turned
    fiery after a rain." "I am ashamed,"
He said dully, "to leave you in sorrow. I can do nothing here,
    not even walk to Mark's room.
A man like me, crippled out of use, hurt out of patience and so
    forth,
May's well go picnics. . . . D'y' see that star?" "What?" "The
    star." "There's no star, Reave." He drew his hand
Over his eyes and said, "No star? None? Oh, yes there is.
Thousands, but in the house we can't see them. Well, Helen.
Move me, ah? March."

That frame of redwood sticks
And canvas was laid on the bed against him, Reave shifted
The living part of his body onto it, the others
The lower part. Helen saw his jaws locked
Not to express pain, she heard the breath
Hiss through his nostrils, and thought that she must detach
Her nerves from feeling with his, or all her remnant
Of strength to help him would bleed away to no purpose: but a
    superstitious
Fear forbade any restraint of sympathy,
It looked too much like betrayal; and Reave might suffer
Some mystic loss. She took one of the whittled
Litter-handles, the old woman another, and Luna
The two at Reave's feet; so they conveyed him forth
And edged him onto the truck-floor. He felt his mother's
Eyes probe him, then to cover pain and the shame
Of helplessness: "You ought to rig up a mast
And tackle," he muttered with flat dry lips,
"To hoist your deck-load aboard." "Reave, for God's sake,"
Helen cried. "What?" he said. "Ships are bad luck I think."
"Fool." "Yes"; and she said panting, "Oh, you're quite right,
Call it a ship. I'll sit on the deck beside you.
Our lives are taken away from luck and given
Higher." The old woman looked at her lifted face
And began fiercely to speak, and looked at Reave's, and clutched
The broken board-ends of the floor of the truck
By his feet, where the steel binding was sprung. "I will stay with
    Mark,"
She said harshly. "It's been promoted," Helen said,
"From being the barge for calves to the butcher.
Now . . ." The mother: "I think, Reave, this woman
Is faithful now." "—A ship," Helen said, "exploring
The open ocean of pain to try if there's any
Shore." "You have not the courage," she answered.
"But as you deal with Reave I will deal with you,
And twice as much. I have nothing to hold me." She turned to
    the house
And the car moved; before she came to the door-step

She fell down in the path; but no one saw her,
For Helen looked at Reave, Reave at the sky,
And Luna drove. The old woman dragged her hands
Through the wet earth and stood up, lifting her yellow
Asturine face: as when a goshawk is caught in a steel trap at a
    pole's end,
That was feathered with a bird for bait, and the farmer comes
    with death in his hands and takes down the pole, she turns
In the steel teeth and outstares her captor with harder eyes.

                        Pitching and slipping on stones
And greasy earth, the truck toiled up the farmlane; Helen
    watched the lines in Reave's face, and risings
Of muscle in his cheek when he locked his jaws when a jolt
    racked him. Once, when the fore-wheels and then the rear
Struck in succession and Reave's lips tightened, she laid her
    hand on his fist: "That was the cable," she said,
And wished that she had kept silence; and said, "It lies in the
    canyon mud like a killed snake: your enemy
Was under your wheels." But whether he heard her or not he
    made no sign.

            At the turn to the county road
Mill creek is bridged; the stream ran full, on the bridge was a
    whirlwind funnel of sticks and splinters, then Helen
Looked up the redwoods and saw the racing sky, and a ray of sun
    plunge like a sword, cut northward,
And be withdrawn. They climbed the cliff-cut zig-zag stair of
    the road; when they neared the crest
The blanket streamed up, stripped from Reave's feet, and Helen
With a sudden sea-gull cry caught it down again
And said "Oh, Reave!" as if waked from a dream
That drove toward some unbearable end. "We can't
Go out to the rock, but if you can bear it
We'll go on farther than that, we'll go on to town.
The doctor will have to do . . . at least something
To still your pain." "All the opium in India.
Brought low enough without that"; he muttered more,

But the streaming wind took it away, then Helen:

"Oh Reave be merciful: spare me once.

We couldn't tell that the storm was stripping the high places

When we planned this, down below, I can't bear it." The wind
tilted the truck on the steep springs

When it gained the crest and turned quartering; Reave struck
the floor with his hand, holding his body with the other to
stay it

From rolling, and groaned, "I guess you can bear it." "You don't
know," she said,

"What stands on the rock . . ." she stoppered her mouth with
her knuckles against the teeth, and breathed through them,
and said,

"You have no mercy: your choice is wise. Here is the gate."

XXII

At the cliff-line, in the lee of one of those heavily

Timbered platforms on the very brow, from which the lime-
kegs used to be slung to the ship's hold,

They rested at length; but only the cripple's insane invincible
stubbornness had brought them to it, by the gullied

Overgrown road. A broken shed on the staging, long ago un-
roofed by some former storm,

Still offered a brittle screen of standing planks, splintered, singing
in the wind; Thurso's companions

Laid him in that shelter on the sea-brow platform. He gathered
and governed pain in a long silence, and said,

"Did you see that riffraff under the floor, in the joists and
braces?"

"What?" Helen said dimly. "Sticks and grass: wood-rats' nests.

Kindling. When this spell of rain ends

We've only to drop a match and all the platform

Flies into ashes: while Luna pries the old engine-boiler

Down the cliff into the sea: we'll have our rock-head

Clean as at first." She answered, "Oh: that?" and shivered

In the whirl of the broken wind, saying, "Reave: listen.

Do you think he minds?" "Hm?" "Your father. Because if he

Lives after his death, envying and doing evil,

Then death, that I have always been sick with fear
To think of, is not an end, and you and I
Might look down at our lives laughing
From a great height." "Dead as a dog," he said.
"I never thought anything else. Grieving for Mark
I may've talked foolishly. We'll erase his leavings
For pleasure and to clean the world." "You don't know.
I don't know. They won't tell," she said grievously.
"Another man, Reave, is dead also. They fall and fall
Like apples in a wind. Johnny Luna told me." She stood up
And called Luna from prying at the truck's mudguard,
Where it was bent to the tire by a stump of oak,
"Was it the Vasquez boys that told you?" she screamed
Down the loud wind. Luna climbed up the platform
And stood with his blank slate face bent from the storm,
Saying "What you want?" "I was so troubled this morning,
I hardly listened to you: didn't you tell me
Armstrong was killed?" He nodded gravely, and Helen:
"I'm glad. Are you glad, Reave?" "No. Rick Armstrong?"
He said groaning, turning himself on his shoulders,
"How did Rick Armstrong die?" "All in a minute,"
She answered, "how was it? In his car, Johnny?"
"He drive too fast at the bridge." "When was that?" Reeve said.
"I don' know. Maybe las' week. Vidal Vasquez
He talking about." Reave said, "It's too bad.
He was a good fellow: but the single fault
I've never understood yet. Well. Time and chance." Helen, sud-
    denly shaking like the erect boards
Behind her in the wind: "Is it nothing, nothing to you? It was
    something to me! Hush. I'll be still. I hoped
You'd feel an old debt paid, and be pleased, and I'd
Be dearer to you. He's dead, you understand? He's gone down.
    You live." Reave gazed up in slight wonder; Helen sighed
And turned to Luna: "That's all. Thank you for lying. It was
    no good." The Indian went carefully down,
And back to the car, clinging by the platform timbers in the
    current of wind.

Helen crouched again
On the planks beside Reave's mattress, she kept jerking her hands
    together and drawing them apart; the screen
Of boards behind her whistled and clapped like something heard
    on a ship; the ragged skies and wreaths
Of mist rushed by, and crescent-moon-shaped flurries of foam
    on the streaked sea; the rock and the platform
Were driving up wind with dreadful increasing speed, the deck
    and the hull. She moistened her lips to whisper
Silently: "Mark's out of it. Oh happy, Oh happy! but the racing
    engines
Will burst with this. Is the time now?"

                    Reave never slept, he
    lay and looked up with broad light eyes
At the driven sky; the upper eyelids cut the blue circles, the
    lower missed them; his face was motionless
Like worn hard wood, but all the while he felt pain. It was hate-
    ful of him to leave the duty to a woman;
Lie there fallen; wait to be saved; what had they come up for!
    And when she killed her lover to please him
He had not cared.

                    She turned herself toward the clattering
    boards and undid the package,
And turned again, holding the things in her hands,
Hidden in her lap. The engine in her side was quieter,
But the ship glided dreadfully faster, giddy with speed.
She swayed upright and went around him to approach him
From the north side, so that her right hand
Was under his chin when she knelt down and kissed,
And babbling something of love drew his own sharp hunting-
    knife
Between the jaw and the jut of cartilage, with such
Hoarded unconscious violence that both the arteries,
And the tubes between them, and much of the muscle sheath
On the right of the throat were severed; his head jerked to the
    left,

The great wound gaped and sighed, all in a moment
Mattress and blanket, the planks, the whole world of sense,
Were painted with blood and foam. He heard her crying
She'd done it for love, he formed his lips to say "Bitch,"
But breath and the light failed; he felt the animal
Flurry of death waggle his arms and head,
No pain from the loins down. Then all was perfect
No-pain.

        Helen stood up from her deed
And said "I have the other thing in my fingers.
Oh Johnny Luna, go down and tell his mother
That the ship has found land." But when she looked,
Luna was still tinkering the truck. She ran
To the platform-end, and the wind threw her on the planks,
She lay on her breasts and thighs, crying "Tell the old woman
To come up here and see him like a king in Babylon
With his slave lying at his feet."

        Her face and the blood
Moved him to flee into the wind and down
The rock-path in the cliff-side.

XXIII

        Reave's mother labored up the
steep face, Luna behind her.
The wind had sagged toward the southwest and somewhat de-
    clined in violence, so that a wide-winged hawk
That had been hungry all day was able to hang in the birdless
    air of the rock-head when they came up,
Probing with her eyes wild buckwheat bushes and sage and the
    polished leaves of the barren strawberry; she looked
Nailed to the firmament, her twitching wings like the spread
    hands of a crucified man fighting the nails;
But Helen imagined her a vulture and was screaming at her.

When Reave's mother came,
Helen made shift to sit up on the planks beside her slain man,
    and staring with enormous violet eyes
From a stained shrunk face, began to make words in a voice that
    was not her own: "I was afraid you'd not come.
I have to tell you. But now I've taken Reave's lifetime of pain
    upon me to spend in an hour or two,
And my throat's burnt, but I have to tell you
As clearly as I might be able, because you ought to understand
    that I am not vile to the very end,
And have done well. His death was rapid. But for mine, after
    I'd done it, if I'd taken any easy way
Out, you'd have scorned me; and the watchful world might 'a'
    thought I'd done it unworthily, what I did out of pure love
And pity; or thought that I die to escape punishment. Don't come
    near me yet, for I've not finished. I read
In the Sunday paper, how they dug out the grave of a king in
    Babylon and found his women about him
With their skulls knocked in; I planned to honor
Reave in that way: he was like a king in some ways, and if he
    had found any great thing to do
He might have done greatly."

                    She fell, drawing up her knees,
    and the mother said: "What poison?" Helen made no answer,
But being asked a third time: "No," she answered faintly, "a
    woman's poison, a white one. The little tablets
I used for fear of having a baby, in our happy time." She fixed
    her eyes on the vacant air
Above the sea-edge: "Why there's that tiny tiny thing with the
    yellow mop
Come up to see us. Keep her off, please.
No, Hester. No. You may watch if you like but I alone
Am allowed to lie at his feet, my love is proved."

The old woman answered, "There's nobody." She crept on the
    platform for the wind threw her down, and crept past Helen
To Reave and said, "How did you do it? Did he let you do it?"
    Helen, coughing with laughter in the poison fever:
"Reave let me? Have you gone crazy? I knifed him while I
    kissed his mouth." She cried with pain
At the end of speaking, and the mother: "I knew he would never
    give in, why did I ask? You have done well,
You always were treacherous, you did it easily." She found the
    hunting-knife
And took it up from the blood against Reave's shoulder,
Then Helen cried, raising herself on her hands,
"You must not! You have no right. I alone saved him,
Alone to die with him." "When you die I will lay it down.
You are not to get well." Helen gasped, laughing
And retching, "Oh *that's* all? Old fool.
Those little white things, meant to fight the seed of our lovers,
Are seed themselves, I'm pregnant and swell fast,
Baby death, darling, darling."

                              She widened terrified
Eyes and said staring: "I can't
Be silent in pain like Reave: Oh, I did hope to.
I never dreamed, Oh, ooh; Oh, ooh." The old woman watched
    her
Attentively across Reave's body, and let the knife
Drop on the planks. Helen heard it, and after a long while
She said, stretching her throat, "Be merciful to me.
As I was merciful to Reave. I can't bear
The next hour. . . . Unless it would seem wrong?
Reave not be honored enough?" "I think your time
Is near," she answered.
"There is an end or I'd help you: it will be braver in us
Not to keep begging death out of the cloud
Before he is ready." But she crept under the wind
Around Reave's body and kissed Helen's hand, and remained
    with her
Tenderly until she died.

The platform is like a rough plank
theatre-stage
Built on the brow of the promontory: as if our blood had labored
all around the earth from Asia
To play its mystery before strict judges at last, the final ocean
and sky, to prove our nature
More shining than that of the other animals. It is rather ignoble
in its quiet times, mean in its pleasures,
Slavish in the mass; but at stricken moments it can shine terribly
against the dark magnificence of things.

Luna came up the platform and stood shaking,
Leaned over against the wind; the old woman said:
"We can do nothing. She had a wasteful gallant spirit.
It is not poured out yet; go down for now."

Toward evening the
seas thundered on the rock, and rain fell heavily
Like a curtain, with one red coal of sundown glowing in its dark.
The old woman stood up
And fell, and stood up and called: "Now come, it is time. . . .
To bear . . . endure . . . are poor things, Johnny; to live
And bear what we can't strike back at: but we come to them
Unless we fall off before. . . . Has the car lights?
Help me: you'll have to carry all the weight. I am the last
And worst of four: and at last the unhappiest: but that's nothing."

357

THE PLACE FOR NO STORY

The coast hills at Sovranes Creek:
No trees, but dark scant pasture drawn thin
Over rock shaped like flame;
The old ocean at the land's foot, the vast
Gray extension beyond the long white violence;
A herd of cows and the bull
Far distant, hardly apparent up the dark slope;
And the gray air haunted with hawks:
This place is the noblest thing I have ever seen.
 No imaginable
Human presence here could do anything
But dilute the lonely self-watchful passion.

FIRE ON THE HILLS

The deer were bounding like blown leaves
Under the smoke in front of the roaring wave of the brush-fire;
I thought of the smaller lives that were caught.
Beauty is not always lovely; the fire was beautiful, the terror
Of the deer was beautiful; and when I returned
Down the black slopes after the fire had gone by, an eagle
Was perched on the jag of a burnt pine,
Insolent and gorged, cloaked in the folded storms of his shoulders.
He had come from far off for the good hunting
With fire for his beater to drive the game; the sky was merciless
Blue, and the hills merciless black,
The sombre-feathered great bird sleepily merciless between them.
I thought, painfully, but the whole mind,
The destruction that brings an eagle from heaven is better than
    mercy.

NOVEMBER SURF

Some lucky day each November great waves awake and are
   drawn
Like smoking mountains bright from the west
And come and cover the cliff with white violent cleanness: then
   suddenly
The old granite forgets half a year's filth:
The orange-peel, eggshells, papers, pieces of clothing, the clots
Of dung in corners of the rock, and used
Sheaths that make light love safe in the evenings: all the droppings
   of the summer
Idlers washed off in a winter ecstasy:
I think this cumbered continent envies its cliff then. . . . But all
   seasons
The earth, in her childlike prophetic sleep,
Keeps dreaming of the bath of a storm that prepares up the long
   coast
Of the future to scour more than her sea-lines:
The cities gone down, the people fewer and the hawks more
   numerous,
The rivers mouth to source pure; when the two-footed
Mammal, being someways one of the nobler animals, regains
The dignity of room, the value of rareness.

WINGED ROCK

The flesh of the house is heavy sea-orphaned stone, the imagina-
    tion of the house
Is in those little clay kits of swallows
Hung in the eaves, bright wings flash and return, the heavy rock
    walls commercing
With harbors of the far hills and the high
Rills of water, the river-meadow and the sea-cloud. You have
    also, O sleepy stones,
The red, the white and the marbled pigeons
To beat the blue air over the pinewood and back again in a mo-
    ment; and the bush-hidden
Killdeer nest against the west wall-foot,
That is fed from many strange ebbs; besides the woodful of
    finches, the shoring gulls,
The sudden attentive passages of hawks.

THE BED BY THE WINDOW

I chose the bed downstairs by the sea-window for a good death-
    bed
When we built the house; it is ready waiting,
Unused unless by some guest in a twelvemonth, who hardly
    suspects
Its latter purpose. I often regard it,
With neither dislike nor desire; rather with both, so equalled
That they kill each other and a crystalline interest
Remains alone. We are safe to finish what we have to finish;
And then it will sound rather like music
When the patient daemon behind the screen of sea-rock and sky
Thumps with his staff, and calls thrice: "Come, Jeffers."

I watch the Indians dancing to help the young corn at Taos
   pueblo. The old men squat in a ring
And make the song, the young women with fat bare arms, and a
   few shame-faced young men, shuffle the dance.

The lean-muscled young men are naked to the narrow loins,
   their breasts and backs daubed with white clay,
Two eagle-feathers plume the black heads. They dance with
   reluctance, they are growing civilized; the old men persuade
   them.

Only the drum is confident, it thinks the world has not changed;
   the beating heart, the simplest of rhythms,
It thinks the world has not changed at all; it is only a dreamer,
   a brainless heart, the drum has no eyes.

These tourists have eyes, the hundred watching the dance, white
   Americans, hungrily too, with reverence, not laughter;
Pilgrims from civilization, anxiously seeking beauty, religion,
   poetry; pilgrims from the vacuum.

People from cities, anxious to be human again. Poor show how
   they suck you empty! The Indians are emptied,
And certainly there was never religion enough, nor beauty nor
   poetry here . . . to fill Americans.

Only the drum is confident, it thinks the world has not changed.
   Apparently only myself and the strong
Tribal drum, and the rockhead of Taos mountain, remember
   that civilization is a transient sickness.

A Celtic spearman forcing the cromlech-builder's brown
    daughter;
A blond Saxon, a slayer of Britons,
Building his farm outside the village he'd burned; a Norse
Voyager, wielder of oars and a sword,
Thridding the rocks at the fjord sea-end, hungry as a hawk;
A hungry Gaelic chiefling in Ulster,
Whose blood with the Norseman's rotted in the rain on a heather
    hill:
These by the world's time were very recent
Forefathers of yours. And you are a maker of verses. The pallid
Pursuit of the world's beauty on paper,
Unless a tall angel comes to require it, is a pitiful pastime.
If, burnished new from God's eyes, an angel:
And the ardors of the simple blood showing clearly a little
    ridiculous
In this changed world:—write and be quiet.

MARGRAVE

On the small marble-paved platform
On the turret on the head of the tower,
Watching the night deepen.
I feel the rock-edge of the continent
Reel eastward with me below the broad stars.
I lean on the broad worn stones of the parapet top
And the stones and my hands that touch them reel eastward.
The inland mountains go down and new lights
Glow over the sinking east rim of the earth.
The dark ocean comes up,
And reddens the western stars with its fog-breath
And hides them with its mounded darkness.

The earth was the world and man was its measure, but our minds
    have looked
Through the little mock-dome of heaven the telescope-slotted
    observatory eyeball, there space and multitude came in
And the earth is a particle of dust by a sand-grain sun, lost in a
    nameless cove of the shores of a continent.
Galaxy on galaxy, innumerable swirls of innumerable stars, en-
    dured as it were forever and humanity
Came into being, its two or three million years are a moment, in
    a moment it will certainly cease out from being
And galaxy on galaxy endure after that as it were forever . . .
    But man is conscious,
He brings the world to focus in a feeling brain,
In a net of nerves catches the splendor of things,
Breaks the somnambulism of nature . . . His distinction perhaps,
Hardly his advantage. To slaver for contemptible pleasures
And scream with pain, are hardly an advantage.
Consciousness? The learned astronomer
Analyzing the light of most remote star-swirls
Has found them—or a trick of distance deludes his prism—
All at incredible speeds fleeing outward from ours.

I thought, no doubt they are fleeing the contagion
Of consciousness that infects this corner of space.

For often I have heard the hard rocks I handled
Groan, because lichen and time and water dissolve them,
And they have to travel down the strange falling scale
Of soil and plants and the flesh of beasts to become
The bodies of men; they murmur at their fate
In the hollows of windless nights, they'd rather be anything
Than human flesh played on by pain and joy,
They pray for annihilation sooner, but annihilation's
Not in the book yet.

        So, I thought, the rumor
Of human consciousness has gone abroad in the world,
The sane uninfected far-outer universes
Flee it in a panic of escape, as men flee the plague
Taking a city: for look at the fruits of consciousness:
As in young Walter Margrave when he'd been sentenced for
    murder: he was thinking when they brought him back
To the cell in jail, "I've only a moment to arrange my thoughts,
    I must think quickly, I must think clearly,
And settle the world in my mind before I kick off," but to feel
    the curious eyes of his fellow-prisoners
And the wry-mouthed guard's and so forth torment him through
    the steel bars put his mind in a stupor, he could only
Sit frowning, ostentatiously unafraid. "But I can control my
    mind, their eyes can't touch my will.
One against all. What use is will at this end of everything? A
    kind of nausea is the chief feeling . . .
In my stomach and throat . . . but in my head pride: I fought
    a good fight and they can't break me; alone, unbroken,
Against a hundred and twenty-three million people. They are
    going to kill the best brain perhaps in the world,
That might have made such discoveries in science
As would set the world centuries ahead, for I had the mind and
    the power. Boo, it's their loss. Blind fools,

Killing their best." When his mind forgot the eyes it made rapid
    capricious pictures instead of words,
But not of the medical school and the laboratories, its late in-
    tense interest; not at all of his crime; glimpses
Of the coast-range at home; the V of a westward canyon with
    the vibrating
Blue line of the ocean strung sharp across it; that domed hill up
    the valley, two cows like specks on the summit
And a beautiful-colored jungle of poison-oak at the foot; his
    sister half naked washing her hair,
"My dirty sister," whose example and her lovers had kept him
    chaste by revulsion; the reed-grown mouth of the river
And the sand-bar against the stinging splendor of the sea . . .
    and anguish behind all the pictures
(He began to consider his own mind again) "like a wall they
    hang on." Hang. The anguish came forward, an actual
Knife between two heartbeats, the organ stopped and then raced.
    He experimented awhile with his heart,
Making in his mind a picture of a man hanged, pretending to
    himself it was to happen next moment,
Trying to observe whether the beat suspended—"suspended," he
    thought—in systole or in diastole.
The effect soon failed; the anguish remained. "Ah my slack
    lawyer, damn him, let slip chance after chance.
Scared traitor." Then broken pictures of the scenes in court, the
    jury, the judge, the idlers, and not one face
But bleak with hatred. "But I met their eyes, one against all."
    Suddenly his mind became incapable
Of making pictures or words, but still wildly active, striking in
    all directions like a snake in a fire,
Finding nothing but the fiery element of its own anguish. He got
    up and felt the guard's eyes and sat down,
Turned side-face, resting his chin on his fist, frowning and
    trembling. He saw clearly in his mind the little
Adrenal glands perched on the red-brown kidneys, as if all his
    doomed tissues became transparent,
Pouring in these passions their violent secretion

Into his blood-stream, raising the tension unbearably. And the
    thyroids; tension, tension. A long course of that
Should work grave changes. "If they tortured a man like a labora-
    tory dog for discovery: there'd be value gained: but by
    process
Of law for vengeance, because his glands and his brain have
    made him act in another than common manner:
You incredible breed of asses!" He smiled self-consciously in
    open scorn of the people, the guard at the door
To observe that smile—"my God, do I care about the turnkey's
    opinion?"—suddenly his mind again
Was lashing like a burnt snake. Then it was torpid for a while.
    This continued for months.

His father had come to visit him, he saw the ruinous white-haired
    head
Through two steel wickets under the bluish electric light that
    seemed to peel the skin from the face.
Walter said cheerfully too loudly, "Hullo. You look like a skull."
    The shaven sunk jaws in answer chewed
Inaudible words. Walter with an edge of pleasure thought "Once
    he was stronger than I! I used to admire
This poor old man's strength when I was a child," and said "Buck
    up, old fellow, it will soon be over. Here's nothing
To cry for. Do you think I'm afraid to die? It's good people that
    fear death, people with the soft streak
Of goodness in them fear death: but I, you know, am a monster,
    don't you read the papers? Caught at last:
I fought a hundred and twenty-three million people. How's
    Hazel? How's the farm? I could get out of this scrape
By playing dementia, but I refuse to, there's not an alienist living
Could catch me out. I'm the king of Spain dying for the world.
    I've been persecuted since I was born
By a secret sect, they stuck pins into me
And fed me regular doses of poison for a certain reason. Why
    do you pretend that you're my father?
God is. . . . Believe me, I could get by with it.
But I refuse."

MARGRAVE

Old Margrave looked timidly at the two guards
listening, and drew his brown tremulous hand
Across his eyes below the white hair. "I thought of going to try
to see the governor, Walter."
"That's it!" "Don't hope for anything, Walter, they tell me that
there's no hope. They say that I shan't even
Be allowed to see him." "By God," the young man said trembling,
"you can if you want to. Never believe that lawyer.
If I'd had Dorking: but you couldn't afford him. Poor men have
no right to breed sons. I'd not be here
If you'd had money to put me through college. Tell the governor
I know he won't pardon, but he can commute the sentence to
life imprisonment. Then I can read and study,
I can help the penitentiary doctor, I can do something to help
humanity. Tell him it's madness
To throw such a brain as mine into the garbage. Don't deny my
guilt but tell him my reasons.
I kidnapped the little girl to get money to finish my medical
education. What's one child's life
Against a career like mine that might have saved
Thousands of children? Say I'd isolated the organism of infantile
paralysis: I'd have done more:
But that alone would save thousands of children. I was merciful;
she died quietly; tell him that.
It was only pithing a little white frog.
Don't you think you can make him understand? I'm not a crimi-
nal: I judge differently from others. I wasn't
Afraid to think for myself. All I did
Was for money for my education, to help humanity. And tell
him if I've done wrong—what's wrong?—I've paid for it
With frightful suffering: the more developed the brain the greater
the agony. He won't admit that. Oh God,
These brains the size of a pea! To be juried
And strangled by a hundred and twenty-three million peas. Go
down on your knees to him. You owe me that: you'd no
right
To breed, you're poor.

But you itched for a woman, you had to fetch me out of the
    happy hill of not-being. Pfah, to hug a woman
And make this I. That's the evil in the world, that letter. I—I—
    Tell the governor
That I'm not afraid of dying, that I laugh at death. No, no, we'll
    laugh in private. Tell him I'm crazy.
I've come to that: after being the only sane mind among a hun-
    dred and twenty-three million peas.
Anything, anything . . ."

        He had let his nerves go wild on pur-
    pose, to edge on the old man to action, now at last
Escaping utterly out of control they stumbled into a bog of thick
    sobs. The guards pulled him up
And walked him away as if he were half insensible. He was not
    insensible, but more acutely aware
Than ever in his life before of all that touched him, and of shame
    and anguish.

        You would be wise, you far stars,
To flee with the speed of light this infection.
For here the good sane invulnerable material
And nature of things more and more grows alive and cries.
The rock and water grow human, the bitter weed
Of consciousness catches the sun, it clings to the near stars,
Even the nearer portion of the universal God
Seems to become conscious, yearns and rejoices
And suffers: I believe this hurt will be healed
Some age of time after mankind has died,
Then the sun will say "What ailed me a moment?" and resume
The old soulless triumph, and the iron and stone earth
With confident inorganic glory obliterate
Her ruins and fossils, like that incredible unfading red rose
Of desert in Arizona glowing life to scorn,
And grind the chalky emptied seed-shells of consciousness
The bare skulls of the dead to powder; after some million
Courses around the sun her sadness may pass:

But why should you worlds of the virgin distance
Endure to survive what it were better to escape?

I also am not innocent
Of contagion, but have spread my spirit on the deep world.
I have gotten sons and sent the fire wider.
I have planted trees, they also feel while they live.
I have humanized the ancient sea-sculptured cliff
And the ocean's wreckage of rock
Into a house and a tower,
Hastening the sure decay of granite with my hammer,
Its hard dust will make soft flesh;
And have widened in my idleness
The disastrous personality of life with poems,
That are pleasant enough in the breeding but go bitterly at last
To envy oblivion and the early deaths of nobler
Verse, and much nobler flesh;
And I have projected my spirit
Behind the superb sufficient forehead of nature
To gift the inhuman God with this rankling consciousness.

But who is our judge? It is likely the enormous
Beauty of the world requires for completion our ghostly incre-
    ment,
It has to dream, and dream badly, a moment of its night.

On the little stone-belted platform
On the turret on the head of the tower,
Between the stars and the earth,
And the ocean and the continent.
One ship's light shines and eclipses
Very far out, behind the high waves on the hill of water.
In the east under the Hyades and rising Orion
Are many cities and multitudes of people,
But westward a long way they are few enough.
It is fortunate to look westward as to look upward.
In the south the dark river-mouth pool mirrors a star

MARGRAVE

That stands over Margrave's farmhouse. The old man has lost it,
   he isn't there any more. He went down to the river-mouth
Last December, when recent rains had opened the stream and the
   salmon were running. Fishermen very solemnly
Stood all along the low sand like herons, and sea-lions offshore
   in the rolling waves with deep wet voices
Coughed at each other; the sea air is hoarse with their voices that
   time of year. Margrave had rambled since noon
Among the little folds of the seaward field that he had forgotten
   to plow and was trying to sell
Though he used to love it, but everything was lost now. He lay
   awhile on his face in the rotting stubble and random
Unsown green blades, then he got up and drifted over the ridge
   to the river-mouth sands, unaimed,
Pale and gap-eyed, as the day moon a clear morning, opposite the
   sun. He noticed with surprise the many
Fishermen like herons in the shallows and along the sands; and
   then that his girl Hazel was with him: who'd feared
What he might do to himself and had come to watch him when
   he lay face down in the field. "I know what they're doing,"
He said slyly, "Hazel, they're fishing! I guess they don't know,"
He whispered, "about our trouble. Oh no, don't tell them." She
   said, "Don't go down, father, your face would tell them.
Sit here on the edge of grass, watch the brown river meet the
   blue sea. Do look: that boy's caught something.
How the line cuts the water and the small wheel sings." "If I'd
   been rich,"
Old Margrave answered, "they'd have fixed the hook for . . .
   Walter . . . with some other bait. It sticks in my mind that
   . . . Walter
Blames me too much." "Look," Hazel said, "he's landing it now.
   Oh, it's a big one." "I dreamed about fishing,
Some time ago," he answered, "but we were the fish. I saw the
   people all running reaching for prizes
That dangled on long lines from the sky. A lovely girl or a sack
   of money or a case of whiskey,
Or fake things like reputation, hackle-feathers and a hook. A man
   would reach up and grab and the line

372

Jerked, then you knew by his face that the hook was in him,
    wherever he went. Often they're played for half
A lifetime before they're landed: others, like . . . my son . . .
    pulled up short. Oh, Oh,
It's not a dream." He said gently, "He wanted money for his
    education, but you poor girl
Wanted boy friends, now you've got a round belly. That's the
    hook. I wanted children and got
Walter and you. Hm? Hooked twice is too much. Let's walk."
"Not that way: let's go up home, daddy.
It makes you unhappy to see them fishing." "No," he answered,
    "nothing can. I have it in my pocket." She walked behind
    him,
Hiding herself, ashamed of her visible pregnancy and her broth-
    er's fate; but when the old man stumbled
And wavered on the slope she went beside him to support him,
    her right hand under his elbow, and wreathed his body
With the other arm.

                            The clear brown river ran eagerly through
    the sand-hill, undercutting its banks,
That slid in masses; tall waves walked very slowly up stream from
    the sea, and stood
Stationary in the throat of the channel before they dissolved. The
    rock the children call Red-cap stood
High and naked among the fishermen, the orange lichen on its
    head. At the sea-end of the sand
Two boys and a man had rifles instead of rods, they meant to
    punish the salmon-devouring sea-lions
Because the fish were fewer than last year; whenever a sleek
    brown head with the big questioning eyes
Broke sea they fired. Margrave had heard the shots but taken no
    notice, but when he walked by the stream
He saw a swimmer look up from the water and its round dark eye
Suddenly burst red blood before it went down. He cried out and
    twisted himself from Hazel's hand
And ran like a squirrel along the stream-bank. "I'll not allow it!"
    He snatched at a rifle. "Why should my lad

Be hanged for killing and all you others go free?" He wrestled
    feebly to gain the rifle, the sand-bank
Slid under his feet, he slipped and lay face down in the running
    stream and was hauled astrand. Then Hazel
Came running heavily, and when he was able to walk she led him
    away. The sea-beast, blinded but a painful
Vain gleam, starved long before it could die; old Margrave still
    lives. Death's like a little gay child that runs
The world around with the keys of salvation in his foolish fin-
    gers, lends them at random where they're not wanted,
But often withholds them where most required.

                                Margrave's son
    at this time
Had only four days to wait, but death now appeared so dreadful
    to him that to speak of his thoughts and the abject
Horror, would be to insult humanity more than it deserves. At
    last the jerked hemp snapped the neck sideways
And bruised the cable of nerves that threads the bone rings; the
    intolerably strained consciousness in a moment changed.
It was strangely cut in two parts at the noose, the head's
Consciousness from the body's; both were set free and flamed;
    the head's with flashing paradisal light
Like the wild birth of a star, but crying in bewilderment and
    suddenly extinguished; the body's with a sharp emotion
Of satisfied love, a wave of hard warmth and joy, that ebbed cold
    on darkness. After a time of darkness
The dreams that follow upon death came and subsided, like
    fibrillar twitchings
Of the nerves unorganizing themselves; and some of the small
    dreams were delightful and some, slight miseries,
But nothing intense; then consciousness wandered home from the
    cell to the molecule, was utterly dissolved and changed;
Peace was the end of the play, so far as concerns humanity. Oh
    beautiful capricious little savior,
Death, the gay child with the gipsy eyes, to avoid you for a time
    I think is virtuous, to fear you is insane.

MARGRAVE

On the little stone-girdled platform
Over the earth and the ocean
I seem to have stood a long time and watched the stars pass.
They also shall perish I believe.
Here to-day, gone to-morrow, desperate wee galaxies
Scattering themselves and shining their substance away
Like a passionate thought. It is very well ordered.

I

The apples hung until a wind at the equinox,
That heaped the beach with black weed, filled the dry grass
Under the old trees with rosy fruit.
In the morning Fayne Fraser gathered the sound ones into a
     basket,
The bruised ones into a pan. One place they lay so thickly
She knelt to reach them.
                              Her husband's brother passing
Along the broken fence of the stubble-field,
His quick brown eyes took in one moving glance
A little gopher-snake at his feet flowing through the stubble
To gain the fence, and Fayne crouched after apples
With her mop of red hair like a glowing coal
Against the shadow in the garden. The small shapely reptile
Flowed into a thicket of dead thistle-stalks
Around a fence-post, but its tail was not hidden.
The young man drew it all out, and as the coil
Whipped over his wrist, smiled at it; he stepped carefully
Across the sag of the wire. When Fayne looked up
His hand was hidden; she looked over her shoulder
And twitched her sunburnt lips from small white teeth
To answer the spark of malice in his eyes, but turned
To the apples, intent again. Michael looked down
At her white neck, rarely touched by the sun,
But now the cinnabar-colored hair fell off from it;
And her shoulders in the light-blue shirt, and long legs like a boy's
Bare-ankled in blue-jean trousers, the country wear;
He stooped quietly and slipped the small cool snake
Up the blue-denim leg. Fayne screamed and writhed,
Clutching her thigh. "Michael, you beast." She stood up
And stroked her leg, with little sharp cries, the slender invader
Fell down her ankle.
                              Fayne snatched for it and missed;

Michael stood by rejoicing, his rather small
Finely cut features in a dance of delight;
Fayne with one sweep flung at his face
All the bruised and half-spoiled apples in the pan,
A fragrant volley, and while he staggered under it,
The hat fallen from his head, she found one thoroughly
Soft-rotten, brown in the long white grass, and threw
For the crown of his dark head but perfectly missed,
Crying "Quits. We're even." They stood and warily smiled at each
    other
In the heavy-sweet apple air.

                  The garden was sunken lower than
    the little fields; it had many fragrances
And its own shadow, while the cows lay in the stream-bed, large
    sycamore leaves dropped on their flanks; the yellow
Heads of the hills quivered with sun and the straining sea-glare.
    Fayne said, "Where did it go, poor thing?"
Looking for the little serpent. Michael said gravely, "That's to
    remember me by. I wish I could do worse.
I'm going away." "What?" "From here again."
"Oh, no." "I am, though." "No, Michael."
"Freckles," he answered, "didn't it ever occur to you
That it's fairly dull here? I'm going up to town again.
I've got to earn money and spend it and hear the motors."
She said dismally, "What about me? Who'll there be to talk to?"
"Lance, of course." "I love him dearly; he's not fun exactly.
He wouldn't stick a rattlesnake up my leg."
"Gopher-snake," he shouted. They stood and laughed at each
    other,
And Michael: "I was over the ridge to Drunken Charlie's,
Fixing up a little party for Saturday.
There'll be a moon in the evening. I leave Monday."
Fayne said unhappily, "Help me pick up the apples
I poured on you."

II

          Michael was taking Mary Abbey;
The Dolmans came, and Will Howard with two girls,

And Leo Ramirez with his sister Nell, so that the youth
Of the coast was all there. They met at Frasers'
And crossed the ridge; and were picketing the horses
Where they could ride no farther, on the airy brink
Above the great slides of the thousand-foot cliff.
They were very gay, colorful mites on the edge of the world.
    The men divided the pack to carry;
Lance Fraser, being strongest, took most.

                    Far down below, the
    broad ocean burned like a vast cat's eye
Pupilled by the track of sun; but eastward, beyond the white-
    grassed hump of the ridge, the day moon stood bleak
And badly shaped, face of stained clay, above the limestone fang
    of one of the Ventana mountains
Just its own color. Lance, looking back, saw his wife talking to
    Michael, her cinnabar-colored hair
Like a flag of life against the pale east. That moment he saw the
    horses plunging against the sky
And heard a noise like a sharp head of water from a narrow pipe;
    a girl cried out,
Lance dropped his pack and returned. Will Howard was looking
    for stones
But found none, but Lance found a burnt fence-post, relic of an
    ancient fire. The snake lay with raised head,
The rattle of its tail making that noise of sharp water running; a
    big rattler, but very small
At bay in the circle of the laughing men. Lance struck for its head,
    but the snake that moment struck at the rope's end
That Michael was flicking at it, so that Lance's blow failed, the
    fence-post broke to bits in his hand,
The snake not harmed; then Michael laughing with pleasure
    whipped the creature to death with the doubled rope
And set his heel on the head; Lance damned all rotten wood, his
    blond face flushing
Dark through the sunburn. Michael cut off the victim's
Tail with the ten rattles to give to Mary;
The other young men quieted the horses, and caught
One that had dragged away the bush it was tied to.

Lance would not wait, he picked up his pack and went
Alone down the zigzag path; but after a moment
His temper cleared.

              Far down, short of the cat's-eye ocean, they
    saw like a brown pebble
Drunken Charlie's hut in a gorge of the cliff, a feather of smoke,
    and his boat like a split berry
Of bladdery seaweed up the thin strand; and Lance stood waiting
    down the wild cliffside, his light-brown hair
Golden with sun, his hat and the pack laid down. The warm wind
    up the mountain was wild with fragrance,
Chiefly the scent of the chiya bushes, that wear rosettes of seed
Strung on the stem. The girls squealed as they scrambled down,
    when the brittle trap-rock broke underfoot,
Small fragments ran over on the next below. When they came to
    the foot of the cliff Michael said, "Now," and offered
A bottle hot from his pocket. "It's time." Mary Abbey refused
    it but the others drank, from mouth to mouth,
Stinging fire from the slobbered bottle-neck.

                   The sun was low
But had played all day on this southwestward
Cliff over the burning-glass water and the air
Still swirled with heat; the headland of Fraser's Point
Stopped off the trade-wind here. Fayne Fraser a little dizzily
Looked seaward, left of the blazing sun-track, and saw the track
    of the northwest gale and the running waves
Like an endless army of horse with banners going by offshore;
    her eyes followed them, a ruled line southward
Of violent water, converging toward the bronze headland beyond
    headland of the mountain coast; and someone was saying,
"It's hot, we'll swim." "Before we eat," someone said.
The girls twittered together and clustered northward
To a little cove beyond a fair spit of rock;
The men remained on this side.

               Fayne undressed beside Mary
    Abbey,
And was careful of words, because she'd sucked from the bottle
    more than she meant to, and had small experience of drinking.

She said carefully, "Where did those girls of Will Howard's
come from?" "Nina told me," she answered; "waitresses
Down from the city on their vacation." "Honestly are they? I
guessed it." "No," Mary said, "they're nice girls."
"That yellow-haired one, she's bad." "No," Mary said. Fayne
said, "Did you see her face when she looked at Michael
Across that bottle?" "Oh, no," Mary answered. ". . . Well. Are
you ready, Mary? Let's go."
They limped down to the waves, giggling and wincing.
Fayne had tied a broad handkerchief around her hair
To shed the spray; she swam out farther than others,
Mary remained along shore.
                              The other side of the rock-spit
The men had bathed, and had come up strand again
To dry by the driftwood fire; all except Michael,
Who loved to swim. Lance Fraser stood by the fire, his broad
smooth chest, grooved between the square plates
Of heavy muscle, steamed and was ruddy in the glowing heat. He
narrowed his eyes to look seaward
And saw Michael's left arm, over the speck of his head, lift, reach
and dip,
Swimming side-stroke; two white arms flashing swanlike on either
side of a handkerchief-hooded head
Emerged from the scales of light on the edge of the sun-dazzle.
The swimmers approached each other,
And met this side the long brown stain of the breathing kelp-bed.
Lance frowned,
But only thinking that they were too far out
And making a show of themselves.
                              On the pleasant water
Michael had called to Fayne, "I've something for you.
Come here a minute." She hardly dared, and thought
In the flashing joy of the sea, "Oh, the water covers us.
What have you got?" "Gin for girls.
We've got a fire on this side." They met laughing,
And reached the bottle from hand to hand and floated decorously
Separate again. Fayne looked toward shore, and saw the vast
cliff in the flare of sundown soaring above

Like beaten gold, the imperfect moon-disk gold on its brow; the
    tiny distinct white shapes of men
Around their spot of fire in the flat blue sea-shadow. She breathed
    hard and said,
"My God, how beautiful. Oh, Michael, stay here at home."
He answered with a watery yell of pleasure, submerging his
    mouth
To roar as the sea-lions do.
                        Fayne trailed the bottle
And swam ashore. There was nothing to dry herself with;
The chill of the water had touched her blood, she sucked breath
    gustily
Through clicking teeth. She sipped from the salted bottle,
And dressed, but shivered still.
                      She sunned herself by the fire,
Watching with fascinated speculation of pain
The antennae of lobsters like spikes of jointed grass
Above the heating water in a five-gallon tin
Writhe at the sky, lives unable to scream.

III

Under the vast calm vaulting glory of the afterglow, low smoky
    rose and delicately
Stratified amber, soaring purple; then rose again, luminous and
    virginal, floating the moon,
High up a scoured hollow of the cliff
Cormorants were settling to roost on the jags and ledges.
They writhed long Negro snake-throats and shot
Sharp heads at each other, shaking out sooty wings
And angry complaining cries.
                    Below, on the thread of beach,
The lonely fisherman who was called Drunken Charlie,
Fire glowing on his drugged eyes, wide beard and lank hair,
Turned meat on the grid over the barbecue-pit
And talked to himself all the time. Michael Fraser knelt
By a turned chest that served for table and poured
From a jug into cups, fierce new distillate
From Charlie's cliff-hidden kettle.

Fayne Fraser shook half-dried hair,

The color of the coals at the heart of the fire

But darkening as light decreased, and went to Lance

Who stood alone at the waves' edge, turning his back on the world, and the wet sand

Raised by his weight on either side of his foot-soles ran water and glistened in the still light. Fayne said

"Are you cross, dear?" She pushed up his rolled sleeve and clasped her fingers on the broad trunk of his arm

Above the elbow, "Dear, are you sad?" "I? No," he said, "What about?" "You haven't spoken to anyone

Since we were swimming." "Why should I? You were out too far, though." "Oh, I can swim.

And Michael was there to help me if I'd got tired." "By God, no," Lance said, with a sharp vision in his mind

Of her bright nakedness, the shining whiteness and the red hair. She understood and said softly, "Well,

I didn't need help. But he's our brother." "Certainly; I didn't mind him," he answered. "But I did hate

To think that rabble of girls could look at you; it isn't decent." She said, "They didn't seem interested.

Come, drink and eat. Those waitress women are passing the paper plates." He saw that vision once more,

The form and whiteness, the little gay-colored flower of the pubic hair, and groaned, as a thick bull

Alone in the field groans to himself, not knowing why the hot brow and the hooves itch for destruction.

Fayne to cure his unhappiness hasted and returned

Fetching two cups of the fire Michael was pouring.

After they had eaten, twilight and moonlight came;

The fire burned smaller and brighter; they were twelve around it; and drinks were poured. The bearded fisherman seemed

Stiffly asleep, with open eyes like a drowned man's

Glazed by the yellow firelight. Tom Dolman and Leo Ramirez

Roughed at each other, and Nina Dolman

Sitting between them cried out; then Michael said,

"Get up and wrestle." All but the fisherman turned
To watch them circle clumsily on the damp sand
And suddenly lock, into one quadruped body reeling
Against the dark band of ocean and the low sky.
Ramirez had the low hold but Dolman was the heavier man;
They tugged and sobbed; Ramirez was lifted high
And writhed on the other's shoulder by the evening star,
But the strained column staggered and crumbled, the Spaniard
Fell uppermost and was the first to rise up.
Michael asked very gravely, "Who was the winner?
The winner may challenge Lance." Ramirez gasping and laughing
Said, "Drunk; not to that extent." "Then gather firewood.
The fire's got low."

                    The yellow-haired one of the two girls Will
    Howard had brought
Sat in the sand beside Lance Fraser; she leaned on his shoulder
    and held a cup to his mouth and said
"Please drink it for me: things are beginning to go 'round in
    circles." He drank; then Fayne on his other side
Grew suddenly cool and quite clear; she leaned across him and
    said, "That hair in the cup! Well, you drank it.
Her bleaches have made it brittle so it keeps falling." "Oh," the
    other gasped, "that's not true." "It's pretty," Fayne said,
"Only the black half inch at the roots. Is your name Lois? What's
    your name?" "Lois." "Lean the other way,
Lois." Then Lance said angrily, "Be quiet, will you," and got up
To fetch more firewood.

                    A timber from one of the four ships
That have broken in half a century off Fraser's Point
Lay near and dry; Ramirez and Howard had brought it,
But the axe was lost in the sand. Lance up-ended it,
An ivory-white pillar under the moon,
Garnished with great iron bolts. He wedged his fingers
Into a crack and suddenly straining tore it in two;
The splitting made a great noise under the cliff,
The sea being quiet. Lance felt himself curiously
Numbed, as if the sharp effort had strained the whiskey
Out of his blood through the sheaths of his nerves;

His body obeyed as ever but felt a distance
Blocked off and alien. He took the halves of the timber
Under each arm and a bolt in his hand,
For two or three had fallen out of the wood,
This one straight, long and heavy. After he had laid
His logs on the fire he saw the fisherman's
Firelight-discolored eyes, and called "Hey! Charlie."
Still the man slept. Lance, wavering a little, reached
Over Will Howard's shoulder and took the cup from his hand,
Drank half, poured the other half on Charlie's long hair;
It dribbled into his beard; he coughed and awoke.
Lance said "D'you ever have rattlesnakes down here?
I snicked at one up the cliff with a rotten stick;
But this'd fix 'em." He gave him the iron bar;
Charlie posted it carefully up in the sand
Between his feet and answered, "Mm; but there's Injuns."
"What?" "All that was cleared out of the country.
Where did you think they got to? They ain't got ships.
Down here they are." The dark-haired girl that Will Howard
    had brought
Suddenly stood up from the fire, she went toward the sea and
    was heard vomiting. Charlie nodded and said,
"There's one o' them now. Most nights I see their fires away
    down the beach." Mary Abbey whispered to Michael,
"Don't take any more. Time to go home." "Ah no," he said,
    "dear, we just got here." Fayne came to Lance
And said, "Don't drink any more. Time to go home." He an-
    swered briskly, "Since when are you giving orders?"
"Since you're not fit to." She knew while the words made in her
    throat, "Now he'll be angry," a pale rush of anger
Ran to meet his; the memory of all his bad-tempered times, his
    heavy earnestness and lack of laughter,
Pierced like a mountain-peak the cloud in her mind, "Oh, I do
    hate you."
He stared, more astonished than angry, and saw her face
Lean, sharp, bled white, each freckle black as a mole
Against its moon-gleam pallor. "That's how you feel, ah?"
He turned his back. She thought, "He'll never forgive me:

Let him not," and saw the Dolmans, Nina and Tom,
Seeking the way up the cliff, Mary Abbey with them,
Fayne went and said, "Michael, I've lost my cup,
Aren't there any more cups?" "I'll hold the jug:
You hold your mouth." "Oo, I need water with it."
"No, you don't." Half of the sip went strangling
Into her throat, half ran by her little chin
And trickled between her breasts. She looked at the fire,
Then at the moon, both blurred fantastically,
Red burrowed, white wavered high. Michael said, "My girl's
    gone."
Fayne said, "Oh, and yours?" He said "That's no sense. That's
    very."
She laughed and answered, "They don't."

                                        The moon suspended
    in her great antelope-leap from the head of the cliff
Hung pouring whiteness along the narrow runway of sand and
    slide-rock under the continent's foot,
A watery glittering and secret place, walled from the world,
    closed by the cliff, ditched by the ocean.
Drunken Charlie dreamed by the dying fire;
Will Howard and Nell Ramirez were one slight point
Far down the white beach. Yellow-haired Lois
Spilled her drink and said, "Seeing is believing.
Come on, I'll show you." She smiled at Lance, "Come, dear.
Sadie's passed out; it's all right wi' Sadie,"
And to Leo Ramirez, "Come if you like, dark boy."
He swayed and stammered, "Responsible; Sister Nell.
Keep an eye on young sister." "Ah, go and find her."
"Not till I see the picture on Sadie's stomach."
They wandered toward Drunken Charlie's little hollow skiff
And its black shadow, drawn up the moonlight strand.
Lance thought, "Here's a boat, let's break it," and thought with
    an ache of shame,
"I wouldn't think that, only being drunk." The center of his
    mind made savage war on rebellious out-liers
In breathless darkness behind the sweating forehead; while Leo
    Ramirez, seeing the bright fish-scales glued

With blood and slime to the boat-thwarts glitter like a night of
  stars, began to sing a stale song: "We'll always,
Be young and gay. We'll always, feel that way." Lois said "Shut
  up," and led them around the boat,
Her friend lay in the moonlight nestled against it. Lois knelt
  down and gently drew her by the shoulder;
She groaned in her sleep, resisting. Lois laughed, "The boys want
  to see it, Sadie," and tugged, and turned her
Onto her back, the stained pale face up to the moonlight; the
  teeth in the opened mouth glittered,
And sour breath crossed them, while Lois turned up the blouse,
  loosened the band and jerked up the linen shift
To show a three-masted sailing-ship tattooed with black and red
  inks on the soft white belly
Below the breasts. "My God," Ramirez said, "there it is."
Lois answered, "A fellow dared her," and looked for Lance,
Who trembled and said, "Cover her up, damn you."
Lois blinking drew down the blouse. Ramirez giggled,
"My God, a U. S. flag at the peak," and reached
Over Lois's shoulder to raise the cloth;
Lance struck and felled him, and stepping across him fallen
Leaned and strode toward the cliff and the red coals
That had been the fire.
　　　　　　　Drunken Charlie lay on the sand,
The iron bolt erect by his feet; Lance caught it up
And smashed the jug, and saw the remnant of whiskey
Glitter among the shards to sink into sand.
He ground his teeth; he saw in his mind in the stream of images
A second jug, and began to search for it.
　　　　　　　　　　The tide had fallen, the
  steep ribbon of beach was but little wider,
But the sea was become so flattened that no waves flashed. Enor-
  mous peace of the sea, white quiet of the cliff,
And at their angle and focus a few faint specks of humanity
  happy in liquor or released in sleep,
But Lance alone. Then noises like the cries of a woman scream-
  ing, bird after bird of sharp-colored sound

Flew on the face of the cliff, tattered wild wings against jagged
    rocks. On the cliffhead the patient horses
Turned their ears, grooving small wrinkles about the roots of the
    cartilage, but did not lift up their heads;
And the sea was not moved, nor the moonlight quivered. Will
    Howard was lying beside Nell Ramirez; they'd fallen asleep
Before he had his desire; they sighed and stirred in the sand. He
    murmured "Oh, somebody's got hysterics,"
And wriggled his fingers, which had grown painfully numb
    between her plump knees. But Lois, Leo Ramirez
And Drunken Charlie heard the sounds nearer; they went in a
    wind of fear to find out their fountain,
And Sadie awoke in the sand and followed heavily,
Falling but once, catching her clothes that slipped,
Whining at the hollow pain in her skull.
                                Beyond a rock
Stood Lance, high white in the moon-glaze, distorted, taller than
    human;
Lois said, "Dearie?" He babbled, "Oh Jesus Christ Oh Jesus
    Christ Oh Jesus Christ,"
Behind him in a great shadow of her hair darkened
By the rock-shadow Fayne turned her white wedge of face
With three holes in it. She was kneeling, bent S-shape,
And seemed to stare up from the very ground. She said, "I think
It is finished. Water please. Water please.
He fell down from the cliff." Then Michael's feet were seen,
And thence the prone extended ridge of his body
Ending indefinitely under Fayne's face.
Lois cried, "He's hurt." But they dared not approach
For Lance standing between, high and twisted
Like a dead tree. Lance said, "I . . ." Fayne cried,
"He fell down from the cliff." They all stood silent,
Lois's mouth opened and closed on silence
Three times, then asked, "Is he hurt?" Lance said, "Oh Christ.
I . . ." Fayne cried so that his words were hidden,
And stood up and said, "He has died. Michael.
He was climbing the cliff and fell, his foot caught on that bush;
He struck his head on that rock, on that edge of rock.

It is all—broken in. Oh, we loved him."
Ramirez said, "What for did he climb up there?"
"Have we drunk *water?*" Fayne said. But Lance began
To shake, like a tall dead mast of redwood that men are felling,
It is half cut through, each dip of the axe the sonorous timber
    quivers from the root up to the cloud,
He said "I caught them . . ." "He caught him," Fayne cried,
"when he fell but he could not save him." "I killed . . ."
"You are wild with sorrow
He fell head down—whether you'd tried to catch him or not.
You are not to blame." He said, "It is horrible
To hear the lies from her mouth like bees from a hot hive: I am
    the one," but Fayne running to him
Made an animal moan in her throat in time to hide what he said.
    She came to Lance, and her face
Like a held spear, and said, "Drunkard.
Too drunk to be understood. Keep still until you can talk and be
    understood." He drew backward from her,
Shuddering like a horse from a snake, but when his back was
    against the rock he stammered, "I
Will find my time." "Yes," she answered, "be quiet now. To-
    morrow when you are better they'll understand you."
"Is he dead?" "Keep still. Will you shame his end
With drunkard babbling? For he was the dearest," she said, "in
    the world to all of us. Lovelier than morning light
On the mountain before the morning. There is not one of us
    would not have died for him: *I* would, *I* would, *I* would,"
She cried writhing, "but not lose Lance too. How can I plan to
    save him, I've got what I can't bear?
You are all our friends."
She set her hands in the masses of red-dark hair, dark in the
    moonlight, and tearing it, with her white face
To the white moon: "*That* eye's blind. Like Juan Arriba's old
    mare he used to beat on the face,
Her eyes froze white like that. He was larking on the cliff and
    fell." She seemed to be treading a tragic dance,
She was scuffling sand to cover the bolt of shipwreck that lay in
    the shadow of the rock; she wrung her hands

And knelt moaning by Michael's head; she rose with blood on her
    hand and fibers of hair, and ran
To the rock under the cliff. "This rock killed him. He fell on this
    edge," she drew her hand on the edge
And the rock was stained. Then Sadie was heard gasping from
    her poor stained face. One or two looked at her. "O-uh,"
She whispered hoarsely, "we was having fun!"

                     Lance moved at
    length, like a dead man walking, toward his dead brother,
And stooped as one stoops to gather a sleeping child. Fayne ran
    and said, "No, the man. No, the man.
He has to come." Lance turned toward her his face like a para-
    lyzed man's
Slack with peace, and said softly, "The man."
"He'd think wrong has been done. I can't think . . . coroner.
Don't take him up." "Home?" he said,
Seeming gently surprised; he gathered the body
Into his arms and walked along the foot of the cliff.
Fayne stayed behind a moment, the others following.
She cast quick looks over the rocks and sand;
One end of the rusty bolt was visible still;
She leaned toward it and fell on her face. She labored up
And went ten steps to the ebb and flung the iron
To the water edge.

              Lance walked along the foot of the cliff.
He turned, not where the path went up, and walked
Into the face of the cliff, and stood there walking
Like an ox in a tread-mill, until Ramirez
Showed him the path. Fayne went up behind him.

                     Half way up
He awoke a moment out of his automatism
To feel failure and pain, his breathing like knives, and the failure
Of his eyes; it was impossible to see the path;
He checked a step and fell forward.

                 Fayne came up to him
And stood; there was nothing that she could do. They lay
Very peacefully together, Lance's face
On his brother's breast. She looked across them;

Terribly far down the moonlight cliff crouched the dark sea.
Ramirez came up and stood. Fayne said they had not the strength
    to carry up either of the fallen, and so
They had to wait. They heard a faint breeze through the dry
    bushes; and the crying of sea-lions far down below,
Where eight or ten were lying in a circle by the softly heaving
    kelp-bed, as their custom is, and gazed
With great mild eyes at the sky and the night of water. Then
    they sing in their manner, lifting up sleek
Dark-shining muzzles to the white moon, making a watery noise
    of roaring and a lonely crying
For joy of life and the night.
                At length Lance
Began to paw with his feet like a dreaming hound,
And some stones fell. He knelt and stood up
And took his burden and went up.
                When they entered the sleep-
    ing farmstead,
Fayne led the horse; Lance held his brother and rode behind him.
It would be hard to tell which one was slain
If the moon shone on their faces. The horse stopped and sighed
By the garden-gate; Lance did not move to dismount,
But sat and held up his brother. Fayne came beside,
Reaching to help; Lance whispered "Ah, ah, thank God."
"What?" "He may be saved, Fayne.
He is hot under the arms and I heard him breathe."
"You heard the horse breathe," she said. They lifted down
The unmanageable weight.
                Oh, ignorant penitents,
For surely the cause is too small for so much anguish.
To be drunk is a folly, to kill may call judgment down,
But these are not enormous evils,
And as for your brother, he has not been hurt.
For all the delights he has lost, pain has been saved him;
And the balance is strangely perfect,
And why are you pale with misery?
Because you have saved him from foolish labors and all the vain
    days?

From desires denied, and desires staled with attaining,
And from fear of want, and from all diseases, and from fear of
    death?
Or because you have kept him from becoming old,
When the teeth drop and the eyes dim and the ears grow dull,
And the man is ashamed?
Surely it is nothing worse to be slain in the overflowing
Than to fall in the emptiness;
And though this moon blisters the night,
Darkness has not died, good darkness will come again;
Sometimes a fog will come in from sea,
Sometimes a cloud will crop all the stars.

IV

The moonlight from the west window was a square cloth
Laid on the floor, with one corner on the bed,
Lying over Michael's hand; they had taken him
To his own room. Fayne whispered: "Now we must tell them.
Your mother may die—her sick heart.
Don't let her die too bitterly. For this one night, dear,
Say nothing worse than 'Michael's gone.' Spare her something
Until she has cried. Four hours' mercy. By morning
That heart of hers will be seasoned." Fayne strained in the dark
To see his face. He answered in a short while,
"How many mornings I've come in here
And routed him out of bed. He always was a late sleeper.
Sound asleep, Mother." Fayne caught his arm. "Can't you hear
    me?"
"You," he said, "keep your hands off! . . . Until morning
I'll say he fell."
                It was not morning, but the moon was down.
The old mother sat by the bed with her hand on Michael's, regu-
    larly her great fat-swollen body
Jerked with a sob, and tears were spurted from her closed eyes.
    Old Fraser sat with his fists evenly
Together on his knees, his bony face held erect, the brown eyes in
    their hollows red with lamplight.
Fayne heard the noise of a motor starting and left the room.

He was backing out the big truck,
The shed was full of the headlight glare, the ruby tail-light
    glowed by the axle. Before she could come
It had crept out; its light swung up the driveway by the stooping
    sycamore
And picked from darkness the heavy timbers of the high corrals
    and the white beehives remote on the hill;
Fayne ran down the river of light to the gate and closed it, and
    stood in the gate for fear he might smash through;
But Lance came wearily to open; stooping, tall,
Black on the light. She said, "Oh, where?" "You know.
Tell dad to come to Salinas and get the truck;
There wasn't enough gas in the little one."
She answered, "Can the sheriff make us happy again?
Or the judge make Michael alive again?" "Open the gate."
"Yes, dear. *Listen* to me. When Arriba and his boys
Stole cows of ours, did you run to the courthouse?
We take care of ourselves down here. What we have done
Has to be borne. It's in ourselves and there's no escaping,
The state of California can't help you bear it.
That's only a herd of people, the state.
Oh, give your heart to the hawks for a snack o' meat
But not to men." When she touched him with her hands,
Pleading, he sighed and said, "If I'd been nearer
My decent mind, it would have been you, not Michael.
Did y' love him? Or was it only because you're female
And were drunk, female and drunk?" "Oh. Hush. I was begging
    him
Not to leave us, as I'm begging you. He promised me, dear.
He said he'd not go away. I kissed him for that; he was our
    brother;
And you came behind." Lance's blackness of his leaning bulk
Vibrated in the light-beam. "It'd be a pity for me then.
I can't see clear, in the dirty streaming memories . . .
Don't be afraid; your part will be secret.
I'll say I killed him for nothing, a flea-bite quarrel,
Being beastly drunk." "He was killed," she answered, "for
    nothing."

"It's a great pity for me then.
Open the gate." She clung to the timber bolt
To hold it home in the slot, and felt his mind
Tearing itself. "Lance. Lance? Sweetheart:
Believe . . . whatever you need to save you.
I won't give you up. You can't remember what happened;
I tell you he fell from the cliff. But if your dreadful
Dream were true, I know you are strong enough
To give your heart to the hawks without a cry
And bear it in lonely silence to the end of life.
What else do you want? Ah. Confession's a coward
Running to officers, begging help. Not you."

                                    She heard
The scrape of slow boots on gravel outside the light-stream,
Across the pulses of the idling motor, and suddenly cried,
"He fell from the cliff." An old man said in the dark,
"They ain't got consideration. Where was you going
This time o' night, after what's happened? Your dad wants you.
Your ma's took bad." Lance moaned and stood still.
Fayne said, "He was going to Lobos to telephone
The doct . . . the coroner. Dearest, you ought to go in.
She suffered great pain before, she was near death.
Old Davie will drive up the coast for you
When daylight comes." "Oh," he said stilly, and turned
His face to the fountains of light; it gleamed without meaning
In the stream of radiance like a stake in a stream,
Except that from exhaustion the pupils of the eyes
Failed to contract, so that their secret interiors
Of their chambers returned the light all sanguine.
At length he kneaded them with his fists and said,
"I can't see well. You'll have to help me find the way in.
It's not a trick of yours, uh?"

V

                         His mother lay on the floor,
For Michael's body lay on the bed. The sun of pain at her heart
   had rays like skewers of anguish

393

Along the left arm and up by the jugular arteries. She dared
not move; her face stood wet-white and still,
With live blue eyes; but the clay-pale lips opened and closed.
Old Fraser had swathed her in hasty blankets.
Fayne entered; Lance behind her stood swaying and stooping
in the door and saw his father
Crouched beside the great cocoon of the blankets; and Michael in
the bed above, and trinkets of Michael's
That hung on the wall, gleam in the lamplight. The violence of
pain was brief; she whispered "better," and breathed
With greedy shallow passion; her eyes found Lance.
                                                    Daylight
    grayed slowly into the room;
The lamp ran dry unnoticed. Lance and his father
Labored and carried the heavy old woman to bed.
Fayne brought them food, but Lance refused it. In the afternoon
He walked outdoors for a time, but nothing farther
Than the cattle-pens. Fayne must have been watching for him,
Because she went and walked by his side, and said,
When they were turned from the house, "Mary Abbey was here.
It seems she expected to marry Michael, though he never told us.
She cried a lot." Lance made no sign of hearing her.
Fayne said, looking up sidelong at his cheek and jaw,
Where the flesh hung thin on the bone: "Her grief's not
Like ours, forever; but sharp at present. If she ever
Imagined that you . . . how could we bear her looks? You are
    too strong, dear,
To lay on weaker persons a burden
That you alone ought to bear." He strode faster
And stopped, muttering, "He lies up there, like that.
And my mother, like that; and I have done it;
And you talk about Mary Abbey." Fayne said, "I have no time
To choose names, for a man is coming to-day
To question us. He's sent for. I have to tell you that you must
    choose whether to relieve
Your own weakness . . . conscience I mean . . . by easy con-
    fession,

Or bear the whole weight unhelped. The first way's easy; you'll
    be acquitted; you'll be left humbled and soiled,
But free; for confession is not enough; and you were too lost to
    remember anything clearly; and I
Am the one witness. I saw him climb on the cliff and fall. So your
    conscience will be well comforted,
And fairly cheap. Only your mother perhaps will die of it; your
    father and I will swallow our portion;
And the crowd at Salinas
Will have had a good time watching your face in court. It would
    be harder, if you've a snake in your heart,
To keep it shut there."

                  He was silent, and drew sharp breath and
    said, "A red-haired one. Ah.
A white one with a red brush. Did you do it with him
Or not?" "Leave that," she said stilly; "this choice is *now*."
He groaned and answered, "My mind's not quick like yours.
. . . I'll not lie to them." "Let me show your mind to you;
Be patient a moment still; if I seem cruel,
That's to save, all that's left. Look at yourself:
A man who believes his own sweet brother's blood
Lies on his hands: yet
Too scrupulous to tell a lie, for his mother's life.
Our minds are wonderful." He meditated, and answered
Heavily, "The sunlight seems dull but red.
What makes it red?" "Your eyes are sick of not sleeping;
Or there's a forest-fire in the south." "Our minds? Little bottles
That hold all hell. I seem too tired to feel it, though.
I'll think, I'll think."
"You have no time for thinking. He will come probably
Within this hour." "Who? Let him come. I'll tell him
God made them male and female but men have made
So-and-so . . . I fall asleep while I talk . . . whiskey eh?
Lighted the sticky fire. It's not possible
I'd ever done it except that I stumbled on you
In the heart of guilt. I know that." "Believe it then,"
She answered shrilly, and stood twitching her lips
In the white freckled face, in the reddish light of her hair,

"If that will help." "Oh," he said.
". . . I wish you had picked from another tree."
She answered: "You are to say that you found him dying.
You heard me cry, and he was down by the rock.
Isn't that the truth exactly, because you remember
No previous thing? You heard me cry out; you came;
Michael was dying or had died. That's all. You carried him home.
. . . I wish he'd come."

                But the man did not come
Until afternoon the next day. Dark weather, for a stagnant ocean
    of cloud was hung on the sky,
And what light shone came colored like the taste of metal through
    smoke of burning forests far to the south,
That veiled the coast, so that it seemed brown twilight
In the house, in Michael's room. A lamp was lighted,
The death-wound viewed. "*Who* saw him fall?" "I alone.
My husband and others came when I cried." "Where is your
    husband?"
"With his mother," she answered faintly. "She had an attack,
Her heart, angina, and has to lie still. Shall I
Call him, sir?" her voice hardening, her eyes
Growing hard and narrow. "Pretty soon. Was this young man
In trouble about anything?" "No." "A girl?" "He was engaged
To Miss Abbey." "They had a quarrel, ah?" "No."
"Did he seem cheerful?" "Very." "They always do.
Yesterday I had to drive by Elkhorn Slough
Because a very cheerful old man opened his throat
With his nephew's pen-knife. I was two hours
Finding that place; the farmers around there they couldn't tell
    you
Whether Jesus Christ died on the cross
Or at the battle of Bull Run."

                Old Fraser had stood
Nerveless and dreaming over the livid face
Since they uncovered it; abruptly he turned his head
Above his bowed shoulder, saying "It's enough.
Dog, blaspheme not. Go to your own place.
My son found death in recklessness, I fear in folly;

Write that and leave us alone; go hence and leave us
To mourn and hope." "Well, Mr. Fraser. You understand . . ."
"I am very patient," the old man said, thrusting
His hollowed face toward the other, the closely set
Inflamed brown eyes pushing like the burnt end of a stick
That has been used to stir fire; the man stepped backward.
"Did he say patient! . . . Well, is your husband here?"
Fayne's mouth jerked and froze hard, her hands quieted.
"I will call him. Come to the room downstairs."
She said at the foot of the stair, "This way, sir. It's dark.
Will you have to go . . . to see the cliff, to see
The cliff?" "Hm, what's that?" "Where he fell."
"Can we drive there?" "No, ride and walk." "Look here,"
He said, "I've come sixty-five miles already.
You're sure it was accidental?" "Yes." "Well.
I always try to save the family feelings
When the case is not clear." He tried his pen,
Shook it, and wrote. Fayne watched, quiet and cold, thinking that
    Lance
Would not have to be questioned; he was saved now;
And saw the man to his car. When he had gone
She thought that now she could laugh or cry if she wanted to,
Now Lance was saved, but her nerves and her mind stood quiet.
    She looked at the dusty gate and the dark house-gable
In the stagnant air against the black cloud, and perceived that all
    events are exact and were shaped beforehand,
And spaced in a steel frame; when they come up we know them;
    there is nothing for excitement.
                  She went in,
And found Lance in the dark at the head of the stair, bent for-
    ward like a great bird. "Has he gone, Fayne?"
"Did you *know* he was here?" "I will live on," he answered,
    "seems to be best. I loved him well; he died instantly,
No anger nor pain. Davis has dug a place by the children's
    graves."
        On account of the dull weather
And closing twilight the group on the hilltop was hardly visible
    in their vast scene. It was quite evident

That not only Pico Blanco against the north, and the gray Ven-
tanas, but even every dry fold
And gully of the humbler hills was almost by an infinite measure
of more importance
Than the few faint figures on the bare height,
The truck, and three saddled horses,
And some persons.
The old man swayed and shook, standing praying
At the head of a dug slot
Beside the pile of pale earth.
The heavy great brown-furred sky that covered all things made
a red point in the west, lost it and darkened,
And the Point Sur lighthouse made a thin stabbing from the
northwest.

Swaying on his heels and toes the old man prayed:
"Oh Lord our God, when thy churches fell off from thee
To go awhoring after organ music,
Singing-women and lecturers, then my people
Came out from among them; and when thy last church,
Thy little band, thy chosen, was turned at length
To lust for wealth and amusement and worldly vanities,
I cried against them and I came forth from among them.
I promised thee in that day that I and my house
Would remain faithful, thou must never despair;
I said, though all men forget thee thou hast a fort
Here in these hills, one candle burning in the infidel world,
And my house is thy people.
                          My children died,
And I laid them in this place and begot more children
To be thy servants, and I taught them thy ways, but they fell
away from thee.
They found their pleasure among the ungodly, and I believe
They made themselves drunk with wine, and my dear son is
fallen.
He died on the shore. One half of the curse of Eli has fallen
upon me."
He covered his face with his knotted hands and stood gasping,

And said, "I loved him. Here he is, Lord.
Surely thou hast forgiven his sins as I have forgiven them,
And wilt lift him to thy glory on the last day."
The old man stood silent, lifting his face, and fixed his deep
    close-set eyes, like the eyes of an old ape,
Small, dark and melancholy under the bar of the brow, between
    the wide cheek-bones, fixed them far off
Across the darkening ridges and ocean upon that single red spot
    that waned in the western sky,
And said "The world darkens and the end is coming.
I cannot beget more children; I am old and empty,
And my wife is old. All men have turned their faces away from
    thee;
I alone am thy church. Lord God, I beseech thee not to despair,
But remember thine ancient power, and smite the ungodly on
    their mouths
And the faithless churches with utter destruction. For Jesus'
    sake, amen." While he prayed, Fayne watched Lance
With pity and fear; and Mary Abbey, who was there with her
    father,
Kept stealing glances at Lance through her wet eyelashes.
She whispered to Fayne: "Oh, Lance looks dreadfully.
I never knew he loved him so dreadfully."
Fayne answered, "Yes, he did"; and looked up at Lance
With pity and fear. "He looks as if he'd fall sick,"
Mary said. Fayne answered, "No, he is strong.
He hasn't eaten since Michael died; maybe
He hasn't slept." Mary said, wiping her eyes,
"His face is so sad and fine, like carved marble.
They say he carried him all the way home, up that cliff."
The old man ended his prayer, the redwood box
Was lowered with ropes; Lance had the weight at one end,
Old Fraser and Davis at the other. The ropes cut grooves
In the earth edges. While they were shovelling earth,
Mary Abbey, with a sudden abandoned gesture
Of the hand that had the handkerchief in it, ran up to Lance
On the scraped ground. "*Don't* grieve so." She reached and
    touched

His hand on the spade-handle. "It makes me afraid for you.
We all loved him; life has to go on." He jerked his hand,
And looked down at her face with startled eyes
So pale gray-blue that all the light that remained in the world
Under the low black sky seemed to live in them,
Stammering, "No. *No.* He fell from the cliff." She said, "I know,
    Lance.
We have to bear it. I loved him too." He gathered his dreaming
   nerves
Into the bundle again and said, "Oh. All right. Please keep out of
    the way for the time.
We have this to do." "Good-bye," she answered patiently. "Fa-
    ther's calling me."
                  The pit was filled full and mounded;
Fayne came and said, "What was she saying to you?" "Nothing.
    Who?" "Mary Abbey." "I didn't see her."
"What, Lance? She came and spoke to you." "I'd rather be there
    with Michael," he answered. "Dear, you must rouse yourself.
Life has to go on." "Somebody was saying so, I think.
There's not a hawk in the sky." She answered from a hoarse
    throat, "After dark? What are you dreaming?
See, Davie's turned on the headlights." "I hate them," he said,
    "killers, dirty chicken-thieves."
                 The farm-truck headlights
Shone on the mounded earth, and cast its enormously lengthened
    shadow and the shadows of a few moving
Persons across the world, with the beam of light, over mound
    beyond mound of bare autumn hills, and black
Ocean under the black-roofed evening.

VI

                 That night he returned
To lie with Fayne in their bed, but like two strangers
Lying in one bed in a crowded inn, who avoid
Touching each other; but the fifth night
She laid her hand on the smooth strength of his breast,
He pretended to be asleep, she moved against him,
Plucking his throat with her lips. He answered, "After all?

You're right. If we're to live in this life
We'll keep its customs." He approached her confidently,
And had no power. The little irrational anger
At finding himself ridiculous brought to his mind
That worse rage, never before clearly remembered,
But now to the last moment; or imagined. He drew
His limbs from Fayne's without thinking of her, and lay still,
    with shut fists,
Sweating, staring up spirals of awful darkness, that spun away up
    and wound over his eyes
Around a hollow gray core with flecks in it. "I am damned un-
    justly. I did it in a moment."

                            But Fayne knew nothing
Of the shut agony beside her; only she was troubled at heart, and
    wondering
Whether he had ceased to love her said tenderly, "Sleep,
Darling. I didn't mean. I didn't want.
Only I love you." He felt her instinctive hand
Move downward fondling along the flat of his belly.
He set it aside and spoke, so low that her ears
Lost every word between the hair and the pillow.
"What, dearest?" "I know it," he said, "they're dogs: that was
    exactly
Fit to tell dogs. I can be damned
At home as well." "Hush, dear." "I don't make a good murderer,"
He said, "I sweat." She was silent and heard him breathing,
And mourned, "Oh, cover your mind with quietness to-night.
In the morning you'll face it down again. This will get well with
    time.
It was really only a dreadful accident." "Very damnable," he said,
"Very true." Fayne said, "We'll live, sweetheart, to feel it
Only a dreadful accident, and the sad death
Of one we loved." "That's your smooth skin.
The fires fester on mine. Will you do something
For me?" "Dearest, with all my heart." "An easy kindness:
Shut up your mouth."

                    He got up after a time;

When he went out she followed, trembling. He turned on her
Outside the door. "I'm not going to Salinas,"
He whispered, "nor bump myself off either.
I'll not starve your hawks of their snatch o' meat.
Now let me alone for Christ's sake." She stood and saw him
Against the starlit window at the end steal down
The hallway, go past the stairhead, and enter the empty
Room of his brother. He slept there from that night on,
And seemed to regain calm strength.

VII

                    In the course of a month
Rain seemed at hand, the south wind whetting his knife on the
    long mountain and wild clouds flying;
Lance and his father set out to burn the hill to make pasture. They
    carried fire in forkfuls of straw
Along the base of the south wall of their valley; the horses they
    rode snorted against it, and smoke
Boiled, but the seaward end of the hill would only be burnt in
    patches. Inland, at the parched end,
A reach of high grass and sage might have led out the fire to the
    forest, and Lance rode up
To watch a flame down the wind to black out the danger.
He carried two barley-sacks and went to the Abbeys' trough
At the hill spring to dip them, to beat down the fire's
Creepings up wind. From that spur of the mountain
He saw the planted pine trees at Abbey's place,
And riding back with the dipped sacks, the vale
Of his own place, the smoke-mist, and Sycamore Creek
Wound like a long serpent down the small fields.
He set his fires and watched them rage with the wind,
Easily stifling their returns, riding herd
On the black line; then from the base of the hill
Red surf, and the dark spray rolled back by the wind,
Of the other fire came up roaring. The lines met
On the fall of the hill like waves at a river's mouth
That spout up and kill each other, and hang white spray
On cold clear wind.

A rabbit with blazing fur broke through the back-fire,
Bounding and falling, it passed by Lance and ran
Straight into the stem of a wild lilac bush,
He saw it was blind from the fire, and watching it struggle away
Up its dark pain, saw Mary Abbey coming down the black hill
    against the white sky,
Treading on embers. Lance turned and hardened in the saddle,
    and saw the vale below him a long trough of smoke
Spilled northward, then Mary came near and said, "I wanted to
    talk to you. I saw you ride by the water-trough."
He shuddered and said, "What? I'll watch the fire." "Fayne
    doesn't like me so well I think
Since Michael . . . indeed I'm ashamed to be always around your
    house."
"I noticed you there," he said, carefully regarding
The dark braids of her hair, and the pale brown face
Seen from above. "I don't know," she said.
"My father says to go away for a time,
His sister lives on a place in Idaho.
But I wouldn't want to forget. But I told Fayne . . .
So I don't know. We could see that you grieved for him
More deeply than anyone else, and all these great hills are empty."
He said, "Is that all?" "Ah . . . ? Yes," she answered,
And turned away and looked back. Lance found that the bridle-
    leather
Had broken suddenly between his hands, and said "You won't get
    anything from Fayne; she's hard as iron.
Why do you follow us around? What do you think you'll find
    out?" She said, "Your grief is greater perhaps,
For you knew him longer. But you have Fayne and I have no-
    body: speak kindly to me. As I remember,
At first it came from seeing you and Fayne so happy in each
    other,
I wanted to be like that. I can't talk well, like Fayne,
But I read a great deal." He stared at her face and began to knot
    the bridle, his hands relaxing,
And said, "I must ride around by the oak-scrub and see that the
    fire has checked. I've got to be watchful always.

Will you stay here?" He went and returned and said, "Come
down to our place whenever you are lonely, Mary.
My mother's quite well again. His death was . . . do people talk
much about it?" She looked in wonder at his face,
And he with numbed lips: "What lies do they . . . can't you
speak out?" "I never
Talked about it with anyone, since Nina Dolman
Told us that day. Truly there's nothing to be said by anyone
Except, he was bright with life and suddenly nothing, nothing,
nothing, darkness."
Lance breathed and said sharply, "I wouldn't bet on it
If I were you. Mary, you are tender and merciful:
Don't come to the house; Fayne is like iron. You'd better
Run home and forget about us. Unless you should hear something
I ought to know." "What do you mean?" "Good-bye."
She saw his bridle-hand lift, she said "I've no pride,
I pray you not to leave me yet, Lance.
I loved him greatly, and now that bond hangs cut,
Bleeding on the empty world, it reaches after
You that were near him, Fayne and you. I was always
Without companions, and now I'd give anything
To be in your friendship a little." "Anything?" he said.
"You faithful women.
Fayne was five days. Mmhm, I have seen a vision.
My eyes are opened I believe."

                      He rode across the burnt hill,
Watching the wind swirl up the ashes and flatten
The spits of smoke. Past the singed oak-scrub he began to wonder,
If there was honey in the little tree, had . . . the dead
Tasted it before he died? "You'd better be off to Idaho.
. . . I shy from his name like a scared horse.
By God, I'd better get used to it; I've got to live with it."
He looked sharply all about the burnt solitude
To be sure of no hearers, and recited aloud:
"I killed Michael. My name is Lance Fraser.
I murdered my brother Michael. I was plastered,
But I caught 'em at it. I killed my brother Michael.
I'm not afraid to sleep in his room or even

Take over his girl if I choose. I am a dog,
But so are all."

        The tall man riding the little bay horse
Along the burnt ridge, talking loudly to nothing but the ash-
    drifting wind; a shadow passed his right shoulder;
He turned on it with slitted eyes, and saw through the strained
    lashes against the gray wind a ghastly old woman
Pursuing him, bent double with age and fury, her brown cloak
    wild on the wind, but when she turned up the wind
It was only a redtail hawk that hunted
On the burnt borders, making her profit in the trouble of field-
    mice. Lance groaned in his throat "Go up you devil.
Ask your high places whether they can save you next time."

VIII

Leo Ramirez rode down on business
About redwood for fence-posts; he asked in vain
For Lance, and had to deal with old Fraser. When he went out
He saw red hair around the corner of the house
And found Fayne in the garden, and asked for Lance.
"I couldn't tell you. I saw him ride to the south.
He'll be home soon for supper." Ramirez stood
In troubled silence, looking at the earth, and said
"I wonder ought I to tell him . . ." Fayne's body quivered
Ever so slightly, her face grew carefully blank.
"What, Leo?" "Will Howard, for instance. Mouths that can't
Shut up for the love of God." "He drives the coast-stage,"
Fayne answered carefully. Ramirez looked over the creek
At the branded flanks of the south hill, and no rain had come
To streak them with gray relentings. "He didn't see it,"
He said; "and those two janes on vacation
Went back to town the next day." He giggled, remembering
The sailing-ship stippled on the white skin,
And fixed his mind smooth again. Fayne said, "How dares he
Lie about us?" Ramirez's brown soft eyes
Regarded her with mournful wonder and slid away.
He said, "You was very quick-thinking." "What?" she said, "You
    were there.

405

And when I cried to him to be careful you looked
And saw him larking on the rock, and you saw him fall,
You could see very plainly in the awful moonlight.
These are things, Leo, that you could swear to." He nodded,
And slid his red tongue along his dry lips and answered,
"Yes'm." "So Howard's a liar," she said. "But don't tell Lance;
He'd break him in two. We'll all do very well,
All wicked stories will die, long long before
Our ache of loss." "Yes'm." She walked beside him
To his tethered horse, and charmed him with an impulsive hand-
      clasp
After he was in the saddle.
                              She stood with her face high, the
      great sponge of red hair
Lying like a helmet-plume on her shoulders, and thought she was
      sure of conquering security but she was tired;
She was not afraid of the enemy world, but Michael would never
      be here laughing again. On the hill,
In the hill he lay; it was stranger than that, and sharper. And his
      killer
Ought to be hated a little in the much love. The smells in the
      wind were of ocean, the reedy creek-mouth,
Cows, and wood-smoke, and chile-con-carne on the kitchen stove;
      it was harder to analyze thoughts in the mind.
She looked at the dear house and its gables
Darkening so low against the hill and wide sky and the evening
      color commencing; it was Lance's nest
Where he was born, and his great white body grew high and
      beautiful. Old Davie shuffled up from the calf-pens
Into the house; then far and high, like a tiny horn on the hill
      against the green-saffron heaven
Lance grew into sight, the man and the horse and the evening
      peace. He was well again; he was sometimes cheerful
Since the early plowing; his muscles needed strong labor. He was
      like this mountain coast,
All beautiful, with chances of brutal violence; precipitous, dark-
      natured, beautiful; without humor, without ever

A glimmer of gayety; blind gray headland and arid mountain,
  and trailing from his shoulders the infinite ocean.
So love, that hunts always outside the human for his choice of
  metaphors,
Pictured her man on her mind. He dropped from sight
In the hill thickets. She thought, "That's the direction
From the Abbeys' or farther south. Mary Abbey's
Quit haunting our house." The sky grew ever more luminous
  pale,
The hills more solid purple. At the valley sea-mouth pale rose
  layered over amber, and over the rose
Pale violet, high over the lifted hawk-wings of divided hills, to
  one fine twist of flamingo-feather
Cloud flying in the wind and arch of the world.

                                A bat flitted up
    the still glimmer.
Fayne went up the drive and opened the gate
For Lance coming across the fields. He looked
As if he had fought, a victory; Fayne was silent;
He nodded, and said, "I've got it over with. You were right."
She saw a thin drift of blood on the bay's foreleg;
A big brown bird hung from the saddle-thongs,
The half-spread sail of one wing clasped Lance's knee;
He had his rifle. "Another hawk, Lance?" "I've been there,"
He answered. "Oh, this? I pick 'em off when I see 'em.
I've been back to that place." "What place, dear?" "The . . .
Slaughter-house. Under the cliff. Ah: I looked around there.
And rubbed that . . . time into my eyes
Until it formed. Now I guess it won't mix
With every mouthful of air; I can call it to memory
Or shut it up." Fayne looked at his drawn face.
But she thought he seemed a degree restored
To natural goodness again, for he dismounted
And walked beside her. She smelled the prickly sweet fragrance
Of whiskey, and said: "That nasty old man was there.
Lance: you were careful with him?" "Care?" he said, "Hell.
We talked about fish. . . . I heard once about a fellow in jail
Kept banging his head on the wall until he died:

I'd liefer have done that than killed my brother.
I often . . . miss him." He stopped to tie up the hawk's feet
To the top wire of the fence; thence they went on
Without speaking.

        At supper he said suddenly across the table,
"Listen, dad.
Are not two sparrows sold for a farthing? When Mikey and I
were little you used to have prayers in the evenings
And flogged us the times we snickered: why did you quit?" Old
Fraser fixed his narrow-set apelike eyes
On Lance's face; they seemed to become one thrusting darkness,
but he said nothing. After a time
Lance said, "But why did you quit?" "Because I grew old and
powerless," the old man answered. Lance: "What was that
You used to read about two sparrows for a farthing?" "The Book
is there." He nodded toward the other room.
"Look it out for yourself." When they stood up from table Lance
said, "I wish you would read it for us,
About the sparrows." "I will not," he said, "read for your mock-
ery. I am utterly left alone on earth;
And God will not rise up in my time." But Lance: "Doesn't it say
No sparrow can fall down without God?" Fayne said, "Oh,
Lance: come on."
"No, no; I want him to read and pray.
What does that mean, fall to earth without God?
Does it mean that God fells it? Fayne and I
Know better than that: ah, Fayne? *We* know, ah?
But God connives.
Do read about the two sparrows." His roving glance
Came on his mother's blanched and full-moon face,
The pouched watery blue eyes, and the mouth always
Thirsting for breath. "No, no, I'll keep still, mother.
I didn't want to tease him, I was in earnest
To have prayers again."

        But he remained in the room
Until his mother had gone up to bed, then instantly
Said, "Listen, dad. Be a good sport.

Are not two sparrows sold for a farthing?" Fayne had watched
 him
Sitting stone-still, only twitching his hands,
His face hollow in the lamp-shadow: she went quickly
And touched his shoulder; she smoothed her hand on his throat,
Saying, "Please, Lance, no more of that. Why will you do it?"
"Sh," he said, "I have him by a raw spot: keep out.
He spooned the gospel down my throat when I was a cub:
Why's he so tight wi' that farthing? Once, dad, you whipped
 Mikey
For spelling the name of God backward
Until the red crucifixion ran down his legs.
Do you remember the brave little brown legs
All smeared and welted?" The old man eyed him and said,
"You lie. He had a thorn-scratch that opened." "Booh," Lance
 answered,
"I won't quarrel with you. I want the truth:
Are not two sparrows sold for a farthing?" Old Fraser
Groaned, and the straight edge of the lamp-shade shadow
That crossed his broad face obliquely over the burning
Blackness of the eyes, but left the stiff mouth and jaw
In the yellow light, shook with his passion. He said, "My Master
 also
Was mocked cruelly by those he loved, desiring to save them.
 You have a strong body, and if I struck you
You'd take me by the wrists like a little child. I am in my house
 and I have no one to help me.
I am old and worn out; my strength is gone and white hair has
 come, but honor has not come. I say that God
Is not mocked; but a feeble ailing old man, who loved his boys
 too indulgently and has seen the blithe hands
Reach out for damnation, and the happy feet . . . Oh . . .
Is rightly mocked. Oh Lance, over Michael's death." Lance, pale
 and mumbling: "We all have troubles, old man;
Yours have come late. Well. Are not two sparrows . . ." Fayne
 cried, "Lance, Lance, for pity
Hush, whatever he did to you when you were little.
He earns peace now." "Mm," he said, "where's that? I've

Been trying to get him to call me about those sparrows:
The old man won't play: we've an ace in the hole too.
Here it is for nothing, old man:
I rode by the Abbeys' line-fence along the steep
Over Wreck Beach, and there's a young deer, a spike-buck,
Hanging dead on the wire, made a bad jump
From the low side. The barbs caught him by the loins,
Across the belly at the spring of the haunches, the top wire.
So there he hangs with his head down, the fore-hooves
Reaching the ground: they dug two trenches in it
Under his suspended nose. That's when he dragged at the barbs
Caught in his belly, his hind legs hacking the air.
No doubt he lived for a week: nothing has touched him: a young
    spike-buck:
A week of torture. What was that for, ah?
D'you think God couldn't see him? The place is very naked and
    open, and the sea glittering below;
He hangs like a sign on the earth's forehead, y' could see him from
    China. . . . But keep the wind side.
For a loving God, a stinking monument." "Bosh," the old man
    answered,
And stood up, and puckering a miminy mouth: "Your little buck!
There is not one soul in hell but would take his place on the wire
Shouting for joy . . . and few men past fifty." Lance also,
Made surly by the slow death of whiskey in his blood,
Stood up: "Your merciful God, that made you whip little boys.
    We're dogs,
But done licking those feet." He bulked in the old man's way to
    the door, towering in the shadow, and forced him
Toward the near corner. Fayne ran between them. "Tell me the
    truth," Lance said, "do you believe in your God?"
Old Fraser, who had stood glaring like a bayed cat, suddenly
    dwindled; and felt outside the walled cube
Of lamplight, under gray stars no Scottish nor Palestinian uplands
    but the godless hills of America
Like vacant-eyed bison lying toward the sea, waiting for rain.
    He moved his lips without breath, he struck

His throat and said feebly: "I am choked and dried up with the
running sands.
I have prayed a great deal in vain, and seen the whole earth
Shed faith like leaves;
And the faces of sin round as the sun and morality
Sneered to death. I cannot
Live unless I believe. . . . I cannot live";
And stood all shrunken. Lance, awed: "My God, who'd ever 'a'
thought
He could be plagued into honesty?" The old man
Cried fiercely: "I believe. Ah: tell your people to be careful
Of the God they have backed into a snarling corner,
And laugh off like a dirty story." "That's it," Lance answered.
"Dogs. We all are." He stood backward, the old man
Passed slowly, staring, saying, "Make yourself ready if you can.
For I see you are changed."

        Fayne shuddered and said,
"What does he mean?" "He? Nothing. He means *two* sparrows
For a farthing." She said, "Lance . . . Lance?"
He moved to leave her; she breathed and said, "Can you hear?
We were doing, what you thought. It seemed . . . usual
That night: both drunk: he was going away . . . So what you
did, Lance,
Was justice." "Agh," he said, "nudge me wi' that, still?
I know it perfectly. What does it matter, what farthing
Sold them?" Fayne, sobbing: "Oh, then, we did not. It is not true.
I lied." "It would not be possible to tell you," he said,
"How little I care." She, with both hands at her white throat, but
lifting her face:
"Yes. I can bear that. We've sailed I think away past the narrows
of common faithfulness. Then care for this:
To be able to live, in spite of pain and that horror and the dear
blood on your hands, and your father's God,
To be able to go on in pure silence
In your own power, not panting for people's judgment, nor the
pitiful consolation of punishing yourself
Because an old man filled you with dreams of sin

When you were little: you are not one of the sparrows, you are
    not a flock-bird: but alone in your nature,
Separate as a gray hawk." "The very thing I was thinking," he
    answered.
"If you'd take your red hair and spindly face
Out of my lamplight I'd be alone: it's like a burst blood-vessel
In the eye of thought."

IX

Old Mrs. Fraser

Caught cold and remained in bed, the bronchial pain
Frightened her heart with memories of worse anguish.
Fayne went back and forth from the stove to the bed
Heating flannels, to lay them on the white upland
Between the blond mountains of falling flesh
That had fed Lance. Going by the curtainless window
She looked whether she could see him, across the fields
Or up the burnt hill. Not Lance, but a smaller figure
Was coming down the black hill under white clouds:
Mary Abbey: her father had horses enough,
Was she walking down here?
                Lance's mother
Wished for that wintergreen oil again; Fayne rubbed it
On the white plain and the roots of the great soft udders.
She could feel in her finger-tips the suck and rattle
Of phlegm in the breathing-tubes, the old woman coughing
And saying "I see there was four sheets in the wash again
From you and Lance; well, dearie, don't fret.
He's just his father all over, crazy as hawks.
They get to thinking Antichrist and the Jews and the wicked
    Pope in Rome
And scunner at every arrangement for human comfort.
Then they come home like hungry sailors from sea.
You're all worn out in the morning; my feet are cold."
She coughed and panted; Fayne rubbed the oil. The old woman
    said,
"My feet are cold." Fayne answered sadly "I'll rub them."
"No, if you'd get me an iron; a fine hot flat-iron

Done up in cloth is a great comfort in bed.
Right often it's been a husband to me when my old man
Was prophesying around and a fresh cow
Cried all the night."

Fayne went downstairs for the iron
And heard a wonderful sound behind the house; she heard Lance
laughing.
She looked from the door and saw old Davie by the limewashed
hen-house, leaning both hands on a long shovel,
Gaze at the ground; Lance crouched near by, with blood on his
hands and something between his knees, red feathers,
That fiery old half-bred game-cock, that sent the dogs
Yelping for mercy. A little Cooper's-hawk was tethered in front
of Lance to a driven peg,
One wing bloodily trailing; Lance pushed the game-cock to-
ward it and the hawk fell, tripped by its wing,
But crutched itself on the other and came up again,
Erect and watchful, holding the earth with its yellow feet.
Lance pushed and freed the game-cock, that eagerly
Staring-hackled in his battle-passion
Leaped up and struck down; the hawk tripped by its wing
Fell quivering under the spurs, but a long-fingered
Lean yellow hand reaching up out of ruin
Plucked at the red king's breast: who charged again: one hawk-
wing
Waved, and the talons mysteriously accomplished
Many quick bitter acts, whence the red king
Reeled out of hope. He crouched beyond tether's reach,
Propping himself on both wings, but the sinking head
Still stretched for fight; then dull-eyed, at strength's end,
Went staggering to it again. The yellow hands
Easily made him what would never any more
Chirp over bright corn to the hens or subdue a rival.
Lance came, and the little hawk ran quickly and fell
Onto its broken shoulder at the tether's end. Lance picked up
the dying game-cock;
Red grains of wheat from the torn crop fell down with the
blood. Fayne watched from the open door; she saw him

Turn at the click of a gate, and Mary Abbey came up from the
creek-bed path. At sight of Lance
She stopped; her hands went up to her throat. He, frowning:
"What do you want . . . Mary?" She lowered her hands
And stepping backward almost inaudibly said, "I . . .
Came the back way. I . . . came to see Fayne." She had hurried
and was breathing hard. Lance stared at her,
And said "Go on in, confess your sins." He turned with his
shoulder toward her; the bleeding bird in his hands
Stretched itself, thrusting back with the spurs as if it were killing
its last rival, and suddenly died,
With a bright bubble of blood in the gaping beak. Old Davie
laughed, but not Lance; the little hawk
Stood up and watched all with intent eyes. Mary stayed wringing
her hands and Fayne came from the door,
Then Mary, half running toward her: "I hardly bear to see
blood: let me go in." Fayne said to Lance:
"It won." "It will lose," he said in his throat, "when my heel is
on it." She, gravely: "It fought well, Lance.
Have you hurt your hands?" "Ugh," he said, "nothing: the ver-
min." He moved toward the little captive, that looked up at
him
With cold intentness; the blood had started again from its broken
shoulder and striped the dead wing. Mary Abbey,
Shrilly, whipping the air with her hands: "Let me go!" Lance
raised his foot to tread, but the victim's intent
Concentration of binocular eyes looked human; Mary cried
shrilly: "They told me, my father said . . .
And Nina told me . . . Oh Fayne!" Lance, suddenly rigid:
"What's that?" Fayne answered steadily and said, "Its life
Is little value to it with a broken wing. Come into the house."
She answered "I am afraid."
But approached the door, whispering "What kind of a house,
with blood sprinkled
Where you enter the door: what have you done?
His hands are red." Lance turned from the hawk and said with
his teeth showing, "Tell your father

That I may soon be with this," he toed the dead cock, "our
    second-sighted old Scotchman has got a hunch,
But not with that, not caught alive." She fled from him
To the open door. Fayne, jerking her face but not
Her shoulders toward him, said low: "You speak of things
Less real than nothing. It is not courage to make
Danger where there is none." She followed Mary Abbey
Into the door, saying: "Lance is not well. He loved his brother
Most deeply, and having heard of venomous talk
Makes the wound burn. Have you too been listening
To our enemies?" Mary, trembling in the house twilight:
"I know you couldn't speak calmly, if, if . . . Oh Fayne.
But every person . . . What have I done?" "Will you hush,"
    Fayne said,
"Mrs. Gomez is probably not interested
In your girl dreams." Then Mary was silent, seeing
The dark ruler of the kitchen. Fayne took the iron,
And said on the stair, "I have to attend to Lance's mother:
You'd better stay with me. Then we'll walk." At the room door:
"Mary Abbey is here, Mother."

                    Mary faltered
At the air of the room, the stove-heat and stale hangings in
    the air
Of wintergreen and eucalyptus. She stood close to the door,
And felt the weary mill turn in her mind,
Unable to think of any definite thing, painfully grinding, turning.
    Old Mrs. Fraser
Sniffed and said, "I can smell scorching cloth,
Did you try it with a wet finger? It ought to sizz
But if it whistles it will burn the sheets; Mary, are you sick?
You look all blue by the mouth," she wagged her head in the
    pillow, "watch your heart." Fayne, kneeling
To slip the iron under the covers of the bed, tossed back her
    bright hair and said, "She's all right, Mother.
Lance was having a kind of cock-fight in the back yard, that
    struck her pale: she's one of those delicate
Natures that die at seeing blood."

                                      The weary mill of the mind
struck a hard kernel and seemed to fall
Down hollow waters; Mary leaned on the door-frame, clenching
    her fists not to go down with it, biting
Her white lip, the circle of sight contracted until only the blood-
    splatch of Fayne's hair was visible
At the hub of the whirlpool. She slid with her back to the steep
    door-frame and did not fall; Fayne helped her
To escape the room, the old woman far off proclaiming "It is her
    heart."

    Mary leaned on the newel
Of the stairhead to find her strength to go down, and said,
"I am so caught. And someone has daubed every
Beam of your house with it. All women have to bear blood
But mine has stopped. Please go first, Fayne,
For you don't hate me yet; now I can't bear
To meet . . . anyone." Fayne slowly said, "It was Michael?"
"I am in terror," she answered, "of every living thing,
And him, and you." Fayne's triangular face,
The high cheek-bones and narrow jaw, thrust in the twilight
Opposite the other's white oval, as a small perching hawk
Thrusts with her head, forcing the shapes of things
To grow alive in the motion of the eyes
And yield up their hunted secrets: Fayne peered at her,
Trembling, and said, "Then follow."
                                      They went out the front
    way;
No one was seen; Fayne said: "It is horrible to be nearing New
    Year's
And still the dust and the sun, as if it could never rain. Would
    you like to be nurse to that old woman?
She's Lance's mother." Mary said faintly, stumbling on the plain
    path, "I have no mother: and the raging
Blue of your eyes hates me." "What you have heard," Fayne said,
    "is only the common lies of the shoie.
It's natural for people to furnish a house with lies if it meets
    misfortune. When a man loses his property

He's called fool, or thief; when they see you crushed
By the sudden death of someone you love they begin to hint
   murder; it's human nature. If you're weak enough,
Believe them; it won't hurt us. But what are you here for?" She
   answered, leaning her hand on the post of the little gate
To steady her body: "I am not strong like you. I am in danger
   of killing myself, if . . .
Or if I believe them." "Better than you," Fayne said, "have died.
   Come on." A little way past the gate,
Mary said, "What is it? You too are trembling!" She answered,
   trembling, "Oh no: *my* life is easy. Dear,
We're friends, we mustn't make mysteries; tell me, won't you,
   what's all this web of trouble
You stare so white through? You can count on my loving friend-
   ship, and my
Forgiveness, if for any reason . . . My worst enemy
Will call me warm-hearted; and if I once had the name
Of being a jealous woman in my love for Lance:
Well," she said with a calm voice, her face twisting
Like a small white flame specked with flying ashes,
"That wears, it softens. And he . . . grows morose and strange,
Is not perfectly a splendor in my eyes any more.
I will confess that I cannot feel so warmly about him
As once I did. . . . Here above the beehives, Mary,
Nobody ever comes, and you could tell me
Everything safely; and if any advice of mine
Could help, though I am not wise."

                              They stood silently,
Turning their faces away from each other,
In a wind acrid with stale honey and the life of bees.
Mary Abbey shuddered and said, "I *came* here
To tell you. Oh, Oh. I used to seem to myself
Locked in, cold and unwishing; but . . . Michael's . . . love
Made April in me, and the sudden emptiness of death
Tore . . . I was much changed: you remember
How I clung to you in the desert of the days afterwards,
And tired you into dislike, until you turned
Hard eyes toward me. The first time I saw Lance alone

He was riding in fire and ashes; he was more unkind
Than you ever were." Fayne tasted
The crack in her bitten lip, and shut her eyes and said softly,
"Go on, sweetheart"; but the dark-haired one
Only wept, and Fayne said, "You've told me nothing,
Sweetheart." She answered, "Are you still really my friend?
Don't look at me," and turned her face from Fayne,
Saying, "I was so aching lonely. I only wanted
To be friends with someone: he really . . . he took me roughly
On the great lonely hill; it hurt, does it hurt at first
If you are loved?" Fayne had stopped trembling and stood
With bones and teeth showing through the skin of her face,
And trying to speak moaned slightly, and avoided
The little blind hand feeling for hers. "But still I
Strain and ache to be near him." Fayne took the hand,
And with her unfleshed mouth kissed Mary's hair,
And tried to speak, and with painful care: "Go . . . on . . .
Sweetheart?" "Then they told me that he killed Michael.
That was not true. Oh yes, I know, but I thought
If I loved where I ought to hate I would kill myself.
I have always been as regular as the new moon,
And this time, twelve days have passed. When I was troubling
About that, that was when they told me. I thought
About a coyote that was caught near our house
In two steel traps at once, so that it couldn't
Stand nor lie down." Fayne touched her teeth with her tongue
Until the stretched white lips came slowly to cover them,
And said, "Do you mean?" She answered, "I am so caught.
I know, I have a book about it. So I came here.
Your dooryard was full of blood." Fayne said, "Maybe you are.
He's travelled away past caring, and would let
Nature fly. I'd naturally . . .
I have to control my starts, because Lance,
Who's worth ten thousand of *you*, hangs on the scale.
D' y' love him, *sweetheart*?" She turned her face toward her,
Saying, "Yes." Fayne mumbled and said, "I'd naturally . . .
It's babies like you . . . Listen to me.
I took Lance in my hand in that bad night

To fling at the world. We do not have to let the dogs judge for
us. I told him that we are our own people
And can live by ourselves: if we could endure the pain of being
lonely. Do you think *you* with Lance
Could strangle time? I am holding the made world by the throat
Until I can make it change, and open the knot that past time
tied. To undo past time, and mend
The finished world: while you were busy teething your young
virginity. I have to control myself.
Last year I'd 'a' let
Nature fly; changed your baby face wi' my hands,
Sweetheart: but I cannot risk: life has changed." "Oh Fayne! why
did you say . . ." "I'm not a tame animal,"
She answered, "the wild ones are not promiscuous. What would
you do," her voice thinning to a wire, "if . . . Lance . . .
If it proved true, that you'd given your little dry heart and care-
ful body
And anxious little savings of honor
For a prize to your lover's murderer: could you walk, eat, sleep,
While you knew that?" She said, "It is true then.
I had made up my mind: indeed I long for it.
Sleep: Oh, you'll see." Fayne drew in breath like one
Drinking in a desert passion, and said, "You've not
Enough courage." "Not for anything else," Mary answered;
"But that"; and began to go back down the dry hill.
Fayne followed, with eyes like the blue flame of sulphur
Under the fever of her hair, and lips reddening.
The moment of joy withered out of her face.
"I am fighting the whole people, do you think I'll risk:
For the pleasure of a small soft fool's removal,
Who'd weep it out to her father or leave a letter. . . . Oh, you:
it's not true.
Lance is no murderer, you're innocent as far as that.
I saw with my eyes your unmourned lover
Clambering up the ledges in his happy drunkenness,
All alone, and the shale broke in his hands;
I saw him pitching down the white moonlight,
And heard the noise like a melon of his head on rock

In the clatter of the falling pebbles. Lance came up the sand
After I screamed." Mary Abbey stood swaying and said,
"If you knew my heart you'd pity me." Fayne, amazed: "Pity
    you
For having had Lance?" and said hoarsely, "When did you tell
    him
That you think you are pregnant?" "Oh, Oh," she stammered,
"Never. You hate me." "You're good at guessing," Fayne said.
"What do you want here, money to bribe a doctor?
We have no money here. Yet it seems I must help you,
Or worse will come. I know a woman in the city . . .
When you start east . . . But you must promise never to come
    back
Into the drawing net of our lives."

X

When Mary had gone,
Fayne went where Lance had been; but only the little hawk
Stood in the dust, hopeless and watchful, with its own misery
And a shadow of its own, between the privy and the hen-house
    and the back door. Fayne thought: would Lance
Be harmed if she should give it the gift? and fetched the axe
    from the wood-block, but forgot to be merciful
And went upstairs. She washed herself, brushed her bright fleece,
    and came down.
                        She found Lance at the fence-corner
Where the north pasture comes down to drink. He had looped
    his belt around the neck of a yearling colt
That had a head like a barrel; the little body and long knotted
    legs of nature, but the head enormous,
Like a barrel-headed beast in a dream. "Oh Lance, what ails it?"
    He stared at her
And answered, faintly smiling, "I guess a little
Message from someone." "What?" she said. "Nothing. We don't
    have rattlers
In the middle of winter." "Is it a rattlesnake bite?"
"They sleep in the rocks and holes, twisted in bunches,
They won't strike if you dig them up: but here

On his lip are the pricks." He unhaltered
The shuddering colt. "Stumble away, poor thing.
That was a mean trick, to sting the innocent."
Fayne said, "Was it a rattlesnake bite?" "Mm: but
What sent it up?" "This weather," she said, "the vicious sun."
"Fine hawk's-weather, ah? Did Mary what's-her-name
Tell you her young sins?" Fayne quivered, closing her eyes,
And answered at length, "She's sick." "So are we all."
"*I* am not. . . . Lance, you are generous: if you found a stranger
Starving, and gave her . . . *him* milk and bread, and came
Home, and you found someone of yours starving;
Your father, whom you don't love, but you have to owe him
A kind of duty . . ." "Why didn't you say brother?"
She fixed her eyes on his face and sighed and said, "I am speaking
Of the living.
. . . And he begged you for the mouthed cup, and what was left
Of the broken loaf?" He made a sound of impatience
And turned, but Fayne took his hand, still marked by pressure
Of the strap that had held the struggling colt: "Would you let
      him starve?"
"No. What about it?" "That . . . stranger . . . you fed seems
      to be sorry about it. I suppose she was starving.
I have some angry rinsings of pride in me
Make begging bitter." "*That's* it," he said. "I could 'a' laughed
      at you
In the days before I was damned. I'm learning. The mares have
      their seasons but women always." "I will bear anything,"
She answered sighing, her narrow white face opaque with toler-
      ance. "I was not always perfectly patient.
If you were safe I'd have twisted a knife in her fluty throat. My
      knife is patience." "I know the very
Place," he said. "Come on, I'll answer his note. The very place."
                              They went up by the dry
Gully through the starved and naked pasture; the autumn hunger
      of horses and the patient hooves had left
Hardly roots of the grass, and the yellow dust was reddened with
      sundown. They saw lean horses drift off
Along the ridges on the darkening sky, and far on the last knoll

Three slabs of redwood standing like erect stones, quite black
  against the red streak and slate-color cloud,
Lonely and strange. Fayne, breathless with labor up the long
  slopes, cried hoarsely, "Where are you going? Oh Lance,
Not there?" "There," he said. "No. I won't. No.
What agony in you . . . not here." "On his earth," he answered.
"It would make us despise ourselves. Oh, do not hate him.
He did no wrong, he was happy and laughing-natured, and dear
  to us all." "Come on," he said, "or go home.
Choose." She went slowly away down the hill, and returned and
  said, "I love you and I want . . . not what you think,
But near enough. And the dead know nothing." "I wouldn't bet
  on it," he said; "the drunk did." "You are wildly wrong,"
She answered, "Oh, horribly," and embracing him strained up
  to his throat
Her whitened lips.
               She felt the bare crumbled earth,
The dark home of the dead and serpents,
Under her back, and gave herself eagerly,
Desiring that gift that Mary meant to destroy,
And herself had never wanted before, but now
To accept what her rival dared not keep,
Take and be faithful where the other fled, had some bitter value;
And faith and the world were shaken; Lance might be lost,
The past might prove unconquerable: no, she could save him:
  but yet
She'd bind the future.
                    This time Lance did not fail.
She feared his caution and schemed against it, quite needlessly,
For he had wandered beyond prudent thoughts;
But when they were going away in the twilight, "Ah vile.
Vile," he said, "your hawks have worse poison in their hook beaks
Than any ground-nest of rattlers." She answered, "I am not to
  tell you
What my hope is." "On top of his bones, dogs in a boneyard."
She answered languidly and bitterly, "I ought to have let you
Go to Salinas. I did not know that your mind . . .
I would have waited for you all the long years.

I did not know that your mind needed men's judgment
And the helpless appraisals of the world to help you. You stood
    so strong,
Separate, clear, free in my eyes: and I did violence to you
When I kept you." She felt a trembling about him
And saw that he did not hear but was watching shadows
Fleet in the air: "Sea gulls. They are gulls, Lance. Look how
    beautiful
The long sharp silent wings in the fading light
On the bare hill." "He took it very quietly," he answered;
"We are all dogs, every one." "Oh," she said, "the world's full
Of evil and foolishness but it is terribly beautiful.
If you could see that, Lance." "What? By God they won't, not
    alive.
But then comes hell." "I pray you, I pray you, dear,
Not to begin to think strangely: that's for your father, who often
Walks his road all staring between hedges
Of Christs and Satans: but you will rub your mind quiet
Like the face of a crystal; there is enough to see
In the dark lovely shoulders of hills, the cows and horses, the
    old gray rocks and the folk around us,
Without tapping strange dreams. . . . Oh, we'll live well."

XI

The rain held off; for two hundred and forty days there had been
    no rain
But one sun-drunken shower. The creek was dry rock and weary
    gray roots; the skin of the mountain crumbled
Under starved feet; the five carcasses of hawks that Lance had
    hung on the fence-wire dried without odor
In the north wind and rages of the sun.
                            Old Fraser walked under
    the moon along the farm-drive beside them,
Saying, "Lord if thou art minded to burn the whole earth
And spat off the dust from thy hands, it is well done,
The glory and the vengeance: but if anywhere
Rain falls on hills, remember I beseech thee thy servant's place,
Or the beasts die in the field." While he was praying

The moon was dimmed; he felt a flutelike exultance
Flow up from the V of his ribs to his wrinkled throat:
He was not abandoned: and looked aloft and saw
A little many-colored man's-palm-size cloud
Coasting the moon from the southeast, the storm-side.
The old man exalted himself; he had power upon God; and
    anxiously
Repressing his joy for fear it waste the event
Beforehand, compelled his heart to remember bitterness,
His two sons lost, one dead, the other in rebellion,
And poverty and scorn and the starved cattle. "Oh Lord God,
As in old time thou didst choose one little people for thine out
    of all the earth,
So now thou hast chosen one man, one old man, foolish and poor:
    but if thy will was made up
To punish the earth, then heed not my voice but arise and punish.
    It is rank with defilement and infidelity
And the music of the evil churches." He saw a shining white
    form at the garden-gate, and for a high moment
Believed that some angel, as unto Abraham . . . It was Lance,
Perfectly naked, and Fayne his wife behind him
Walking in her white nightdress, who spoke pleadingly,
But Lance went on. He came with stiff hesitance,
And seemed not to look down at the latch but opened the gate.
The old man watched and waited in the tool-house shadow.
Lance passed the gate and stood in the open dust
Like a blind marble pillar-stone, the icy moonlight
Washing his body, pouring great shadows
Of the heavily moulded muscles on the hairless breast,
And the ripple of strength on the smooth belly; he stood
And babbled and called: "Mikey. Oh Mikey. Come home.
I'll be *it* to-morrow again. It's getting too dark to play,
Don't hide any more, buddy, for the owls are out.
If you'll come in I'll let you have my cornelian,
And the heron's eggs that I found." Fayne took his hand,
"Lance, Lance, wake up," and stroked the smooth power of
    his arm,

Her face caressing his shoulder. He said, "Hurry, they're blam-
  ing me.
They think you're lost." Fayne said, "I can't bear it, Lance.
Mikey's in the house. He's come in already." The old man
Came forward out of the shadow; Fayne heard and stared at him.
Lance said, "Damned liar. Ma's not . . . mare.
People ain't made like . . . dirty . . ." and babbled words
That could not be understood. Fayne said, "Sleep-walking.
Did he ever before . . . what can I do?" Lance moaned,
She reached her arm around him and stroked his face
With the other hand; the old man saw her hair
Against the wide white breast like a burst of blood
Deep in the moonlight, then Lance flung her aside
As white foam flies from the oar, saying still in the dream-drunken
Sing-song, "Oh no you don't: this is not dog's meat.
Or you'll have to kill it before you paw it.
The angels wi' the hooky beaks . . . What in hell," he said
Sharply, "who's there?" "I, Lance. Oh come to bed, dear.
You wandered out in your sleep." "No: that spying devil,"
He said, "Hm?" "Your father, your father, Lance.
He was here when you came." "Oh. . . . Did I talk?"
"Hardly a word. Nothing, dear." "I sleep better
Alone," he said, "now."
                          The old man looked up at cloud-flecks
Like algae breeding on clear deep well-water around the moon,
And looked at Lance, and returned up the drive. Lance said,
    "Do you wear white? Hitch it up on your breast,
The teat is bare. Why did he turn away without speaking?" "He
    saw you'd wakened." "Black will look fine,"
He answered, "wi' the fiery hair. I want you to marry again,
    you'll have chances."
                    The sky in the morning
Was layered with cloud, and it drove from the southeast; the
    old man kept working his mouth in silent thanksgiving
For answered prayer; and the wind came down from heaven and
    smoked in the fields. The sky cleared for a time,
But that was natural; the wind increased. It ran quartering the
    little valley; ashes from the hill

And mountain dust entered all cracks of the house. It raged on
    the salt pool at the creek sea-mouth
By the caverned crag that storms have worn spongelike; it reaped
    the heads of the waves on the wide sea, and lay
Like a quivering steel blade on the necks of the herbless moun-
    tains.
          Far away northward in San Francisco
It blew the filth of the street into the faces
That walked there; one was Mary Abbey's little pale oval
Lost among thousands. She moved unevenly, fast and lagging,
And looked with terrified eyes at the gilt street-number
Scribed on a window; beyond a mean plush-curtained restaurant
The number stood over a door. She stood choking,
And read on a brass plate in the doorway: "Dr. Eisendraht,
Eye, ear, nose, throat"; a wind-scoop of sudden dust
Blurred the letters and filled her eyes. She went on
With faint small steps, and at the street-corner
Tried to stand still, and was jostled. Not wearing gloves
She spurred blood from the back of her left hand
With the nails of her right: the pain helped her go back
And enter the door and find the stairway. She had to sit long,
Waiting her turn; she was served impersonally
And dismissed, fainting or able, to the desert wind
And dust and multitude down the mean street.
                      At Sycamore Creek
Lance's mother was wiping the table oil-cloth
For the noon meal, the film of the wind's dust, and suddenly
Fell into a chair; Mrs. Gomez came in with knives and forks on
    the plates and found her, and Fayne
Came at the cry; they couldn't take her upstairs until Lance came
    in. They helped her slip to the floor,
And brought a pillow, then Lance came in. Fayne said, "She is
    weak but better, the pain is passing." The old woman
Mountainous laid on the floor wished to lie still for a time. Lance
    knelt by her side. "All right, Mother.
As long as you like. Fayne," he said gravely,
"Will you come to the door a minute?" Fayne went, and outside
    the door said, "What do you want, Lance? You scare her

Wi' that secret look." "I was not afraid to go in after him, I want
  you to see him. The question is
Whether my eyes have begun to sing lies to me.
He came from the orchard walk and went in the shed.
I know you have courage. A frightful branding. Oh," he sighed,
"That's the point." She looked at his face and followed him,
And reeled in the dry fierce wind in front of the house;
But he leaning his back on the stiff wind,
So that his shirt moulded the groove between
The great bands of lean power from the shoulders: "Well. Do
  you see him?
In the shed door." "No." "It was closed, he opened it.
You can see that it's open? Now I'll catch him.
Come." He ran suddenly and leaped the garden gate.
But Fayne must stop to unlatch it, and when she came
Lance had gone into the shed and around the motor-truck
That stood within. Fayne said, "Wind broke the peg
That held the clasp of the door: see, here's one piece.
That's why it's open." She heard the roof straining
Over the imprisoned storm. Lance said, "Did he pass you?
Ah?" She answered, "We must go away from this place.
For you, it's haunted. Your mother, whom I think you love, is
  just now
Lying low between life and death, and you leave her
To chase the wind, and the foxes of your eyes. Do you love
  him so?
Or hate him?" He answered, "The fire's burnt through his cheek,
His back teeth grinned at me through the horrible scar.
I'll be there soon." "What fire? . . . Are you dreaming punish-
  ment?
Oh, that's the vainest craziest falsehood of all.
Leave that to your poor old father." "We go down
Into blackness," he stiffly answered,
"And neither you nor I nor the old man
Knows what happens there. This was Michael: if I should dream
  him
I'd dream the skull knocked in, hm? What I saw's

The cheek burnt through." "I will not let go and lose you," she
answered. "Probably," Lance said, "he'd have lied
If I could have caught him."

In the afternoon
Fayne saw from the window above the kitchen a small gray object
Making a singular dance in the flying dust.
The little hawk which Lance had shot but not killed
Was dying; they had dropped it a strip of beef that dried in the
sun,
And given it a dish of water, and not again
Remembered it, though it stood up grimly and watched
Whoever passed to the privy. The water was blown
Out of the dish; no matter, it had never drunk.
Now it was flapping against the wind,
Fluttering the natural wing and trailing the broken one,
Grotesque in action as the blackcock at dawn
Making his dance of love; but this was of death.

In the night Fayne said: "That little hawk died. Oh, be quiet now;
You've shot them out of the sky. . . . Dear, I am to blame
Like you, and yet I'd be as happy at heart
As a fed bird that glides through the high air
If you were not tearing yourself." He made no answer,
She heard the wind tear at the roof, and said,
"I love this place. But time has changed, let old Davie
And your dad farm it now, it is full of memories
And very fit for old men. You and I
Will take three horses for all our share of it,
And travel into the south by that deer-track
Where the planted foot is on the face of the mountain and the
lifted foot
High over the gray face of the sea: four or five days
Only the eagles will see us, and the coasting ships
Our fires at evening, and so on southward. But when we get to
Los Angeles, dear,
You'll put your great white shoulders to work
For passage-money, we'll sell the horses and ride
In a ship south, Mexico's not far enough,

The Andes are over the ocean like our hills here,
But high as heaven." "Fancy-work," he mumbled. "Ah. Low as
    hell."
Fayne said, "No. Listen: how the air rushes along the keel of the
    roof, and the timbers whining.
That's beautiful; and the hills around here in the cloud-race moon-
    glimmer, round rocks mossed in their cracks with trees:
Can't you see them? I can, as if I stood on them,
And all the coast mountain; and the water-face of the earth, from
    here to Australia, on which thousand-mile storms
Are only like skimming swallows; and the earth, the great meteor-
    ball of live stone, flying
Through storms of sunlight as if forever, and the sun that rushes
    away we don't know where, and all
The fire-maned stars like stallions in a black pasture, each one
    with his stud of plunging
Planets for mares that he sprays with power; and universe after
    universe beyond them, all shining, all alive:
Do you think all *that* needs us? Or any evil we have done
Makes any difference? We are a part of it,
And good is better than evil, but I say it like a prayer
That if you killed him, the world is all shining. It does not
    matter
If you killed him; the world's out of our power, the goodness
    and splendor
Are things we cannot pervert, although we are part of them
And love them well." He heavily answered: "Have you finished?
Don't speak of . . . him . . . again." She began to answer,
Thought, and was silent.

XII

                    She fetched a pair of rawhide panniers
From the harness wall in the barn, remembering that Michael
Less than two years ago had whittled the frame, and Lance
Shaped the hairy leather and stitched it with sinew thongs.
That was the time they three in delight and love
Rode south by the sea-eagle trails to Point Vicente and Gamboa
For seven days' hunting, when Fayne shivered with happiness,

Riding between the most beautiful and strongest man
For husband, and the gayest in the world for brother, on per-
fectly
Wild hills and by rushing streams.
                              She packed the panniers,
And balanced the weight, mixing her things with Lance's.
The wind had ceased and no rain had fallen, but the air grown
colder
Whipped up her courage to believe Lance would go,
And find life, in new places. His mother was well again;
And on the farm all things had come to a pause; he was not
needed.
The hay-loft was emptying fast; but Lance could not make it
rain by staying!

While she packed the panniers
A little agony was acting under the open window, between the
parched lips of the creek.
One of those white-crowned sparrows that make sweet voices in
the spring evenings in the orchard
Was caught by a shrike and enduring death, not the bright sur-
gical mercy of hawks, but slow and strangling.
Its little screams quivered among the gray stones and flew in the
window; Fayne sighed without noticing them,
And packed the panniers.
                    When Lance came up at evening she
showed him what she had done: "We'll go to-morrow."
He said he'd not leave the place in trouble, "Even dogs are faith-
ful. After the first good rain I'll go."
The reasons she made only angered him.
                              Late in January
Fell rain mingled with hail, and snow in the nights. Three or four
calves died in a night, then Lance
Had occupation with what survived; and the north slopes of
hills were sleeted with magic splendor
That did not melt.
                    Fayne was drying dishes while Mrs. Gomez
washed them; she dropped a cup

With the dazzle of the white hill in her eyes when the sun came
     out;
Then Lance's mother filled up the door and said,
"That Mary Abbey is here." Fayne answered clearly,
"I broke a cup. She is in Idaho I think."
The old woman: "She's thinner. Oh Fayne, there were only seven
Left of the dozen"; she gasped, remembering Michael: six were
     enough.
"She's got something to tell you." Fayne said, "Being out of our
     net
Has she flown back? Where's Lance?" and passed the old woman
As one moves a door to pass through a doorway,
But found no one; neither in the front rooms
Nor on the garden path when she opened the house-door.
Then she returned to Lance's mother and asked,
"Where has she gone? Where was she?" but found no light in
     the answers,
Only that Mary looked waxy as a little candle,
Her heart must be terribly weak, she looked all blue by the
     mouth,
And must have come a wet way.
                         Fayne felt the jealous
Devil fingering her throat again, tightening her breath,
And hasted and found Lance; but he was alone;
In the lower creek-bed, lopping all the twigs from the willows,
     making a load, to be chopped fine
And mixed with little portions of hay. She saw him reaching up
     the dwarf stems, as tall as the trees,
The sky-cold knife, the purple twigs at his feet, and said, "Have
     you seen Mary Abbey?" "What?" "Mary Abbey."
"You said she'd gone." "Well, she did go: she was up at the house
     just now"; and knowing her own bitter absurdity
Fayne trembled, saying, "Was she here?" He looked into the
     hollow creek-bed behind him; what was Fayne seeing
To make her tremble? "No," he said. Fayne, trembling with
     anger: "I'll tell you what she went east for: she was pregnant.
She stopped in San Francisco to be fixed up." "That's bad," he
     said; "poor child";

431

He slashed the twigs. Fayne tortured her hands together until
the pain in the knuckles made her able
To smell the wounds of the willows and say steadily, "What
will you do,
Now she's come back?" "Oh," he answered. She stood waiting;
he slashed the twigs and dropped them, saying, "Let her
stay there.
I've been thinking, Fayne. I've been able to think, now the heat's
broken. We have no outlet for our bad feelings.
There was a war but I was too young: they used to have little
wars all the time and that saved them,
In our time we have to keep it locked up inside and are full of
spite: and misery: or blindly in a flash:
Oh," he said stilly; "rage
Like a beast and kill the one you love best. Because our blood
grows fierce in the dark and there's no course for it.
I dream of killing all the mouths on the coast, I dream and dream."
She said, "Will you go to-morrow?"
"No. When the grass grows up. I'm bound to save what I can for
the old people, but knives and axes
Are a temptation. Two inches of grass." She stood gazing; he
saw the blue of her defenseless eyes
Glance at his knife-hand. "Don't be a fool," he said, "I can be
quiet forever. Have you seen the old man
When he looks at me? I think he knows." "That is impossible,"
Fayne answered. "Why?" "For his mind is like
A hanging rock; he'd go mad when you crossed his eyes. But if
he learned it after you'd gone away
He could absorb it, like the other dreadful dreams that he eats."
He answered, "Davis has known for weeks.
I can tell that." "We have friends," she said; "faithful ones."
"Did you say that poor child
Was . . . what did you say?" Fayne hardened and answered,
"Your mother saw her."
"I mean . . . no matter," he said.
In the night she lay
Unable to sleep; she heard the coyotes howl
And shriek on the white hill, and the dogs reply.

Omens and wraiths waked in her night-weakened nerves,
Reminders of the vague time when wolves were terrible
To one's ancestors; and through all the staring-gaps of the night
She kept thinking or dreaming of Mary Abbey,
Who had come to the house and then lacked courage to stay,
    and must no doubt
Be suffering something.
But Lance to-night slept quietly; he'd enjoyed the good fortune
Of useful and active labor outdoors, in the cold
Beautiful weather. He was so concentrated
On the one spot of anguish
That nothing else in the world was real to him. The Abbey girl
Was never real to him; not even while . . . Fayne heard her
    own teeth
Chipping each other in the angry darkness . . .
Nor whether she'd been in trouble.
                  The little wolves on the hill
Lifted their tumult into a tower of wailing; Fayne saw clearly
    in her mind the little muzzles
Lifted straight up, against the starlit gray shoal of snow, and the
    yellow-gray clamor shot up the night
Like a church-spire; it faded and floated away, the crackling
    stars remained. "They smell," Fayne thought,
"The dead calves, and no doubt have found them. They've
    feasted,
And now they sing. . . . Nothing is real to Lance but his wound;
But when we get away from this luckless place,
Which yet I love,
Then gradually the glory of the outer world
Will become real; when he begins to perceive the rushing and
    shining storm and fragrance of things,
Then he'll be well."
               A drift of thin rain fell in the morning;
The white vanished from the hill. The third day,
Fayne, going to spy for fear Mary might come
Where Lance was working, found old Davis in the driveway
Talking to a tall thin man on a red horse;
A Spanish man whom Fayne had not seen before,

But felt that she'd seen the horse. She eyed them and said,
"What does he want?" Davis, turning his back on the stranger,
Covertly touched his forehead and drooped an eyelid.
"He works at Abbey's. This is the famous Onorio Vasquez,
The cowboy that sees the visions. He wants to tell you: you can
send him off if you want to. Have you heard
About Abbey's girl?" "What?" Fayne asked, her eyes narrowed,
lips thinned. "He says she put herself out.
The young they ain't got consideration for nobody." "What do
you mean?" "Jumped off a pier I believe.
A telegram came in their mail yesterday. Her dad's gone up to
San Francisco to view the body.
—So his hired man can roam." Fayne's mouth jerked, her eyes
widened. "I cannot understand what you mean,
Davie," she said; but gazed at the Spanish-Indian, the hollow
brown eyes
With a bluish glaze across them, in the shadow of his hat, in his
bony face. "Jumped off a pier,"
Davis answered with patient enjoyment; "it seems she kept her
address in her hand-bag on account of traveling,
So they telegraphed." "Did you say that she died?" He nodded,
"Mmhm: wa'n't made for a fish, didn't have gills.
The young ain't got consideration for things like that." "Mary!"
Fayne said, her hand at her throat.
She drew deep breath, and sharply lifting her face toward the
silent horseman: "What are you waiting for,
Your news is told?" He, in better English than one expected,
In the soft voice of his race: "You are very sorry:
Excuse me, please. I only saw her a little and she went away
After I came to work; she was beautiful with patient eyes but
I think it is often good to die young.
I often wish." "She came to this house," Fayne said, "two days
ago: how could she . . . in the city? She was here
The day before yesterday." "No, that was the day," he answered,
"she died." Fayne stared at him
Without speaking; he was half dazzled by the wide blue of her
eyes below the fire-cloud of hair,
He looked at the brown earth. "What time did she . . .

What time?" Fayne asked. "Don't know." She said slowly,
"I think it is . . . strange." She hardened. "Nothing. Have you
come
To tell us any other thing?" "Yes," he said proudly,
"I ride on the hill and see a vision over this house. You have
heard of Onorio
Vasquez? That is my name." Old Davis made a derisive noise
in his throat; Fayne, thinking "Visions?
Apparently we too . . ." said quietly, "I never heard of you."
He, saddened: "It does not matter." But Davis, the grizzled
Thatch of his lip moving to make a smile:
"Now that's too bad: for the man's famous. He's got six brothers
And every one of them knows him, every Vasquez on the coast.
If they can't steal meat nor borrow a string of peppers they listen
to brother Onorio
Telling his dreams all through a winter night;
They don't need nothing." She answered, "If you have nothing
to do here,
Go and help Lance." And to Vasquez: "Tell me what it is
You have to say." "You know a place in the south call' Laurel
Spring? No?" he said. "Near Point Vicente.
I never been: my brother Vidal has been. He told me a rock and
an old laurel tree
Is cut by the wind into the shape of the rock, and the spring runs
down. He made a beautiful place
The way he told; we are much Indian, we love such places."
Fayne answered, "I am busy just now." He: "Excuse me, please.
I ride on the hill and every day
Watch the old war in the sky over this house;
I hurt my heart with my eyes. Sometimes a naked man
Fighting an eagle, but a rattlesnake bitten him;
Sometimes a lion fighting a tide of dogs;
But sometimes terrible armies out of the east and west, and the
hacking swords." Fayne gazed at him
And said, "Is that all?
I have just heard that my best friend has died:
I cannot think of these things." He said "The two armies
Destroyed each other, except one man alone

Walking among the bodies of horses and men
That blocked the sky; then I heard someone say,
'Let him lie down with the others.' Someone say, 'No.
At Laurel Spring he will wash off the blood,
And be cured of his wound.' I cannot live
Until I tell you." "Is it on the way
Into the south?" Fayne said. "Yes: on the trail.
My brother Vidal . . ." "I believe many lies
Are told about us," she said. "Have you heard talk
About this house?" He picked at the hair rope of the halter
On the horn of the saddle. She said, "I can guess
What you have heard. . . . May I call you Onorio?
Because it was kind of you to come down; and thank you
For telling me about your vision." She went nearer to him,
To reach his eyes under the eaves of his hat.
"Do you know Leo Ramirez?" "Him? Yes." "Have you talked
to him?
He could tell you about it. He and I alone
Saw my husband's brother climb on the cliff and fall.
Ask him and he will tell you the truth. The others lie:
To amuse idleness, I guess. If they had your great power
And saw the spirits of the air, they'd never do so.
But would you think the spirits of the dead?" Her face
Flashed at him, soft and hard at once, like a wet stone.
"Nothing," she said. "This present world is enough
For all our little strength. Good-bye, Onorio. If you hear any-
thing
Come down and tell me . . . at Abbeys' or anywhere . . .
For nobody comes down to see us any more,
On account of those wicked . . . lies . . ." While she spoke
A sob broke through and she hid her face. He from above
Looked down at her bent head and the wild color
And foam of her hair; he reached and touched her hair
As if it were a holy thing. Fayne, in a moment
Quelling her tears: "I'll remember
About the way south, that fountain. I am very unhappy
For my lost friend." She turned hastily away
And left him, and found Lance.

She sobbed, "Mary Abbey
Will never come back. I . . .. I liked her well enough
If she had not . . . Oh Lance." He was flaying the leather from
   a white and red calf, kneeling to work.
He rested his red-stained hands on the carcass and looked up with
   vague eyes. Fayne remembered, "At Laurel Spring
He'll wash the blood . . ." "Hm?" he said, "what?" "Mary . . .
   What am I doing," Fayne thought, "I oughtn't to tell him
While his mind is like this"; and clearing her face if she could,
   making a smile, said carefully, "What
Do you want the skin for?" "I've nothing to do," he said, "for
   the time. Rawhide has uses. I ground my knife
After all the willows were cut. Occupation." "A sort of bloody
   one," Fayne said carefully. "Well," he said,
And tugged at the skin with his left hand, making small cuts with
   the knife against the cling of the flesh.
She stood and watched, and furtively wiped her eyes. He looked
   up again: "No fat to scrape off." He dipped
The knife in the shrunken flesh between ribs. "Amazing," he
   said, "how the beasts resemble us, bone for bone,
And guts and heart. What did you say about Mary Abbey?"
   "No," she answered, "nothing. I was too unkind.
I think how lonely she was." "Oh. You mean Mary Abbey. I
   wish to God . . ."
He stopped speaking and tugged the skin, making small cuts
At the tearing-place. Fayne said, "Did you ever hear
Of Laurel Spring, down the coast?" She saw his wide shoulders
Suddenly stiffen, a shadow shot over in the air
And Lance's white-blue eyes rolled after the bird,
A big black one, with bent-up wing-tips, a flesh-color head
That hung and peered. He sighed and pulled at the skin, slicing
   the fiber.
Fayne said, "A vulture. They're living high now." "Mm," he
   said, *they know:* they're always stooping over my head.
I thought it was something else." "You've shot them out of the
   sky," she answered, "there are no hawks." "Aren't there!"
He said, and hushed.

　　　　　　　　After a time Fayne left him, and looked
back
When she came to the ridge of the hill. She saw the brown breast
　　of earth without any grass, and the lean brown buckeye
Thicket that had no leaves but an agony of stems, and Lance
Furiously stabbing the flayed death with his knife, again and
　　again, and heard his fist hammer
On the basket-work of the ribs in the plunges of the hiltless
　　blade. She returned; when he saw her he was suddenly still.
She said, "Whom were you thinking of?" He gazed in silence
　　as if he thought that he ought to remember her
But could not. "Who was being stabbed . . . in your mind,
　　Lance?" "Nobody. We are all dogs. Let me amuse myself."
"Me?" she said steadily. "No." She sighed and said, "I was going
　　to tell you . . . I will. Mary Abbey's dead."
She watched his blood-flecked face and his eyes, but they stood
　　still. "Oh," he said coldly. "What did she die of?"
"Unhappiness. She drowned herself." "Too bad." He said no
　　more, and Fayne stared and said: "When your mother
　　saw her
That day, she was not real but a pleading spirit; she was dying
　　in the north. We never pitied her."
"Is she frightened?" he said. "Who? Your mother? I have not
　　told her." "Don't then."

XIII

　　　　　　　　He stood up slowly,
And wiped the knife on the hair side of the skin;
He looked up the darkening wind and said, "It is going to rain."
Fayne said, "Then will you go?" seeing his fixed face
Against the lit cloud, so that the sanguine flecks
And smear under the cheek-bone were not apparent,
Only the ridge of the face, the unrounded chin
Higher than her eyes. He turned in silence and passed
Heavily over the grassless earth, but soon
Fayne had to run to keep up. Near the house
They came to Davis pouring water into the hand-pump
Of the old well to prime it; who said, "The water's

Quit in the pipes; the crick's not dry up yonder,
I guess a rat in the intake . . ." Lance answered hoarsely,
"Fish it out then. Where's the old man?" Fayne said,
"What do you want, Lance?" "The old man." Old Davis gaped
At his changed face; Fayne saw the water clamber
Up the sides of the can in the shaking hand
In little tongues that broke and ran over, "Hey, hey,"
Davie stammered, "y' got to consider," but Lance touched him
With only the finger-tips, then the man raised
One arm and pointed northwestward, slant up the hill.
Lance turned and ran; Fayne followed him, but could not now
Keep up, old Davis hobbled panting behind them;
At lengthening intervals the little ridiculous chase
Crossed over the creek-bed under sycamore trees,
Past buckeye clumps, and slant up the bare hill
Below the broad moving sky.

                    Tall spikes of a tough weed
With leather leaves grew at a place on the hill;
A few staring-flanked cows tongued the gray leaves
But would not crop them, and broke the stalks. Old Fraser stood
Against a fence-post and watched; he saw the herd
A red and white stippling far down the slope, and the serpent-
    winding creek-bed, the salt pool of its end
Behind the sand-bar, and the sandstone fang in the mouth of the
    valley, from which the shore hills over sky and water
Went up each way like the wings of a sombre archangel. Lance
    came from behind
And said, "I have run my course. I cannot go on forever." The
    old man, broken out of his revery,
Looked blindly at the wide chest, red hands and stained face, as
    if a pillar of mist had come up and stood
Threatening above him. "You," he said harshly, "what do you
    want?" "Judgment. I cannot go on alone,"
And in a boy's voice, "Oh, judgment. I have done . . .
I need, I need." The old man's brown apelike eyes got him clear
    at length, and became after their manner
A force of thrusting, like a scorched bar of fire-hardened wood.
    "Go home," he said, "drunkard.

If there is no work in the field for your . . . hands . . . what
blood is that?" "My brother's," Lance said. Fayne came too
late,
And sobbed for breath, in her throat a whining, and said, "He
was skinning a calf down there, he was . . ." Lance passed
Between them and leaned on the fence-wire with his hands to-
gether and dragged the palms of his hands to the right and
left
So that the barbs of the wire clicked on the bones of his hands
through the torn flesh. "And mine," he said.
Fayne heard the tough noise of tearing, and felt in her own
entrails through the groin upward an answering anguish.
Lance turned, hissing with pain, and babbled: "For no reason on
earth.
I was angry without a cause and struck him with iron and killed
him. The beast in me
That wants destruction. I mean Michael you know, Michael I
mean." Old Fraser staggered, saying quietly,
"Has he had drink?" Fayne said, "He . . ." she looked up at
Lance's beautiful head and stained gray face,
But the lower zone of her vision could not avoid his hands, and
thick blood falling from the shut knuckles:
Where was that readiness of mind, her thoughts were wailing
away on the wind like kildeer, which flitter singly,
Crying all through the white lofts of the moonlight sky, and
you never see them. "Am I going to tip over
For blood, like Mary?" She stammered: "He . . .
Ah God. I'll tell you . . ." Lance said, "This is mine. I have
come. Keep that woman away from me until I speak.
She fooled me into concealment, time and again, Oh cunningly.
I have fallen through flight after flight of evil
And harmed many." Fayne gathered her mind and said,
"This is it. This is the thing. He made love
With a girl and she has just died: now he hates me and he hopes
To take all the sins of the world onto his shoulders, to punish
himself. It is all like a mad saint.
You trained him to it. But I saw Michael . . ." Lance said, "I
remember an iron bolt for my shipwreck

Stood in my hand": he opened the ripped palm and the red
  streamed: "I struck." "Climb," Fayne said,
"Up the awful white moon on the cliff and fall, I saw him. It is
  Mary Abbey
Has killed herself." Lance said, "How your power's faded. You'll
  never
Fool me or the world again. I would not die
Until I had told."

            Davis came up, and saw
Lance head and shoulders against the sky like a dead tree
On which no bird will nest; the others at his base
On the brown hill, Fayne saying "Oh weak as water,
How will this help you bear it?" Davis, choked
With haste on the hill: "Ah. Ah. What's he been doing?" Lance
  held
His two hands toward his father, suppliant, but clenched
To save the blood. "What shall I do?" The old man
Stepped backward without an answer. Fayne said, "Because
The Abbey girl drowned herself, Lance thinks his finger
Helped push her down; but she was sick in her dreams
And might 'a' done it for anyone: the rest's invention
To punish himself. I am the one to hate him
Meddling with that sick child, but I love him
And will not lose." Davis, eyeing certain flakes
And scraps on the red thorns of the wire, sighed "Ah
That was a ghastly thing," and stood swaying,
Yellow and withered. Old Fraser's burnt wandering eyes
Fixed on him, the old man said: "Which is the liar?
Did Lance do it?" Lance opened his palms toward him
As if they would take and hold, saying "Tell the truth.
I will not bear to live in the dark any more."
Davis groaned, "Ay. It's true I guess." Fayne: "Ah, Ah, coward.
Because he held his hands at you." She said to old Fraser:
"People hate you and your enemies made this story
Because you still had a son after Michael died.
This is what they have whispered so long, and Lance has heard it
And uses it to stab himself." Lance said, "It is horrible
To hear the lies from her mouth like bees from a hive

Hot in the sun. I was Michael's death;
And I cannot bear it in silence. Only I pray you all to keep it
Hidden from my mother; you can do that
With a little care, with a little care, she cannot live long.
Make a story to save her." Old Fraser, suddenly
Covering his face: "Me . . . has anyone cared a little to save
Lest I live to the bitterness?" He passed among them
With tottering steps, tasting the way with his hands,
And down the hill toward home. Lance stood and muttered,
"What did he say, did he answer me?
He's honest, I bank on that."

A short way down
The old man stumbled and nearly falling stood still a moment;
Then turned his course up the hill and seemed to make haste
With short weak steps. Lance watched him and followed soon,
But turned fiercely on old Davie: "Back to work. Off.
That rat in the intake." And to Fayne: "How death
Makes even a rat powerful, they swell like clouds.
Leave me, will you." She answered, "I will never leave you.
But you, Davie, go home." "Hm?" Lance said, "never? You take
        your time.
Tie up my hands then; I think the seepage dulls me
More than the hurt helps. Here's a handkerchief:
Your dress is old." She tore it, and while she bandaged him
They stood, the old man trotted on. Lance dully wondered:
"Why did I come to him; because he believes in God?
What the hell good is that? Hm? Oh, to put it
Out of its misery." "I know you have been in torture," Fayne
        said.
"And now you have done unwisely but yet we'll live: not here,
        but certainly, fully
And freely again. You might have spared that old man.
Our joined lives are not weak enough to have gone down
In one bad night. . . . Oh Lance," she prayed suddenly, "have
        mercy on me. While you tear and destroy yourself
It is me that you tear."

He went on, she followed. On the high
        knoll ahead

442

Stood the bleak name-posts of those three burials, one new and
two old, erect against the sinking gray sky,
And seemed to rise higher as the clouds behind went down. The
old man was struggling across a gully this side.
Fayne breathlessly said, "Lance, Lance, can you hear me? He is
going up to Michael's grave, where his wild mind, that
you've
Not spared, is to find some kind of fall, some kind of decision.
Do you remember, dear, that you took me
To Michael's grave a while back? You were so angry.
But that was the break of our bitter frost.
And maybe there, or maybe afterwards at home in bed: some-
time you put new life in my body.
Do you remember that I begged you for it? I could not bear
That that sick child and not I . . .
Through *me* you go on, the other threw you away. Remember,
whatever destroying answer
Is to gore us now,
A spark of your life is safe and warm in my body and will find
the future. There is some duty in the parcel
With being a father; I think some joys too. But not to destroy
yourself,
Not now I think." "Sing to yourself," Lance answered.
"I am sorry if she died sadly, I've worse to think of."

Fayne saw old Fraser, crooked and black against the light cloud,
Totter up the hilltop and drop himself down
By the new name-post, but he stood up again
Before Lance and Fayne came. He screamed, "Keep off,"
And picked up clods of the herbless earth and threw them,
But Lance went up without noticing. "What must I do?"
He prayed, "I cannot live as I am." Old Fraser
Suddenly kneeling covered his face and wept,
And said, "What has God done? I had two sons and loved them
too much,
And he is jealous. Oh Lance, was there no silence in the stream-
ing world
To cover your mouth with, forever against me?

I am not. Not hangman. Tell your story
Where it belongs. Give yourself up.
Must I take you?" "That's what I thought of at the very first,
But have been deluded awhile," Lance answered quietly,
And turned to go down. Fayne cried, "What good is this? Oh,
  but how often,
Father, you have spoken of the godless world: is that what Lance
  is to go to for help and punishment?
When they came to put a serum into your cows, what did you
  say? You would not trust an old cow to them,
Will you trust Lance? If he were as red as Cain . . . when
  hunters come and break down your fences here
Do we run to the law? Must we run to it
For a dearer cause? What justice or what help or what under-
  standing? I told him to give his heart
To the wild hawks to eat rather than to men." Lance gripped her
  elbow with the tips of his fingers,
And pointing at the empty air past the old man: "See, he looks
  pleased wi' me,
And happy again." She looked first at Lance, then at the vacant
  air. "How could he help but forgive you,"
She answered, "he knows it was not hatred but madness.
Why must you punish yourself, you loved each other"; and to
  the old man: "Is God's hand lamed? Tell Lance
To lean on your God; what can man do for him? I cannot re-
  member," she said trembling, "how Cain ended.
There were no prisons I am sure?" Lance said, "He looks well.
No scar at all and his eyes laughing. Ah, Ah, look:
He waved his hand at his grave and laughed. I'll tell you, though,
He's not real. Don't mistake him. It makes me glad,
But it's bright nothing. Now it's gone: see?" The old man, sud-
  denly
Erect and shaking against the gray cloud: "I will have no part in
  this matter.
It is written that sevenfold vengeance on the slayer of Cain. Go.
  Go. To be a fugitive and be a vagabond,
And tramp the earth hard that has opened her mouth for thy
  brother's blood. No wonder the sweet rain could not fall.

I say flee quickly, before the dogs . . . should I give
My son to be judged by dogs?" Fayne said, "Do you hear him,
Lance, he has answered you. We must go away south,
As I've been praying." Lance said, "It has all been useless and
blind. I am back in hell." He sighed and went down
The way Fayne led, old Fraser behind them crying:
"If you had listened in the days before: now it is night,
And who shall hear? but the sharp feet of pursuers: yet look
how Christ's blood
Flows like a fiery comet through heaven and would rain sweet-
ness
The fields refuse."

             Fayne said, "I am going to tell your mother
That you've got work as foreman on a farm in the south,
A dairy I'll say, near Paso Robles. You've got to go and earn
wages
Because we're to have a baby. But next summer
She'll see us again: we'll come visiting: do you understand?
You must not let her think that you're going for good;
She couldn't bear that perhaps; but cheerfully say good-bye,
You'll save the sorrow, that's your wish, perhaps even
The ticking of her tired heart. Can you do it, Lance?
No," she said sadly when she looked at his face.
"I'll say that you've gone ahead. You had to go suddenly
To get the job." "By God," he said, "I can do my own lying,
And smooth a face of my own, come on and watch me.
It is *my* mother." "Your hands, Lance." He moaned impatiently
"How will you say they were hurt?" He moaned, "Hobbled,
hobbled.
Never an inch. That's the first rule in hell,
Never to step one inch until it is planned.
. . . In the feed-cutter." Fayne said "I daren't. Yes, at the end.
I'll find clean cloth to bandage them. You must wash.
Get Davie to help you ready the horses.
The pack is ready, only we must put food in it."
He answered, "I am sick of life. I have beaten at the last door
And found a fool."

XIV

Beyond Abbey's place
The trail began to wind up to the streaming cloud.
Fayne looked back: Abbey's was hidden, the awful memoried cliff
Crouched indistinguishable. Lance said fiercely,
"What do you see?" "Nothing." Fayne led the packhorse
To save torture of his hands; Lance rode behind.
He stopped on the rounding of a high fold of the hillside
And turned himself in the saddle, with his finger-tips
On the withers and on the croup. Fayne stopped. "Did you see," Lance said,
"The look of the man that watched us by Abbey's fence?"
"What, Lance? I am quite sure you are wrong: there has been no one
Since we left home." "Then I was mistaken.
. . . I see nobody following. If they come after me
I'll kill them; I am not going to be interfered with now.
My trouble's my own affair. I'd cut my heart out
To make him live: that's out of the question. I have beaten like
a blind bird at every window of the world.
No rational exit. No cure. Nothing. Go on. No," he said, "wait.
You know it's our last chance to see home. There are our hills
but the valley's hidden. There's Fraser's Point,
Do you see? The small jag: like a beak, ah? And," he said slowly, "the curve
On this side, glimmering along . . . that cliff you know.
Looks like flat shore." "Dear," she said faintly, "it would be better
not to look back. We're going far. Come."
"Worn flat I suppose by my thoughts, walking around, up and
down, walking around. Don't talk about it.
I can even pick out the hill where we stood this morning, that
posted hill. I'm a little run down in health,
Perhaps these haggles in my hands will poison. Go on: I've seen enough."
Around the corner of the hill, where wet earth hushed
The stony hooves, "Did you tell me," Lance said,

"That my mother saw Mary . . . what did you tell me
When she died?" Fayne felt a tired hope of joy:
He was thinking of someone else than Michael at least.
"Your mother saw her the day she died; probably the hour
And very moment. She thought that she asked for me,
But when I came, the presence had disappeared."
"What about it?" he said, "there's no sense in it." "No.
That's the manner of . . . spirits. She had a clear sweet nature,
Candid and loving." Lance answered, "I am much troubled
About leaving my mother. The skin looked bluish again
Around her nostrils; we ought not to have left her." Fayne heard
An angry repeated crying high up in the air;
She was careful not to look up, but stealthily
Looked back at Lance; and said, "She was happy, dear,
When I told her about the baby; she was full of plans.
And we'll write often." He was glaring up at the sky,
His face menacing and pale. Fayne said, "Lance?"
And when he did not answer, herself looked up and watched a
     great soaring bird,
White-tailed, white-headed, a bald eagle, wide over the moun-
     tain and shore scribing his arc of flight,
Tormented by a red-tail hawk that sailed above. The hawk dived,
     screaming, and seemed to strike,
The eagle dipped a wing with reluctant dignity
And sailed his course. "Oh, you can't kill them all,"
Fayne said, "from here to Mexico." "I don't want to.
They win, damn them."
                         They climbed at length to the cloudy
     ridges
Where the high trail went south; they rode through the clouds
     and in windy clearings
Would see enormous declivities tilting from the hooves of the
     horses down wells of vapor to the sudden shore's
Thin white surf on a rock like a grain of sand. Two or three times
Fayne heard Lance stop; she sat in the cloud and waited until he
     came. When the ridge and the trail widened
They rode abreast; then she saw that he'd stripped
The bandage from his right hand, but one thin layer

They rode like flies upon the face of a wall;
The tired horses must stick if they could, and go in darkness
Until some flat place found. Fayne was tired too,
And shook in the cold. "Lance, Lance, ride carefully.
If you should fall I'll follow. I will not live
Without you." He laughed, "Ha!" like the bark of a dog.
"No danger here, we are going in the perfect owl's eye.
Michael has gone ahead to make ready for us.
You know: a camp." "What?" she said. "*You* know: a camp.
We'll come to it." "Oh Lance, ride carefully." A kind of shoulder
  on the wall
Showed in the dark, and a little noise
That Fayne thought was the sea. Lance called behind her,
"Hello. Are you there?" She said, "Here, Lance." "Uhk-hm.
The other fellow; not you." She thought "I can't bear it,"
And said quietly, "It's water my horse has found.
It must be a little creek; I can hear it falling."
They stopped and drank under the whispering bushes,
And found no place to lie down. There were no stars,
But three ships' lights crept on the cavernous depth
And made a constellation in the under-world;
Lance said, "Damn you, go on." Fayne understood
By the useless curse how his mind stared. The horses
Paced on with heads down, and around the fold of the hill
Stopped of themselves. Here in a shallow gully
There seemed to be room to camp, between the sharp slope
And a comb of bushes.
                          Fayne saw a glimmer move in the dark
And sobbed to restrain a cry; it was Lance's hand
From which he had slipped the bandage; the wound and its wet
  exudate
Shone phosphorescent: the right hand: the hand that had done it.
    Or can pain shine? In a moment Fayne thought more quietly:
"Is it infected, could infection shine in the dark like decaying
  wood?" He was feeling the earth for sticks
To start a fire: she dipped in the pannier and found the matches.
  In the red firelight she examined his hand:

Feverish, a little; but less than his lips and eyes: Oh, when would
    the strain end? "Let's make a big fire,
This our first night of freedom, and keep ghosts away." She took
    the short-handled axe from the pannier side
And broke dead wood with it. "We'll make a bright eye up here
    for the night, in the high blackness, for the hollow night,
For the ships to wonder what star . . . I'll tell you what star,
You streaming ships: the camp-fire of Lance and Fayne is the
    star; we are not beaten, we are going to live.
We have come out of the world and are free, more hawk than
    human, we've given our hearts to the hawks to keep
In the high air." Lance laughed, "Ha! Owls you mean. Wel-
    come." He kept his hands
From the fire-heat, and would take no food.

XV

                             The famished horses
Moved in the dark; Lance ground his teeth in sick sleep;
Wind whispered; the ocean moaned; that tinkling water
Fell down the rock. Fayne lay and was cold; she wondered
Whether it was Laurel Spring perhaps; then perfectly knowing
That all the leaves were oak, she was compelled
To creep away in the darkness and crush leaves
To smell their nature. "I was not like this
A year ago," she thought wistfully, "to lie wakeful
And stare at the words of a fool; in the high sweetness
Of mountain night." Her solitary mind
Made itself a strange thought: that Lance would be saved and
    well,
But she herself would die at the baby's birth,
After some happy months: it seemed to lead hope
Into the line of nature again; for nobody ever
Comes off scot-free.
               She slept a little; Lance woke
And felt his hands aching, and thought, "It cannot be true
That I killed. Oh yes, it is. At every waking.
And there is no way to change it." Night was grown pale
In the way to dawn, and many dark cold forms

Of bush and rock stood quietly. But moving creatures
Troubled the stillness, Lance heard the steps of pursuit
Along the trail from the north, more than one rider;
Then his long-frustrate and troublesome life
Flaming like joy for the meeting, shook its bewildered elements
To one sharp edge. He was up, and moved quietly,
Willing to let Fayne sleep, in the sunset cloud
And pillow of her hair. His puffed hot fingers buckled
In a moment without fumbling the holstered belt
That had the gun; he caught the short-handled axe
That magnetlike drew his hand; and the world was suddenly
Most cool and spacious.
                        Four lean steers
Led by a barren cow were along the path.
They had come to drink in the dawn twilight, and now
Remembered a grass-plot southward. Where Lance met them
The trail was but a hair of passage stepped in the face
Of a leaning clay cliff; the leader stopped,
Was pushed from behind, and trying in her fear to turn,
Splayed with both forefeet over the slippery edge,
Felt the axe bite her neck; so leaping out blindly
Slid down the pit. They were horsemen to Lance, his enemies,
Albeit a part of his mind was awake and faintly
Knew what they were; the master part willed them to be
Men pursuing a murderer; they were both cattle and men
At the one moment. For being men, hated; for being cattle,
The hand was more free to strike, the fiery delight
More pure of guilt. The steer came on, not angrily,
Dull and unable to turn, dipping his new-moon horns,
Lance whining with joy and reckless of his own body
With both hands on the axe-helve drove the sharp steel
Into the shoulder; it broke right through the shoulder-blade
And nicked the broad ribs below. At the same moment
The curve and base of a horn found Lance's thigh
And pushed; but he with his weight flung forward
In the fury of the axe-blow went over the head
Onto the shoulder, and a moment clung there, as when an old
    mountain-lion

Has hunted under the spite of fortune for many days, until his
    bright hide is ruffled, and the ribs
Lift up the hair; he comes by a secret way and crouches in the
    alder leaves an hour before dawn
Over a pool where the deer drink; but not a deer but a cow-elk
    comes to the pool,
And stands in the glimmer and the trembling twilight, and stoops
    her head: the puma watches, his lustful mind
Can even taste the hot flesh through the rough hide, and smell the
    soft heavy fountain of blood: he springs,
And sticks on the shoulder, blunting his teeth against the great
    bones of the neck; but the elk does not fall,
But runs, and beats her death against the low branches, and scrapes
    him off:
So Lance fell off from the steer's shoulder, and was ground
Between the flank and the cliff, as the numbed foreleg
Failed and recovered. The weight lifting, he stood
With his back to the steep wall and violently
Pushed the great hairy quarters with all his power
Of both his arms; the hind hooves fell over the edge,
And the forelegs, one crippled, scraped the stiff clay
In vain for foothold, the great hurt bulk went down
Standing, but fell in a moment and slid in the chasm.
The others had turned and fled.
                      Fayne saw her lover
Come swaying and shining against the gray sky
Over the abyss of darkness, and she had seen the steer fall.
Lance held the axe. "Ah, Ah," Fayne cried, "strike then. Strike.
    Finish it. We have not lived pleasantly,
And I have failed." He threatened her, laughing with pleasure.
    "I have not had such pleasure in the days of my life.
Did the dogs think they were hunting rabbit? Surprised them, ah,
    ah?" She said, "Your hands have opened again
And dripping fast." "More?" he said, hearing the horses that
    stamped and snorted beyond. "Oh, good. If they get me,
Remember it's a grand end." He ran and struck
The nearest; it was holding its head ready for the axe, backing and
    straining

On the taut halter, and went down on its knees; the second stroke
Chopped horribly along the neck, the third ended the pain. Lance
    crouched and looked at the head, and wearily
Rose, and said slackly, "There was no way out, here, either. My
    own horse you see.
I must 'a' been . . . I have been troubled.
Beating my face on every glass gap and porthole . . .
And get a beaten face.
Were those more horses?" Fayne had stood rigid; she said,
"Steers." "Why didn't they shoot? . . . Oh . . . Steers. *That's* it.
Yet I hate blood.
See how it springs from the ground: struck oil at last, ah?
I felt like this, that time. So we've tried a long time
And never found
My exit: I think there's none: the world's closed.
A brave fellow, a tethered horse.
A natural butcher."

                One of the fallen forelegs
Paddled its hoof on the earth and Lance said faintly, "I've come to
    the point
I cannot even put him out of his pain."
He dropped the red axe; Fayne saw his own blood spring from his
    palm
When he let go. "I think," he said, "have I got the gun on me?
Will *you* finish him off?" "He is dead," she answered.
"Listen, Lance." Her throat was twisting and beating upward
    with hot nausea; she swallowed and said,
"Dearest. This is only a stumble on the way. We are going on.
    You will be well after this.
You are dreadful with blood but you are too beautiful
And strong to fail. Look, dear,
How the clear quivering waters and white of dawn fill the whole
    world; they seem to wash the whole mountain
All gently and white, and over the sea, purifying everything. If
    I were less tired
I could be full of joy." She pressed her hands to her throat and
    swallowed and said, "Where you and I

Have come to, is a dizzy and lonely place on a height; we have to
peel off

Some humanness here or it will be hard to live. If you could think
that all human feelings, repentance

And blood-thirst too, are not very important in so vast a world;
nor anyone's life;

Nor love either, the unlucky angel

That has led me so far: we'll go on, we'll not fail. All over the
mountain

The eagles and little falcons and all the bright cold hawks—
you've made friends with them now—are widening

Their wings to wash them in the cool clearness, and over the
precipices launching their bodies like ships

On the high waves of dawn. For us too

Dawn brings us wandering; and any ghost or memory that wants
to follow us will be sore in the feet

Before the day's end. We're going until the world changes, you
and I like the young hawks

Going hunting; we'll take the world by the throat and make him
give us

What we desire."

        He stood bent over, smiling sidewise, watch-
ing the drip from his hands, and said,

"You do it quite bravely. No doubt you are right, and I must
take your guidance without a word

From this time on. What next? I'll go wash. Faugh.

What a hell of red to be stuck in; you're out o' luck,

Loving a butcher." She answered with her hands at her mouth,
struggling against her sickness, "I'll come in a moment

And help you to clean your hands and bandage them again." He
went back by the trail, but she

Vomited with grievous labor a little water and followed him.

        Now all the world was quite clear

And full of dawn, so that Fayne saw from the trail

The jutting shoulder of the hill, guessed at in darkness,

Was a great rock, lengthened by thick hard foliage

Of mountain laurel, which grew above it, and the wind had
carved

Into the very nature and form of the rock
That gave it shelter, but green for gray. She remembered
With a wild lift of the heart, "He'd wash the blood
In Laurel Spring, and be healed of his wounds,"
But Lance had not gone to the stony basin, but stood
Out on the ledge of the rock, and was looking down
The straight vast depth, toward the beauty of the ocean
Like a gray dove's breast under the dawn-light. She could not
   call to him
Before he leaped and went down. He was falling erect
With his feet under him for a long time,
But toward the bottom he began turning in the air.
One of the roots of the mountain concealed his end
On the shore rocks. Fayne lay down in the trail
And thought that when she was able she would go down to him,
One way or another. ". . . That would be happiest.
But then he'd be extinguished forever, his last young spark
That lies warm in my body, bought too dear
For gulls to eat : . . and I never could help you at all,
And now has come the wild end.
I could not keep you, but your child in my body
Will change the world."
                     She climbed slowly down,
Rock to rock, bush to bush. At length she could see him
Lying softly, and there was somebody bending above him,
Who was gone in a moment. It was not so dreadful
As she had feared; she kissed the stained mouth,
And brought smooth stones from the shore until she had covered
Her love against the vultures and salty gulls;
Then climbed up, rock to rock, bush to bush.

A LITTLE SCRAPING

True, the time, to one who does not love farce,
And if misery must be prefers it nobler, shows apparent vices;
At least it provides the cure for ambition.
One does not crave power in ant-hills, nor praise in a paper forest;
One must not even indulge the severe
Romance of separateness, as of Milton grown blind and old
In his broken temple against the drunkards:
The ants are good creatures, there is nothing to be heroic about.
But the time is not a strong prison either.
A little scraping the walls of dishonest contractor's concrete
Through a shower of chips and sand makes freedom.
Shake the dust from your hair. This mountain sea-coast is real,
For it reaches out far into past and future;
It is part of the great and timeless excellence of things. A few
Lean cows drift high up the bronze hill;
The heavy-necked plow-team furrows the foreland, gulls tread
     the furrow;
Time ebbs and flows but the rock remains.
Two riders of tired horses canter on the cloudy ridge;
Topaz-eyed hawks have the white air;
Or a woman with jade-pale eyes, hiding a knife in her hand,
Goes through cold rain over gray grass.
God is here, too, secretly smiling, the beautiful power
That piles up cities for the poem of their fall
And gathers multitude like game to be hunted when the season
     comes.

INTELLECTUALS

Is it so hard for men to stand by themselves,
They must hang on Marx or Christ, or mere Progress?
Clearly it is hard. But these ought to be leaders . . .
Sheep leading sheep, "The fold, the fold.
Night comes, and the wolves of doubt." Clearly it is hard.

Yourself, if you had not encountered and loved
Our unkindly all but inhuman God,
Who is very beautiful and too secure to want worshippers,
And includes indeed the sheep with the wolves,
You too might have been looking about for a church.

He includes the flaming stars and pitiable flesh,
And what we call things and what we call nothing.
He is very beautiful. But when these lonely have travelled
Through long thoughts to redeeming despair,
They are tired and cover their eyes; they flock into fold.

TRIAD

Science, that makes wheels turn, cities grow,
Moribund people live on, playthings increase,
But has fallen from hope to confusion at her own business
Of understanding the nature of things;—new Russia,
That stood a moment at dreadful cost half free,
Beholding the open, all the glades of the world
On both sides of the trap, and resolutely
Walked into the trap that has Europe and America;—
The poet, who wishes not to play games with words,
His affair being to awake dangerous images
And call the hawks;—they all feed the future, they serve God,
Who is very beautiful, but hardly a friend of humanity.

STILL THE MIND SMILES

Still the mind smiles at its own rebellions,
Knowing all the while that civilization and the other evils
That make humanity ridiculous, remain
Beautiful in the whole fabric, excesses that balance each other
Like the paired wings of a flying bird.
Misery and riches, civilization and squalid savagery,
Mass war and the odor of unmanly peace:
Tragic flourishes above and below the normal of life.
In order to value this fretful time
It is necessary to remember our norm, the unaltered passions,
The same-colored wings of imagination,
That the crowd clips, in lonely places new-grown; the unchanged
Lives of herdsmen and mountain farms,
Where men are few, and few tools, a few weapons, and their
    dawns are beautiful.
From here for normal one sees both ways,
And listens to the splendor of God, the exact poet, the sonorous
Antistrophe of desolation to the strophe multitude.

CRUMBS OR THE LOAF

If one should tell them what's clearly seen
They'd not understand; if they understood they would not
 believe;
If they understood and believed they'd say,
"Hater of men, annihilating with a sterile enormous
Splendor our lives: where are our lives?"
A little chilled perhaps, but not hurt. But it's quite true
The invulnerable love is not bought for nothing.
It is better no doubt to give crumbs than the loaf; make fables
 again,
Tell people not to fear death, toughen
Their bones if possible with bitter fables not to fear life.
—And one's own, not to have pity too much;
For it seems compassion sticks longer than the other colors, in
 this bleaching cloth.

SHANE O'NEILL'S CAIRN

TO U. J.

When you and I **on the** Palos Verdes cliff
Found life more desperate than dear,
And when we hawked at it on the lake by Seattle,
In the west of the world, where hardly
Anything has died yet: we'd not have been sorry, Una,
But surprised, to foresee this gray
Coast in our days, the gray waters of the Moyle
Below us, and under our feet
The heavy black stones of the cairn of the lord of Ulster.
A man of blood who died bloodily
Four centuries ago: but death's nothing, and life,
From a high death-mark on a headland
Of this dim island of burials, is nothing either.
How beautiful are both these nothings.

OSSIAN'S GRAVE

PREHISTORIC MONUMENT NEAR CUSHENDALL
IN ANTRIM

Steep up in Lubitavish townland stands
A ring of great stones like fangs, the shafts of the stones
Grown up with thousands of years of gradual turf,
The fangs of the stones still biting skyward; and hard
Against the stone ring, the oblong enclosure
Of an old grave guarded with erect slabs; gray rocks
Backed by broken thorn-trees, over the gorge of Glenaan;
It is called Ossian's Grave. Ossian rests high then,
Haughtily alone.
If there were any fame or burial or monument
For me to envy,
Warrior and poet they should be yours and yours.

For this is the pure fame, not caged in a poem,
Fabulous, a glory untroubled with works, a name in the north
Like a mountain in the mist, like Aura
Heavy with heather and the dark gray rocks, or Trostan
Dark purple in the cloud: happier than what the wings
And imperfections of work hover like vultures
Above the carcass.

                I also make a remembered name;
And I shall return home to the granite stones
On my cliff over the greatest ocean
To be blind ashes under the butts of the stones:
As you here under the fanged limestone columns
Are said to lie, over the narrow north straits
Toward Scotland, and the quick-tempered Moyle. But written
    reminders
Will blot for too long a year the bare sunlight
Above my rock lair, heavy black birds
Over the field and the blood of the lost battle.

OSSIAN'S GRAVE

Oh but we lived splendidly
In the brief light of day
Who now twist in our graves.
You in the guard of the fanged
Erect stones; and the man-slayer
Shane O'Neill dreams yonder at Cushendun
Crushed under his cairn;
And Hugh McQuillan under his cairn
By his lost field in the bog on Aura;
And I a foreigner, one who has come to the country of the dead
Before I was called,
To eat the bitter dust of my ancestors;
And thousands on tens of thousands in the thronged earth
Under the rotting freestone tablets
At the bases of broken round towers;
And the great Connaught queen on her mountain-summit
The high cloud hoods, it creeps through the eyes of the cairn.

We dead have our peculiar pleasures, of not
Doing, of not feeling, of not being.
Enough has been felt, enough done, Oh and surely
Enough of humanity has been. We lie under stones
Or drift through the endless northern twilights
And draw over our pale survivors the net of our dream.
All their lives are less
Substantial than one of our deaths, and they cut turf
Or stoop in the steep
Short furrows, or drive the red carts, like weeds waving
Under the glass of water in a locked bay,
Which neither the wind nor the wave nor their own will
Moves; when they seem to awake
It is only to madden in their dog-days for memories of dreams
That lost all meaning many centuries ago.

Oh but we lived splendidly
In the brief light of day,
You with hounds on the mountain
And princes in palaces,

I on the western cliff
In the rages of the sun:
Now you lie grandly under your stones
But I in a peasant's hut
Eat bread bitter with the dust of dead men;
The water I draw at the spring has been shed for tears
Ten thousand times,
Or wander through the endless northern twilights
From the rath to the cairn, through fields
Where every field-stone's been handled
Ten thousand times,
In a uterine country, soft
And wet and worn out, like an old womb
That I have returned to, being dead.

Oh but we lived splendidly
Who now twist in our graves.
The mountains are alive;
Tievebuilleagh lives, Trostan lives,
Lurigethan lives;
And Aura, the black-faced sheep in the belled heather;
And the swan-haunted loughs; but also a few of us dead
A life as inhuman and cold as those.

THE LOW SKY

No vulture is here, hardly a hawk,
Could long wings or great eyes fly
Under this low-lidded soft sky?

On the wide heather the curlew's whistle
Dies of its echo, it has no room
Under the low lid of this tomb.

But one to whom mind and imagination
Sometimes used to seem burdensome
Is glad to lie down awhile in the tomb.

Among stones and quietness
The mind dissolves without a sound,
The flesh drops into the ground.

THE BROADSTONE

NEAR FINVOY, COUNTY ANTRIM

We climbed by the old quarries to the wide highland of heath,
On the slope of a swale a giant dolmen,
Three heavy basalt pillars upholding the enormous slab,
Towers and abides as if time were nothing.
The hard stones are hardly dusted with lichen in nobody knows
What ages of autumns in this high solitude
Since a recordless tribe of an unknown race lifted them up
To be the availing hero's memorial,
And temple of his power. They gathered their slighter dead
    from the biting
Winds of time in his lee, the wide moor
About him is swollen with barrows and breaks upon many stones,
Lean gray guardians of old urned ashes,
In waves on waves of purple heather and blithe spray of its bells.
Here lies the hero, more than half God,
And nobody knows his name nor his race, in the bee-bright
    necropolis,
With the stone circle and his tribe around him.
Sometimes perhaps (but who'd confess it?) in soft adolescence
We used to wonder at the world, and have wished
To hear some final harmony resolve the discords of life?
—Here they are all perfectly resolved.

THE GIANT'S RING

BALLYLESSON, NEAR BELFAST

Whoever is able will pursue the plainly
False immortality of not having lived in vain but leaving some
    mark in the world.
Secretly mocking at his own insanity
He labors the same, he knows that no dead man's lip was ever
    curled in self-scorn,
And immortality is for the dead.
Jesus and Cæsar out of the bricks of man's weakness, Washington
    out of the brittle
Bones of man's strength built their memorials,
This nameless chief of a knot of forgotten tribes in the Irish dark-
    ness used faithfuller
Simpler materials: to diadem a hilltop
That sees the long loughs and the Mourne Mountains, with a ring
    of enormous embankment, and to build
In the center that great toad of a dolmen
Piled up of ponderous basalt that sheds the centuries like rain-
    drops. He drove the labor,
And has earmarked already some four millenniums.
His very presence is here, thick-bodied and brutish, a brutal and
    senseless will-power.
Immortality? While Homer and Shakespeare are names,
Not of men but verses, and the elder has not lived nor the
    younger will not, such treadings of time.
—Conclude that secular like Christian immortality's
Too cheap a bargain: the name, the work or the soul: glass beads
    are the trade for savages.

IN THE HILL AT NEW GRANGE

ONE OF THE THREE GREAT PREHISTORIC BURIAL MOUNDS ON THE RIVER BOYNE

Who is it beside me, who is here beside me, in the hollow hill?"
A foreigner I am. "You've dug for nothing. The Danes were here
A thousand years before you and robbed me of my golden bracelets,
Stinking red-haired men from the sea, with torches and swords."
Dead king, you keep a better treasure than bracelets,
The peace of the dead is dearer than gold, no one can rob you.

What do you watch, old king, from the cave? "In the north the
   muddy chippers of flint on the Antrim coast,
Their chests covered with hair and filth, shrewd eyes under
   bushes of brow, clicking the flints together.
How we used to hate those hunters. One squats in a cave-mouth
   and makes an axe, one in a dune shapes bolt-heads."
They have all (and we too, old king) been dead for thousands of
   years. I see in the north a red-haired woman
Meeting her lover by Shane O'Neill's cairn, her peasant husband
   is drunk at home, she drifts up the hill
In the sleeve of twilight. "Mary Byrnes is that you?" "Ye may
   kiss a hure but not name her. Ah, lad, come down.
When I was a wee maid I used to be loving Jesus,
All helpless and bleeding on the big cross. I'd never have married
   my drunkard only the cart ran over him.
He lay helpless and bleeding in the black lane. Och, laddie, not
   here now.
Carry me up to the cairn: a man lies bloodily under the sharp
   black stones, I love that man."
Mary Byrnes, when her lover has done and finished, before he
   stands up
To button his clothes together, runs a knife in his throat. "Oh
   Shane O'Neill it's you I was loving,

Never one else. You helpless and bleeding under the stones.
Do ye weary of stretching quiet the four long centuries? Take
    this lad's blood to hearten you, it drops through the stones.
Drips, drops in the stones.
Drink, Shane; drink, dear: who cares if a hure is hanged? We kill
    each other in Ireland to pleasure the dead."

Great upright stones higher than the height of a man are our walls,
Huge overlapping stones are the summer clouds in our sky.
The hill of boulders is heaped over all. Each hundred years
One of the enormous stones will move an inch in the dark.
Each double century one of the oaks on the crown of the mound
Above us breaks in a wind, an oak or an ash grows.

"I see in the south Cloyne round tower burning: the Christians
    have built a spire, the thieves from the sea have burnt it,
The happy flame streams roaring up the stone tube and breaks
    from the four windows below the stone roof
Like four bright banners.
The holy men scream in their praying, the golden reliquaries are
    melted, the bell falls clanging."
They have all (and we too, old king) been dead for a thousand
    years. I see on the island mountain Achill,
In the west where wave after wave of the beaten tribes ran up
    and starved, an old woman, her head
Covered with a shawl, sits on Slieve Mor. Two thin sharp tears
    like knives in the yellow grooves of her face,
"My cow has died," she says, "and my son forgets me." She
    crouches and starves, in the quivering Atlantic wind,
Among the great skulls of quartz on the Achill mountain.

What do you watch, old king, from the cave? "A cause of mighty
    laughter in the mound on the hill at Dundalk.
They piled the earth on the blood of one of their spitfire princes,
    their bold watchdog of the Ulster border.
After two handfuls of centuries
One Bruce, a younger drinker of battles, bloodily ceasing to be
    king of Ireland was buried above him.

Now a rich merchant has built his house on the mound's head,
    a living man. The old capon perches there trembling,
The young men of Ireland are passionate again, it is bad for
    a man of peace to have built on the hill of battles,
Oh his dear skin, Oh the papers of his wealth.
Cuchulain looks up at Bruce and Bruce at the sweating merchant.
    By God if we dead that watch the living
Could open our mouths, the earth would be split with laughter."

I hear like a hum in the ground the Boyne running through the
    aging
Fields forever, and one of our great blue spiral-cut stones
Settle in the dark a hair's breadth under the burden of the hill.
"We hear from cairn to cromlech all over Ireland the dead
Whisper and conspire, and whinnies of laughter tinkle in the
    raths.
The living dream but the dead are awake."

High in Donegal, in the bitter waste north, where miles on miles
    of black heather dwindle to the Bloody Foreland,
Walks an old priest, near crazy with solitude and his peasants
    like cattle, he has wrestled with his mental Satan
Half his lifetime, and endured and triumphed. He feels the reward
    suddenly await him, the churchyard wall
Looks light and faint, the slabs and mounds by the entrance. In
    the midst of mass the crucified image trembles
Above the altar, and favorably smiles. Then Father O'Donnel
Gabbles the Latin faster to an end and turns himself once more
    and says to the people, "Go home now.
Missa est." In the empty church he screams and spits on the Christ,
He strikes it with his hand. Well done, old priest. "Is the man on
    the cross his God, why does he strike his God?"
Because the tortured torturer is too long dying; because the strain
    in the wounded minds of men
Leaves them no peace; but here where life is worn out men should
    have peace. He desires nothing but unconsciousness,
To slip in the black bottomless lake and be still. Time for us also,

Old king, although no strain so many thousands of years has
    wounded our minds, time to have done
With vision, as in the world's youth with desire and deed. To lie
    in the dark in the hill until the stones crumble,
And the earth and the stars suck into nothing, the wheel slopes
    and returns, the beautiful burden is renewed.
For probably all the same things will be born and be beautiful
    again, but blessed is the night that has no glowworm.

ANTRIM

No spot of earth where men have so fiercely for ages of time
Fought and survived and cancelled each other,
Pict and Gael and Dane, McQuillan, Clandonnel, O'Neill,
Savages, the Scot, the Norman, the English,
Here in the narrow passage and the pitiless north, perpetual
Betrayals, relentless resultless fighting.
A random fury of dirks in the dark: a struggle for survival
Of hungry blind cells of life in the womb.
But now the womb has grown old, her strength has gone forth;
    a few red carts in a fog creak flax to the dubs,
And sheep in the high heather cry hungrily that life is hard; a
    plaintive peace; shepherds and peasants.

We have felt the blades meet in the flesh in a hundred ambushes
And the groaning blood bubble in the throat;
In a hundred battles the heavy axes bite the deep bone,
The mountain suddenly stagger and be darkened.
Generation on generation we have seen the blood of boys
And heard the moaning of women massacred,
The passionate flesh and nerves have flamed like pitch-pine and
    fallen
And lain in the earth softly dissolving.
I have lain and been humbled in all these graves, and mixed new
    flesh with the old and filled the hollow of my mouth
With maggots and rotten dust and ages of repose. I lie here and
    plot the agony of resurrection.

NO RESURRECTION

Friendship, when a friend meant a helping sword,
Faithfulness, when power and life were its fruits, hatred, when
the hated
Held steel at your throat or had killed your children, were more
than metaphors.
Life and the world were as bright as knives.

But now, if I should recall my ruins
From the grass-roots and build my body again in the heavy grave,
Twist myself naked up through the earth like a strong white
worm,
Tip the great stone, gulp the white air,

And live once more after long ages
In the change of the world: I should find the old human affections
hollowed.
Should I need a friend? No one will really stab me from behind,
The people in the land of the living walk weaponless.

Should I hate an enemy? The evil-doers
Are pitiable now. Or to whom be faithful? Of whom seek faith?
Who has eaten of the victor's feast and shared the fugitive silence
Of beaten men on the mountain: suffer

Resurrection to join this midge-dance
Of gutted and multiplied echoes of life in the latter sun?
Dead man, be quiet. A fool of a merchant, who'd sell good earth
And grass again to make modern flesh.

DELUSION OF SAINTS

The old pagan burials, uninscribed rock,
Secret-keeping mounds,
Have shed the feeble delusions that built them,
They stand inhumanly
Clean and massive; they have lost their priests.
But the cross-bearing stones
Still foot corruption, and their faces carved
With hopes and terrors
At length too savagely annulled to be left
Even ridiculous.
Long-suffering saints, flamelike aspirers,
You have won your reward:
You sleep now as easily as any dead murderer
Or worn-out lecher.
To have found your faith a liar is no thorn
In the narrow beds,
Nor laughter of unfriends nor rumor of the ruinous
Churches will reach you.
As at Clonmacnoise I saw them all ruined,
And at Cong, at Glendalough,
At Monasterboice; and at Kilmacduagh
All ruined, all roofless
But the great cyclopean-stoned spire
That leans toward its fall.
A place perfectly abandoned of life,
Except that we heard
One old horse neighing across the stone hedges
In the flooded fields.

IONA: THE GRAVES OF THE KINGS

I wish not to lie here.
There's hardly a plot of earth not blessed for burial, but here
One might dream badly.

In beautiful seas a beautiful
And sainted island, but the dark earth so shallow on the rock
Gorged with bad meat.

Kings buried in the lee of the saint,
Kings of fierce Norway, blood-boltered Scotland, bitterly
     dreaming
Treacherous Ireland.

Imagine what delusions of grandeur,
What suspicion-agonized eyes, what jellies of arrogance and
     terror
This earth has absorbed.

SHOOTING SEASON

The whole countryside deployed on the hills of heather, an army
    with banners,
The beaters whoop the grouse to the butts.
Three gentlemen fling up their guns and the frightened covey is
    a few wings fewer;
Then grooms approach with the panniered horses.
The gray old moorland silence has closed like water and covered
    the gunshots.
Wave on wave goes the moor to the great
Circle of the sky; the cairn on the slope names an old battle and
    beyond are
Broad gray rocks the grave-marks of clans.
Blond Celtic warriors lair in the sky-line barrows, down toward
    the sea
Stand the tall stones of the Danish captains.
We dead that handled weapons and hunted in earnest, we old
    dead have watched
Three little living gentlemen yonder
With a bitter flavor in the grin of amusement, uneasily remem-
    bering our own
Old sports and delights. It is better to be dust.

GHOSTS IN ENGLAND

At East Lulworth the dead were friendly and pitiful, I saw them
    peek from their ancient earthworks on the coast hills
At the camps of the living men in the valley, the army-mechanics'
    barracks, the roads where they try the tanks
And the armored cars: "We also," they say, "trembled in our
    time. We felt the world change in the rain,
Our people like yours were falling under the wheel. Great
    past and declining present are a pitiful burden
For living men; but failure is not the worm that worries
    the dead, you will not weep when you come,"
Said the soft mournful shadows on the Dorset shore. And those
    on the Rollright ridge by the time-eaten stone-circle
Said nothing and had no wish in the world, having blessedly aged
    out of humanity, stared with great eyes
White as the hollowed limestone, not caring but seeing, inhuman
    as the wind.

           But the other ghosts were not good,
But like a moon of jackals around a sick stag.
At Zennor in the tumbled granite chaos, at Marazion and the
    angel's Mount, from the hoar tide-lines:
"Be patient, dead men, the tides of their day have turned," from
    the stone rings of the dead huts on Dartmoor,
The prison town like a stain of dirt on the distant hill: "We not
    the last," they said, "shall be hopeless,
We not alone hunger in the rain." From Avebury in the high
    heart of England, in the ancient temple,
When all the cottages darkened themselves to sleep: "Send it
    along the ridge-ways and say it on the hilltops
That the bone is broken and the meat will fall."

                There was also a
    ghost of a king, his cheeks hollow as the brows
Of an old horse, was paddling his hands in the reeds of Dozmare
    Pool, in the shallow, in the rainy twilight,

Feeling for the hilt of a ruinous and rusted sword. But they said
"Be patient a little, you king of shadows,
But only wait, they will waste like snow." Then Arthur left
hunting for the lost sword, he grinned and stood up
Gaunt as a wolf; but soon resumed the old labor, shaking the
reeds with his hands.

Northeastward to Wantage
On the chalk downs the Saxon Alfred
Witlessly walks with his hands lamenting. "Who are the people
and who are the enemy?" He says bewildered,
"Who are the living, who are the dead?" The more ancient dead
Watch him from the wide earthworks on White Horse Hill,
peer from the Ridgeway barrows, goggle from the broken
Mound and the scattered stones in the oval wood above Ashbury.
They whisper and exult.

In the north also
I saw them, from the Picts' houses in the black Caithness heather
to the bleak stones on Culloden Moor,
The rags of lost races and beaten clans, nudging each other, the
blue lips cracking with joy, the fleshless
Anticipatory fingers jabbing at the south. And on the Welsh
borders
Were dead men skipping and fleering behind all the hedges. An
island of ghosts. They seemed merry, and to feel
No pity for the great pillar of empire settling to a fall, the pride
and the power slowly dissolving.

INSCRIPTION FOR A
GRAVESTONE ·

I am not dead, I have only become inhuman:
That is to say,
Undressed myself of laughable prides and infirmities,
But not as a man
Undresses to creep into bed, but like an athlete
Stripping for the race.
The delicate ravel of nerves that made me a measurer
Of certain fictions
Called good and evil; that made me contract with pain
And expand with pleasure;
Fussily adjusted like a little electroscope:
That's gone, it is true;
(I never miss it; if the universe does,
How easily replaced!)
But all the rest is heightened, widened, set free.
I admired the beauty
While I was human, now I am part of the beauty.
I wander in the air,
Being mostly gas and water, and flow in the ocean;
Touch you and Asia
At the same moment; have a hand in the sunrises
And the glow of this grass.
I left the light precipitate of ashes to earth
For a love-token.

Doggerel," he thought, "will do for church-wardens,
Poetry's precious enough not to be wasted,"
And rhymed it all out with a skew smile:
"Spare these stones. Curst be he that moves my bones—
Will hold the hands of masons and grave-diggers."
But why did the good man care? For he wanted quietness.
He had tasted enough life in his time
To stuff a thousand; he wanted not to swim wide
In waters, nor wander the enormous air,
Nor grow into grass, enter through the mouths of cattle
The bodies of lusty women and warriors,
But all be finished. He knew it feelingly; the game
Of the whirling circles had become tiresome.
"Annihilation's impossible, but insulated
In the church under the rhyming flagstone
Perhaps my passionate ruins may be kept off market
To the end of this age. Oh, a thousand years
Will hardly leach," he thought, "this dust of that fire."

THE DEAD TO CLEMENCEAU:
NOVEMBER, 1929

Come (we say) Clemenceau.
Why should you live longer than others? The vacuum that sucked
Us down, and the former stars, draws at you also.

No wrench for a man near ninety.
They were younger who crowded us out of distinction the year
    you drove them
Like flies on a fire. We don't say it was wrong.

We don't say it was right.
These heavy choices are less than verbal, down here, to us dead.
Never a thorn in the crown of greatness down here.

Not even Wilson laments here
The cuckoo brood of design. This is the cave you conjectured;
Nothing in death, as nothing in life, surprises you.

You were not surprised when France
Put you aside, when the war was finished, as a sick man mending
Puts aside the strong poison that turned his fever.

You'd not be surprised to hear
Your enemies praising your name and the Paris cannon applaud
    you;
Not surprised, nor much pleased, nor envious of more.

Your negative straightness of mind—
And bleached like a drowned man's cast-up thigh-bone by erod-
    ing age—
Hardly required the clear corrections of death.

SUBJECTED EARTH

Walking in the flat Oxfordshire fields
Where the eye can find no rock to rest on but little flints
Speckle the soil, and the million-berried hedges
Tingle with birds at evening, I saw the sombre
November day redden and go down; a flight of lapwings
Whirled in the hollow of the field, and half-tame pheasants
Cried from the trees. I remembered impatiently
How the long bronze mountain of my own coast,
Where color is no account and pathos ridiculous, the sculpture
    is all,
Breaks the arrows of the setting sun
Over the enormous mounded eyeball of ocean.

                        The soft alien twilight
Worn and weak with too much humanity hooded my mind.
Poor flourishing earth, meek-smiling slave,
If sometime the swamps return and the heavy forest, black beech
    and oak-roots
Break up the paving of London streets;
And only, as long before, on the lifted ridgeways
Few people shivering by little fires
Watch the night of the forest cover the land
And shiver to hear the wild dogs howling where the cities were,
Would you be glad to be free? I think you will never
Be glad again, so kneaded with human flesh, so humbled and
    changed.

Here all's down hill and passively goes to the grave,
Asks only a pinch of pleasure between the darknesses,
Contented to think that everything has been done
That's in the scope of the race: so should I also perhaps
Dream, under the empty angel of this twilight,
But the great memory of that unhumanized world,
With all its wave of good and evil to climb yet,
Its exorbitant power to match, its heartless passion to equal,
And all its music to make, beats on the grave-mound.

483

It seems hardly necessary to stipulate that the elegiac tone of these verses reflects the writer's mood, and is not meant for economic or political opinion.

Shane O'Neill's cairn and the dateless monument called Ossian's Grave stand within a couple of miles of each other on the Antrim coast.

A dolmen is a prehistoric burial-house made of great stones set on end, roofed by a slab of stone. There are many still standing in Ireland and England.

Newgrange is one of three great artificial hills, on the Boyne west of Drogheda. Passages and cells were made of megalithic stonework, decorated with designs cut in the great stones, and the hills were heaped over them. No one assigns a reasonable date to these erections. Evidently they are burial mounds, like the pyramids.

The Irish round towers are well known, of course, slender, tapering spires of stone and lime mortar, of mysterious origin, but probably belfries and towers of refuge, built between 600 and 1200 A.D. They are associated with the earliest Christian churches.

Antrim is the northeasternmost county of Ireland, only a few sea-miles from Scotland. Iona is the sacred island of the Hebrides.

Avebury is a little Wiltshire village inside a great prehistoric stone-circle and fosse. It was the religious and perhaps the political capital of southern England before Stonehenge was built, i.e., before 2000 B.C., probably. The circle and the remaining stones are greater than those at Stonehenge, but the stones were not hewn to shape. Most of them are gone now; broken up to build the village.

Dozmare Pool is in Cornwall, a little flat mere in a wide wilderness, said to be the water where the sword Excalibur was cast away when King Arthur died.

The ridgeways are ancient grass-grown roads on the ridges of the hills, used by the pre-Celtic inhabitants of England, when the lowlands were impassable swamp and forest.

(The story of Achilles rising from the dead for love of Helen
is well enough known. That of Polyxo's vengeance may be less
familiar; it can be found in Pausanias' "Description of Greece,"
explaining the Rhodian worship of Helen as Dendritis, the tree-
goddess.)

The scene is the fore-court of a noble dwelling on the island of
Rhodes. Portico of the house, with steps of heavy stone and
painted wooden columns, but all worn and old. Black pine-forest
on the hill behind. One great pine stands to the left of the steps,
near the house-wall; it is old, with contorted boughs, one of
which overhangs the steps. The time is nearly twenty years after
the fall of Troy.

> *Enter a shepherd and his little son, the shepherd leading a re-
> luctant lamb by a noosed thong. They come from the right
> foreground, and go toward the left.*

THE SHEPHERD The gods get hungry like you and me, so it has
to die.

THE BOY But you called her mine; you promised that I might
rear her. Oh father.

THE SHEPHERD I can't help that. You have a shepherd's eye and
you chose the perfect one. *We* eat the runts and the lame,
the gods want perfection; the run of the season, that is
neither poor nor perfect, is for wool and breeding. Choose
again.

THE BOY Only to lose again.

A man comes in running, from the left.

THE SHEPHERD Hey. Fisherman?

THE FISHERMAN (breathless) You had better fetch in your flock,
and tell cowboy. Pirates I think.

THE SHEPHERD What, what, what?

THE FISHERMAN   Ohey, the house! Who is at the door? A ship
has landed.

THE PORTER   Who's there? A ship?

THE FISHERMAN   Armed men coming ashore from a black ship.
I left Calcho watching.

*The porter turns in the doorway. Shouting is heard from
within the house. The shepherd and boy scurry away out of
sight, tugging the lamb.*

THE PORTER   What kind of a ship?

THE FISHERMAN   (breathless)   Akh. Akh. The kind that people
sail in.

*A few men with spears or pikes begin to come down between
the columns; one is adjusting a leather helmet, another strug-
gles clumsily with his shield.*

*Calcho comes in from the left. He is a fisherman too, and car-
ries the trident fish-spear of his trade.*

THE FIRST FISHERMAN   Oh, here is Calcho. Didn't they catch
you?

THE PORTER   Where are they, Calcho? Raiding the pasture?
Speak, man.

CALCHO   They are coming quietly up the path.

*The spearmen begin to form across the courtyard, at the foot
of the steps. The first fisherman edges around behind them.*

THE PORTER   What? Armed men? (*turning*) My lady . . .

*He moves to the side, to stand by one of the columns. Polyxo,
the lady of the house, comes to the head of the steps, and
speaks across the spearheads below her.*

POLYXO   Tell me what you have seen, Calcho.

CALCHO   We dare not launch; the west is too full of wind; we
drop our lines from the rock. I heard oars groaning;
That long black ship glided below us like a dream and came in
and landed. These are some great lord's men;
I watched when they leaped the strake. They have fierce obedi-
ent faces; their life is outside them; they would do anything
Without winking. As for the woman with them . . .

POLYXO   A woman?

CALCHO
For whom they laid the plank to the strand;

I watched and her beauty was like the thoughts of God, burning and calm.

POLYXO   We knew one like that:

Gold and fire and ivory; King Menelaus his adulterous wife: that
Helen, for whose lawless luxury

Ten thousand died; the lord of my love and of this island among
them . . . for a wanton. If this were that fountain

Of death! We've prayed for it; did the men speak like Spartans?
I dream too much.

CALCHO   Not a word.

*He looks behind him, and joins the defenders of the house,
holding his trident as they hold their pikes. The strangers
come in, masked identically, moving like one machine. The
woman with them might be either their captive or their
queen; a fold of her cloak is drawn over her face.*

POLYXO

Who are you, strangers? It is peace I think?

*The woman drops her cloak from her face and head; the hair
is golden and the face ivory. An exclamation like a sigh of
wonder is heard among Polyxo's people.*

HELEN   Peace and love, dear.

POLYXO (*shuddering*)   Ah. Yes. Your
face, Helen,

Has been much in my dreams. . . . My eyes are too old to see
only the beauty among the tricks of the world.

What are these warriors?

HELEN   I'll tell you that in the house, when you
are kind. Do you remember, Polyxo,

A day in spring, you and I were laughing together beside the
flooded Eurotas? I garlanded

Your dear dark head with flowers before we bathed together,
parting the green reeds of the bank.

Our skies were clear and no grief had come; you were my guest
then.

Now I am yours.

*The household spearmen have moved to right and left of the
steps at the word "peace," so that the space between the two*

*women is cleared; Polyxo standing at the head of the steps and
Helen in front of her guard.*

POLYXO   Grief has come; and that day is dead. . . . A man was
here last year from Laconia
Passing to Egypt, who boasted that neither time nor grief nor
weariness touched Helen's face. We judged him
A liar.

HELEN   You find me much changed, Polyxo.

POLYXO   Changed? A woman
who has been a wild cause of misery and death
Will surely be pale with repentance; a woman famously unfaith-
ful, surely purple with shame; a woman
Pursued by the ghosts of slaughtered men and a screaming city—
could hardly escape marking I think:
The cheeks furrowed, and the eyes a haggard stare between the
red eyelids . . . Nothing—nothing—nothing—
Not a line, not a mark. You have wandered through life uncaring,
untouched, heartless, unmarked, and all your wickedness
Is like a song.

HELEN   Must I not love you any more, once my dear friend?

POLYXO   Whilst I . . . Oh, your beauty is pure,
Young and burning and holy; you are not changed from the
bride Menelaus unveiled or the young wife
The long soft eyes of Paris lustfully lingered on; whilst I—look
at me.
   *She uncovers her head, throwing down the Tyrian headdress;
   her thin gray-white hair, corded throat and wrinkled cheeks
   are seen.*
   It was no trick of mine
That drew ten thousand down to black death and burnt the chief
towers of Asia. But you the gods have made
To look pure forever. The gods do strangely.
Perhaps . . . they leave justice to men.

HELEN   .   They are in their cloud;
we know too little about them. We know
They love and surely reward the hospitable house. May I go
into your house, Polyxo? I am homeless.
We have come far; weary are the waves.

POLYXO   Not yet. I am think-
ing what gift . . . Is Menelaus behind you
Baying on the trail? He will find it hard perhaps to raise the Greek
    princes a second time.

HELEN   My lord
Grew old, and has left me, in the aging world. Carved stones con-
    tain him, with all the careful honors of death,
In high Therapnæ.

POLYXO   Well—old. Some have died
Young. You are all alone then? If any evil-disposed or remem-
    bering person should do you hurt,
No husband would come, nor no fierce lover, to find the quarrel
    and avenge you? It is bitter to be left alone.
I have learned that.

HELEN   Very bitter. Worse to be exiled. Old friends
    I see begin to regard you
Strangely and coldly; they let you stand at the door.

POLYXO   I have not
only myself to think of, but all
This island people. You come questionably. Tell me who exiled
    you, for what new . . . we'll not say crime: the . . .
Adventures of one so immortally beautiful must not be called . . .

HELEN Call them, Oh my lost friend, by any
Bleak shameful name that your heart can bear, but not me beau-
    tiful. That name is my hill of miseries. Many
Women are beautiful; and some have peace; and a few are happy.
    I am exiled indeed, but for no crime.
The sons of Menelaus by that other woman have always hated me.
    They inherit the kingdom, and I
Am exiled.

POLYXO   Not without reason; they would give the people a
    reason.

HELEN I am not here to be judged. A storm
That struck Therapnæ, and the living dead, perhaps had fright-
    ened them.

POLYXO What is this? You shall tell me all the story
Before you come in my door.

HELEN (*turning to her guardsmen*)
Servants of Achilles: you see that
friendship is a fading and fragile hope
Among the living. With you in the high sepulchres
It stands, if anything does. Oh soldiers, where will you take me, to
what refuge, if I refuse
To humble myself before this woman, but turn and shake off the
eyes of Rhodes and enter the ship,
Where will you sail to?

THE CAPTAIN OF THE GUARD   Queen: to the mound on the Asian
foreland. You know our condition: that we have no home
But the high, holy and quiet sepulchre. A ship is made to sail
home; we shall hasten home.

HELEN (*shuddering*)   Ah, Ah.
I knew that!

THE CAPTAIN   The west wind still wildly blows.

HELEN   Oh soldiers: you
know that Achilles your master loved me. Look north;
You can see from here like a blue shadow on the raging sea
Ancient Crete, and the snows of Cretan Mount Ida; take me there
and leave me; leave me on the sand
Like a beggar woman, and hasten home.

THE CAPTAIN   We must not beach the
black prow again, we must hasten home.

HELEN
To the burial-hill. To the wailing Trojan ghosts. To dust and
ashes. (*She turns toward the house.*) I will contrive to be
humble.
Polyxo: I am the woman
Whom Theseus loved, and high-born Menelaus, and beautiful-
throated Paris, and Deiphobus,
And one greater than these more terribly, whom I shall name. I
would rather have been a shepherd's daughter
To run barefoot and milk the mountain ewes, and pat the curd
into cheeses.

POLYXO   Far better for you;
Or else to be strangled at birth.

HELEN   Yet I remember the good gray
elders of Troy, having seen their sons
For my sake slain, and knowing me the poison in the city's heart—
yet when they passed me, walking like kings,
They would look at my face with love, they never reproached
me. I have memories of men doing nobly, to make me patient
In the day of humiliation.
(*She stands in silence, struggling with her pride, while Polyxo
bitterly watches. Helen continues:*)
But Achilles,
Violent and fierce, whom nothing could bind: for while he lived
he dared affront Agamemnon the king,
And had no reverence for beautiful human flesh, but pierced the
shining feet of Hector slain
And dragged him about and about the city at the chariot's tail,
defiling the beautiful heroic body;
But after he was dead he opposed
The purpose of God. . . . He said my remembered face tor-
mented him, he had no reverence but lusted for me,
In his life he had never known me, in his death he lusted. He
wrestled with Death in the shut darkness; he broke
The mighty wrists and the mound of burial. He stood on the
broken head of the mound and shouted to his men,
Whose graves pit the wide plain. They had never failed to obey
him, they heard and rose. All the fierce Myrmidons,
Dark faces and fire in the hollow eye-sockets and earth-matted
hair; staring they stood. These men here
Are of those that stood up.
(*Movement of Polyxo's people. They retreat a little, but a
line of the best draws across the foot of the steps again, so that
Polyxo is seen again above spearheads. She herself shows fear,
but says:*)
POLYXO   Go on. Tell it all. Whatever I resolve
to do will not be shaken
By the lies of the poets you listen to in idle Sparta
Or lonely Therapnæ in the long evenings.
HELEN   I would to God it
were lies. Why do you hate me, Polyxo?

POLYXO

Tell your tale.

HELEN   I cannot. I will not. Soldiers:
Will you not speak?

THE MYRMIDONS (*clashing their shields, and making a heavy
pacing dance, as of bronze puppets; but I think only the
leader speaks.*)
                              We that broke the walls
And tore open the citadel of Asia,
And the holy city of Priam like a gored ship
Foundered in the roaring seas of our blood:
We have sacked the empire of Death also.
They planted strange seed in Asia who buried Achilles.
The earth had received us and we broke the earth;
The hands of God were upon us to hold us under;
We broke the fingers of God and Fate;
They planted wild seed in Asia who buried Achilles.
When we camped in the dead
Metropolis, we dead, there was nothing living but a wolf and
          a dog;
The very swallows were burnt
That used to twitter in the eaves of Troy.
Where Priam and the silken processions
Went delicately
By the great hewn stones; in the morning
We pissed on the stones and knew that we dead lived,
And went south from there
Fasting, until we came to a town and killed it.
Punic ships lay on the shore.
They planted strange seed in Asia who buried Achilles.
Oh high blue water
And whirling currents in the lee of islands,
Purple nights and blue days,
Were you not pierced, were you not trampled?
Bear witness how his great heart burned you,
Toward this woman he burned.

HELEN

Stand farther, soldiers. I cannot bear. . . . Oh Polyxo, save me,
    Though love is dead and friendship forgotten,
The living should guard the living, and a woman ought to have
    pity on a woman . . .

THE MYRMIDONS   We beached at sundown
And struck in the night, in the gathered storm.
King Menelaus said "What are these?"
And the spear-point was at his beard.
"Dorian barbarians?"
Look under the torches, Oh King, that flare in the wind in the
    gates,
Look under the torches.
The Dorians have yellow hair; ours is earth-dark.
The Dorians have black iron helmets, ours are green bronze.
They planted strange seed in Asia who buried Achilles.

HELEN

Be silent, be silent! It is all true. There was only a little guard at
    Therapnæ. Our troops were north
On the borders, in the doors of the north. They took the high
    house and held Therapnæ. The storm raged, and the thunder
Shook the towers, while Achilles possessed me. It is true: he
    came and possessed me. His body was not like death—
Only his eyes.

THE MYRMIDONS We were the door-holders.
Our master went in and laid off his armor, and the queen of
    Laconia
Screamed once, and then sweetly smiled.
The wild male power of the world
Was mated with the perfect beauty.
While Menelaus outside the gate
Howled like a dog in the violet lightnings in the gaps of night
For spears, but all his were fleeing to the mountain.
And the Gods came down against us and we held the doors.

HELEN

You are not a rock but a woman: let me go in, let me go in!
From public shame, and this furnace of eyes.

POLYXO   Menelaus died?

493

HELEN   Not that night.
He did die,
Of old age, the next day. . . . I was compelled, undefended.

POLYXO   We are not
blind, we can see you are beautiful
Enough to have stung the body of a violent man in the very
    ashes. But I am a woman, and not
A loving woman. Tell me, you dead and stationed soldiers, where
    is your master, this woman's lover?
I desire not to offend him by . . . any act toward this woman,
    if she is still claimed. We have no force
In our pastoral island to oppose the power
That humbled warlike Therapnæ bristling with spears.

THE LEADER OF THE MYRMIDONS   You hide
a knife in your mind, but not too darkly
For eyes that have looked through hollow death, and are whetted
    and disillusioned, nor too dreadful. We are charged
To keep this woman whom our lord has enjoyed intact of any
    less lover until she dies.
When she dies we may hasten home.

HELEN   Will you plot against me
before my face? And vainly. I can pity delusion
Even in dead men; whatever it is you would sell, she will not
    buy. My friend has grown cold, but not
Wicked; not monstrous; one can see that without looking
    through hollow death. . . . As to Achilles,
I will tell you, Polyxo. He went away from Therapnæ in the
    stormy dawn, gathering his men,
Only detaching these few to guard me. He returned to the
    ships; and one had been burned, he took one of ours;
And sailed away to fetch west for the island Leuke, that white
    Atlantic splendor in the waves, to find there
The peace, he said, that even the most beautiful woman never
    can give. For there one is free of death's
Dreams as of life's. He will never return. I tell you because I
    trust you.

POLYXO   That is true. Whatever you've done,
Your blood is noble. The free-born

494

Trust gayly where a slave trembles. I have determined what
    I will do.

HELEN Why are you trembling, Polyxo?

POLYXO

We are not accustomed to seeing the dead land on this island.
    Come into the house. Come in. Let Helen
Pass, but not those bronze corpses.

THE LEADER OF THE MYRMIDONS   We deliver her to you.

A VOICE AMONG POLYXO'S MEN   Oh beautiful
    woman trust her not!

POLYXO   Who spoke?

HELEN

I will go in without fear, although I think that you hate me for
    some reason. I'd not seek shelter
In a house of cold welcome, but choice has been taken from me.
    The ship I came from goes home to black
And quiet death. One endures a cold welcome liefer than death;
    I will lay down all pride
And like a suppliant go in. But why do you tremble, Polyxo?

POLYXO   Surely with
    eagerness. My house is honored.
    *Helen approaches the steps, and the spears part to let her
    pass. Calcho leans from among the spears and whispers as
    she passes in.*

CALCHO

Beautiful woman turn back. Look: her pressed lips mean evil.

HELEN Thank you, fisherman.

POLYXO   What did that man
Whisper across the trident?

HELEN   Why, nothing, dear. He would bring
    me a speckled sea-trout or a great lamprey.
He thinks I am used to kindness. Oh, why do you tremble so?

POLYXO   The chill at
    sundown. Time brings all things.
    They go into the house.

CALCHO Evil is planned. Shall we let the most beautiful woman
    in the world fall into a trap, while we stand idle?

ONE OF THE MEN Well, it's a pity . . .

ANOTHER You think our lady lays traps because she had you
whipped once; but well you deserved it.

THE MYRMIDONS

Is there any stir in the house?
Listen: or a cry?
Farm-boys with spears, you sparrows
Playing hawk, be silent.
Splendid was life
In the time of the heroes, the sun went helmeted, the moon was
    maiden,
When glory gathered on Troy, the picketed horses
Neighed in the morning, and long live ships
Ran on the wave like eagle-shadows on the slopes of mountains.
Then men were equal to things, the earth was beautiful, the
    crests of heroes
Waved as tall as the trees.
Now all is decayed, all corrupted, all gone down.
Men move like mice under the shadows of trees,
And the shadows of the tall dead.
The brightness of fire is dulled,
The heroes are gone.
In naked shame Agamemnon
Died of a woman.
The sun is crusted and the moon tarnished,
And Achilles has chosen peace.
Tell me, you island spearmen, you plowboy warriors,
Has anyone cried out in the dark door?
Not yet. The earth darkens.

*Slate gray twilight has come; but later a high cloud catching
light fills the scene with a confusing red radiance.*

At the fall of an age men must make sacrifice
To renew beauty, to restore strength.
We say that if the perfect beauty were sacrificed,
The very beauty that makes our death-cleansed eyes
Dazzle with tears, would be spread on the sky
And earth like a banner.
All men would begin to desire again, and value
Come back to the earth, and splendor walk there.

There is one perfection to be poured out, one lonely beauty
Left in the world, as lonely as the last eagle.
Has anyone groaned in the house? There it sounds.
A sharp clear broken-off cry like a snapped arrow.

CALCHO
Dead wolves, will her death feed you?

THE MYRMIDONS   Our trade was death.
And now we have known it, it is nothing evil.

CALCHO Can we endure this?
   He and a few others are going up the steps, when Polyxo
   comes out and stands above.

POLYXO Clear the stones.
   Armed men are at her side; Calcho and his few followers
   return down.

POLYXO You need not press in, you shall see all. I have caught
   the panther.
Oh men of Rhodes, we sometimes exclaim against the great gods,
   when the guilty seem to flourish, and the innocent
Fall unavenged. We are always rebuked at last. A murderer may
   flee to Caucasus but the broad eyes
Hardly turn and behold him constantly, and see the knife
   whetting or the noose hanging, in the very gorge
He runs to hide in, under the snow-shining walls and towers of
   the world. Do you remember my lord
Tlepolemus, the husband of my soul and my body? I have caught
   his murderer. Numberless thousands have died
By the war-making act of this one woman, the powers of Greece
   and the house of Priam; they are not perfectly
Important to us here enisled, but Righteousness counted them;
   and while I avenge Tlepolemus the gods are here
Avenging all. I have two black men I bought from Egypt, whose
   minds are not made like ours, they feel
No shudder where a Greek would flinch; I bid them lead forth
   the murderess, so stripped and shamed as men who were
   stricken
On the plain by Troy . . . as Tlepolemus . . .
Ah Ah . . . was robbed

Of the hacked and dinted armor . . . all . . . that corselet I
    gave him: in the days when I was able to weep,
And prayed it keep safe his breast; the Greeks retreated from his
    body fallen in the dust, and grooms and foot-soldiers
Despoiled and stripped him, and left him naked under the glaring
    lion of heaven and the Trojan eyes,
White flower in the foul dust, the body I had held in my arms,
    the flesh that my mouth had clung to. . . . Shall I not
Shame this dead woman? . . . Come.
*Helen is led by slaves from the door, her hands bound behind
her back. The confusing red twilight somewhat veils her
nakedness. Her head is held high, and the eyes clear, though
she struggles against the bonds, breathing hard through
parted lips. Her yellow hair is disordered, and hangs like a
heavy fleece on one shoulder.*
HELEN (*straining at the cords*) Are you the stronger? Yet
    wretched to the end of time:
Contempt and a hissing: whilst I overcome by treachery am
    more than equal to all that may hurt me.
POLYXO   Here
Is what made war. Look at it, because it will not be beautiful
    to-morrow. No warriors will quarrel for it.
No one will cut through death to come to it. Now, now, I say,
    the old aching hatred, the very bitterness
That fouled my wine with aloes and stained my meat with spilt
    gall, morning and evening all the empty years,
Is turned sweet; it is better to taste than honey; it smells more
    lovely than myrrh and frankincense
Hot from the south. You caught panther!
I am glad that you were a queen in haughty Therapnæ; it will
    be harder to die; I am glad you are beautiful
Beyond fault, beyond nature: the ridiculous ugliness of death
    and corruption look the more dreadful to you;
I am glad you had many lovers, you will lie alone; I am glad time
    could not touch you nor age deflower you,
That your beauty is like the African crystal no point can scratch,
    unwoundable, uncontaminable;
For what comes now shall very suddenly unpolish it. Ah, Ah, Ah,

I am sick with delight. Call the black ravens, you beautiful
  woman.
Oh Helen, black crows and heavy-beaked ravens to be your
  lovers, to kiss your eyes. Call the mountains
Of Asia to look at you.

HELEN   Rhodians: your mistress you see has
  gone mad, you must prevent her—not for my sake,
For your own honor—from making this place forever abominable.

POLYXO (*to a slave*) Cast the rope over that branch.
I shall sleep sound at last, who have lain year after year tortured
  remembering. To-morrow, coming
From the door at dawn, I shall see my enemy's face puffed
  purple and her breasts blackening, and the dragged neck
Not like a dove's, and those fine white feet
Perhaps all shrivelled, perhaps all swollen, who knows? God,
  who sent her here, knows. Why do you wait?
Fling the coil, slave, keep the noose in your hands. Hup! A good
  cast. I shall not sleep, but call
Torches, and feast all night.

HELEN   I see my dark shameful death. Hear
  me, Rhodians . . .

POLYXO Let her speak, haltered.
  *The slave makes to hang the noose on her neck, but when
  she looks at him he stands back in awe of her.*

VOICES AMONG THE PEOPLE
We cannot suffer this. Oh Oh Oh.
Spear the black men, hang up the old woman.
Pikes and fire, ah? Like spitted pigs. We dare.
  They move toward the steps.

POLYXO
I thought that you herd of dogs and peasants . . . Here, the
  guard. Peasants: here are the men
Who fought at Troy, men to be trusted, my house garrison.
  *Fully armed soldiers, old men but dangerous, move mechan-
  ically in two files from the door, right and left of the group
  formed by* POLYXO *and* HELEN *and the slaves, and make a
  fence of spears at the foot of the steps. They are masked with*

identical faces of old grim warriors; between them and the
Myrmidons the island militia seethe like a rabble.

POLYXO   Rabble, you
know your boundary: the soldiers
Of Tlepolemus. Few, but enough. These will not lust for a har-
lot. These are the men that saw
The gods fighting, when the rivers of the plain flowed fire and
the earth roared like water. . . . Veterans of Troy:
It is mine to avenge your labor and pain and your leader's death;
it is yours to keep those plowboys in awe
And herd those herdsmen.

THE MYRMIDONS
Old men you ought to have died
In your good years, not wearily
Gone home to rust.
If you had died and revived again
Your hair would not be snowed under but brown as ours,
And your eyes as fierce.

POLYXO (*to the slave*)   I said, halter that woman. Between the
dead and the living my hatred stands.

HELEN
Will you stand and let me be slain, you men of Rhodes?

POLYXO
What, is life sweet? Cry out. Weep publicly. Show all your
mind, make all your grief like your body naked.
Surely it is all as beautiful as your body, and I shall be merciful.

THE MYRMIDONS
It is beautiful to see men die by violence, but to watch a woman
Killed, is the crown. Oh Queen, die boldly.

HELEN   I pray you on my knees, Polyxo.
Life is too dear to be spent on pride. I am not afraid, but I love
life.

POLYXO   I tell you, kneeling's
Not half enough. You must act fear, if you feel none. Plead,
scream.

Helen stands again, and wrenches at the cords, twisting her
body.

THE MYRMIDONS (*coming nearer the house, pressing on the demoralized crowd*)

Queen, life and death are no better than the two ears of a carrion-
Battening dog; there is nothing to choose.

We know them both, and their beauty is beyond them, their
beauty is the value,

As yours is your beauty. We also were sacrificed.

HELEN

Dead wolves, fight for me. Save me. You could blow down this
brittle stubble of Rhodian spears like summer

Fire in the stubble. Flash your fangs, wolves. Fight, you bronze
wolves. For I have the seed of Achilles in me.

For your lord, for your leader's blood, not for me make war.

THE MYRMIDONS

Beautiful blossoms of battle again and forever unfolding
Star the earth, but we dropped petals of one
Shall endure peace, not even to behold them again nor to hear
them,

In the quiet places, in enormous neutrality.

Oh perfectly beautiful, pain is brief, endure to be sacrificed.

This great age falls like water and a new
Age is at birth, but without your pain it could never be beautiful.

The golden fleece of your hair, the straining
Shoulders, the dove-throat, the breasts thrust forward by the
strain of bonds,

Shall yield their beauty to the earth and sky,

The wonderful breasts their soul to all the flushed hills of earth,

The long white thighs to the marble mountains.

Mycenæ is down in corruption but Athens will stand instead,

The Dorians will make Laconia a land of helots.

HELEN

Dogs, not wolves. Death-whipped dogs. Hear me, veterans

Of Rhodes, old valiant warmen that fought in Asia—from the
wall I watched you. . . . No help, no help anywhere?

I am brought to bay here between the bony mercy of unmanned
old age and the eyeless pity of the dead.

Do you see this ebony tool of murder hangs the halter on my
throat, the strangling death?

POLYXO   Helen:
Speak quickly, for your end hastens.

HELEN   I will speak. I have lived
and seen the great beauty of things, and been loved and
honored.
If now I must die, it is come. Nothing on earth nor in ocean is
hatefuller than death; at least I have not
Wasted my life like this gray murderess, fouling with age, lying
twenty years in the pit of time
Grinding the rust on a knife.

POLYXO   Take for your portion agony and
shame. Sweep room there below, guardsmen.
Haul, slaves. May all that cause war, thus perish. . . . It is dark;
torches, torches! People of Rhodes, we have caught
And hanged a panther. Pelt the white body with pine cones, pelt
it with clods.

While she is hanged, confused struggle in the brown twilight
between the old guardsmen and the people. The Myrmidons,
chanting in their pacing dance, take no part in it.

THE MYRMIDONS
Wild swan, splendid-bodied,
Silent at last, silent and proud, fly up the dark.
Clash bronze, beat shields, beauty is new-born.
It is not to be whispered in Argos that Helen died like a woman,
Nor told in Laconia that sickness killed her.
Strike swords, blade on blade, the daughter of God
Hangs like a lamp, high in the dark, quivering and white.
The breasts are thrust forward and the head bows, the fleece of
gold
Shakes on the straining shoulders, writhes to the long white
thighs.
When God looked down from heaven the mound in the Troad
Swarmed like an anthill, what spears are those?
Power that will pierce your people, God of the living,
The warrior-ants of the anthill, the spears from the dark bar-
row . . .

Torches are being brought from the house.

Look under the torches, Oh King, that flare in the wind of night,
Look under the torches.
No Dorians are we; they planted strange seed in Asia who buried
    Achilles,
Power to pierce death, helmeted heads cracking the grass-roots,
Power to be born again.
Come down and behold us Oh King of heaven and Oh hawks of
    Caucasus
Come down and behold us,
You African lions in the tawny wilderness roar in the storm,
For our master is joined with the beauty he remembered in
    death, with the splendor of the earth,
While the King of Laconia howls like a starved dog
In the rain, in the violet lightnings, in the gaps of night, and we
    hold the gates.
    Polyxo comes between torch-bearers to exult.
POLYXO
High violent wind let the tree stand, leave me my vengeance.
    Slaves, hold the flaring torches up high;
I can see a hanging whiteness in the wind and smoke. She ought
    to be hideous now? How beautiful she is.
Hair veils the face. Where is my triumph? I am very happy.
    The high wind swings her slowly spinning
As if to show all her beauty. I did not wantonly, Oh beautiful
    woman; my need compelled me. I have done
More than I dared; I have put my pain outside me; it is time to
    exult. White mountains, ice-helmeted peaks
That wall the ends of the world, come here and behold my
    triumph. Where is my triumph, has the wind snatched it?
There is no woman on earth so happy as I am, having slain my
    pain: yet it seems that all present things
Slip away down hill, and I could weep for them.
CALCHO (*coming behind her in the darkness and confusion*)
                                      Old woman,
    revenge is a slippery fish. This from Calcho.
    *He drives the trident into her side, and tries to escape. One
    of the guard strikes him down. Polyxo has groaned and fallen
    on the steps.*

THE MYRMIDONS (*who have not ceased from their pacing dance*)
Roar in the night, storm, like a lion, spare not the stars.
They have planted wild seed in the air who lifted God's
Daughter on high, wavering aloft, blessing the new
Age at birth with the beauty of her body . . .

POLYXO (*slowly, gasping*)
Three spears?—that fish-spear—ah, ah, like a shark or tunny.
    Drag . . . the points, black man, the barbed points, out.
Ah. Ah. Ah. No. Their claws catch in my entrails; her death was
    kinder. What whiteness
Wavers up there over fires and anguish? Rhodes: I have no
    son . . .

THE MYRMIDONS (*turning and going back by the way they
    came*)
All is accomplished. Islanders, gather the slain.
Seed has been planted in Asia, seed in Therapnæ,
High in the dark, seed for the white eagles of dawn.
For us the black ship on the shore, for us the black waters, the
    black
Hollow of the mound. Heavily beat, bronze upon bronze.
Clash, bronze; beat, shields; beauty is new-born.
    The flame is blown from the torches by the violent wind.

The story is derived from the closing chapters of the Volsung Saga, the action of which refers itself to a date fairly correspondent with the end of the Greco-Roman age and the beginning of this one.

The theme of self-contradiction and self-frustration, in Gudrun's nature, intends to express a characteristic quality of this culture-age, which I think should be called the Christian age, for it is conditioned by Christianity, and—except a few centuries' lag—concurrent with it. Its civilization is the greatest, but also the most bewildered and self-contradictory, the least integrated, in some phases the most ignoble, that has ever existed. All these qualities, together with the characteristic restlessness of the age, its energy, its extremes of hope and fear, its passion for discovery, I think are bred from the tension between its two poles, of Western blood and superimposed Oriental religion. This is the tension that drew taut the frail arches of Gothic cathedrals, as now it spins the frail cosmogonies of recent science and the brittle utopias of economic theory. This tension is really the soul of the age, which will begin to die when it ceases. In modern times the direction of the tension has shifted a little; the Christian faith is becoming extinct as an influence, compensatorily the Christian ethic becomes more powerful and conscious, manifesting itself as generalized philanthropy, liberalism, socialism, communism, and so forth. But the tension is relaxed, the age prepares for its long decline. The racial pole is weakened by the physical and especially the spiritual hybridization that civilized life always brings with it; the Christian pole is undergoing constant attrition, steadily losing a little more than it gains.

I believe that we live about the summit of the wave of this age, and hence can see it more objectively, looking down toward the troughs on both sides, than our ancestors could or our more remote descendants will. . . . Is it necessary to add that I am not speaking as one of the prophets? These are only ideas that came to me while I was writing what follows, when I wondered "Why

does Gudrun act this way?" Thence they added themselves to
the thought of the poem, and are noted here to explain one
tendency of its thought. The others seem clear enough.

When the north and the east crawled with armed tribes to-
ward mindless wars,
Barbarians like a shieldful of knives flung random, clashing to-
gether, stabbing, gashing or missing
Through the north darkness, Goth, Hun and Vandal, Saxon and
Frank, and down the hopeless frontiers of Rome:
Three men leading three hundred came to the edge of the forest
to a murdered farm. Hoegni said laughing,
"Hey for the owner!" And Gunnar: "Ay. He hangs there." For a
haltered man
Hung in the oak above the fire-crumbled walls. "This is the
place she named to us: the dead man's farm,
A hill over a plain, a hanged man, a choked well, a stream at the
hill-foot. Let them drop the gear."
But Hoegni: "I say go on," jutting his chin to the south, the sharp
yellow beard,
"We'll meet the sooner. Aah, camp here waiting
While they loot Gaul?" "Wolf-eagerness is a treasure in war-
riors, caution in kings," answered Gunnar,
Called king for being the head of a little clan between the Saxons
and Franks; his eyes were royal
Over the thick brown beard, deep and ice-blue, dark-browed,
"If Gudrun comes, and gives bonds and promises,
Yet I shall probably turn you back and lead home. I am not in
love with letting my naked face
Into the bear's mouth." His brother Hoegni groaned and laughed
but not spoke. Then Carling his youngest brother,
A boy still, beardless, brave face, wide eyes, bright hair: "I shall
not turn. Look, brother, how it is clouded
With herds of horses like a summer heaven, clouds beyond
clouds, I never saw anything nor heard a poem
So beautiful as this plain.

Yonder must be the Horde's encampment: like a hundred cities:
and the horses, the horses, the many-colored,
At pasture around it like a vast wheel. There, there, and there,
are the towers of smoke from the burnt towns.
Yonder a band of war-men far off goes galloping on some great
raid. Sigurd had a horse;
He called him Grayfell." Gunnar said: "Listen, boy. You shall
have horses to ride if we go down there.
But Sigurd is not to be named. Sigurd is not to be named. Re-
member we are making peace with Gudrun,
Who is our sister, and has grown powerful too." Hoegni laughed,
Carling said, "I know. It is a pity.
Oh Gunnar it seems to me that my spirit,
After the close fields and forest at home, flies towering up to
the sun like a noon eagle
Above this plain, the space the distance, the immense green free-
dom glimmering to blue: as if I could almost
See Rome from here." Hoegni said, "Live and we'll see it; if those
Goths have left anything. Meanwhile we'll feed.
They'll have to hack firewood from the owner's oak, it's all that's
left him. *He* will not care." "Oh Hoegni!" Carling
Answered, "Oh Gunnar! When Gudrun comes and we've dearly
greeted her, then let us
Not seek the Hun's camp nor friendship with him, but suddenly
help ourselves to keen horses and alone together
Go and see Italy.
Oh Gunnar! *that* would be the high path for heroes, no talk, no
alliances. I know Sigurd would do it
If he were living. Ride southward like a pointed storm of wild
swans, like a flying lance-head, an axe-head,
Carve our own valley through the Huns and Romans." "What
a pity," Hoegni said,
"To be a fool at sixteen. I warned you Gunnar,
Leave Fool at home." "A flight of horsemen," the youth said
gladly, "this way. Oh look, Oh the lovely fellowship,
Like a long arrow burning with dust for smoke." "You have
young eyes. Ay.

That will be Gudrun. How many?" He answered, "They ride by
fours, less or more. Some ten ranks: forty perhaps."
"Hardskin and Swayn," Gunnar said. "Ay," they answered.
"Patrol the wood-path until I call you.
You east and he west.
Not to be embraced from behind as well. She left us in white
anger, I will not trust her yet."

II

Gudrun dismounted and came to her brothers; tall, blonde and
pale, clad in a wine-dark gold-threaded
Wide cloak, snatch of some Byzantine altar, sweetly smiling
came Gudrun; a black-haired slave-woman,
A face like white wax, walked at her side; on the other a
swarthy sword-wearing Hun, who scowled and spoke.
Two more behind him watched hard under slant brows. Then
Gudrun: "*Dear* brothers! Gunnar: will you bid your men
Go ten steps back? Timor here . . . this dark-browed battle-
rememberer
Is Timor, he is lofty in my lord's attendance. My three brothers,
Timor. He is full of safeguards, being as he says
Accountable for the priceless treasure of my person.
GUNNAR (*waving his men back*)   Well, sister. Twenty.
GUDRUN   My Timor is very faithful,
And fears . . . never death . . . torture. Can that be Carling?
Oh my dear, Carling, how beautiful you have grown!
I always loved you.
GUNNAR   We were most happy, Gudrun,
In your dear message. Jealousies die but love is immortal. We
have come at great pains through the wet woods
Only to see your face. I say *only*,
Because it is certain that we are wealthy enough
Without Hunnish alliances. Our thought in coming is toward
you only; to see the loved face, salute
The dear lips, and return.
HOEGNI   And ask you how it feels to be mar-
ried to a toad, for every man told us

Huns look like toads: and by God it's true. Pop eyes, no noses,
    toad color . . .

GUDRUN   Hoegni!

Be wary of your words a little.

HOEGNI   Not *I.*

GUNNAR   As to the precious gather-
    ings of Gaul and Italy: what's gold?

We came for love's sake.

GUDRUN (*to Hoegni*)   He understands it well enough,

Though for scorn he won't speak it.

HOEGNI   Tim—Timy you mean?

    For scorn you say? I am telling you . . .

GUDRUN   *Understand me,*

Hoegni. My lord and his race are not mocked. The emperor of
    northern and middle Europe, all from the Caspian

To the North Sea.

HOEGNI   Not a toad? Nose-holes

Where a nose ought to be . . .

GUDRUN   And soon I believe to conquer
    and rule the whole nation-written

War-weary tablet, all the king-scarred earth.

HOEGNI   Not *me.* . . . That
    is a marvelous piece of a victory

Worn on your shoulders, Gudrun. Well, you look young still.

GUDRUN   And for gold: look at these

Bracelets that bruise my arms; and this neck-chain.

HOEGNI   Oh, he loads
    you. Save up, save up,

Lest winter come.

GUDRUN   The chain's for King Gunnar. No: I pray
    you, brother, take it with my love. Though I was bitter,

That was quite long ago. And now I live among foreigners . . .

GUNNAR   How your lips writhe!
    Don't cry, my dear,

I'll not refuse it nor the love either, but joyfully. . . . Let me
    kiss you Gudrun, why do you cover your face?

I'll kiss the tears.

GUDRUN   It was caught in my hair. There. You've a
    tress with it. Ah, Gunnar,
Little you know!

GUNNAR   Dear sister. I am far more glad that our love
    is born again
Than for all these great links of gold.

GUDRUN   And for my . . . brother
Hoegni, these . . .

HOEGNI   Don't do it
If it hurts you so. You're white as death,
Snow-girl.

GUDRUN I remember you used to call me that. We were near
    the same age.

HOEGNI But now those blue eyes of yours
Have wolves in 'em.

GUDRUN   The better to see you with, dear! Well,
    I've been through . . . and seen stark battles: but if
These eyes grow hard: not toward my brothers, Hoegni. By-
    gones are by-gones, that wound's hid . . . healed I mean.
You never knew me to lie I believe? So take the bracelets. I guess
    them nearly the weight in gold
Of Gunnar's chain.

HOEGNI   Thank you, Gudrun. I wish to do you some-
    time a worthy service. Why, men
Have fought to death for less than a hundredth fraction
Of this heavy glitter.

GUDRUN   It's nothing: we swim in it. Carling dear:
    I've something . . . I find myself
Wet-eyed to look at you.
Because you were much younger than me and Hoegni. . . . I'm
    not false, I'll hide no thought, if you'd been tall
At that time, I believe you'd have helped me. Who knows?
    Hush, dear, let me dream. This is very vain talk
About an old woe. The snows of that year are melted and so is
    my heart, and I am Attila's wife.
You look like ghosts, ah? All but Carling. Oh, it's wiped out.
I thought you, Carling, too noble-minded . . . young I should
    say . . . to care about gold, and so have chosen you

A steel jewel, only a sword, yet a rare one. Give it to me, Jukka.
(*She takes it from one of the dark warriors behind her.*) It
is said there were great enamel-workers
And godlike smiths in Gaul before the back-and-forth grovellings
and wash of war
Wiped out all.

CARLING   Oh Gudrun! What are these gems? Why, the
hawk-head hilt
Is like a firebrand.

GUDRUN   The blade, the blade. The hilt's nothing, a
gem-crust. Nor the scabbard either. See
How cunningly they let the delicate-colored threads of enamel
Into the fierce blank steel.

CARLING   Oh Gudrun.

GUDRUN   Hawk or eagle the pretty
tracery, who cares? It's pretty, ah?
I begged it of my lord when he was merry.

CARLING   I cannot tell you.
. . . Oh Gudrun.

GUNNAR   By God, what a smith. I think
You've the best, brother. (*to Hoegni, quietly, nodding toward
the oak*) I don't like those two, the ravens.

HOEGNI   Mm? Those?
Children of nature, attracted by meat like you and me. They
take the eyes first.

GUNNAR   Caw caw, damn them!
Though they're God's birds. Is she true?

HOEGNI   It's true gold.

CARLING (*admiring the sword*)   Oh Gudrun,
the beauty, the power, the balance! And as for the edge:
Look at my thumb: I barely touched it to feel it.

GUDRUN   Oh, Oh, my gift!

CARLING   But
I love the slight cut.
I think it's magical: see, I streak my own blood on the silky
blade, that makes it mine for my life-days
Faithfully. Oh sister, I'll do such deeds with it . . . some **deed**
for the poets to remember in all the fire-lit music-filled

Evenings of time. Sigurd's great beautiful bone-biter, the sword
That he called Anger, never did such a deed . . . Oh! . . .
I didn't mean, I didn't want . . .
I adore his memory.

HOEGNI   Fool.

GUDRUN   I know, dear. Hush, Hoegni, let
him alone. We may love Sigurd and yet
Not hate his . . . killers. He was too great to need any memory
but thoughts of love . . . to need any
Reprisal. His fame's not slain. . . . What'll you call the sword,
Carling?

CARLING   I thought of calling him
Sea-eagle. Ah Sea-eagle you'll fly in Rome,
You'll dazzle the south.

ONE OF GUNNAR'S MEN (*shouting from a distance*)
Troop of horse, a long one.

ANOTHER   From the west by the wood's edge.

HARDSKIN (*farther off*)   A thousand horse.

HOEGNI   Bitten, by God. (*Gunnar and Hoegni draw sword, so
do the Huns.*)

GUNNAR   I will never believe, Gudrun, no never.
. . . Timor: we are here
As friends, probable allies . . .

HOEGNI   Baited and trapped,
with a yellow glitter
And milky talk. (*shouting*)   Stand to it. Ham-string'em, that
stops'em. (*to Timor*) . . . Well?
Toad? Let's begin.

GUDRUN (*cuffing her slave-woman, who was about to scream*)
           You are too excitable, you shame me red,
brothers, before
These quiet dark lords of the East. Those are the horses to mount
you. Each man of that troop leads a spare horse.
And thus you trust me! I could not allow you to *walk*, you and
your people,
To the Emperor's camp.

GUNNAR   Ay? why do they come from behind
and cut us off from the wood?

GUDRUN   They come from the pasture.
GUNNAR   So it takes five hundred men
To bring us mounts?
GUDRUN   For your escort also. There's rough work
On the plain.
GUNNAR   There'd be rougher
If my poor woodsmen forked themselves over horses.
No, Gudrun.
GUDRUN   The Huns despise you if you come walking.
GUNNAR   Are we your prisoners?
GUDRUN   Why, brother!
GUNNAR   No? Then
      farewell, Gudrun.
We carry back to the great fir-woods, the lonely tarns
And little clearings, magnificent memories
Of wealth and kingly splendor and kindness, and a sister's great
Forgiving heart.
HOEGNI   And toads. . . . Come home with us,
We'll make you queen of the North.
CARLING   Oh. I want to ride with her.
GUDRUN   But since I . . . love you, my brothers: how could
      I let you go? I'd even keep you
By force. You see: by force . . .
Of loving persuasion. I could hardly persuade my Huns
To let such warriors as you . . . not join the Horde.
Gunnar: he will conquer the whole world, there's not a doubt:
All the wealth, all rings of gold, all tribes of men, all the meat
      and drink:
It rolls to his feet like a ball. . . . Hoegni:
Do you love battles?
HOEGNI   In moderation, in moderation.
GUDRUN   This would
      be out of scale for you, then.
Now the great crowning battle of the world is making, to
      dazzle all war
Before and after, will be fought on this plain within three days.
      For Rome has bandaged all her sick legions

Into one sword, ransacked her waning moon for man-power,
   and bought peace with the West Goths
(Whose king Theodoric is eight feet tall) to try odds against
   us. They have joined the two armies like axe and helve
For one huge stroke. Their last one.

HOEGNI   Is Caesar a tall man too?

GUDRUN   Which Caesar?
   None fights. They've an active general,
What's his name? I can't think. They are hundreds of thousands
   together, and ours are three hundred thousand, with the
   East Goths,
Vandals, Gepidae, Franks . . .

HOEGNI   Boo, said the goose
Counting duckweed.

GUDRUN   What?

HOEGNI   Tell it to the Swedes, not to us.

GUNNAR   No, no, we don't doubt
Your good faith, sister: yet there's a dreamy quality
About these numberings of multitude. How could such hordes
   be fed?

GUDRUN   Ours, are experienced.
They tap their horses' neck-veins and suck the blood, then stop
   the wound and ride on. Or a man's at a pinch,
Ah, Timor? The Goths and Romans I imagine starve. . . . Oh,
   this
Meeting will exceed all measure, enormous, a sword-mountain:
   you'll stay and see it? And, Carling, after we force them—
For the sun will fall out of heaven before Attila
Fails of a victory—the whole fragrant south will lie open, un-
   locked and helpless, all the sun, all the honey,
Rich gardens, rare fruits, all kinds of artist-work. We'll ride on
   the golden strands of blue seas and drink nothing
But purple wine, hear nothing but little Greek slaves
That sing like nightingales.

GUNNAR   Will you swear by the holiest,
By Woden hanged on tree; and by all the Gods of the Huns too,
   and all other Gods,
That you mean well by us?

GUDRUN   I cannot imagine why you mistrust
me.

GUNNAR Will you swear?

GUDRUN Why should I? You have no choice.
And you mistrust me vilely. And what are the Gods, who sees
    them? My Huns have travelled the whole world and now
Laugh at the Gods. Yes, I will swear.

GUNNAR   By Woden hanged on
    the tree?

GUDRUN   Oh, clearly. And by all the Huns' Gods,
And the Roman Christ.

GUNNAR   You will be sick and die
If you break oath. Well, Hoegni?

HOEGNI   I want to see old Hardskin
    straddling a horse, that's what I want.

CARLING   They'll go. Oh Gud-
    run how beautiful you look. One to stand shining
And sworded for the Decider of Battles in the eagle sky
In the poem that I've been making.

GUDRUN   Do you make poems, Carling?

CARLING Things are so beautiful. Your face, like a white sword
Lifting against the blue. I'll make better ones.

GUDRUN   Sing me a poem
While we ride down. I need it. Life narrows on me,
All its events are vicious, whichever I choose.

III

In front of the curtains. Sentinels post themselves in the midst.
Men enter and stand conversing at the extreme right. Gudrun and
her brothers, her slave Chrysothemis, and the Hun Jukka, come
in from the left.

GUNNAR . . . The pastures are wide and rich, yet all the grass
    is bitten to the roots. What was that river we forded?

GUDRUN I told you. The Marne. We have to wait here until
    the trumpet is blown; no one may enter before Attila.

HOEGNI I wish him joy of it.

GUNNAR Marne; the Marne. What a language. Hoegni: did you
    notice the herd of thick-flanked brood-mares? I believe there

were at least two thousand. These things are out of our scale of thought.

HOEGNI Bah!

GUDRUN This building is an old broken place, curtained for the feast. The broken country-house of some dead Roman. The curtains look richly purple in the evening sun, don't they, Carling? If blood would keep its color, what a dye. And cheap.

CARLING Does he not come to bring you in? As I remember Sig . . . I remember Sigurd used to?

GUDRUN No.

GUNNAR Tell me, sister: what do they do when their mares foal on the march?

GUDRUN (*impatient*) Ah! Another time. Ask Jukka.

GUNNAR I have asked him a number of questions, he only gabbles. It is essential for a ruler to understand . . .

GUDRUN Will you . . . I am trying to make a quietness in my mind.

HOEGNI Yes. I have watched you, Gudrun. You are mad with pride.

You think you have married the mountain of the world. Sigurd was not enough . . .

GUNNAR   By the honor of God, brother!

Keep the peace, will you?

HOEGNI   Aahh . . .

GUDRUN   I'll tell you plainly then.

I am ill in my mind.

Pride? No: hardly. I was proud while Sigurd lived, before you killed him, but as things are

I've won back a little . . . power . . . not pride. Perhaps you will be able to tell me, being wise, Gunnar,

Why it is that I. For it seems that I still love you, for all your. I am not able. We're the one blood,

And were gay when we were little together,

Yet, when the warmth wins, I remember that yours was the cold contemptible mind that planned his death

Because your woman wound you up to be envious. And the cynical hand

Was my brother Hoegni's. And how cowardly it was done.

HOEGNI (*handling his sword-hilt*)

I guessed you. Bring on your niggers.

GUNNAR   You are bound by the highest and most dangerous of oaths, Gudrun.

GUDRUN (*impassively*)   So that my heart is in heavy trouble between love and hatred.

Two snakes in one coil. Which can neither endure nor destroy
  each other, but each is swollen to bursting with venom

From the other's jaws, it spurts on my heart. Ah? Well? . . .
  Well, that's how it is wi' me.

I was saying, to do you a harm would never make Sigurd live,
  nor be any comfort to myself, so breathe easily. Carling's
  a poet: do you think killed men want justice, Carling? Don't
  answer. I think they're nothing, they're lucky. I believe
  nothing.

After you've travelled and seen ten thousand corpses

You'll keep your poems in the way of nature.

GUNNAR   Indeed, sister, these questions about death are mysteries to all of us; it is wisest perhaps . . .

GUDRUN   The men with the red straps wound to the knees are
  East-Goth nobles. That tall man, who is talking to the Hun,
  is Alberic the Frank. Yonder are two lords of the Gepidae.
  I love to see kings cooling their heels at my husband's
  pleasure.

GUNNAR   And those to the left, Gudrun?

GUDRUN   Huns. Don't question me! I am not patient.

A TRUMPETER *appears between the parting curtains. He sounds
  the trumpet, and announces in Hunnish and in Gothic:*

The Lord of Lords has taken his seat. The Masters of War have
  taken their seats.

HOEGNI   The Toads have squatted.

The curtains draw aside, and they enter.

IV

*It is the atrium of a ruined Roman country-house. The walls at
this end are broken down; the wall seen slant on the left is ar-
caded with freestone columns, the near ones broken, the farther*

entire. Strange guests have stopped here since the owner fled. The wall at the back has no colonnade but is adorned with wall-paintings; the panels to left and right indistinguishable, the great central painting scarred but clear. It represents Prometheus bound on Mt. Elboros, the snow-veined rocks, the wound and the vultures.

Planks on trestles range parallel to the walks, making an L-shaped table. On the far limb of the (inverted) L, below the colossal Prometheus, Attila is seated among his generals. He is swarthy, thick, gray-haired, with a flat Mongolian face, and robed in barbarian magnificence. He is already feeding and drinking.

Gudrun will take a place near the angle of the L, keeping Carling on her right, allowing Gunnar to sit on her left, toward Attila and beside Timor. Gudrun's slave stands behind her. Hoegni sits between Carling and Jukka. The other guests, Huns, Ostrogoths and so forth, are coming in and finding places, and servants are busy.

GUDRUN (*standing at her place*) My lord. . . . My lord.

ATTILA (*at length turning his face toward her*) All right?

GUDRUN This is King Gunnar, my brother, of whom I spoke.
  And my other brothers.

ATTILA Mm. Welcome. (*turning back to one of the Huns*)
  I say if Arval fails taking Troyes as he slacked at Orleans,
  that is the end for him.

GUNNAR Noble Attila:
Our sister having by message invited us
We come with clear good will and kingly confidence
To behold her face, and yours, and the glory of the Horde.
She has flown high, she was nourished in a high nest.
We have strong places northward and power of warriors,
Though fewer . . . horses, I believe . . .
And not as a guest from wandering, but as the king
Your brother-in-law, retinued with quiet swords . . .

ATTILA (*turning and staring*)   Hm?

GUNNAR We acknowledge your hospitality.

ATTILA   Well, well.
Sit down. I remember she spoke of you.

HEOGNI (*aloud*)   Toad of toads.

GUNNAR   But as
for alliance,
And to ride with your host . . .

ATTILA   Jukka! Converse with him for
me. (*turning to Blada, who sits next him*) So you'll sweep
the banners around their loose end, curl it up and cut for the
center: the plain is wide.

BLADA Ay, Master. They'll have reserve, I must have more
weight than can be delayed . . .

JUKKA (*to Gunnar*) He say he ver' glad you here.

GUNNAR He seems a laconic man. Between kings, courtesy
should be religion.

HOEGNI Whisper, Gudrun. How does it feel? They say the
Black Forest women have to do wi' wolves, but a toad, my
God! Have you got warts?

GUDRUN Do not tempt me . . .

JUKKA (*to Gunnar*) He make plan 'bout . . . big fighting.
Soon he drink more, then make speech to you maybe.

GUDRUN . . . toward a black duty. I have what I sought in
marriage, that's power. I am not hardened yet
To its uses. . . . Oh Oh, Carling, I wish I had died with him.
There were blue campions around him beside the spring,
All changed in color, his blood had filled all their cups.
I wish the wet red earth sweet with young flowers
Had swallowed my life with Sigurd's, for I am not strong enough
to be his avenger. (Nothing, Jukka,
Oh nothing: an old feud of our tribe.) Gunnar:
Look down the table, you see the three boys beyond Blada and
Bela-Nor?
They are sons of Attila. He has no other male relatives, for he
killed his brothers, it is their custom. These fresh boys will
cut each other's throats when the time comes.
You'll leave early to-morrow, I shall arrange it.
Tell Hoegni . . . tell Hoegni his hand . . . was crueller than
mine. Carling:
Stay with me?

CARLING   I long to. You are good and beautiful, and here
is the main door of the world. . . . I am Gunnar's man.

GUDRUN Because I am lonely and hate myself. And though this
  camp-life is always dangerous, and has no root
In nature, nothing but wars, rapine and wandering; this people
  would need ennobling to pass for wolves:
But Gunnar too and Hoegni are murderers. If you should ever
  do anything glorious they'd knife you for it.
In the back.

GUNNAR I am glad you are not an oath-breaker. You cannot
  have him.

GUDRUN Can I not?

GUNNAR You'll go home with us, Carling.

GUDRUN You make him unhappy and nothing is decided. Drink,
  brother.

*The trumpeter comes in, on the serving-side of the table, drops
on one knee before Attila, and whispers to Blada.*

BLADA The bishop of Troyes, Master. One of those Roman
  holy-men. He came through the lines at Troyes saying he
  had gifts for you, so they brought him here. What was his
  name? What?

THE TRUMPETER Lupus, my lord. Bishop Lupus.

ATTILA We lack entertainment since the juggler was brained.
  Ah? Bring him in.

HOEGNI (*to Gudrun*) Are you done raging? What's a juggler?

GUDRUN (*to Carling*) The poor man was doing tricks for them.
  At first they threw pennies, but when they were drunk they
  threw bones.

*Bishop Lupus and his followers are led in, and set to stand facing
Attila. The bishop is a tired white-bearded old man, noble in
distress. His robe is torn and soiled; he carries a crozier.*

ATTILA Well, old beard? Talk.

BISHOP LUPUS . I come to plead for a Roman
  town
Your troops are troubling; that your majesty may deign to spare
  it for a fit ransom. I am the unhappy shepherd
That has to kneel to the wolf.

ATTILA Your name?

LUPUS I thought they had
  told you. I am the unhappy Bishop of Troyes,

Which lies like an egg in your hand to spare or crush.

ATTILA (*like a play-actor, pretending vast anger*)
Spy! Do you hide your name?

LUPUS   Lupus, my lord.

ATTILA Lupus. I thought so. Unmasked, ah? This seeming-reverend benign old man, that styles himself
A shepherd: what kind of shepherd? A stealthy ravening and murderous wolf. I'll pluck that mock-saintly beard,
See the great fangs grin in the jaws.

LUPUS   It is only my name, my lord,
I cannot help it. Your majesty
Delights in mockery.

GUNNAR (*to Gudrun*) What is this ah-ah-ah talk, so smooth and soft? Do you understand it?

GUDRUN (*who has drawn a straight bright dagger from a hidden sheath, and plays with it on the table before her, regarding it gravely, as if she were reading it like a sad poem, in silence but with moving lips*)
Roman. No.

GUNNAR I wish I could understand it. (*seeing the dagger*) That is a nice brave thing, do you cut your meat with it?

GUDRUN I keep it clean. (*turning to her slave-woman*) Chrysothemis:
What are they saying? (*Chrysothemis interprets in her ear from time to time, Gudrun does not listen, but reads her knife.*)

ATTILA (*continuing, to the bishop*) Well, then: what ransom?

LUPUS All that we have in the city, except a few loaves of mercy
Against starvation. For if you destroy the hive you'll have the honey, my lord, but burnt and damaged.
Much rather take the honey and let the hive live, and season after season returning take
New tribute.

ATTILA   You have a great store of wealth then.

LUPUS   Oh, little,
my lord. The Goths have stripped us yearly, and the Alans
Before them: we can only give all that we have.

ATTILA   All, hm? That's
  to say, *all*. Including your virgins,
Young wives, all other livestock.
LUPUS   My lord, I have stood humbly
  before you bearing your mockeries.
ATTILA   Very well.
Open your gates to-morrow in the morning, my officers will ex-
  amine your houses.
LUPUS   You are right, Attila,
To judge me both fool and coward, that I have prayed mercy
Where no mercy is.
ATTILA You guess badly again. I am as full of mercy as the
  comb is of honey. But unfortunately I have not enough wine
  for all my people, nor beer either. We must drink the rivers.
LUPUS I doubt your meaning, my lord. We will roll out all we
  have, every keg, every jug.
ATTILA It is not enough. Your misfortune is that your city is on
  the Seine and pollutes the water. My horses bloated when we
  passed there. And now that we move west again: you under-
  stand? For sanitation, for sanitation. Man, woman, and child:
  every soul that drops excrement.
LUPUS You are great and cruel, and are pleased to mock at us.
I have borne it humbly. I have been deceiving you, Attila: you
  are not the mighty one here. You range the dark world
From the Danube to the western sea; no man resists you, no
  power confines you; your numbers like the shore sands,
And deadlier and crueller than the sea waves; so that the tall white
  ignorant heathen that humble Rome
Horde upon horde fall helpless before you.
They fall and scream at your feet; you ride them like horses or
  you drive them like deer. . . . Yet I say to you
That the King whom I serve sometimes weeps in his sleep, pity-
  ing Attila.
ATTILA Ho! In the pillow?
Paternoster, ah? Paternoster. We know you. . . . What is that
  hook?
LUPUS For though you are great on earth,

And seem to prosper invincibly: alas, there is only one little step
    for a man between life and death,
Vast pride and bloody destruction.

ATTILA   I step, but not down. What
    is that hook in your hand? Answer.

LUPUS   My crozier. The shep-
    herd staff, the sign of my office.

ATTILA   Hm? . . . Dog!
*Attila glares at him in silence, with a stagy look of black
ferocity. Lupus begins to tremble, but returns the stare with
courage.*

GUNNAR (*to Gudrun*) What now, what now? What did he say?

GUDRUN He is trying to scare the old man.

HOEGNI Eh: Gudrun. What d' y' keep reading your knife for?
    Has it runes in it?

GUDRUN This? . . . I will tell you.
It is clean and straight. It speaks to me. It says: "Justice.
Faithfulness. Honor. Courage. Duty." . . . But I am not able.
I am not just, but a woman with kindred.
Not honorable, not faithful to the eagle I loved.
But passive, corrupt, merciful.

HOEGNI   *Do* you say so! Sheathe it then.

ATTILA Hear me, companions. I have wound this babbler in the
    net of his own words, and he has confessed. He is the spy of
    a great king (that soaks pillows), and he is sent to hook me
    down with that hook: do you see that hook? See it jiggle
    in his hand. Judge.

HUNS AND GOTHS   (*some in earnest, others shouting with laughter*)
Death. Flaying.
The blood-eagle. By his beard hang him.

LUPUS Lord Christ, I entrust my spirit to thy wounded hands
Very cheerfully. Speak to thy Father, Lord,
For the poor people of my city; and that he have mercy
Even on Attila.

ATTILA You tremble, however. Wait! . . . Reprieved, old man.
    I never offend a God on the eve of battle. My secretary
    Gratiano will arrange a fair ransom with you before you go
    home: he is a Christian too. Now . . . What's this picture

on the wall behind me? Is it your God? Gratiano thinks so. *The sun is setting, its level rays burn on the painting. Attila's imposing shadow, at the feet of the Prometheus, moves as he turns.*

LUPUS No. (*He wavers, as if to fall.*)

I have tasted death. I wish to remember that it holds no bitterness;
But lined with eternal life, solemn with joy.
As for that picture . . . The picture, my lord?

ATTILA Come, come.

LUPUS (*wearily, passing his hand over his forehead*)

A fable of the pagans; we read it in school. A wise giant that loved mankind: the God of the pagans crucified . . . I mean hanged him for it.

ATTILA Bah. I took the ransom because I thought your God was here.

Drink, friends, it's a sick world! . . . Why was *yours* hanged?

LUPUS What did you say, my lord?

ATTILA Yours too was hanged for loving mankind.

LUPUS Yes . . . yes. I am terribly tired. He gave himself willingly.

ATTILA It is all the same thing. Keep your feet, old man! If you fall your city falls. (*The bishop sways and faints, but is held up from falling by the priests with him*) Ricimer: why was yours hanged?

RICIMER, A GOTH Who? Me, master?

ATTILA When you swear by your hanged God, when you promise me faithfulness.

Was he hanged for loving mankind?

RICIMER Ho! We love our friends, not mankind.

GUNNAR (*to Gudrun reading her dagger*) *You* have sworn, Gudrun.

RICIMER We say that he hanged himself up as a sacrifice to himself. They hang up heroes and white horses to him but that's not enough; he wanted the greatest sacrifice. There is nothing greater than himself, so he hanged himself up. Or another story . . .

GUDRUN (*suddenly standing*) I, my lord! I, my lord!

ATTILA Eh? Go on.

GUDRUN   I was brought up in it. We think there's a great wisdom
in pain that's hidden from the happy.

Woden's our God of Gods and no power could hurt him: then
he must hurt himself to learn it: how else,

Wisdom's higher half? It's false, though; I learn nothing. I . . .
Oh tell me, my lord, do the dead care

What the living . . . what we do?

ATTILA   Take care of your words; we
are feasting, not prophesying.

GUDRUN   Or even a punishment

Is death? Quick pain and eternal quietness: that's a reward. Or do
they lie groaning? Ignorant, my lord?

But I can't act without knowing! Ask your companions, Attila,
ask your lords of war, Attila!

What: have you sent so many thousands to death, and not know
what death is?

Never frown at me, my lord, I am not drunk,

Or only on the bitterness. Because my spirit's been rushing back
and forth all day and dashing itself

On both sides of decision like a fish in a doubled net. I can neither
do it nor not do it . . .

I'll speak quietly.

ATTILA   (*scowling*) Do what?

GUDRUN   I will tell you. . . . I pray you
to let the old man lie down, my lord. We are cruel

In needs and nature, but not to use it for amusement. That old sick
innocence.

HOEGNI   (*to Carling*) Boy: slip away before it explodes. Gunnar
and I are hanging on a widow's hair: never fear, we'll take
some with us: but you . . . survive, survive. Do as if you
were drunk and must find a place to relieve yourself.

CARLING   You mistake her terribly.

ATTILA   Gudrun: we never allow women to drink with us: I hon-
ored you because you seemed white and still and well-bred.
I was wrong to make an exception. You do for the bed but
not the board.

Keep standing, old man; on your feet! or all's lost.

When it grows dark I'll set a torch-bearer by you

To light you all night: if you fall we sack Troyes. I am not to be
    moved by women. You old white weariness,
Can you not watch with me for one night?
I too am aging, the snows of time in my hair like winter on the
    black pinewoods that wind that Grecian
Fire-mountain Aetna: the frightful heart never cools, and when
    the fire bursts forth where is the snow?
But still I am aging, and carry the enormous burden of the world.
    Night after hollow night my friends here
Eat flesh, drink and wax merry, my armies that cover all the plain
    feed by straw fires and sleep, my companions
Rest in their tents; but for me no slumber, no rest, no relief. My
    herds of horses
Lie down under the stars before dawn, the herders forget to herd
    them, all the mounted sentinels
Nod lower, their heads droop over to the horses' manes. The
    last drunkard sleeps in his song; the inveterate
Gamblers dicing for bits of conquest, by a candle hooded with
    double leather, let fall their yellow
Eyelids, their fingers relax. Even the little flowers of the fields
    have closed their faces and sleep . . .
Who watches then? Who takes care? Who upholds
The troublesome and groaning earth, revolving it like a vast iron
    ball in the torrent of his mind, devising
Its better courses? Which one of your Caesars? Or does a Goth
Uphold the whole earth, night and day, never sleeping? Is it
    Attila? And yet your thankless Romans and brutal
West Goths conspire. Whom I shall crush with one mangling
    battle, in streams of blood exterminate rebellion
And settle the world; no man again to make war, no man to be
    masterless, but laboring in orderly peace
Under my lordship, the peace and happiness of the whole earth.
    . . . Hold up your face, man.
If you fall, or fail to attend me, remember: every roof burnt,
    every man slain, each woman and child
For a sport to the horse-herders. Eh, old man? . . . Tell me:
I, watching all the nights through, toiling all day, sustaining the
    earth: am I not like your God

That gave himself up to torture to save humanity, because he
loved them? . . . Take off your hands from him!
Let him stand alone. . . . Eh? Answer.

LUPUS   Have mercy . . .

ATTILA   And
who, except my own people stuffed with incessant spoils,
Has any gratitude? You in Troyes, shutting your gates? The
Romans, that opened their mouths to swallow the earth
And have choked on it? Or Theodoric the Goth, bought with
Rome's gold? I shall not leave one alive.

HOEGNI (*to Carling, as Gudrun rises again*) Make off, will you.
Warn our folk if you can.

CARLING She is good. You are dreaming.

GUDRUN My lord, you are great and men are ungrateful. You
have told your sufferings, our pity is moved. May I mention
mine?
I shall make no disturbance; I have found decision and can speak
quietly. My prayer is for simple justice,
And you only in the world have power. I have stood in your
favor.

ATTILA Promotion for your brothers, I suppose. Let them earn
it in the near battle, it will taste the sweeter.

GUDRUN (*sighing sharply*) Ah. A kind of promotion. Yes, my
lord.
My youngest brother is perfectly without guilt in the matter: he
must be saved. And my brother's men
Are guiltless: I pray you let them go home.

ATTILA   Hm? Stop there.
Twilight's a bad counsellor. Bring in the torches.

HOEGNI (*gently*)   Snow-girl:
Snow-girl: do you expect to outlive us?
We are not disarmed.

GUNNAR (*out of the corner of his mouth, to Hoegni*)
                          Hold your hand, brother. That would
finish it.
Patience and cunning may find the ford yet. . . . Gudrun . . .
sister . . .

*Torch-bearers have come in. Some take their places behind
the top of the table, so that the Prometheus is illuminated, but
Attila a thick overbearing bulk against the light; others, at
Attila's gesture, stand opposite Gudrun and her brothers, and
one by Lupus; much of the company is in shadow, but these
brightly lighted.*

GUDRUN Carling dear, can't you quiet them

Until I have finished speaking? . . . You remember, my lord,
how curiously I inquired (and never an answer!)

On the subject of death? But now I think that if it is good I will
do them good, for I love them.

If evil, evil: for I hate them too. The thing they did to Sigurd
I will do to them. (And quite ready

To tempt it myself, Hoegni. Jukka: watch him. He threatens my
life.)

Ah but this is a miserable story, my lord, of spites and jealousies

In a back-woods corner between the swamp and the trees. In
winter we have no sun and bleach white, in the spring

We kill each other; blue campions blossom. You can hardly
imagine our heavy narrowness, one thought a year

And there it sticks. You plains-riders pass over and look at new
things.

I knew an eagle in my youth, but the warrior-woman

Brynhild had enjoyed him when he was a boy.

She married my brother Gunnar here, still loving Sigurd,

Who was mine. . . . Wave the torch-man, my lord, nearer my
face

While I speak of him, because I must praise him

For Brynhild's reasons. Myself being wedded to the Hun-king,
the captain of the earth,

Would hardly . . . care . . . to remember

How beautiful (to that bison-boned woman I mean) Sigurd ap-
peared. Oh, he was tall, and rather

Pale than ruddy, with golden brown hair and eyes like the . . .

He was like a lonely eagle in the van of attack and like an iron
tower (Brynhild

Believed) in the closed battle when it bled at his base. Yet gayer
at the feast and gentler than any girl . . .

At least of such as we breed northward . . . She preferred him
    to Gunnar and wooed him secretly and he disdained her.
I too was a little scornful, because the woman was built too big
    and masculine to go about sighing
With eyes like a sick wood-pigeon's,
Then Brynhild in a cold and patient fury wrought on her hus-
    band, my brother here, saying daily
That Sigurd outbraved him, Sigurd was the better man, Sigurd
    plotted to wrench his kingdom away,
And so forth, and we in ignorance. The more noble are the more
    helpless in these whispering wars. So they killed Sigurd.
Gunnar my brother and my brother Hoegni knifed him from
    behind, while he was kneeling to drink
At a spring in the forest and you observe, my lord,
That my face has not twitched nor my tongue faltered; the wrong
    I suffered led me up to the sun
Of your countenance and burns to a benefit.

ATTILA   Gives you that icicle
    look: Hm?

GUDRUN   The whole world is injured
If wickedness flowers unpunished.

ATTILA   What do you want?

GUDRUN   The woman, my lord, killed herself.
Here are the men. I told the story to amuse you.

ATTILA   You have a crooked mind. If you know what you want
    I will do it.

GUDRUN   That my brother Carling be spared, because he had no
    part in the matter, he was then a young child.

CARLING   Oh . . . *Gudrun?*

GUNNAR   (*standing*) My lord she has not shown you the half of
    this business.
We are here as your guests and hers . . .

HOEGNI   (*laying his sword on the table in front of Jukka*) Take
    it, toad. (*rising while Jukka reaches for it*) I have its little
    twin.

    *He leans across Carling, striking at Gudrun with his dagger;
    but Carling, his right arm engaged under Hoegni's weight,
    catches the blade of the dagger in his left hand.*

*Chrysothemis screams. Jukka and others overpower Hoegni
from behind. Gunnar, leaping back and half drawing his
sword, is overpowered by Timor and others.*

ATTILA (*roaring with angry laughter*) Ho! . . . Are you hurt?

GUDRUN (*to Carling*) Your hand, your hand!

CARLING (*his hand raining blood on the table*)
What have you done, Gudrun!

ATTILA (*angrily shouting*) I say are you hurt?

GUDRUN My . . . No, my lord. My little brother . . . Oh,
Chrysothemis, tear your linen and tie it up. Here, here.
(*Gudrun gives her the dagger that she had been playing
with*) Cut strips. . . . Not hurt, my master. My brother
took in his hand the blade . . .

ATTILA What kind of death will you choose for them? . . .
Drink, friends, it's no harm.

GUDRUN I . . . (*moaning over Car-
ling's hand*) Does it hurt? Oo, Ooh . . . I am so awakened
From such a dream . . . *I* was not the one
That wanted them, that wanted . . . Oh no, my lord; and I do
pray you . . .

ATTILA *By God*, again?

GUDRUN As in a nightmare
We do what day would damn us for,
I have been wanting . . . What have I done!
My brothers, my lord: I grew up wi' them. . . .
As if I had walked in the narrow cave of a dream and could never
turn,
But now have wakened. No, no, no. If he struck at me,
He knew that I was mad and trying for his life. . . . Oh, truly
my lord
It was only a play of mine to amuse you. I have sisterly grudges,
I sought to frighten them.

ATTILA Ay? We've drunk too much
For you to jest with.

GUDRUN It went too far. Yes, my lord.

ATTILA Well, Timor?
Ah? Whatever she wants,

They have brawled at our table. Take them out, do what my law
    requires. Leave the pale boy.

HOEGNI   *Damn* you, Carling, that saved the toad's slut! But there,
    boy. Take heart. Live merrily.

JUKKA   *(to Hoegni)* Come on, you. Your last walk.

TIMOR   *(to Gunnar)* Come.

GUDRUN   *(who has been standing death-white and passive, with
eyes staring at no mark)* I am in such a hell . . .

GUNNAR   Nobles of the Goths: is this justly done? You princely
    East Goths and Franks . . .

It was sworn to me by Woden hanged on the tree, by the agony
    of God . . . *(A hand is clapped on his mouth.)*

ATTILA   *(sharply, to Lupus) Keep on your feet,* Bishop the
    beard.

GUDRUN   *(to Chrysothemis) Give* me that! *(She takes the dagger
and sets the point against her breast)* Attila, my master! If
anyone comes near me before I speak . . . or if they are
taken off before you have heard me . . . I know not that
you care, but I'll do this.

ATTILA   Fool.

GUDRUN   Perfectly, my lord. That is my name. One who swore
    vengeance by the great self-tortured God

I then believed in; and consecrated my helpless life to it, went
    spying through the world for power to accomplish it . . .
    (Her eyes rove continually, watching against interference)

Tell your servants to stand away from me, my lord,

Or in goes the needle-point. . . . I heard that the power in the
    world was Attila: I knew not then that I was to love you,

But solely playing my life to kill Sigurd's murderers . . . That
    was my constant passion, whether we rode

In Greece or pleasured in Persia, or on the mirage-

Glimmering Hungarian plain. At length we campaign in Gaul;
    I laid the trap when we crossed the Rhine,

And sprung it by the Marne, and I cannot bear it.

I seem contemptible to Sigurd but let him lie. Let them go!

Oh, Oh, quietly. I promise.

For two reasons, my lord: for if I have accomplished my brothers' destruction it will seem to all men that I love Sigurd dead more than you living. And also I shall kill myself.

ATTILA   These are dreams from the wine-cup bottoms. You have drunk yourself mad.

GUDRUN   Forgive me, Carling. . . . Hands off!

RICIMER THE GOTH   Master. . . . For undoubtedly they are guests; and it seems a crooked occasion. Might it be well to wait judgment until the morning?

Two messengers have come in. They are dressed for the field, capped with iron and stained with riding. The gaudily dressed trumpeter is with them, trying to prevent them.

THE TRUMPETER   No, no, no, let me announce you.

ONE OF THE MESSENGERS   It is haste.

GUDRUN   Oh noble Ricimer! Pray to my master!

The messengers stand beside Bishop Lupus and his companions.

ATTILA   What. You're well splashed. You, Haiga?

HAIGA   Master. They have made forced marches and have forded the Seine at five miles from Troyes. Your servants there are vigilant.

ATTILA   It is time.

HAIGA   I have ordered raids, we shall have a few captives for questioning. The horses are being brought in.

ATTILA   This is not courage. These wretches rush on their fate like trembling culprits

That pray the executioner to hurry the stroke. Dear hearts! it's ready. I shall so hug you, Theodoric,

And you, Roman Aetius . . . (*to Haiga*) You will tell me the rest after we clear the hall. . . . Out, you unneeded. For the forest-men: take them and tie them up and set a guard: your business, Jukka. Except that pale boy: treat him with honor. Set a strong watch on their people. . . . For this old white-muzzled sheep-dog . . . go pray, totter-knees. Give him a tent. Out with you. (*As they go out*) Close the curtains, we take counsel.

V

GUDRUN   (*standing this side of the closing curtains; with Chrysothemis. Carling has left her, going with his captive brothers*)

Do you see him forget me, that pale bright thankless boy? Yet
    his blood's
What washed my courage away and made me a merciful . . .
    piece for contempt. We are all four
That bright foul blood. That foul bright . . .
Am I insane or what? Look how Attila lights for action like a
    joy-fire, how Hoegni flamed up for it . . . (*tearing at her-
    self*) Oh! Wet punk. You were born a Roman.

CHRYSOTHEMIS I? Yes, my lady, a Greek.

GUDRUN Men stole from your parents when you were ten years
    old.

CHRYSOTHEMIS Yes.

GUDRUN You were beaten without mercy, raped and starved and
    sold to a trader, and so began your pilgrimage. If your rob-
    bers were laid at your feet, what would you do?

CHRYSOTHEMIS Alas, my lady. Nothing.

GUDRUN How, nothing?

CHRYSOTHEMIS I would let them go. We were taught to forgive
    evil and love our enemies. But also I have known too much
    suffering ever to wish to inflict it, even on the wickedest . . .

GUDRUN (*striking her*) Coward. Slave. A slave by nature.

> (*They go out.*)

VI

*The scene is empty and darkened. Again and again horses are
heard galloping from a sudden start: Attila's messengers to the
four quarters of the field. The curtains are darkened out of sight,
so that the person who comes in seems to walk abstract and alone,
on a great plain at night. He sweeps the plain with a broom.*

THE SWEEPER

I am sweeping the Catalaunian plain,
Seine to Marne, Marne to Seine.
Back and forth, south and north,
For another battle this old earth.
North and south,
Blood of your sons will fill your mouth.
West and east,
Warrior's fall is worm's feast.
East and west,

Who can say but death's best?
Here a track for the Hun stallions,
Here a stand for Goth battalions,
I must make all smooth and plain
Along the Catalaunian plain.
Here the legions, here for a king . . .
To fall . . . here for a king . . .
I forget the rhyme, I cannot help it. At every new era we have to
learn a new set of verses, but damn this tinkle-tankle.
God curse all rhymes
I have to learn because of changing times.
Fair, ah? I made it out of my head. Times change and we have to
tag along,
Learn a new song.
I am the wind, I am the rain
Over Chalons and along the plain,
The tortured grass to grow again . . .
Wi' poppies in it too. The stars shine weakly . . . Stop. What
are *you*? (*Two heroic shadows pass in the air.*)

ONE OF THE SHADOWS
Weep for the living, Brynhild, not for us dead.
We cannot be betrayed nor betray ourselves;
We have power, though unwilled; and only shadows of pain.
(*They fade and pass.*)

THE SWEEPFR (*shivering*) Booh!
I am the wind, I am the rain,
Sweep the Catalaunian plain,
The dead they flit, the living remain,
Lives like grass and blood like water,
The women will breed and it's no matter.
(*He goes out, sweeping.*)

VII

Starlight. A few distant red campfires.

CARLING (*entering alone*) What was that? . . . Nothing. But
their guards never sleep. Gunnar and Hoegni are held in a
pit under a wall, bound hand and foot, and I am not allowed
to come near them. I will glide through the army and rouse

our people. We'll show these brown men whether the western
axe has an edge, whether Gunnar is a king or a servile Goth.
We are few, but the many sleep. What does it say in the poem?
Let only a few but resolute arise,
The tyrannies of darkness are not invincible. The soul of man is
greater than the winter giants. Ah sweet sword,
Sea-eagle how you vibrate against my thigh. We never guessed
that so soon . . . Ah? We are going to act
A nobler poem than any sung one: if I shake it's with eagerness.
That red torch Antares
Stands high in the south of summer midnight and we shall hew
out of here before dawn. Now. Quietly.   (*He goes out.*)

VIII

*Interior of a tent, lighted by a small lamp. Darkness outside.
Chrysothemis lies asleep in a corner of the tent.*

GUDRUN   A slave's dream, but a sweet one,
That love is her law and God. She has slept on it, with a little
breath of a Roman prayer, her hand
Under her cheek.
                    "Snow-girl," he called me, the pet-name, even
in his hissing anger. And poor Gunnar's
Pitiful bewildered kingliness. . . . Yes? Was not Sigurd
Pitiable too? No, never, in his life or death. Betrayed, then? Be-
trayed and stabbed, cowardly and shamefully.
I have given my life and lived with a loathed husband, made
myself the Hun's flattering harlot, to avenge it.
Lived in the filth of the camp, lain in the sweat of his bed, my
cold white body accepting entrances
It ought to have died not to endure. No wonder my mind's
divided in two: how can I tell
Which half's the real one? . . . It's because I've lost religion;
travel and the Christians corrupt me. I see the armies
Like worms crawling, and the Gods a cloudy growth of decep-
tion, and laws and justice only habitual
Fear and imposed violence.
                    I'll kill the half of my mind and not
change again: how they'll laugh at me

When safe at home. But Oh, the futile proceedings of life hence-
    forward, its purpose gone, disgraced
And beggared, sold for nothing, empty and vile. Empty and vile.
    Yes, but
Lordly Sigurd is nothing either; Sigurd is ashes. What value in
    ashes? that desire nothing,
And are not desired; no courage in ashes, no joy, no loveliness, no
    eyes, no song. Am I to have killed
My brothers for the sake of a cup of ashes? . . . Yes, but if
    Sigurd and the wish to serve him die out of me,
Then Sigurd is dead indeed. Oh . . . (*staring*) I am in such a
    hell of emptiness . . .
I will not change. I have forgiven them. Wake up, will you.
    (*shaking Chrysothemis by the shoulder*) Up!

CHRYSOTHEMIS   Ah, no, my
    lady, I am sure
It can't be lost. I laid it in the cinnamon-wood casket
With the other silver.

GUDRUN   You must get up.

CHRYSOTHEMIS   Yes, my lady.

GUDRUN   They took my brothers to that cellar-hole
Under the broken wall by the linden tree, near Blada's encamp-
    ment. You'll bear them a message for me.
Tell them I pledge my life for theirs and will see them safe. Tell
    them that, as you say so grandly,
"Love has conquered." I have the will and the power. . . . But
    after that. After that, woe to me harborless,
Without direction or virtue. Well. Go.

CHRYSOTHEMIS   How long I have prayed
    to die. Oh not at night, my lady,
Through the fierce camp!

GUDRUN   Poor doll, what do you fear, you were deflowered
    twenty years ago. No one will touch you, you are known
    for mine. And you are old, you are old.

CHRYSOTHEMIS (*kneeling*) I dare not. I cannot, though you kill
    me. They are horrible.

GUDRUN   You are not wise, my dear. There is a worse wolf here

than in the hundred thousand. I have tied up his jaws as well
as I can, but speak softly.

*Chrysothemis goes, but stops outside the tent, in the light
from the tent-flap, wringing her hands.*

GUDRUN Assure them they're safe, and will soon be free.

. . . Little Christ-God of hers: apparently you are the last of
the Gods for Gudrun, who has sloughed them all. You'll
never go far in the world: I wish you could. A few women,
a few slaves; but the nature of things is a wolf and your throat
in his.

A woman and the Roman slaves. I was a little more than a woman,
and not a slave, though put to it

To do craftily, when I made the plan and brought it perfect. I
have played the slave's part until it fits;

Ah? Slaved myself to the Hun and sold away my body's and
spirit's nobility for an exact

Payment of nothing, what a bargain.

I have been bewildered. This is the curse of having been childless;
the unspent milk swims in my blood,

Honor, action, fierce faithfulness cannot live in me; but female,
female mercy, female compunctions,

And be inferior forever. You! Chryso!

CHRYSOTHEMIS (*wringing her hands*) I stand between death and
death.

GUDRUN She's gone: I forgot. No matter.

This other message is mine to carry, on my knife's point.

*She goes through the tent-flap and comes on Chrysothemis,
who drops to her knees.*

GUDRUN (*coldly*) Baby. Get up and follow. (*Noise of horses
galloping*) Wait while the horsemen pass: Attila's message-
birds

That fly all night when killing's in the air. He is filthy to touch
or smell but a man of war. I

Could respect him. Come . . . Ah? *That's* something.

(*Distant shoutings and anger in the darkness. Clash of arms, as of
an enemy raid driven into the encampment.*) Have they
pulled open the iron flower of battle

537

Untimely under weak stars? Listen (*A stampede of horses is heard.*
Men calling from all directions. The central anger seems mov-
ing distantly, from left to right) it's pretty. Shine, killers.
What! Will your Christians
Fight? It makes Tyr and Woden itch in my blood, all the unbe-
lieved absurdities like thirsty fleas.
Wonderful, to feel one's mind for a moment unfixed from misery.
Baby, come. I want to see it.
(*drawing Chrysothemis by the wrist*) Come I say.
Gudrun's tent-sentinel has been standing motionless in the
darkness. He comes into the light that shines from the tent-
door.

SENTINEL   Regret, my lady, it is not fitting that our lord's
lady . . .

GUDRUN   Quiet, you. Guard my gear. (*shuddering*) What was
that?

SENTINEL   . . . wander through the night camp . . . My lady?

GUDRUN   Blind I have been. I never thought of it, mixed in my
misery. My own folk's death-shout. My own blood spilling
Made me merry just now. I drove 'em to it: Carling has called
their troop and I am the fool.

SENTINEL   My lady . . .

GUDRUN   Follow down then. (*They go into the darkness.*)
Men are heard roundabout, moving in the darkness, calling to
each other.
Which way?—I said the bridle.—Is it you, Katta?

A VOICE   (*farther back*) Nothing: some riotous captives. They
are being dealt with.

A VOICE   Go back to your places and lie down.

A VOICE   Help me turn the horses if you are mounted, Katta. This
is no storm.

IX

A length of broken wall. There are many dead at the wall-foot. A
campfire flickers to one side; toward the center, warriors of the
Huns, and men with torches. Others are investigating the fallen.
Blada enters.

A HUNNISH CAPTAIN   My lord Blada! They brought it on themselves, we only quelled them. . . . The Chief will understand.

BLADA   I hope so. You are responsible. You must understand that this was the clan of the Lady Gudrun.

THE CAPTAIN   They started up suddenly and attacked.

BLADA   Have you questioned your prisoners? And there are live men in the heap, I can hear them gasping.

THE CAPTAIN   I have sent for a Frankish man who can gather their language. Here he comes I think.—Merovech? Come here.

A HUN SOLDIER   (*lifting up Carling from among the slain*)
Here is one living, an arrow right through him. And still grips a broken sword-hilt.

ANOTHER SOLDIER   Oh! That youth was their leader.

BLADA   Question him, Frank. What were they attempting?

MEROVECH   Were you their leader, young man? What is your name?

CARLING   (*painfully*) A free . . . fool. Whoever you are, you had better be lying here . . . than serve the Hun.

MEROVECH   Come, come, your name.

CARLING   Nobler than yours.

MEROVECH   (*to Blada*) I cannot do well with him: his mind wanders.

ANOTHER SOLDIER   (*turning over a wounded man*)
Ho! Here is one of the two that were bound in the cellar-pit, whom they set free.

BLADA   (*to Merovech*) Try that one. Quick: he is going out.

MEROVECH   (*kneeling over the wounded*) Were you a chief of theirs? Your name, your name.

HOEGNI   (*whispering*) Go to hell.

MEROVECH   I wish to be your friend. You have death in your belly.

HOEGNI   (*whispering*) I will tell my name . . . to your master the Hun but not to you.

MEROVECH   (*to Blada*) He says he will tell you his name, but not to me.

Blada stoops close to hear him. Hoegni strikes a dagger into his skull and shouts:

Hoegni! Do you like it?

MEROVECH God!

THE CAPTAIN Ah . . . rat . . . (*driving the lance he carries through Hoegni's body*)

MEROVECH You need not have troubled: both dead already, both dead.

THE CAPTAIN Oh noble Blada. He can't have died thus: help me!

MEROVECH He can't have lived very well, the long blade in his brain and the hilt his horn. My God, a one-horn, a unicorn.

THE CAPTAIN Oh tent-pole of battles we shall miss you to-morrow.

Oh star of the horses. . . . God, God, it's not possible. (*To a soldier*) Report this to Lord Timor . . . no, no, to Jukka first. Oh dreadful accident! Straighten his body, draw out the dagger.

A SOLDIER How the dead forest-man grins in his yellow axe of a beard.

Gudrun comes, with her tent-sentinel and Chrysothemis.

GUDRUN I know what has happened. Are any living?

THE CAPTAIN The noble Blada! Murdered, murdered.

MEROVECH My lady!

GUDRUN (*quietly*) I see.

I have come to ask about my brothers: have you killed them all? I bear the blame: but for pity . . .

I am slack and patient you know, I can bear anything and smile at it, so answer me. Two of them were

Captive, one a brave boy. (*She sees Hoegni's body*) Oh. . . . It was cruel. . . . Is anyone alive?

THE CAPTAIN   My lady: a dreadful accident.

The noble Blada . . .

GUDRUN   I see. Where's Ca . . . King Gunnar?

Were any taken

Alive?

MEROVECH I have come just now. There's a fair boy still breathing . . . If you look carefully

You'll see twin flecks of light in the heap: he's down but his head's
    lifted: his eyes in the torchlight . . . strange, eh? . . .
Fixed on us.

CARLING   Gudrun: come here. But do not touch me for the
    pain . . . I never guessed: nobody speaks
About the pain . . .

GUDRUN   (*moaning above him*) Oh, Oh.

CARLING   I roused our men, hop-
    ing to save my brothers. You and I between us
Ha' done it, we've done it. . . . I dreamed of being a poet and a
    warrior and am a piece of skewered meat. The sword
You gave me snapped, it was rotten with enamellings. I hate you,
    but not for that. Look along by the wall-foot,
Gunnar like a dead lion.

GUDRUN   Oh his mouth bleeds and fills: beasts! help
    me will you . . .

CARLING   (*painfully*) Drown yourself, Gudrun. Save pain.

GUDRUN   Die, dear . . . dear . . . dear . . .
    Quietly; like sleeping. Poor wet forehead. Oh, never? Oh
    how you shudder.
Again? . . . Again? . . . The last. (*rising*) Now
Blood-men be quiet. One beautiful and innocent, worth all your
    Horde
And smoky victories, has died. (*seeming to weep*) Oh. Oh. . . .
    I am false to the bones: I feel nothing: only weariness
And sticky fingers.

MEROVECH   My God! the Chief!
    *A stir among the soldiers. Attila enters, with Jukka and
    others.*

ATTILA   Where? (*seeing Blada's body and Gudrun standing near
    it*) To your tent. A *man* has died.

GUDRUN   Many have, my lord: from time to time.

ATTILA   (*to the captain*) Are you of Blada's men?

THE CAPTAIN   Oh, master. Timor's.

ATTILA   (*to a soldier*) You?

THE SOLDIER   Truly.

ATTILA   Can you follow Bela-Nor as boldly? Your master would
    have led the encircling charge to-morrow, the hook that

brings home the battle: he was my right hand and is cut off:
Bela-Nor must lead it. You and your comrades will know
that he is in Blada's place, it is Blada's soul in him. You will
know. Your leader is not dead, his soul has gone into Bela-
Nor. Do you hear, Blada's men?

SOLDIER   Ay! Master. Bela-Nor!

ATTILA   For these rioters: if any lives, kill. (*to Gudrun*) And
you . . . T' your tent!

GUDRUN   Well, I bear the whole blame. I have managed neither
justice nor mercy; slacked and let happen.

I am one of those cowards that let go the bridle and brutal chance
rule all. I ought to be whipped to death.

But who's to do it, Attila? You?

ATTILA   Are you mad?

GUDRUN   No. Slacking
again. Look, I pray you: this one's

The best corpse of them all, his hand still bandaged from saving
my precious life, his brave sword snapped.

A lovely boy but not formed for war. He had beautiful music
in his breast, and if he had lived might possibly . . .

Ha' charmed cockroaches.

And take care of my poor little slave-woman: be kind, be kind.
I've lived wi' masterly killers,

Taking instruction. (*Her knife-blade winks in the torchlight.*)

ATTILA   Catch her hand!

GUDRUN   Do this to the Romans to-
morrow.

*She has carefully placed the point on her breast, and drives it
in convulsively with both hands, a gesture of straining em-
brace, and falls. The bystanders cry out. Chrysothemis
kneels by her.*

CHRYSOTHEMIS   Oh. Dearest . . .

JUKKA.   (*stooping by the body*) Master.

ATTILA   It is deep?

JUKKA   To the bottom. It is finished.

ATTILA   (*furiously*) Stand away from her then! . . . Ah the
white beast.

What ailed her in God's name? She wanted her brothers killed
. . . wanted, not wanted, gets what she wanted,
And drinks a knife. It makes me mad, Jukka: I liked her well.

CHRYSOTHEMIS Dear Savior, care for her spirit.
She was bewildered, and she was kind. She might have come to
thee.

ATTILA   All these long white women have devils.
Pah—the eve of battle—the same spiteful hour—
My right-hand friend and my favorite too. A cursed omen.

> *He stands, blackly brooding.*
> *Meanwhile a thin, fractional, insubstantial Gudrun disengages
> herself from the body of Gudrun and stands beside it, among
> the living but neither seen by them nor seeing them, and
> stares with wide empty eyes.*

ATTILA (*to Gudrun's tent-sentinel*) Why did you not catch her
hand? Whose man are you?

THE SOLDIER (*in terror*) My lord my lord. I was not near
enough. Timor's.

ATTILA He can spare you. (*to the Captain*) Have him bound:
and bind the slave-woman. Bury them living in the Lady
Gudrun's grave, not to lack attendance.

CHRYSOTHEMIS (*moaning*) Oh. Oh. (*But neither she nor the
soldier offers resistance.*)

ATTILA For high-born Blada whom I loved: bury him not until
after the battle. There will be thousands of Goths for him,
thousands of Romans.

GUDRUN'S SHADOW (*with vague monotonous voice delirious after
the shock of death*)
I know not moon nor stars,
How low you lie, lynx.
You must 'a' bled in the wars.
Edgyth to whom he drinks,
Or Fredegond:
Me to womb he thinks . . .

JUKKA (*to Attila*) May I speak? . . . Shall we convey the bod-
ies to their tents, master?

ATTILA Do it. Their tents? Yes, do it.

JUKKA I'll have beds brought to carry them. (*To a soldier*) You,
Elvi. And you. You. From Blada's quarters: hide stretched on
spears, or what you can find, but hastily.

GUDRUN'S SHADOW Tall sit the wolves around
The lynx in the snow,
Hanging their tongues beyond
Their tails I know. (*calling*) Chrysothemis! (*quietly*) No, no.
I know.
In a row around the red pool
In the snow. (*calling*) Sigurd? (*quietly*) Snow, no.

ATTILA (*over Gudrun's body*) She looks less than tall now.
Lying wantonly with what a craving mouth. I ought to have . . .
what she asked for . . . whipped to death . . .

GUDRUN'S SHADOW (*which has already moved to some distance
from the body*)
Oh when my (mother's) maiden lynx
Bled on the spear in the snow. (*calling*) Father? (*quietly*) No:
snow.
Folded close will my petals open
When the tenth moon has broken
Silence? (*calling*) Mother? (*quietly*) No snow either.
I am in the whom alone.

ATTILA (*touching with his fingers the face and throat of the
body*) I ought to 'a' killed you when you came riding that
first time. You were damned from the first. Farewell,
Harlot-gold hair.
　　　*He withdraws from the body and turns his back on it, while
　　　men come in with stretchers.*

GUDRUN'S SHADOW My darkness begins to crawl. . . . Lynx are
you there? . . . I begin to remember a loathsome thing
That the living call life. (*She stands staring.*)

ATTILA (*to Jukka*) D' y' think it'll dawn clear?

JUKKA Master? Oh, ay, I think so. There were low clouds but
the moon outsoars them. I think we shall have perfect
weather, my lord.

ATTILA We had better. (*fiercely*) Attend to that business: see it
done with dignity.

GUDRUN'S SHADOW   Am I to go down the darkness eternally
Chewing such a filthy cud of memories between my eyelids?
  Poor youth-broken Carling whimpering
In the dead men's haycock . . . and Hoegni the poison-white
  sidelong slayer . . . the plain careful fool
Gunnar making a speech. Or a horrible beater of drums like
  Attila. Or myself, whored and treacherous
Plotter too weak to see it through. (*tearing at herself*) Shadow
  cannot hurt shadow,
No knife can save me.

> *The bodies are being borne away, accompanied by torch-*
> *bearers: and with Gudrun's, Chrysothemis and the tent-sen-*
> *tinel are led. Chrysothemis screams suddenly, and Attila*
> *turns.*

JUKKA   Stop that. Strike her mouth.

> *She is silenced; the bodies are taken out. Attila shudders and*
> *draws his cloak to his face.*

THE CAPTAIN   (*to Jukka, quietly*) The Chief . . . look.

JUKKA   Oh master. If I dare: what is it . . .

ATTILA   (*making a noise like anger*) There was none like Gudr
  . . . Blada. . . . Things are not right here, do you feel that?
  There is no tension in the air. Always before a battle we've
  lain
Twitching in the stored womb of thunder, where the hair starts
  from the skin, men ha' snapped at each other
Like famished hounds, horses neighed all night. Now: by God,
  listen. Not a fierce note in the camp.

GUDRUN'S SHADOW   Ah, but
My eagle. Conquering Sigurd, for whose dead sake . . . I sup-
  pose there is no meeting among the dead;
But each in his lonely darkness, after the drunken insanity and
  sweat of life, remembers disgust.

ATTILA   Nothing. Murmurs. Sleepy patience, walking horses,
  stinking omens.

JUKKA   Master, we have Attila.

ATTILA   Oh, ay, we'll cook them and eat them. Come. . . .
  Aetius and his Romans: Theodoric his West Goths and so
  forth: when I gather them in my mind, then they are under

my hand. I am still Attila. (*Attila and Jukka go out with their following.*)

GUDRUN'S SHADOW (*while soldiers heap the fire, and hold torches to strip the better-furnished of the slain*)
For my killed eagle. Love, the base instinct, the leader of cap-
  tivities. How low you lie, lynx, I've sweated pleasure
Under Attila's brown bag of a body when I thought of his power.
  Love? . . . I think my deformity
Was only ambition: to fly at the highest.
Therefore I valued Sigurd, famous for killing, but horrible Attila's
  ten thousand to him. Oh, vile
Vile heroic flesh. Brynhild have him
If any residue's to find, I know he hankered. Worthy of each
  other, both heroes, dog-wolf and bitch-wolf.
But I will give myself to the earth-hating wind, in hope to be
  washed clean of the stains and scalding
And that crime of being born; and praying to find the black
  honey of annihilation in some comb of darkness
Back of the stars. At worst I shall find no deeper defilements nor
  no worse captivities. Fling me far, wind. (*She goes out.*)

X

The Sweeper, as in VI, passes along the closed curtain, carrying his broom. He seems inhumanly remote and tall, in spite of the bonhomie of his mask.
THE SWEEPER A fair field, as they say, well swept.
I've labored all night and seen the yellow lions of day
Creep on the Argonne hills peering for prey.
Plenty: they're breaking each other's bones already. Go it, Goth.
  Sick 'em, Hun. Now I can take a few hours off and back to
  work in the afternoon, for—
Hun brag and hound bay,
This broom decides the day.
Roman hold and Hun ride,
My broom will decide.
Strictly according to orders: I'll recite them for you. First: to
  blow Attila back to the Danube. Second: to clear the air of

the chittering ghosts of the slain. Third: to pat down the
battle-corpses and gloss over everything.
So much anger, so much toil,
All to make soil.
So much fury to feed grass
Comes to pass.
All the horror, all the pain . . .
What's horror and pain? If I could understand the words I might
remember the rhyme. (*scratching his head*) . . . Well, but
Some day cabbages and vineyards
Will spring out of the warriors' inwards.
(*He goes out, absent-mindedly sweeping.*)

XI

Gudrun, at first alone. The factors of the scene do not become
visible until she perceives them.

GUDRUN Thin storm, no farther? The air hisses and fails, dying
like a sick snake. Far down below me the meteors
Spin green fire-threads; almost infinitely far down, the glaciers
make faint light at the mountain-foot.
The peak is hidden in that cloud of stars. . . . Ah, it's not here,
What I was hoping. My knife was a fool and could only thread
the meat of the breast, missed this unlucky
Point it was sent to find . . . spirit, soul . . . *me* apparently . . .
the dead body's lost dog,
Howls in the silence. Will it starve at last? Or is it perhaps . . .
Immortal? . . . that would be a sick thing.
                                        I thought this height
had no human stain: but someone . . . The star-vapor
Drifts off and clears him. Another of death's white lies I suppose.
(*A figure becomes visible, standing on a rock a little higher*
than Gudrun) Red stars in his hands and feet, a blood-comet
Cut in his side. He is berserk-naked, young and gray-haired, one
of the shieldless that burn young.
He seems to be praying to the peak, as our childish priests used to
pray to oak trees . . . and other handless Gods . . .(*ad-*
dressing the young man)

And get the same answer. What are you praying for, annihilation? If you find it, tell me.

THE YOUNG MAN Did you believe in me once, that you rub salt in my wound?

GUDRUN What? No. If you are the Roman God that my slave described to me: how bleak your heaven is.

THE YOUNG MAN I was deceived; and love is a fire; I cannot end until my banked longing burns itself out.

SINGERS (*coming up from below, and going about the rock the young man stands on*)

. . . No angel flew
To unwind us when the flesh died,
No light no song for a guide,
I cannot guess how we knew
The way up to you.
I died in childbirth crying to you.
I died of old age in your faith.
I of a crueller death.
All my life was my flying to you.
We on the spear and sword,
Fighting for Christian Rome.
The running pestilence, Lord.
Open the enchanted home,
Open the glory of God.
Savior, I on the road
Running to your wars.
Open the joy, break back the stars.
Because my faith
Haughtily trampled on death.
The wings, the victory, the shrill
Song on the height.
The violent blossoming, the life the light
After the mortal strife.
He will tell us the gate is open: be still.
The star-gates. Endless life.

THE YOUNG MAN When I could not bear it . . . Betrayed children, I was deceived before I deceived you. I have stood here long

And seen my betrayed come to my feet, and bitterly seen the soul
    more mortal than flesh, and found
No blood to weep for it. When the earlier dead came crying to
    me, my first martyrs, from jails and gibbets,
Who had endured all evil for my sake, led by my words to
    misery, my promises to death by torture:
And even my own dear friends whom I had touched with my
    hands . . . when I could not bear it,
I lied and said "Life is here. Wait but a little, my Father is pre-
    paring your places behind the stars."
They waited in hope, soon they were nothing. They faded and
    wasted and were gone away, but not into joy.
I will not lie to you. You are dead; your lives are finished; there
    is nothing more. The spirit is a distant echo
From the other mountain, dying in a moment. Or a blown fading
    smoke of burnt grass. My dream was a fool.
My promises were a love-drunken madness. Alas that you are too
    weary shadows to cry out and curse me
And drown my long self-torment in your seas of bitterness. If
    Judas for a single betrayal hanged himself,
What for me, that betrayed the world?
SINGERS Our Saviour says
Wait, for the star-gates move;
While I gaze on his face,
While I faint on his love.
THE YOUNG MAN You have not understood me. I would not de-
    ceive any soul
Again forever. While I lived I saw my people beaten and de-
    prived, therefore I imagined a world
Beyond life, out of time, righteousness triumphing. I saw it so
    clearly, towers of light, domes of music,
God's love the wings and the flame. But sometimes I thought my
    vision was only a symbol of much greater realities.
Thus passionately I raised myself up to be mocked and pitied.
    . . . There is nothing good after death.
As to God: I know not whether he is good. I know not whether
    he exists. I have stood and gazed at the star-
Swarming cloud. . . . Out of huge delusion

My truth is born. It has nothing to do with the dead; I loved the
living and taught them to love each other.

Even now on earth my love makes war upon death and misery,
not like a sword, like a young seed,

And not men's souls, but far down the terrible fertile future their
children, changed and saved by love,

May build the beauty of an earthly heaven on all our dead an-
guishes, and living inherit it.

SINGERS Do you hear? He says that we inherit
Heaven on the instant and the roofs are tiled
With the flame-wings, the high-singing angels, the rose-color
wings, the wild
Fire-color wings, the violet-fire feathers and spirit over spirit
For tile over tile overlapping from the ridges downward . . .

OTHER SINGERS (*hoarse voices; a heavier tune*)
The arrow is like air but the held spear enters.
The pike is a pearl, pushes its path.
Ha! says the sword, ham-strings the horses.
The hooking halberd, the Hun from the saddle-ridge,
Ha! says the halberd . . . (*more quietly*) the fear, the pain.
The knees that sag while the blood runs out, the dizzy sickness,
The choking struggle, the horror of death . . .

GUDRUN Another variety of dreamers. They pass like pulses from
a cut artery. I saw Hoegni in the press
Furiously stabbing imaginary princes; and Blada leading his
lonely fancy of ten thousand horse,
His private death-dream.

OTHER SINGERS Claw, green cat,
Roll it home to Roua.
Cat of the standard!
You have felt the claws, Goth?
The teeth excel them.
(*quietly*) Oh, the terror.
The darkness of wounds, the fallen riders, the red agonies.

OTHER SINGERS Wolves for your hunger horse-meat and Hun-
meat.
Weary not, West-wolves, worry to the bone.

(*quietly*) The horror, the hidden cowardice,
The stifling agonies.

GUDRUN What a wretched fisherman is death,
That lets his catch lie kicking in the nets of delusion like living
men. . . . A sudden silence has covered them.

THE YOUNG MAN The cloud that veiled it: Oh breaking, break-
ing. The stars like dust flee apart, perhaps for the face of
God . . .

*The height clears. It is the great cliff under the mountain-
peak, precipitous, with a shallow concavity and over-balance,
like the face of a breaking wave. A vast form, in appearance
youthful and human, beautiful and powerful, is bound
against the rock, hanging on heavy chains from the wrists,
and bleeding from wounds. The figure resembles the Pro-
metheus painted on the wall of the ruined house where Attila
feasted; but this is more beautiful, and not a painting.*

THE YOUNG MAN I hoped. I am finally betrayed and perfectly
fooled to the end. It is only my dream of my own death
Hanged on the sky. Blind stars, return.

SINGERS Oh stars return, Oh mind
Remember the earth or be suddenly blind.
I see the pride of an eagle nailed up alive.
A leopard pierced with spears that transfix the stone.
Enormous helpless shoulder-storms of an eagle nailed there: yet
strive, wings, strive.
Sharp strength come down, be free. Oh lonely virtue, Oh alone
Beauty and power. Bright snake nailed on the stone.

GUDRUN Leopard, serpent, eagle? Wounded power? Oh, but
lovelier. The hanged God that my childish blood loves.
This is my barbarous blood from the north, from the sick swamps
and the heavy forest, white fogs and frosts,
My vicious blood . . . was it spilt? . . . my vicious love flies
to him like sighing fire like the tides of the sea.
I know not moon nor stars, how low you lie, lynx, I have come
to my love, I have found him. Here is the dignity
We adored in rocks and waters, the reticent self-contained self-
watchful passion of the gray rock

The greatness of high rivers going west; here is the comeliness
    I knew in heroes, the high beauty of the helmets,
The praise of Sigurd; here is the pain in myself and all. Here is
    reality,
All that my living eyes ever saw was phantom
Shadows of this. Myself too: I was nothing but only a sigh
    toward him. For this I killed my brothers,
For this I let Sigurd be killed: I never knew myself
Before this moment: I know that I consented in Sigurd's death.
    Layer after layer I am stripped
Of falsehood under falsehood and fear under fear, and know my
    naked center in the flame of reality,
The sun of this beauty, the song of burning. To this I am will-
    ingly sacrificed, I have come to my love, I have found him,
I have aped him and shared his life, like the white horses the
    Swedes hang up to Odin, from the porch lintels
Of pillared Upsala.
THE YOUNG MAN   He is not a phantom. The stubborn violent
    rays and strain of reality
Glow from those tortured limbs, I know them, I have found
    what I was all my life seeking, and all my death,
The power my life-delusion called Father, and never feared him
    and never . . . hated him . . . before this time.
I wish the waters of Palestine had been white fire, devouring the
    flesh with the spirit before I sought to him.
I wish my mother had been slain with a sword before she con-
    ceived me, or shame had killed her when the unknown seed
Knocked at the womb. He is terribly beautiful.
He is like a great flower of fire on a mountain in the night of
    victory, he is like a great star that fills all the night,
He is like the music and harmony of all the stars if all their shin-
    ing were harp-music. He has no righteousness,
No mercy, no love.
SINGERS   Peace, and the vast
Expanse of the soaring storms, the peace of the eagle
Forever circling
Perfectly forever alone, no prey and no mate,
What peace but pain?

His eyes are put out, he has fountains of blood for eyes,
He endures the anguish.
But if he had eyes there is nothing for him to see
But his own blood falling,
He is all that exists. . . .

GUDRUN   It is bitter in me
That I fled out of life, while I see the beauty of power over-
    coming pain, and the earnest eyes.
I think that Gunnar was born a fool, and now I know Carling.
    Hoegni had a glimmer of the beauty, he burned
A little pure, if pure killer. And Brynhild beautifully did evil
    and died. Sigurd . . . a noise
Flung up by fortune. I have come to my love, if only in a par-
    tial vision: his greater part
No poet can know.

THE YOUNG MAN   The fire on the mountain
Lights all my depth: I see the ridiculous delusion that gave me
    power and the ways that led up to Golgotha,
The delusion dies, the power survives it. I am not conquered. I
    set myself up against you, Oh merciless
God not my father. On earth an old wave of time is fallen and
    a new one draws
From the trough to tower higher: my spirit is the light in it,
    I am remembered, this age is mine.
I have bought it with the stubborn faith of my people, and my
    own
Insane idealism, the wine of my wounds, the tension of intolerable
    hope. Let me remembered
Be a new spirit of mercy in the new age, a new equality between
    men, that each
Unblinded behold the beauty of all others: thence happiness and
    peace . . . my longing chokes me. . . . When men are
    happy
Let them cut the crosses out of the churches, no man remem-
    ber me.

GUDRUN   He is beautiful, this easterner, but like a child
Desiring what men despise. Happiness? For all the living? How
    shamefacedly we should have to kill it

As if it were evil. Hoegni'd run white and stabbing through the
world, and well stabbed, Hoegni. I can't think why.

SINGERS (*Scattered multitude, seen moving among the rocks at
the Hanged God's feet, or like meteors across the sky at his
knees*)
If once I could see the poplars again that ring the cistern
Whiten their leaves
I could bear to have died.
They are fed with sun and the flashing water, from the high
thunder-cloud
Falls a stray wind
To the mountain foot.
—What enemy has maimed you and nothing perfect?
The cloud on the mountain is black, on the plain a small golden
dust-cloud
Where men race horses;
The cool round cistern's
Blue eye glitters, the pale poplars for eyelashes; dark
Rises the mountain
To the roaring cloud.
—Oh wounds of God, storm of stars, broken wings.
At Cartagena on the broken sea-wall spikes of white grass
Used to be shuddering,
You saw blue water
Through the spikes of dry grass, Oh why must I weep for those
Pale rays wavering
In sea-cloud wind?
—I would the enemy that wounded him had killed him.
The Christmas fir-trees crack with burdens of snow, how low
Low you lie, lynx,
The torn throat's flow
Is red but the wolves glitter with frost and snow, their spears
Red in a row
Around the red pool.
—He is beautiful, I fear his wounds are not mortal.
Ah Sigurd that I was mourning Adonis the mistletoe lance,
Hoegni nail hard
The hero's hands

To the eagle wings, make him more than a man, die for me Christ,
Thammuz to death,
Dermot go down.
What boar's tusk opened God's flank; what enemy has bound
his wrists,
Nailed him on the eagle
Wave of the mountain?
Die, dear . . . dear . . . quietly like sleeping, Carling, drink
sleep.
Oh how you shudder.
Again? Again?
The cool black water Oh red lips of fever, burning harsh lips,
Dear, die. Oh dreadful
Agony of God can you never die?
The mountain storm-cloud of stars, mounded and towering, mul-
titude, thunder-cloud
Dark with the blinding arrogance of light: what a black
Lightning from that!
—I say have you learned from the Roman Christ to be meek and
hang there,
For love of humanity perhaps!
Hanged like a beast's hide?
Bound captive who looks like power, like the eagle of battles,
when you shudder in the agony huge bands of strength
Move in the arms to the groove of the breast as if you might
conquer many but an enemy has conquered you. By craft
then?
Or like the young Jew
For you loved your enemy perhaps!
—Why do you call him impure, there is no impurity in fire there's
pain,
Me Attila and Christ defiled in vain.
The grave slow sunset bleeding at the end of enormous lands,
Always to bleed,
Never go down,
I would I had worn my life with a little valor while I lived
And the earnest beauty of things
Was always reproaching me.

—O sola beatitudo,
Lonely bleeding star
So high, so high
Over the multitudes.
I believe because it is unbelievable, there is my victory.
—What is that rushing in the air,
That moaning on earth?
—Witches and Maries at the foot of the gallows
And over the post and the peak and the superscription in the
  furiously pouring
Rage of the stars
Riding Valkyries.
—Come up Grimalkin my long-nosed sister.—Is it you, Birdalow?
—Naked and greased
Swim in the storm.
—I am old and have flapping breasts.—Bind a birth-strangled man-
  child's
February bud
In the hollow between them.
—Oh hell's the horror.—*Hush!*—Hell's the horror.—Shut your
  mouth, woman!
Lord Satan wishes
That hell hushes.
—Blood fire in the mouths of eternal furnaces, Oh Oh no hope
  no help no end, save me Christ.
—No. You must be sacrificed.
—I'll hang with my lord then, my beautiful honey-love Satan.
  —Snow no. It's God.
Satan was burnt.—Ah!—but to nothing.
Gone, destroyed, nothing.
—Loathing?—Snow, nothing.
—Oh lucky prince.
—Do you hear the storm of the wind rattling the gibbet
Chains? The lynx has got out of chains, what reins
Will now bridle him?—The wind's idle hymn,
The girls on black horses, the chaste Valkyries.
—And who is to lead us in that day?
The gnomes of the chaste machines?—Not they.

—What, the scared rich?
—Snow: the sword.
—Into the ditch.
—Man has no nobler lord.
—Now the age points to the pit, all our vocation
Is to teach babes to jump.—Oh sterile
Process of Caesars, all the barren Caesars.
—Look at us, God, we are part of you: not defiled? not imbecile
Children sold for the seventh
Share in a toy, a motor or a music-box, push-button comforts,
     a paper world?
I would the enemy that wounded you had killed you.
I would the shores and the valleys were sheeted with fire and the
     mountain volcano's
Vomit on the plains, when the feet were burnt off we should
     fall on our hands and fire
Lap at the wrists and cut them and the faces fall in it. We are
     many, and strangely
Powerful, knowing metals, knowing drugs, we have counted
     the stars, we have conquered the mastery of wings, and
     there's not one of us
Worthy to live, pure enough, proud enough.—So they say.
What, they think life is great?
I have had my day:
Life is too little to love, too little to hate.
Temperately share the house
With beetle and louse.—At the head of the beautiful glen
The mountain is crowned with dawn and his purple shoul-
     ders . . .
There are fox-gloves here, at the foot
How the sea flames.
—The sun will come through it in a moment,
Saying "I desire to die, let me die.
I hate myself, I writhe from myself in fountains of fire
And fall back frustrate, something escapes, wastes into light,
     waste is my want,
I pour my body on the eyeless night
And a few planets the rain

Of golden pain,
But knowing that annihilation's no promise, but on and on
New flesh catches old bone . . ."
INHUMAN VOICES I am the whale's way. What, for *their* woes?
I am the old
Dragon of blue water.
—Rock and the snow, Aconcagua, Gosainthan, Kinchinjunga, all
High-builded cloud-knives,
Heads of the earth, here is our sky-head.
—Blazing I gaze, I am the sun, never to find
Purpose nor worth: why do I shine? Why shall I die? I am the
sun.
—Fire-swarm of wheeling vultures of light, torch-multitude
Turning in the emptiness,
Hungry for darkness, I am the galaxy.—Darkness for all-heal?
I am an old
Out-lier, a cloud of
Coal-black vultures, universe of slag, caught in the fork. I have
eaten darkness.—I am the shoreless
Ocean of stars, crazy to shed
My desire from me.—I am power,
Pushing so close against the fountain that I can hardly
Distinguish myself from him; I am the doer, pale with desire,
never to know
What is my want, where is the end; stone-eyed and lightning-
Handed and sleepless.
VOICES What horse will you ride, Katta?—The crazy black.
I was broken yesterday.
Life was an idiot dreaming, death's his kept ape.
—Sir, we guessed that last August in Macedonia,
The night we turned atheist by a dry-weed campfire
Drinking bitterness and spitting vinegar.—Hush it thunders.
THE HANGED GOD Pain and their endless cries. How they cry to
me: but they are I: let them ask themselves.
I am they, and there is nothing beside. I am alone and time passes,
time also is in me, the long
Beat of this unquiet heart, the quick drip of this blood, the whirl
and returning waves of these stars,

The course of this thought.

My particles have companions and happy fulfilments, each star has stars to answer him and hungry night

To take his shining, and turn it again and make it a star; each beast has food to find and his mating,

And the hostile and helpful world; each atom has related atoms, and hungry emptiness around him to take

His little shining cry and cry it back; but I am all, the emptiness and all, the shining and the night.

All alone, I alone.

If I were quiet and emptied myself of pain, breaking these bonds,

Healing these wounds: without strain there is nothing. Without pressure, without conditions, without pain,

Is peace; that's nothing, not-being; the pure night, the perfect freedom, the black crystal. I have chosen

Being; therefore wounds, bonds, limits and pain; the crowded mind and the anguished nerves, experience and ecstasy.

Whatever electron or atom or flesh or star or universe cries to me,

Or endures in shut silence: it is my cry, my silence; I am the nerve, I am the agony,

I am the endurance. I torture myself

To discover myself; trying with a little or extreme experiment each nerve and fibril, all forms

Of being, of life, of cold substance; all motions and netted complications of event,

All poisons of desire, love, hatred, joy, partial peace, partial vision. Discovery is deep and endless,

Each moment of being is new: therefore I still refrain my burning thirst from the crystal-black

Water of an end.

My lips crack with their longing for it,

My wounds are fires, the white bones glitter in my iron-eaten wrists, blood slowly falls, blinding white bands

Of fire flow through the strained shoulder-blades, so that I groan for an enemy to kill: there is none: I alone.

Stars are condensed from cloud and flame as it were immortally, and faint and have ceased, and their slag finds

After enormous ages the mother cloud; self-regenerating universes
    all but eternally
Shine, tire, and die; new stars fling out new planets, strange
    growths appear on them, new-formed little lamps of flick-
    ering
Flesh for the same flame.
                . . . On earth rise and fall the ages
    of man, going higher for a time; this age will give them
Wings, their old dream, and unexampled extensions of mind; and
    slowly break itself bloodily; one later
Will give them to visit their neighbor planets and colonize the
    evening star; their colonies die there; the waves
Of human dominion dwindle down their long twilight; another
    nature of life will dominate the earth,
Feathered birds, drawing in their turn the planetary
Consciousness up to bright painful points, and accuse me of in-
    flicting what I endure. These also pass,
And new things are; and the shining pain. . . .
                     Every discovery
    is a broken shield, a new knife of consciousness
Whetted for its own hurt; pain rises like a red river: but also
    the heroic beauty of being,
That all experience builds higher, the stones are the warring
    torches, towers on the flood. I have not chosen
To endure eternally; I know not that I shall choose to cease; I
    have long strength and can bear much.
I have also my peace; it is in this mountain. I am this mountain
    that I am hanged on, and I am the flesh
That suffers on it, I am tortured against the summit of my own
    peace and hanged on the face of quietness.
I am also the outer nothing and the wandering infinite night.
    These are my mercy and my goodness, these
My peace. Without the pain, no knowledge of peace, nothing.
    Without the peace,
No value in the pain. I have long strength.
SINGERS The long river
Dreams in the sunset fire
Shuddering and shining.

—All the drops of his blood are torches.

I am one with him, I will share his being.

—Alas to me the deep wells of peace are a dearer water.

GUDRUN   I will enter the cloud of stars, I will eat the whole serpent again.

SINGERS   His beauty redeems his acts, it is good for God

Not to be quiet, but for men not to live long.

—Forever if I could: his intelligencer

Spying the wild loveliness.

—But after I have rested as it were a moment

Against the deep wells, and then

I am willing to eat the whole serpent again . . .

The river down the long darkness

Shining writhes like a fire,

The stars return.

THE CRUEL FALCON

Contemplation would make a good life, keep it strict, only
The eyes of a desert skull drinking the sun,
Too intense for flesh, lonely
Exultations of white bone;
Pure action would make a good life, let it be sharp-
Set between the throat and the knife.
A man who knows death by heart
Is the man for that life.
In pleasant peace and security
How suddenly the soul in a man begins to die.
He shall look up above the stalled oxen
Envying the cruel falcon,
And dig under the straw for a stone
To bruise himself on.

ROCK AND HAWK

Here is a symbol in which
Many high tragic thoughts
Watch their own eyes.

This gray rock, standing tall
On the headland, where the seawind
Lets no tree grow,

Earthquake-proved, and signatured
By ages of storms: on its peak
A falcon has perched.

I think, here is your emblem
To hang in the future sky;
Not the cross, not the hive,

But this; bright power, dark peace;
Fierce consciousness joined with final
Disinterestedness;

Life with calm death; the falcon's
Realist eyes and act
Married to the massive

Mysticism of stone,
Which failure cannot cast down
Nor success make proud.

Spirits and illusions have died,
The naked mind lives
In the beauty of inanimate things.

Flowers wither, grass fades, trees wilt,
The forest is burnt;
The rock is not burnt.

The deer starve, the winter birds
Die on their twigs and lie
In the blue dawns in the snow.

Men suffer want and become
Curiously ignoble; as prosperity
Made them curiously vile.

But look how noble the world is,
The lonely-flowing waters, the secret-
Keeping stones, the flowing sky.

REARMAMENT

These grand and fatal movements toward death: the grandeur
    of the mass
Makes pity a fool, the tearing pity
For the atoms of the mass, the persons, the victims, makes it
    seem monstrous
To admire the tragic beauty they build.
It is beautiful as a river flowing or a slowly gathering
Glacier on a high mountain rock-face,
Bound to plow down a forest, or as frost in November,
The gold and flaming death-dance for leaves,
Or a girl in the night of her spent maidenhood, bleeding and
    kissing.
I would burn my right hand in a slow fire
To change the future . . . I should do foolishly. The beauty
    of modern
Man is not in the persons but in the
Disastrous rhythm, the heavy and mobile masses, the dance of the
Dream-led masses down the dark mountain.

WHAT ARE CITIES FOR?

The earth has covered Sicilian Syracuse, there asphodel grows,
As golden-rod will over New York.
What tragic labors, passions, oppressions, cruelties and courage
Reared the great city. Nothing remains
But stones and a memory haunting the fields of returning as-
phodel.
You have seen through the trick to the beauty;
If we all saw through it, the trick would hardly entice us and
the earth
Be the poorer by many beautiful agonies.

AVE CAESAR

No bitterness: our ancestors did it.
They were only ignorant and hopeful, they wanted freedom but
　　wealth too.
Their children will learn to hope for a Caesar.
Or rather—for we are not aquiline Romans but soft mixed
　　colonists—
Some kindly Sicilian tyrant who'll keep
Poverty and Carthage off until the Romans arrive.
We are easy to manage, a gregarious people,
Full of sentiment, clever at mechanics, and we love our luxuries.

SHINE, REPUBLIC

The quality of these trees, green height; of the sky, shining, of
water, a clear flow; of the rock, hardness
And reticence: each is noble in its quality. The love of freedom
has been the quality of Western man.

There is a stubborn torch that flames from Marathon to Concord,
its dangerous beauty binding three ages
Into one time; the waves of barbarism and civilization have
eclipsed but have never quenched it.

For the Greeks the love of beauty, for Rome of ruling; for the
present age the passionate love of discovery;
But in one noble passion we are one; and Washington, Luther,
Tacitus, Aeschylus, one kind of man.

And you, America, that passion made you. You were not born
to prosperity, you were born to love freedom.
You did not say "en masse," you said "independence." But we
cannot have all the luxuries and freedom also.

Freedom is poor and laborious; that torch is not safe but hun-
gry, and often requires blood for its fuel.
You will tame it against it burn too clearly, you will hood it
like a kept hawk, you will perch it on the wrist of Caesar.

But keep the tradition, conserve the forms, the observances, keep
the spot sore. Be great, carve deep your heel-marks.
The states of the next age will no doubt remember you, and edge
their love of freedom with contempt of luxury.

THE TRAP

I am not well civilized, really alien here: trust me not.
I can understand the guns and the airplanes,
The other conveniences leave me cold.

"We must adjust our economics to the new abundance . . ."
Of what? Toys: motors, music-boxes,
Paper, fine clothes, leisure, diversion.

I honestly believe (but really an alien here: trust me not)
Blind war, compared to this kind of life,
Has nobility, famine has dignity.

Be happy, adjust your economics to the new abundance;
One is neither saint nor devil, to wish
The intolerable nobler alternative.

PRAISE LIFE

This country least, but every inhabited country
Is clotted with human anguish.
Remember that at your feasts.

And this is no new thing but from time out of mind,
No transient thing, but exactly
Conterminous with human life.

Praise life, it deserves praise, but the praise of life
That forgets the pain is a pebble
Rattled in a dry gourd.

Like mourning women veiled to the feet
Tall slender rainstorms walk slowly against gray cloud along the
far verge.
The ocean is green where the river empties,
Dull gray between the points of the headlands, purple where
the women walk.
What do they want? Whom are they mourning?
What hero's dust in the urn between the two hands hidden in
the veil?
Titaness after Titaness proudly
Bearing her tender magnificent sorrow at her heart, the lost
battle's beauty.

GRAY WEATHER

It is true that, older than man and ages to outlast him, the Pacific surf
    surf
Still cheerfully pounds the worn granite drum;
But there's no storm; and the birds are still, no song; no kind of
    excess;
Nothing that shines, nothing is dark;
There is neither joy nor grief nor a person, the sun's tooth
    sheathed in cloud,
And life has no more desires than a stone.
The stormy conditions of time and change are all abrogated, the
    essential
Violences of survival, pleasure,
Love, wrath and pain, and the curious desire of knowing, all per-
    fectly suspended.
In the cloudy light, in the timeless quietness,
One explores deeper than the nerves or heart of nature, the womb
    or soul,
To the bone, the careless white bone, the excellence.

LOVE THE WILD SWAN

"I hate my verses, every line, every word.
Oh pale and brittle pencils ever to try
One grass-blade's curve, or the throat of one bird
That clings to twig, ruffled against white sky.
Oh cracked and twilight mirrors ever to catch
One color, one glinting flash, of the splendor of things.
Unlucky hunter, Oh bullets of wax,
The lion beauty, the wild-swan wings, the storm of the wings."
—This wild swan of a world is no hunter's game.
Better bullets than yours would miss the white breast,
Better mirrors than yours would crack in the flame.
Does it matter whether you hate your . . . self? At least
Love your eyes that can see, your mind that can
Hear the music, the thunder of the wings. Love the wild swan.

SIGNPOST

Civilized, crying how to be human again: this will tell you how.
Turn outward, love things, not men, turn right away from humanity,
Let that doll lie. Consider if you like how the lilies grow,
Lean on the silent rock until you feel its divinity
Make your veins cold, look at the silent stars, let your eyes
Climb the great ladder out of the pit of yourself and man.
Things are so beautiful, your love will follow your eyes;
Things are the God, you will love God, and not in vain,
For what we love, we grow to it, we share its nature. At length
You will look back along the stars' rays and see that even
The poor doll humanity has a place under heaven.
Its qualities repair their mosaic around you, the chips of strength
And sickness; but now you are free, even to become human,
But born of the rock and the air, not of a woman.

WHERE I?

This woman cannot live more than one year.
Her growing death is hidden in a hopeless place,
Her death is like a child growing in her,
And she knows it, you see it shine in her face.
She looks at her own hands and thinks "In a year
These will be burnt like rags in the crematory.
I shall not feel it. Where I? Where I? Not anywhere."
It is strange, it gives to her face a kind of glory.
Her mind used to be lazy and heavy her face,
Now she talks all in haste, looks young and lean
And eager, her eyes glitter with eagerness,
As if she were newly born and had never seen
The beauty of things, the terror, pain, joy, the song.
—Or is it better to live at ease, dully and long?

RETURN

A little too abstract, a little too wise,
It is time for us to kiss the earth again,
It is time to let the leaves rain from the skies,
Let the rich life run to the roots again.
I will go down to the lovely Sur Rivers
And dip my arms in them up to the shoulders.
I will find my accounting where the alder leaf quivers
In the ocean wind over the river boulders.
I will touch things and things and no more thoughts,
That breed like mouthless May-flies darkening the sky,
The insect clouds that blind our passionate hawks
So that they cannot strike, hardly can fly.
Things are the hawk's food and noble is the mountain, Oh noble
Pico Blanco, steep sea-wave of marble.

FLIGHT OF SWANS

One who sees giant Orion, the torches of winter midnight,
Enormously walking above the ocean in the west of heaven;
And watches the track of this age of time at its peak of flight
Waver like a spent rocket, wavering toward new discoveries,
Mortal examinations of darkness, soundings of depth;
And watches the long coast mountain vibrate from bronze to
   green,
Bronze to green, year after year, and all the streams
Dry and flooded, dry and flooded, in the racing seasons;
And knows that exactly this and not another is the world,
The ideal is phantoms for bait, the spirit is a flicker on a grave;—
May serve, with a certain detachment, the fugitive human race,
Or his own people, or his own household; but hardly himself;
And will not wind himself into hopes nor sicken with despairs.
He has found the peace and adored the God; he handles in
   autumn
The germs of far-future spring.
                        Sad sons of the stormy fall,
No escape, you have to inflict and endure; surely it is time for
   you
To learn to touch the diamond within to the diamond outside,
Thinning your humanity a little between the invulnerable dia-
   monds,
Knowing that your angry choices and hopes and terrors are in
   vain,
But life and death not in vain; and the world is like a flight of
   swans.

STEELHEAD

The sky was cold December blue with great tumbling clouds,
   and the little river
Ran full but clear. A bare-legged girl in a red jersey was wading
   in it, holding a five-tined
Hay-fork at her head's height; suddenly she darted it down like
   a heron's beak and panting hard
Leaned on the shaft, looking down passionately, her gipsy-lean
   face, then stooped and dipping
One arm to the little breasts she drew up her catch, great ham-
   mered-silver steelhead with the tines through it
And the fingers of her left hand hooked in its gills, her slender
   body
Rocked with its writhing. She took it to the near bank
And was dropping it behind a log when someone said
Quietly "I guess I've got you, Vina." Who gasped and looked up
At a young horseman half hidden in the willow bushes,
She'd been too intent to notice him, and said "My God,
I thought it was the game-warden." "Worse," he said smiling.
   "This river's ours.
You can't get near it without crossing our fences.
Besides that you mustn't spear 'em, and . . . three, four, you
   little bitch,
That's the fifth fish." She answered with her gipsy face, "Take
   half o' them, honey. I loved the fun."
He looked up and down her taper legs, red with cold, and said
   fiercely, "Your fun.
To kill them and leave them rotting." "Honey, let me have one
   o' them," she answered,
"You take the rest." He shook his blond head. "You'll have to pay
   a terrible fine." She answered laughing,
"Don't worry: you wouldn't tell on me." He dismounted and
   tied the bridle to a bough, saying "Nobody would.
I know a lovely place deep in the willows, full of warm grass,
   safe as a house,

Where you can pay it." Her body seemed to grow narrower
    suddenly, both hands at her throat, and the cold thighs
Pressed close together while she stared at his face, it was beautiful,
    long heavy-lidded eyes like a girl's,
"I can't do that, honey . . . I," she said shivering, "your wife
    would kill me." He hardened his eyes and said
"Let that alone." "Oh," she answered; the little red hands came
    down from her breast and faintly
Reached toward him, her head lifting, he saw the artery on the
    lit side of her throat flutter like a bird
And said "You'll be sick with cold, Vina," flung off his coat
And folded her in it with his warmth in it and carried her
To that island in the willows.

                        He warmed her bruised feet in
    his hands;
She paid her fine for spearing fish, and another
For taking more than the legal limit, and would willingly
Have paid a third for trespassing; he sighed and said,
"You'll owe me that. I'm afraid somebody might come looking
    for me,
Or my colt break his bridle." She moaned like a dove, "Oh Oh
    Oh Oh,
You are beautiful, Hugh." They returned to the stream-bank.
    There,
While Vina put on her shoes—they were like a small boy's, all
    stubbed and shapeless—young Flodden strung the five fish
On a willow rod through the red gills and slung them
To his saddle-horn. He led the horse and walked with Vina,
    going part way home with her.

                      Toward the canyon sea-mouth
The water spread wide and shoal, fingering through many chan-
    nels down a broad flood-bed, and a mob of sea-gulls
Screamed at each other. Vina said, "That's a horrible thing."
    "What?" "What the birds do. They're worse than I am."
When Flodden returned alone he rode down and watched them.
    He saw that one of the thousand steelhead

Which irresistible nature herded up stream to the spawning-
  gravel in the mountain, the river headwaters,
Had wandered into a shallow finger of the current, and was
  forced over on his flank, sculling uneasily
In three inches of water: instantly a gaunt herring-gull hovered
  and dropped, to gouge the exposed
Eye with her beak; the great fish writhing, flopping over in his
  anguish, another gull's beak
Took the other eye. Their prey was then at their mercy, writh-
  ing blind, soon stranded, and the screaming mob
Covered him.

            Young Flodden rode into them and drove them
  up; he found the torn steelhead
Still slowly and ceremoniously striking the sand with his tail and
  a bloody eye-socket, under the
Pavilion of wings. They cast a cold shadow on the air, a fleeting
  sense of fortune's iniquities: why should
Hugh Flodden be young and happy, mounted on a good horse,
And have had another girl besides his dear wife, while others
  have to endure blindness and death,
Pain and disease, misery, old age, God knows what worse?

THE COAST-ROAD

A horseman high alone as an eagle on the spur of the mountain
over Mirmas Canyon draws rein, looks down
At the bridge-builders, men, trucks, the power-shovels, the teem-
ing end of the new coast-road at the mountain's base.
He sees the loops of the road go northward, headland beyond
headland, into gray mist over Fraser's Point,
He shakes his fist and makes the gesture of wringing a chicken's
neck, scowls and rides higher.

I too
Believe that the life of men who ride horses, herders of cattle on
the mountain pasture, plowers of remote
Rock-narrowed farms in poverty and freedom, is a good life. At
the far end of those loops of road
Is what will come and destroy it, a rich and vulgar and bewildered
civilization dying at the core,
A world that is feverishly preparing new wars, peculiarly vicious
ones, and heavier tyrannies, a strangely
Missionary world, road-builder, wind-rider, educator, printer and
picture-maker and broadcaster,
So eager, like an old drunken whore, pathetically eager to impose
the seduction of her fled charms
On all that through ignorance or isolation might have escaped
them. I hope the weathered horseman up yonder
Will die before he knows what this eager world will do to his
children. More tough-minded men
Can repulse an old whore, or cynically accept her drunken kind-
nesses for what they are worth,
But the innocent and credulous are soon corrupted.

Where is our
consolation? Beautiful beyond belief
The heights glimmer in the sliding cloud, the great bronze gorge-
cut sides of the mountain tower up invincibly,
Not the least hurt by this ribbon of road carved on their sea-foot.

GOING TO HORSE FLATS

Amazingly active a toothless old man
Hobbled beside me up the canyon, going to Horse Flats, he said,
To see to some hives of bees. It was clear that he lived alone and
craved companionship, yet he talked little
Until we came to a place where the gorge widened, and deer-
hunters had camped on a slip of sand
Beside the stream. They had left the usual rectangle of fired
stones and ashes, also some crumpled
Sheets of a recent newspaper with loud headlines. The old man
rushed at them
And spread them flat, held them his arm's length, squinting
through narrowed eyelids—poor trick old eyes learn, to
make
Lids act for lens. He read "Spain Battle. Rebels kill captives. City
bombed Reds kill hostages. Prepare
For war Stalin warns troops." He trembled and said, "Please read
me the little printing, I hardly ever
Get to hear news." He wrung his withered hands while I read;
it was strange in that nearly inhuman wilderness
To see an old hollow-cheeked hermit dancing to the world's
echoes. After I had read he said "That's enough.
They were proud and oppressed the poor and are punished for
it; but those that punish them are full of envy and hatred
And are punished for it; and again the others; and again the
others. It is so forever, there is no way out.
Only the crimes and cruelties grow worse perhaps." I said, "You
are too hopeless. There are ways out."
He licked his empty gums with his tongue, wiped his mouth and
said
"What ways?" I said "The Christian way: forgiveness, to forgive
your enemies,
Give good for evil." The old man threw down the paper and
said "How long ago did Christ live? Ah?

Have the people in Spain never heard about him? Or have the Russians,

Or Germans? Do you think I'm a fool?" "Well," I said to try him, "there's another way: extermination.

If the winning side will totally destroy its enemies, lives and thoughts, liquidate them, firing-squads

For the people and fire for the books and records: the feud will then be

Finished forever." He said justly, "*You're* the fool," picked up his bundle and hurried through the shadow-dapple

Of noon in the narrow canyon, his ragged coat-tails flapping like mad over the coonskin patch

In the seat of his trousers. I waited awhile, thinking he wished to be quit of company.

                               Sweet was the clear

Chatter of the stream now that our talk was hushed; the flitting water-ouzel returned to her stone;

A lovely snake, two delicate scarlet lines down the dark back, swam through the pool. The flood-battered

Trees by the stream are more noble than cathedral-columns.

                                           Why

do we invite the world's rancors and agonies

Into our minds though walking in a wilderness? Why did he want the news of the world? He could do nothing

To help nor hinder. Nor you nor I can . . . for the world. It is certain the world cannot be stopped nor saved.

It has changes to accomplish and must creep through agonies toward new discovery. It must, and it ought: the awful necessity

Is also the sacrificial duty. Man's world is a tragic music and is not played for man's happiness,

Its discords are not resolved but by other discords.

                                  But for each man

There is real solution, let him turn from himself and man to love God. He is out of the trap then. He will remain

Part of the music, but will hear it as the player hears it.
He will be superior to death and fortune, unmoved by success
 or failure. Pity can make him weep still,
Or pain convulse him, but not to the center, and he can conquer
 them. . . . But how could I impart this knowledge
To that old man?

    Or indeed to anyone? I know that all men
 instinctively rebel against it. But yet
They will come to it at last.
Then man will have come of age; he will still suffer and still die,
 but like a God, not a tortured animal.

Ed Stiles and old Tom Birnam went up to their cattle on the
    bare hills
Above Mal Paso; they'd ridden under the stars' white death,
    when they reached the ridge the huge tiger-lily
Of a certain cloud-lapped astonishing autumn sunrise opened all
    its petals. Ed Stiles pulled in his horse,
That flashy palamino he rode—cream-color, heavy white mane,
    white tail, his pride—and said
"Look, Tom. My God. Ain't that a beautiful sunrise?" Birnam
    drew down his mouth, set the hard old chin,
And whined: "Now, Ed: listen here: I haven't an ounce of
    poetry in all my body. It's cows we're after."
Ed laughed and followed; they began to sort the heifers out of
    the herd. One red little deer-legged creature
Rolled her wild eyes and ran away down the hill, the old man
    hard after her. She ran through a deep-cut gully,
And Birnam's piebald would have made a clean jump but the
    clay lip
Crumbled under his take-off, he slipped and
Spilled in the pit, flailed with four hooves and came out scram-
    bling. Stiles saw them vanish,
Then the pawing horse and the flapping stirrups. He rode and
    looked down and saw the old man in the gulley-bottom
Flat on his back, most grimly gazing up at the sky. He saw the
    earth banks, the sparse white grass,
The strong dark sea a thousand feet down below, red with reflec-
    tions of clouds. He said "My God,
Tom, are you hurt?" Who answered slowly, "No, Ed.
I'm only lying here thinking o' my four sons"—biting the words
Carefully between his lips—"big handsome men, at present lolling
    in bed in their . . . silk . . . pyjamas . . .
And why the devil I keep on working?" He stood up slowly and
    wiped the dirt from his cheek, groaned, spat,

And climbed up the clay bank. Stiles laughed: "Tom, I can't tell
  you: I guess you like to. By God I guess
You like the sunrises." The old man growled in his throat and
  said
"Catch me my horse."

This old man died last winter, having
  lived eighty-one years under open sky,
Concerned with cattle, horses and hunting, no thought nor emo-
  tion that all his ancestors since the ice-age
Could not have comprehended. I call that a good life; narrow,
  but vastly better than most
Men's lives, and beyond comparison more beautiful; the wind-
  struck music man's bones were moulded to be the harp for.

GIVE YOUR WISH LIGHT

By day and night dream about happy death,
Poor dog give your heart room, drag at the chain,
Breathe deep at dawn, wish it were the last breath,
Imagine the leaden ball planted in the brain,
The seed of that superb flower, dream the brave noose
That loves the neck so dearly it lets the life loose,
Dream the fierce joys of war where men like drunken
Jesuses fling the supreme gift at each other,
"Take blessedness, take it deep in your breast, brother . . ."
Dream on, dream all these joys, life might look shrunken
In lack of dreams. Give your wish light, give it room.
You know you will never untimely attempt the tomb.
—Go in to your bride by daylight before the crowd
As if sweet death were a whore? You are too proud.

THE PURSE-SEINE

Our sardine fishermen work at night in the dark of the moon;
   daylight or moonlight
They could not tell where to spread the net, unable to see the
   phosphorescence of the shoals of fish.
They work northward from Monterey, coasting Santa Cruz; off
   New Year's Point or off Pigeon Point
The look-out man will see some lakes of milk-color light on the
   sea's night-purple; he points, and the helmsman
Turns the dark prow, the motorboat circles the gleaming shoal
   and drifts out her seine-net. They close the circle
And purse the bottom of the net, then with great labor haul it in.

                              I cannot tell you
How beautiful the scene is, and a little terrible, then, when the
   crowded fish
Know they are caught, and wildly beat from one wall to the
   other of their closing destiny the phosphorescent
Water to a pool of flame, each beautiful slender body sheeted
   with flame, like a live rocket
A comet's tail wake of clear yellow flame; while outside the
   narrowing
Floats and cordage of the net great sea-lions come up to watch,
   sighing in the dark; the vast walls of night
Stand erect to the stars.

                     Lately I was looking from a night mountain-top
On a wide city, the colored splendor, galaxies of light: how could
   I help but recall the seine-net
Gathering the luminous fish? I cannot tell you how beautiful
   the city appeared, and a little terrible.
I thought, We have geared the machines and locked all together
   into interdependence; we have built the great cities; now
There is no escape. We have gathered vast populations incapable
   of free survival, insulated

From the strong earth, each person in himself helpless, on all
    dependent. The circle is closed, and the net
Is being hauled in. They hardly feel the cords drawing, yet they
    shine already. The inevitable mass-disasters
Will not come in our time nor in our children's, but we and our
    children
Must watch the net draw narrower, government take all powers
    —or revolution, and the new government
Take more than all, add to kept bodies kept souls—or anarchy,
    the mass-disasters.

                These things are Progress;
Do you marvel our verse is troubled or frowning, while it keeps
    its reason? Or it lets go, lets the mood flow
In the manner of the recent young men into mere hysteria, splin-
    tered gleams, crackled laughter. But they are quite wrong.
There is no reason for amazement: surely one always knew that
    cultures decay, and life's end is death.

THE GREAT SUNSET

A flight of six heavy-motored bombing-planes
Went over the beautiful inhuman ridges a straight course north-
   ward; the incident stuck itself in my memory
More than a flight of band-tail pigeons might have done
Because those wings of man and potential war seemed really in-
   trusive above the remote canyon.
They changed it; I cannot say they profaned it, but the memory
All day remained like a false note in familiar music, and suggested
   no doubt
The counter-fantasy that came to my eyes in the evening, on the
   ocean cliff.

            I came from the canyon twilight
Exactly at sunset to the open shore, and felt like a sudden exten-
   sion of consciousness the wild free light
And biting north-wind. The cloud-sky had lifted from the west-
   ern horizon and left a long yellow panel
Between the slate-edge ocean and the eyelid cloud; the smoky
   ball of the sun rolled on the sea-line
And formless bits of vapor flew across, but when the sun was
   down
The panel of clear sky brightened, the rags of moving cloud took
   memorable shapes, dark on the light,
Whether I was dreaming or not, they became spears and war-
   axes, horses and sabres, gaunt battle-elephants
With towered backs; they became catapults and siege-guns, high-
   tilted howitzers, long tractors, armored and turreted;
They became battleships and destroyers, and great fleets of war-
   planes . . . all the proud instruments
Of man imposing his will upon weaker men: they were like a
   Roman triumph, but themselves the captives,
A triumph in reverse: all the tools of victory
Whiffed away on the north-wind into a cloud like a conflagra-
   tion, swept from the earth, no man

From this time on to exploit nor subdue any other man. I thought,
  "What a pity our kindest dreams
Are complete liars," and turned from the glowing west toward
  the cold twilight. "To be truth-bound, the neutral
Detested by all the dreaming factions, is my errand here."

The proletariat for your Messiah, the poor and many are to
seize power and make the world new.
They cannot even conduct a strike without cunning leaders: if
they make a revolution their leaders
Must take the power. The first duty of men in power: to defend
their power. What men defend
To-day they will love to-morrow; it becomes theirs, their prop-
erty. Lenin has served the revolution,
Stalin presently begins to betray it. Why? For the sake of power,
the Party's power, the state's
Power, armed power, Stalin's power, Caesarean power.

                                                          This is
        not quite a new world.
The old shepherd has been known before; great and progressive
empires have flourished before; powerful bureaucracies
Apportioned food and labor and amusement; men have been
massed and moulded, spies have gone here and there,
The old shepherd Caesar his vicious collies, watching the flock.
Inevitable? Perhaps, but not new.
The ages like blind horses turning a mill tread their own hoof-
marks. Whose corn's ground in that mill?

THEBAID

How many turn back toward dreams and magic, how many
    children
Run home to Mother Church, Father State,
To find in their arms the delicious warmth and folding of souls.
The age weakens and settles home toward old ways.
An age of renascent faith: Christ said, Marx wrote, Hitler says,
And though it seems absurd we believe.
Sad children, yes. It is lonely to be adult, you need a father.
With a little practice you'll believe anything.

Faith returns, beautiful, terrible, ridiculous,
And men are willing to die and kill for their faith.
Soon come the wars of religion; centuries have passed
Since the air so trembled with intense faith and hatred.
Soon, perhaps, whoever wants to live harmlessly
Must find a cave in the mountain or build a cell
Of the red desert rock under dry junipers,
And avoid men, live with more kindly wolves
And luckier ravens, waiting for the end of the age.

Hermit from stone cell
Gazing with great stunned eyes,
What extravagant miracle
Has amazed them with light,
What visions, what crazy glory, what wings?
—I see the sun set and rise
And the beautiful desert sand
And the stars at night,
The incredible magnificence of things.
I the last living man
That sees the real earth and skies,
Actual life and real death.
The others are all prophets and believers
Delirious with fevers of faith.

THE ANSWER

Then what is the answer?—Not to be deluded by dreams.
To know that great civilizations have broken down into violence,
and their tyrants come, many times before.
When open violence appears, to avoid it with honor or choose
the least ugly faction; these evils are essential.
To keep one's own integrity, be merciful and uncorrupted and
not wish for evil; and not be duped
By dreams of universal justice or happiness. These dreams will
not be fulfilled.
To know this, and know that however ugly the parts appear the
whole remains beautiful. A severed hand
Is an ugly thing, and man dissevered from the earth and stars
and his history . . . for contemplation or in fact . . .
Often appears atrociously ugly. Integrity is wholeness, the great-
est beauty is
Organic wholeness, the wholeness of life and things, the divine
beauty of the universe. Love that, not man
Apart from that, or else you will share man's pitiful confusions,
or drown in despair when his days darken.

Staggering homeward between the stream and the trees the un-
    happy drunkard
Babbles a woeful song and babbles
The end of the world, the moon's like fired Troy in a flying
    cloud, the storm
Rises again, the stream's in flood.
The moon's like the sack of Carthage, the Bastile's broken, ped-
    lars and empires
Still deal in luxury, men sleep in prison.
Old Saturn thinks it was better in his grandsire's time but that's
    from the brittle
Arteries, it neither betters nor worsens.
(Nobody knows my love the falcon.)
It has always bristled with phantoms, always factitious, mildly
    absurd;
The organism, with no precipitous
Degeneration, slight imperceptible discounts of sense and faculty,
Adapts itself to the culture-medium.
(Nobody crawls to the test-tube rim,
Nobody knows my love the falcon.)
The star's on the mountain, the stream snoring in flood; the brain-
    lit drunkard
Crosses midnight and stammers to bed.
The inhuman nobility of things, the ecstatic beauty, the inveter-
    ate steadfastness
Uphold the four posts of the bed.
(Nobody knows my love the falcon.)

HOPE IS NOT FOR THE WISE

Hope is not for the wise, fear is for fools;
Change and the world, we think, are racing to a fall,
Open-eyed and helpless, in every newscast that is the news:
The time's events would seem mere chaos but all
Drift the one deadly direction. But this is only
The August thunder of the age, not the November.
Wise men hope nothing, the wise are naturally lonely
And think November as good as April, the wise remember
That Caesar and even final Augustulus had heirs,
And men lived on; rich unplanned life on earth
After the foreign wars and the civil wars, the border wars
And the barbarians: music and religion, honor and mirth
Renewed life's lost enchantments. But if life even
Had perished utterly, Oh perfect loveliness of earth and heaven.

NOVA

That Nova was a moderate star like our good sun; it stored no
    doubt a little more than it spent
Of heat and energy until the increasing tension came to the
    trigger-point
Of a new chemistry; then what was already flaming found a new
    manner of flaming ten-thousandfold
More brightly for a brief time; what was a pin-point fleck on a
    sensitive plate at the great telescope's
Eye-piece now shouts down the steep night to the naked eye,
    a nine-day super-star.

                    It is likely our moderate
Father the sun will some time put off his nature for a similar
    glory. The earth would share it; these tall
Green trees would become a moment's torches and vanish, the
    oceans would explode into invisible steam,
The ships and the great whales fall through them like flaming
    meteors into the emptied abysm, the six mile
Hollows of the Pacific sea-bed might smoke for a moment. Then
    the earth would be like the pale proud moon,
Nothing but vitrified sand and rock would be left on earth. This
    is a probable death-passion
For the sun's planets; we have no knowledge to assure us it may
    not happen at any moment of time.

Meanwhile the sun shines wisely and warm, trees flutter green
    in the wind, girls take their clothes off
To bathe in the cold ocean or to hunt love; they stand laughing
    in the white foam, they have beautiful
Shoulders and thighs, they are beautiful animals, all life is beau-
    tiful. We cannot be sure of life for one moment;
We can, by force and self-discipline, by many refusals and a few
    assertions, in the teeth of fortune assure ourselves

Freedom and integrity in life or integrity in death. And we know
that the enormous invulnerable beauty of things
Is the face of God, to live gladly in its presence, and die without
grief or fear knowing it survives us.

Farther up the gorge the sea's voice fainted and ceased.
We heard a new noise far away ahead of us, vague and metallic,
  it might have been some unpleasant bird's voice
Bedded in a matrix of long silences. At length we came to a little
  cabin lost in the redwoods,
An old man sat on a bench before the doorway filing a cross-cut
  saw; sometimes he slept,
Sometimes he filed. Two or three horses in the corral by the
  streamside lifted their heads
To watch us pass, but the old man did not.

                                    In the afternoon we
  returned the same way,
And had the picture in our minds of magnificent regions of space
  and mountain not seen before. (This was
The first time that we visited Pigeon Gap, whence you look
  down behind the great shouldering pyramid-
Edges of Pico Blanco through eagle-gulfs of air to a forest basin
Where two-hundred-foot redwoods look like the pile on a Turk-
  ish carpet.) With such extensions of the idol-
Worshipping mind we came down the streamside. The old man
  was still at his post by the cabin doorway, but now
Stood up and stared, said angrily "Where are you camping?"
  I said "We're not camping, we're going home." He said
From his flushed heavy face, "That's the way fires get started.
  Did you come at night?" "We passed you this morning.
You were half asleep, filing a saw." "I'll kill anybody that starts
  a fire here . . ." his voice quavered
Into bewilderment . . . "I didn't see you. Kind of feeble I guess.
My temperature's a hundred and two every afternoon." "Why,
  what's the matter?" He removed his hat
And rather proudly showed us a deep healed trench in the bald
  skull. "My horse fell at the ford,

I must 'a' cracked my head on a rock. Well, sir, I can't remember
   anything till next morning.
I woke in bed the pillow was soaked with blood, the horse was
   in the corral and had had his hay,"—
Singing the words as if he had told the story a hundred times.
   To whom? To himself, probably,—
"The saddle was on the rack and the bridle on the right nail.
   What do you think of *that* now?" He passed
His hand on his bewildered forehead and said, "Unless an angel
   or something came down and did it.
A basin of blood and water by the crick, I must 'a' washed my-
   self." My wife said sharply, "Have you been to a doctor?"
"Oh yes," he said, "my boy happened down." She said "You
   oughtn't to be alone here: are you all alone here?"
"No," he answered, "horses. I've been all over the world: right
   here is the most beautiful place in the world.
I played the piccolo in ships' orchestras." We looked at the im-
   mense redwoods and dark
Fern-taken slip of land by the creek, where the horses were,
   and the yuccaed hillsides high in the sun
Flaring like torches; I said "Darkness comes early here." He an-
   swered with pride and joy, "Two hundred and eighty-
Five days in the year the sun never gets in here.
Like living under the sea, green all summer, beautiful." My wife
   said, "How do you know your temperature's
A hundred and two?" "Eh? The doctor. He said the bone
Presses my brain, he's got to cut out a piece. I said 'All right,
   you've got to wait till it rains,
I've got to guard my place through the fire-season.' By God,"
   he said joyously,
"The quail on my roof wake me up every morning, then I look
   out the window and a dozen deer
Drift up the canyon with the mist on their shoulders. Look in
   the dust at your feet, all the little hoofprints."

SELF-CRITICISM IN FEBRUARY

The bay is not blue but sombre yellow
With wrack from the battered valley, it is speckled with violent
  foam-heads
And tiger-striped with long lovely storm-shadows.
You love this better than the other mask; better eyes than yours
Would feel the equal beauty in the blue.
It is certain you have loved the beauty of storm disproportion-
  ately.
But the present time is not pastoral, but founded
On violence, pointed for more massive violence: perhaps it is not
Perversity but need that perceives the storm-beauty.
Well, bite on this: your poems are too full of ghosts and demons,
And people like phantoms—how often life's are—
And passion so strained that the clay mouths go praying for de-
  struction—
Alas, it is not unusual in life;
To every soul at some time. *But why insist on it? And now*
For the worst fault: you have never mistaken
Demon nor passion nor idealism for the real God.
Then what is most disliked in those verses
Remains most true. *Unfortunately. If only you could sing*
That God is love, or perhaps that social
Justice will soon prevail. I can tell lies in prose.

HELLENISTICS

I look at the Greek-derived design that nourished my infancy—
  this Wedgwood copy of the Portland vase:
Someone had given it to my father—my eyes at five years old
  used to devour it by the hour.

I look at a Greek coin, four-drachma piece struck by Lysimachus:
  young Alexander's head
With the horns of Ammon and brave brow-ridges, the bright
  pride and immortal youth and wild sensitiveness.

I think of Achilles, Sappho, the Nike. I think of those mercenaries
  who marched in the heart of Asia
And lived to salute the sea: the lean faces like lance-heads, the
  grace of panthers. The dull welter of Asia.

I am past childhood, I look at this ocean and the fishing birds, the
  streaming skerries, the shining water,
The foam-heads, the exultant dawn-light going west, the pelicans,
  their huge wings half folded, plunging like stones.

Whatever it is catches my heart in its hands, whatever it is makes
  me shudder with love
And painful joy and the tears prickle . . . the Greeks were not
  its inventors. The Greeks were not the inventors

Of shining clarity and jewel-sharp form and the beauty of God.
  He was free with men before the Greeks came:
He is here naked on the shining water. Every eye that has a
  man's nerves behind it has known him.

II

I think of the dull welter of Asia. I think of squalid savages along
  the Congo: the natural

Condition of man, that makes one say of all beasts "They are
    not contemptible. Man is contemptible." I see

The squalor of our own frost-bitten forefathers. I will praise the
    Greeks for having pared down the shame of three vices
Natural to man and no other animal, cruelty and filth and super-
    stition, grained in man's making.

III

The age darkens, Europe mixes her cups of death, all the little
    Caesars fidget on their thrones,
The old wound opens its clotted mouth to ask for new wounds.
    Men will fight through; men have tough hearts.

Men will fight through to the autumn flowering and ordered
    prosperity. They will lift their heads in the great cities
Of the empire and say: "Freedom? Freedom was a fire. We are
    well quit of freedom, we have found prosperity."

They will say, "Where now are the evil prophets?" Thus for a
    time in the age's afterglow, the sterile time;
But the wounds drain, and freedom has died, slowly the machines
    break down, slowly the wilderness returns.

IV

Oh distant future children going down to the foot of the moun-
    tain, the new barbarism, the night of time,
Mourn your own dead if you remember them, but not for civili-
    zation, not for our scuttled futilities.

You are saved from being little entrails feeding large brains, you
    are saved from being little empty bundles of enjoyment,
You are not to be fractional supported people but complete men;
    you will guard your own heads, you will have proud eyes.

You will stand among the spears when you meet; life will be
    lovely and terrible again, great and in earnest;

HELLENISTICS

You will know hardship, hunger and violence: these are not the
    evils: what power can save you from the real evils

Of barbarism? What poet will be born to tell you to hate cruelty
    and filth? What prophet will warn you
When the witch-doctors begin dancing, or if any man says "I
    am a priest," to kill them with spears?

OH, LOVELY ROCK

We stayed the night in the pathless gorge of Ventana Creek,
   up the east fork.
The rock walls and the mountain ridges hung forest on forest
   above our heads, maple and redwood,
Laurel, oak, madrone, up to the high and slender Santa Lucian
   firs that stare up the cataracts
Of slide-rock to the star-color precipices.

                                        We lay on gravel and
   kept a little camp-fire for warmth.
Past midnight only two or three coals glowed red in the cooling
   darkness; I laid a clutch of dead bay-leaves
On the ember ends and felted dry sticks across them and lay
   down again. The revived flame
Lighted my sleeping son's face and his companion's, and the ver-
   tical face of the great gorge-wall
Across the stream. Light leaves overhead danced in the fire's
   breath, tree-trunks were seen: it was the rock wall
That fascinated my eyes and mind. Nothing strange: light-gray
   diorite with two or three slanting seams in it,
Smooth-polished by the endless attrition of slides and floods; no
   fern nor lichen, pure naked rock . . . as if I were
Seeing rock for the first time. As if I were seeing through the
   flame-lit surface into the real and bodily
And living rock. Nothing strange . . . I cannot
Tell you how strange: the silent passion, the deep nobility and
   childlike loveliness: this fate going on
Outside our fates. It is here in the mountain like a grave smiling
   child. I shall die, and my boys
Will live and die, our world will go on through its rapid agonies
   of change and discovery; this age will die,

OH, LOVELY ROCK

And wolves have howled in the snow around a new Bethlehem:
   this rock will be here, grave, earnest, not passive: the energies
That are its atoms will still be bearing the whole mountain above:
   and I, many packed centuries ago,
Felt its intense reality with love and wonder, this lonely rock.

THE BEAKS OF EAGLES

An eagle's nest on the head of an old redwood on one of the
   precipice-footed ridges
Above Ventana Creek, that jagged country which nothing but a
   falling meteor will ever plow; no horseman
Will ever ride there, no hunter cross this ridge but the winged
   ones, no one will steal the eggs from this fortress.
The she-eagle is old, her mate was shot long ago, she is now mated
   with a son of hers.
When lightning blasted her nest she built it again on the same
   tree, in the splinters of the thunderbolt.
The she-eagle is older than I; she was here when the fires of
   eighty-five raged on these ridges,
She was lately fledged and dared not hunt ahead of them but ate
   scorched meat. The world has changed in her time;
Humanity has multiplied, but not here; men's hopes and thoughts
   and customs have changed, their powers are enlarged,
Their powers and their follies have become fantastic,
The unstable animal never has been changed so rapidly. The
   motor and the plane and the great war have gone over him,
And Lenin has lived and Jehovah died: while the mother-eagle
Hunts her same hills, crying the same beautiful and lonely cry and
   is never tired; dreams the same dreams,
And hears at night the rock-slides rattle and thunder in the throats
   of these living mountains.
                              It is good for man
To try all changes, progress and corruption, powers, peace and
   anguish, not to go down the dinosaur's way
Until all his capacities have been explored: and it is good for him
To know that his needs and nature are no more changed in fact
   in ten thousand years than the beaks of eagles.

The world's as the world is; the nations rearm and prepare to
change; the age of tyrants returns;
The greatest civilization that has ever existed builds itself higher
towers on breaking foundations.
Recurrent episodes; they were determined when the ape's chil-
dren first ran in packs, chipped flint to an edge.

I lie and hear
dark rain beat the roof, and the blind wind.

In the morning perhaps
I shall find strength again
To value the immense beauty of this time of the world, the flow-
ers of decay their pitiful loveliness, the fever-dream
Tapestries that back the drama and are called the future. This
ebb of vitality feels the ignoble and cruel
Incidents, not the vast abstract order.

I lie and hear dark rain beat
the roof, and the night-blind wind.

In the Ventana country darkness and rain and the roar of waters
fill the deep mountain-throats.
The creekside shelf of sand where we lay last August under a
slip of stars,
And firelight played on the leaning gorge-walls, is drowned and
lost. The deer of the country huddle on a ridge
In a close herd under madrone-trees; they tremble when a rock-
slide goes down, they open great darkness-
Drinking eyes and press closer.

Cataracts of rock
Rain down the mountain from cliff to cliff and torment the
stream-bed. The stream deals with them. The laurels are
wounded,
Redwoods go down with their earth and lie thwart the gorge. I
hear the torrent boulders battering each other,
I feel the flesh of the mountain move on its bones in the wet
darkness.

Is this more beautiful
Than man's disasters? These wounds will heal in their time; so
will humanity's. This is more beautiful . . . at night . . .

DECAYING LAMBSKINS

After all, we also stand on a height. Our blood and our culture
    have passed the flood-marks of any world
Up to this time. Our engineers have nothing to learn from Rome's,
    Egypt's, China's, and could teach them more
Than ever their myth-makers imagined. Our science, however
    confused, personal and fabulous, can hardly
Lean low enough, sun-blinded eagle, to laugh at the strange
    astronomies of Babylon, or at Lucretius
His childish dreams of origins, or Plato's
Lunatic swan. While as for our means and mastery of warfare, at
    sea, on land, in the air . . .
                      So boastful?
Because we are not proud but wearily ashamed of this peak of
    time. What is noble in us, to kindle
The imagination of a future age? We shall seem a race of cheap
    Fausts, vulgar magicians.
What men have we to show them? but inventions and appliances.
    Not men but populations, mass-men; not life
But amusements; not health but medicines. And the odor: what
    is that odor? Decaying lambskins: the Christian
Ideals that for protection and warmth our naked ancestors . . .
    but naturally, after nineteen centuries . . .

O Mort, vieux capitaine, est-il temps, nous levons l'ancre? It is
    perhaps
Time, almost time, to let our supreme inventions begin to work.
    The exact intelligent guns
Can almost wheel themselves into action of their own accord, and
    almost calculate their own trajectories.
The clever battleships know their objectives; the huge bombing-
    planes and meteor pursuit-planes are all poised for . . .
    what?
Vanity. This also is vanity; horrible too, but a vain dream.
Our civilization, the worst it can do, cannot yet destroy itself;
    but only deep-wounded drag on for centuries.

SHIVA

There is a hawk that is picking the birds out of our sky.
She killed the pigeons of peace and security,
She has taken honesty and confidence from nations and men,
She is hunting the lonely heron of liberty.
She loads the arts with nonsense, she is very cunning,
Science with dreams and the state with powers to catch them at
    last.
Nothing will escape her at last, flying nor running.
This is the hawk that picks out the stars' eyes.
This is the only hunter that will ever catch the wild swan;
The prey she will take last is the wild white swan of the beauty of
    things.
Then she will be alone, pure destruction, achieved and supreme,
Empty darkness under the death-tent wings.
She will build a nest of the swan's bones and hatch a new brood,
Hang new heavens with new birds, all be renewed.

NOW RETURNED HOME

Beyond the narrows of the Inner Hebrides
We sailed the cold angry sea toward Barra, where Heaval mountain
    tain
Lifts like a mast. There were few people on the steamer, it was
    late in the year; I noticed most an old shepherd,
Two wise-eyed dogs wove anxious circles around his feet, and a
    thin-armed girl
Who cherished what seemed a doll, wrapping it against the sea-
    wind. When it moved I said to my wife "She'll smother it."
And she to the girl: "Is your baby cold? You'd better run down
    out of the wind and uncover its face."
She raised the shawl and said "He is two weeks old. His mother
    died in Glasgow in the hospital
Where he was born. She was my sister." I looked ahead at the
    bleak island, gray stones, ruined castle,
A few gaunt houses under the high and comfortless mountain;
    my wife looked at the sickly babe,
And said "There's a good doctor in Barra? It will soon be winter."
    "Ah," she answered, "Barra'd be heaven for him,
The poor wee thing, there's Heaval to break the wind. We live
    on a wee island yonder away,
Just the one house."
                The steamer moored, and a skiff—what they
    call a curragh, like a canvas canoe
Equipped with oars—came swiftly along the side. The dark-haired
    girl climbed down to it, with one arm holding
That doubtful slip of life to her breast; a tall young man with
    sea-pale eyes and an older man
Helped her; if a word was spoken I did not hear it. They stepped
    a mast and hoisted a henna-color
Bat's wing of sail.
               Now, returned home
After so many thousands of miles of road and ocean, all the hulls
    sailed in, the houses visited,

NOW RETURNED HOME

I remember that slender skiff with dark henna sail
Bearing off across the stormy sunset to the distant island
Most clearly; and have rather forgotten the dragging whirlpools
of London, the screaming haste of New York.

THEORY OF TRUTH

(Reference to Chapter II, *The Women at Point Sur)*

I stand near Soberanes Creek, on the knoll over the sea, west of
the road. I remember

This is the very place where Arthur Barclay, a priest in revolt,
proposed three questions to himself:

First, is there a God and of what nature? Second, whether there's
anything after we die but worm's meat?

Third, how should men live? Large time-worn questions no
doubt; yet he touched his answers, they are not unattainable;

But presently lost them again in the glimmer of insanity.

How
many minds have worn these questions; old coins

Rubbed faceless, dateless. The most have despaired and accepted
doctrine; the greatest have achieved answers, but always

With aching strands of insanity in them.

I think of Lao-tze; and the dear beauty of the Jew whom they
crucified but he lived, he was greater than Rome;

And godless Buddha under the boh-tree, straining through his
mind the delusions and miseries of human life.

Why does insanity always twist the great answers?
Because only
tormented persons want truth.

Man is an animal like other animals, wants food and success and
women, not truth. Only if the mind

Tortured by some interior tension has despaired of happiness:
then it hates its life-cage and seeks further,

And finds, if it is powerful enough. But instantly the private
agony that made the search

Muddles the finding.
Here was a man who envied the chiefs of
the provinces of China their power and pride,

And envied Confucius his fame for wisdom. Tortured by hardly
    conscious envy he hunted the truth of things,
Caught it, and stained it through with his private impurity. He
    praised inaction, silence, vacancy: why?
Because the princes and officers were full of business, and wise
    Confucius of words.

Here was a man who was born a bastard, and among the people
That more than any in the world valued race-purity, chastity, the
    prophetic splendors of the race of David.
Oh intolerable wound, dimly perceived. Too loving to curse his
    mother, desert-driven, devil-haunted,
The beautiful young poet found truth in the desert, but found
    also
Fantastic solution of hopeless anguish. The carpenter was not his
    father? Because God was his father,
Not a man sinning, but the pure holiness and power of God.
    His personal anguish and insane solution
Have stained an age; nearly two thousand years are one vast poem
    drunk with the wine of his blood.

And here was another Saviour, a prince in India,
A man who loved and pitied with such intense comprehension of
    pain that he was willing to annihilate
Nature and the earth and stars, life and mankind, to annul the
    suffering. He also sought and found truth,
And mixed it with his private impurity, the pity, the denials.

                       Then
    search for truth is foredoomed and frustrate?
Only stained fragments?

                Until the mind has turned its love from
itself and man, from parts to the whole.

INDEX OF POEMS

INDEX OF POEMS

INDEX OF FIRST LINES

INDEX OF FIRST LINES